03.5
7
39
.192

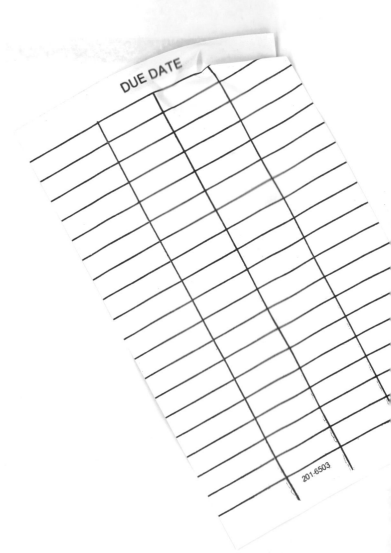

Popular Reading and Publishing in Britain
1914–1950

JOSEPH McALEER

CLARENDON PRESS · OXFORD
1992

Oxford University Press, Walton Street, Oxford OX2 6DP

Oxford New York Toronto
Delhi Bombay Calcutta Madras Karachi
Petaling Jaya Singapore Hong Kong Tokyo
Nairobi Dar es Salaam Cape Town
Melbourne Auckland

and associated companies in
Berlin Ibadan

Oxford is a trade mark of Oxford University Press

Published in the United States
by Oxford University Press, New York

British Library Cataloguing in Publication Data
Data available

Library of Congress Cataloging in Publication Data
McAleer, Joseph.
Popular reading and publishing in Britain, 1914–1950 / Joseph McAleer.
p.   cm. — (Oxford historical monographs)
Includes bibliographical references and index.
1. Books and reading — Great Britain — History — 20th century.
2. Popular literature — Great Britain — History and criticism.
3. Literature publishing — Great Britain — History — 20th century.
I. Title.   II. Series.
Z1003.5.G7M39   1992   028'.9'0941—dc20   92–19004
ISBN 0–19–820329–2

Typeset by BP Integraphics Ltd., Bath, Avon
Printed and bound in Great Britain by Bookcraft Ltd.,
Midsomer Norton, Bath

for
MY FAMILY

ACKNOWLEDGEMENTS

THIS book could not have been written without the assistance, advice, and encouragement of many people. Special thanks are reserved for Ross McKibbin, who supervised this book in thesis form, and for its examiners, Lord Briggs and Dr Paul Johnson. I would also like to express my appreciation to Philip Waller, Colin Matthew, Rosemary Giedroyć, Walter Tyson, George Cooper, and Mrs Henry J. Heinz II.

I am grateful to the publishers, archivists, authors, and editors (several of whom became friends) who tolerated and facilitated my research and interviews, including Mr John Boon and Mr Alan Boon of Mills & Boon Ltd.; the Directors of D. C. Thomson & Co., Ltd., and the firm's librarian, Mr Douglas M. Spence; the Reverend Alec Gilmore, General Secretary of the United Society for Christian Literature; Dorothy Sheridan, archivist of the Tom Harrisson Mass-Observation Archive; and Mr T. W. Baker-Jones, archivist of W. H. Smith Ltd.

Archival material and illustrations are reproduced with permission from D. C. Thomson & Co., Ltd., Mills & Boon Ltd., W. H. Smith Ltd., and the United Society for Christian Literature. Mass-Observation material remains the copyright of the Trustees of the Tom Harrisson Mass-Observation Archive, reproduced by permission of Curtis Brown Ltd., London.

This book was written over several years in three different locations: amid the dreaming spires of Oxford, the haunting beauty of Hawthornden Castle, and the comforts of home in Connecticut. To my many friends in England and Scotland I say, simply, Thank you. My family in America, including my father, three brothers, sister-in-law, niece, and (in spirit) my mother, has supported my academic and literary endeavours with enthusiasm, patience, and a sense of humour. It is a privilege to dedicate this book collectively to them.

JOSEPH MCALEER

Stamford, Connecticut
February 1992

CONTENTS

LIST OF ILLUSTRATIONS

(Unless otherwise stated, plates are reproduced from the author's own originals.)

LIST OF FIGURES

LIST OF TABLES

ABBREVIATIONS

B	*The Bookseller*
BOP	*The Boy's Own Paper*
GOP	*The Girl's Own Paper*
M-O	The Tom Harrisson Mass-Observation Archive, University of Sussex. Location of material is indicated by Topic Collection (in quote marks), box number, and file letter; e.g. 'Reading' Box 8 File C. Interview subjects were coded according to sex (F, M), age group, class, and (sometimes) location: e.g. M/25/D, Chelsea. Mass-Observation used standard sociological groupings: Class B: Upper and middle classes; Class C: Artisan, lower-middle, and upper-working classes; Class D: Unskilled working class.
PC	*The Publishers' Circular*
TC	*The Trade Circular* (W. H. Smith)
USCL	The United Society for Christian Literature Archives, School of Oriental and African Studies, University of London. Location is indicated by the classification number; e.g. USCL 135.

INTRODUCTION

THE preoccupations of this book have been anticipated by two authors: Wilkie Collins and George Orwell. As novelists they are poles apart, but as essayists each contributed an important work which blended literary criticism with social commentary and which has changed the way we look at 'popular' (i.e. 'lower-middle/working-class') culture. As one was published close to the beginning of the period discussed in this book, and one towards the end, their common points of reference are significant. It is important here to recount briefly their arguments, as both are central to any study of popular publishing and reading habits.

Wilkie Collins's essay was published anonymously in *Household Words*, Charles Dickens's weekly journal, in 1858, two years before *The Woman in White*.[1] The title of the essay coined a phrase frequently used often by later critics: 'The Unknown Public'. Collins was anxious to dispel the illusion: that the 'great bulk of the reading public of England' was composed of 'the subscribers to this journal, the customers at the eminent publishing-houses, the members of book-clubs and circulating libraries, and the purchasers and borrowers of newspapers and reviews'. His discovery that this was not so was made after closer inspection of what he called 'penny-novel Journals', publications which filled the windows of stationers' and tobacconists' shops in 'the second and third rate neighbourhoods' of London, and in 'every town, large or small', around England. These nameless papers contained, for a penny, a mixture of serial and short stories, 'snippets' of information (household hints, riddles, trivia), and answers to readers' queries (resembling, in other words, any number of modern weekly entertainment magazines). Collins was informed ('without exaggeration') that five of these journals had a combined weekly circulation of one million copies. Estimating three readers to each copy sold, he was

---

[1] [Wilkie Collins], 'The Unknown Public', *Household Words*, 18 (21 Aug. 1858), 217–22.

amazed at the result—'*a public of three millions*—a public unknown to
the literary world . . .'.

'Arguing carefully by inference', after interviews with shop-owners
and a quasi-sociological analysis of published replies to readers,
Collins drew several conclusions as to the composition of this 'Unknown Public'. These readers were clearly working-class, judging
from 'the social and intellectual materials' evident in their queries ('A
reader who is not certain what the word Poems means . . . A speculative
reader, who wishes to know if he can sell lemonade without a license
. . . Two timid girls, who are respectively afraid of a French invasion
and dragon-flies'). Apparently, they read for their own amusement
rather than for information, and quantity was more important than
quality: shop-owners could not advise on the contents of the journals,
only that they were 'good pennorths'. In fact, any improvement in the
type of fiction published spelled commercial disaster: an attempt by one
journal to serialize *The Count of Monte Cristo* resulted in a 'serious
decrease' in circulation. The serial story, which Collins ascertained
was the chief attraction of the papers, was conventional, melodramatic,
sentimental, undistinguished—but moral. 'The one thing which it is
possible to advance in their favour is, that there is apparently no
wickedness in them', Collins wrote. 'There seems to be an intense
in-dwelling respectability in their dulness [*sic*]. If they lead to no
intellectual result, even of the humblest kind, they may have, at least,
this negative advantage, that they can do no moral harm.'

Collins concluded on a surprisingly optimistic note. Although he
pitied the ignorance of this reading public, which clearly had never
been taught *how* to read and was therefore unaccustomed 'to the de-
licacies and subtleties of literary art', he was convinced that, in time
and with proper guidance, this group would develop into a formidable
market for literary genius. 'The largest audience for periodical fiction,
in this age of periodicals, must obey the universal law of progress, and
must, sooner or later, learn to discriminate', he wrote. Collins awaited
the time when even the humblest of readers would know the difference
between a 'good' book and a 'bad' book:

When that period comes, the readers who rank by millions, will be the readers
who give the widest reputations, who return the richest rewards, and who will,
therefore, command the service of the best writers of their time. A great, an
unparalleled prospect awaits, perhaps, the coming generation of English
novelists. To the penny journals of the present time belongs the credit of
having discovered a new public. When that public shall discover its need of a

great writer, the great writer will have such an audience as has never yet been known.

It should be remembered that Collins was writing at a time when the mass-market publishing industry was still in its infancy. He could not have foreseen the prodigious expansion of the periodical press after 1870, when a spate of new publications encouraged not discrimination and refinement but demand for more of the same, 'light' entertainment.

George Orwell's classic essay on 'Boys' Weeklies' was first published in *Horizon* in March 1940.[2] As an examination of publications which appealed to working-class readers, Orwell's essay can be regarded as a direct descendant of Collins's. Although he was not the first critic since 1858 to explore this subject (Helen Bosanquet, Edward Salmon, Margaret Phillips, and Q. D. Leavis, for example, had already done so), Orwell's essay has attracted much attention; he was an author and literary critic of stature and persuasion, and his essay was published at a time when interest in the sociology of popular culture was high.

Like Collins, Orwell first became interested in working-class reading habits through close scrutiny of the newsagent's shop, a fixture in 'any poor quarter in any big town'. He was clearly impressed by the 'unbelievable' quantity and variety of the tuppenny weekly magazines. 'Probably the contents of these shops is the best available indication of what the mass of the English people really feels and thinks. Certainly nothing half so revealing exists in documentary form.' With this in mind, Orwell proceeded to examine one type of publication which was then very popular: 'boys' papers', commonly called 'dreadfuls' or 'bloods'. Looking in turn at titles published by the Amalgamated Press (*Gem*, *Magnet*), and by D. C. Thomson (*The Wizard*, *The Hotspur*), Orwell sought to highlight differences as well as similarities. In general, he criticized the unrealistic, over-optimistic world-view expressed in these papers, which excluded any mention of contemporary political, social, and moral issues. Consequently, they failed to prepare young men for their future responsibilities as citizens. 'The clock has stopped at 1910. Britannia rules the waves, and no one has heard of slumps, booms, unemployment, dictatorships, purges or concentration camps.' Instead, anachronistic views and stereotypes were reinforced, especially in terms of class relationships and a jingoistic

[2] George Orwell, 'Boys' Weeklies', in Sonia Orwell and Ian Angus (eds.), *The Collected Essays, Journalism and Letters of George Orwell*, vol. i (Penguin edn., Harmondsworth, 1987), 505–31.

patriotism. The Amalgamated Press titles (which, Orwell admitted, were no longer as popular in 1940 as they had been in the 1910s and 1920s) were wholly concerned with a middle-class fantasy world of public schools, cricket matches, silly masters, huge teas, and funny pranks. 'Everything is safe, solid and unquestionable. Everything will be the same forever.' Although the contents of the Thomson papers (the best-selling titles throughout the interwar period) were more varied and stylistically superior, they perpetuated these same attitudes. They were, however, more influenced by the cinema and the 'bolder' magazines published in America, in their promotion of bully-worship and a cult of violence:

> Instead of identifying with a schoolboy of more or less his own age, the reader of the *Skipper*, *Hotspur*, etc. is led to identify with a G-man, with a Foreign Legionary, with some variant of Tarzan, with an air ace, a master spy, an explorer, a pugilist—at any rate with some single all-powerful character who dominates everyone about him and whose usual method of solving any problem is a sock on the jaw.

Orwell admitted that 'on its level the moral code of the English boys' papers is a decent one. Crime and dishonesty are never held up to admiration, there is none of the cynicism and corruption of the American gangster story.' But while conceding that no one 'in his senses would want to turn the so-called penny dreadful into a realistic novel or a Socialist tract' ('An adventure story must of its nature be more or less remote from real life'), Orwell none the less was disturbed by the huge demand for such inferior fiction among boys of all classes, and the distorting view of a sanitized reality which they were absorbing:

> To what extent people draw their ideas from fiction is disputable. Personally I believe that most people are influenced far more than they care to admit by novels, serial stories, films and so forth, and that from this point of view the worst books are often the most important, because they are usually the ones that are read earliest in life.

It was, in effect, a form of social control, which was even more worrying given the obvious right-wing bias in the magazines.

> . . . in England, popular imaginative fiction is a field that left-wing thought has never begun to enter. *All* fiction from the novels in the mushroom libraries downwards is censored in the interests of the ruling class. And boys' fiction above all, the blood-and-thunder stuff which nearly every boy devours

at some time or other, is sodden in the worst illusions of 1910. The fact is only unimportant if one believes that what is read in childhood leaves no impression behind.

In concluding, Orwell called attention to a similar type of publication for women (*Peg's Paper*, *Family Star*). These also avoided any mention of current affairs, sex, and domestic problems in their 'escapist' fiction, usually rags-to-riches tales involving office workers or factory girls. The ubiquitous happy ending added to the lack of realism. 'Always the dark clouds roll away, the kind employer raises Alfred's wages, and there are jobs for everybody except the drunks. It is still the world of the *Wizard* and the *Gem*, except that there are orange-blossoms instead of machine guns.'

This book is concerned with the reading public which Collins and Orwell tried to describe, during the period when Orwell wrote and which Collins would have recognized: from 1914 until 1950. A number of questions will be considered. Was reading as popular a leisure activity among the lower-middle and working classes as both writers contended? How extensive, and exclusive, was this demand? Did the 'Unknown Public' learn to 'discriminate', as Collins hoped, and graduate to the works of the 'best' writers? Were the publishers of 'popular' fiction, in both book and magazine form, guided purely by commercial concerns, or did they seek to influence their innocent readers, 'censoring' fiction as Orwell claims? Indeed, what was the relationship between publisher and reader: were their tastes and views compatible? To what extent can the social and cultural views of the lower-middle and working classes be inferred from what they read?

In considering these (and other) questions, I have selected three publishing houses to examine in detail, noting in particular their complicated editorial policies within the increasingly 'mass' market. These are Mills & Boon, D. C. Thomson, and the Religious Tract Society. Mills & Boon and D. C. Thomson were the quintessential publishers of the early twentieth century: essentially commercial enterprises, each firm reflected changing social values within its publications while courting their readerships. The Religious Tract Society was less successful: a nineteenth-century foundation embodying the spirit of Victorian liberalism, it failed to adapt to a changing (and increasingly secular) world, with disastrous results. In each case, the publisher took seriously his role *in loco parentis*, whether dealing with adults or children, in promoting a perception of both reality and the ideals of the reader, which was characteristically 'middle-class' in its endorsement of the status quo.

Mass reading habits have not been the subject of much sustained historical inquiry, although something can be learned, for example, from Q. D. Leavis, Richard Hoggart, and Richard Altick.[3] Histories of leisure have considered the development of public libraries, for instance, but not of the magazine and fiction trades. One reason, perhaps, why reading habits and popular fiction have been overlooked is their diminished scholarly appeal when compared with two other leisure activities, the wireless and the cinema, whose impact has been more dramatic. Despite this, historians have recognized their social importance. Detective stories, according to A. J. P. Taylor, 'often provide for the historian clearer and more accurate social detail than can be found in more literary works'.[4] Rowntree and Lavers believed that 'the reading habits of a nation have a double significance, for what a man reads not only reveals his present intellectual and cultural standards, but also helps to determine what they will be in the future'.[5] More recently, Kirsten Drotner, in examining children's magazines, found these to be 'excellent "seismographs of child taste", for an unwelcome change in characters or an unexpected development of events may immediately be registered by a sudden drop in circulation figures'.[6]

Like Orwell (a contemporary), the founders of Mass-Observation[7] believed that popular fiction had a great influence upon its readers beyond the obvious entertainment value. 'I have always felt that the

---

[3] Q. D. Leavis, *Fiction and the Reading Public* (London, 1932); Richard Hoggart, *The Uses of Literacy* (London, 1958); Richard Altick, *The English Common Reader: A Social History of the Mass Reading Public 1800–1900* (Chicago, 1957).

[4] A. J. P. Taylor, *English History 1914–1945* (Oxford, 1965), 312.

[5] B. Seebohm Rowntree and G. R. Lavers, *English Life and Leisure: A Social Study* (London, 1951), 286.

[6] Kirsten Drotner, 'Schoolgirls, Madcaps, and Air Aces: English Girls and their Magazine Reading Between the Wars', *Feminist Studies*, 9 (Spring 1983), 34.

[7] The name given to this organization is fitting, as its purpose was indeed to observe the masses, in a quasi-anthropological and psychoanalytical way. Founded in 1937, Mass-Observation comprised a team of investigators ('Mass-Observers'), who surveyed behaviour patterns, conducted interviews, and wrote reports, and a 'National Panel' of volunteers who kept detailed diaries and responded to specific questions from the organization. The mass of material gathered is a rare source of popular opinions and attitudes, particularly for the period 1937–46. Mass-Observation's studies of Bolton and Blackpool (the Worktown Project), the day survey of the coronation of George VI, and the war diaries of Naomi Mitchison are perhaps best known. The firm and its observations continue today.

literary weeklies have dangerously ignored the growth of a mass literature', Tom Harrisson, the organization's co-founder, wrote in 1941.[8] Harrisson and his colleagues argued that popular fiction could promote specific attitudes (such as patriotism) and stereotypes (the 'intelligent tough' or the 'mad scientist'), through repetition. Kathleen Box, a full-time investigator and author of several of the early reports on reading habits, prefaced a 1940 study on book-reading in Fulham with similar observations on magazine-reading:

Book buyers and members of book clubs are largely middle class and largely intellectual . . . That there is a gulf between the types of books read and what 'reading' means to middle class (especially intellectuals) and working class people is evident especially from the types of magazines stocked in the shops in different districts . . . Intellectuals may imagine that 'pamphlets' are a force in determining public opinion. Few working class people even know what these are. Much more can be found out (about) what people like reading from public libraries, twopenny libraries, and grubby little sweet shops, than from Charing Cross Road.

She concluded that weekly papers such as *Red Star Weekly* and *Oracle* 'must have an enormous influence in forming opinion and determining shape(s) of wish-pictures and symbols in people's minds'.[9]

The period 1914–50 has been selected as it represents the first time the mass reading public was commercially managed and exploited in a recognizably modern way. It was also in some respects a calm interval between two turbulent periods: the foundation and consolidation of the Unknown Public and the popular publishing industry before 1914, and the challenge to reading by such persuasive entertainments as television during the 1950s. The outbreak of war in 1914 can be considered a turning point. Forty years after the 1870 Education Act, the market for popular fiction had matured; the war and its restrictions on trading and paper supplies pared the number of publishing houses and accelerated the trends towards concentration of ownership and cheaper-priced fiction which dominated the period to 1950. Similarly, the market after 1950 is distinctive, in part because of the new types of publications which emerged from the lifting of wartime bans which

[8] Tom Harrisson, Report, M-O 'Reading' Box 3 (22 June 1941), 2–4.
[9] Kathleen Box, 'Wartime Reading', M-O File Report 37 (Mar. 1940), 27; Box, Report, M-O 'Reading' Box 3 File A (4 Mar. 1940), 1.

had retarded development. These included fiction of a more 'realistic' nature, and the picture-story paper.[10]

What was the market for popular fiction? 'Popular' does not imply 'common'; in book and magazine form, it did not attempt to appeal to all classes. D. L. LeMahieu has identified the cinema and such high-circulation newspapers as the *Daily Mail* and the *Daily Express* as the best examples of 'common culture'. The wireless, moreover, saturated British homes in a way television would after the Second World War.[11] Rather, popular fiction was directed principally at what the critic Sidney Dark (like Collins) in 1922 called 'the New Reading Public . . . that ever-increasing company drawn from what we commonly call the lower-middle class and the working class'.[12] Popular fiction implied 'low-brow',[13] often sensational and critically unacclaimed works (and therefore not 'common' in the LeMahieu sense). Romantic novels and tuppenny magazines were targeted at middle and working-class readers in a way that (say) Graham Greene and *The Lady* were not.[14] John Boon, a director of Mills & Boon, perhaps best characterized the market for this type of fiction when in 1945 he condemned a movement in the industry to ban 'popular' books in order to release more rationed paper for 'quality' works. Boon claimed an important role for such fiction in the general market and the distinctive nature of its readership:

The dealers in popular books do a service to the trade. They are the missionaries who preach the reading habit. The readers of quality books form a fairly constant group; they are less set in their tastes, and less inclined to be distracted by cheap modern entertainments. The popular reader more often than not represents what is called in politics the 'floating vote'. He has to be won from football pools, the dogs, the cinema, the wireless and kindred temptations. In fact, the popular trade bears the brunt of the competition with those

[10] Fiction in women's magazines, for example, became less flowery and romantic and more challenging and thought-provoking. The great success of the *Eagle*, from 1950, marked the decline of prose-story papers and the proliferation of picture-stories (or 'comics') for children.

[11] D. L. LeMahieu, *A Culture for Democracy: Mass Communication and the Cultivated Mind in Britain Between the Wars* (Oxford, 1988), 227.

[12] Sidney Dark, *The New Reading Public* (London, 1922), 5–6.

[13] The adjectives 'low-brow' and 'high-brow', used by literary critics throughout this period, are American in origin, first popularized in Britain by H. G. Wells (Robert Graves and Alan Hodge, *The Long Week-End: A Social History of Great Britain 1918–1939* (London, 1941), 50).

[14] The exception was detective fiction, which (as today) seemed to attract all classes of readers. Sir Arthur Conan Doyle, Agatha Christie, and Dorothy L. Sayers were especially popular.

forces which tend to make people read less . . . Every new reader of Edgar Wallace does not mean one less of Proust.[15]

Philothea Thompson, a former editor of *The Bookseller*, graphically described what she called 'the cheap stuff'. Referring to a novel by E. Phillips Oppenheim in the 'Yellow Jackets' series published by Hodder and Stoughton, she said, 'It really is representative of the period: in appearance, in absolutely ghastly writing, in ghastly sentiment—you know, money. All that was revolting.'[16] Occasionally, some novels, periodicals, and authors transcended these barriers: most notably, *Gone with the Wind* and *Rebecca*;[17] the *Picture Post*; Georgette Heyer and P. G. Wodehouse.

Popular fiction embraces many genres, from romantic fiction and detective stories to Westerns, thrillers, adventure stories, historical fiction, and books for children. Each genre, in turn, is expressed in the form of novel, novelette, short story, and the serial. Variations of these, moreover, are aimed at certain audiences: women, or children, for example. Given such scope and scale, some kind of concentration has had to be made here in terms of genre and readership. In this book I will look specifically at two types: romantic fiction for women (novels and weekly magazines) and weekly prose papers for boys. Of all the popular reading genres these two especially were 'managed' and 'targeted'. From 1870 and the launch of a 'quality' movement in literature, publishers, parents, and critics alike believed that popular fiction had to be regulated with great care. The more successful publishers (including D. C. Thomson and Mills & Boon) adopted a paternalistic approach towards their readers, dispensing conventional attitudes and ideals in their publications, which were often marketed as a kind of personal companion or guidebook. The affinity between publisher and reader was reinforced by vigorous market research; publishers constantly tested the waters in order to maintain an up-to-date and interesting product in a competitive market. The failure to do so contributed to the downfall of the Religious Tract Society. It is because we can see how publishers both managed their 'products' and reacted to changing tastes of the readership that popular fiction—however it was

---

[15] John Boon, 'A Plague O' Both Your Houses!', *B* (18 Oct. 1945), 498–9.

[16] Philothea Thompson was interviewed in 1987. She joined *The Bookseller* in 1945.

[17] Thompson claimed that Daphne du Maurier's 1938 bestseller was a publishing enigma which appealed to all readers and would have broken sales records in every class. Published by Gollancz, *Rebecca* has never been out of print.

managed—can also be regarded as a useful barometer of the tastes, ideals, and aspirations of its readers (here, the lower-middle and working classes). In the case of boys' weeklies, these may also have reflected the desires of the parent, the unseen but all-powerful factor in children's publishing, as much as those of the child.

It is, furthermore, legitimate to study book and magazine reading together, as often no distinction was made between the two by their readers, of any age. 'Reading' frequently meant magazine reading; tuppenny weeklies were referred to as 'books', just as for most people 'books' meant works of fiction. 'It is not an exaggeration to say that for most people "a book" means a novel', Q. D. Leavis observed in 1932.[18] Similarly, during the 1940s a typical reply to the question, 'Do you read books?', posed by Mass-Observation, was: '"Yes. What you call magazines. I call them books . . . well, girls' books".'[19] Interviewers preparing a Gallup Poll in February 1940 were surprised by the 'large' number (15 per cent) of people who said they had bought the book they were reading. Gallup suspected—almost certainly correctly— that some people included magazines and periodicals in their definition of 'books'.[20]

Perhaps not unexpectedly, given the nature of this subject, the historian encounters many problems, not only in obtaining information but in interpreting sources. In one sense, the natural preference for 'high' over 'low' culture has engendered a kind of literary snobbery. On the death of the romantic fiction writer Ethel M. Dell in 1939, *The Times* made a rare admission in citing her, with Charles Garvice, Nat Gould, and Edgar Wallace, as 'the most popular novelists in the English-speaking world'.[21] And yet these authors—the favourites of the 'New Reading Public'—are rarely found in surveys of English literature. The book which probably had the largest sale and widest readership of any novel in Britain during the Second World War—James Hadley Chase's grisly thriller *No Orchids for Miss Blandish*—has received similar treatment, as has Mills & Boon. The firm even admitted so in a 1950 advertisement: 'Many people still disapprove of romantic fiction. Perhaps you are one, but all the same it remains a necessary part of any circulating library.' John Boon expressed his resentment over such treatment by literary critics. 'I

---

[18] Leavis, *Fiction and the Reading Public*, 6.   [19] F/25/D, Chelsea; M-O.
[20] *B* (21 Mar. 1940), 380.
[21] Penelope Dell, *Nettie and Sissie: The Biography of Ethel M. Dell and her Sister Ella* (London, 1977), 164.

suppose of any genre we have the biggest readership in the world, but you'll never see us mentioned.'[22]

Similarly, investigators of reading habits during this period were sometimes reluctant to admit that the poorer classes, and especially children, were reading—and enjoying—'inferior' fiction. Some conclusions reached, therefore, were largely 'wishful thinking' and must be regarded with care. In 1916, for example, the reading habits of factory employees aged 21 and under were surveyed by their company supervisor. Given only the run of his private library (which was well stocked with 'boys' books . . . temptingly displayed'), these workers preferred *Queen Mary's Gift Book*, *Scotland for Ever* (a Red Cross volume), and *Princess Mary's Gift Book*, among others. The investigator was cheered by these selections made by members of the 'humbler but intelligent classes'; his conclusion is unwarranted and absurd.[23] In 1927 Foyle's, the London bookseller, distributed questionnaires to schools and clubs in England to determine the most popular authors of boys' books. The top ten were R. M. Ballantyne, G. A. Henty, Sir Arthur Conan Doyle, H. Rider Haggard, Herbert Strang, Jules Verne, Captain Marryat, Rudyard Kipling, Charles Dickens, and (the first of the 'moderns') Percy Westerman. 'The result seems to indicate that the average boy is conservative in his reading tastes, that he is quite satisfied with his father's old favourites, and is slow to adventure into new literary fields', according to *The Publishers' Circular*. What was not mentioned, however, was that the field of twenty-five authors listed on the questionnaire was selected by Foyle's, and that a number of critics, including *The Publishers' Circular*, suspected that many ballot papers had been completed by parents. In a reply, Gunby Hadath, a writer of school stories, added that six of the twenty-five authors in the list—Conan Doyle, Kipling, Stevenson, Dickens, Rider Haggard, and Sir Walter Scott—could not truly be classified as 'boys' authors'.[24]

---

[22] John Boon was interviewed in 1988. Sir John Betjeman was an exception among literary critics. 'He got so fed up with reviewing what he called obscene books or unpleasant subjects, he was always pleased when he got a Mills & Boon—not that I think he got very many of them', Boon said.

[23] Peter Playfair, 'The Literary Tastes of Working Lads', letter, *Times Literary Supplement* (30 Nov. 1916), 574.

[24] 'Who Are the Most Popular Authors of Boys' Books?', *PC* (16 Apr. 1927), 452; (1 Oct. 1927), 477, 479. John Stevenson, in *British Society 1914–45* (London, 1984), refers to a 1926 survey with the same results (p. 399); this may be the Foyle's study.

POPULAR READING AND PUBLISHING
1870–1914

'FOR very many Englishmen of all classes, the periodical, daily, weekly, or monthly, is practically an exclusive synonym for literature itself', T. H. S. Escott wrote in 1897.[1] Lady Bell, in her 1907 survey of Middlesbrough, concluded that it 'seems undeniable that for the great majority of people reading means recreation, not study: it is a pity we have only the one word to designate the two pursuits'.[2] Both observations would surely have dismayed Wilkie Collins, and both suggest that his hopes had not been fulfilled even before the era of the modern mass market. In order to understand the market for light fiction and its mass readership which were an established part of British culture after the First World War, it is necessary here to consider the growth of the Unknown Public and the development of the publishing industry in the nineteenth century. Many factors stimulated a boom in reading and in publishing. These included the abolition of the 'taxes on know- ledge', extension of education and literacy, and the development of new (and cheaper) methods of production and distribution. The char- acteristic of the period is, indeed, 'cheapness', for it was through a fall in retail prices and costs of production that reading, and the publishing industry, expanded.

Between 1870 and 1914 two schools of thought, frequently inter- twined, influenced the expanding market for popular fiction. One of these, the 'improving' or optimistic school, was a by-product of Vic- torian liberalism. Reformist in aspiration, publishers such as the Religious Tract Society hoped to edify the newly literate masses by replacing the popular 'dreadful' publications with 'wholesome' papers, often with specifically religious leanings. The other school was wholly commercial and entrepreneurial. New and ambitious publishers seized

---

[1] T. H. S. Escott, *Social Transformations of the Victorian Age: A Survey of Court and Country* (London, 1897), 375.

[2] Florence Eveleen E., Lady Bell, *At the Works: A Study of a Manufacturing Town* (Virago edn., London, 1985), 170.

the opportunities presented by the growing market for the greatest financial gain. Although it is not difficult to predict which of the two would emerge the stronger, the state of the publishing industry and the reading market by 1914 was not that simple. The more successful publishers of the twentieth century, including D. C. Thomson and Mills & Boon, represented a synthesis of these two attitudes: preserving (in spirit) a Victorian editorial paternalism within finely tuned and cleverly marketed publications which dominated their markets. The continuities which can be established between the pre-1914 period and the post-war era, therefore, are as important as the discontinuities.

I

The year 1870 is often cited as a watershed in the history of publishing in Britain. In this year Forster's Elementary Education Act was passed, technically bringing elementary education within the reach of every child. Overnight—or so it seemed—the masses were literate and de-manded copious amounts of reading matter. The fledgling publishing industry boomed in response, and the mass market in 'popular' fiction was born. Contemporary critics often referred to the 1870 Act, casting upon it the entire blame for the bad reading tastes of the poor. Joseph Ackland, writing on 'Elementary Education and the Decay of Litera-ture' in 1894, was not surprised by this state. 'The intellectual faculties of the bulk of the nation were too long in bondage; it should not cause any wonder that when the shackles of ignorance were struck off there was a rush to the Elysian fields of fancy and pleasure.'[3] In 1906 James Haslam measured the optimistic expectations of the Education Act against working-class reading habits in Manchester. '"The Three Rs" were to lead magically to higher planes of morality, politer man-ners, purer thoughts', he wrote. 'The contrast between these expecta-tions and the present reality is enough to make the most robust optimist a temporary cynic.'[4] George Gissing's classic novel of the publishing world, *New Grub Street* (1894), aired both sides of the controversy. 'Your Board schools, your popular press, your spread of education! Machinery for ruining the country, that's what I call it', John Yule

---

[3] Joseph Ackland, 'Elementary Education and the Decay of Literature', *The Nine-teenth Century*, 35 (Mar. 1894), 423.

[4] James Haslam, *The Press and the People: An Estimate of Reading in Working-Class Districts* (Manchester, 1906), 3. Haslam, an idealist, correlated poor living conditions with low-brow reading tastes. 'When the slum-dweller delights in reading Milton and Shakespeare then there will be no more slums', he believed.

declares, although Mr Whelpdale, publisher of *Chit-Chat*, is proud to serve 'the quarter-educated', 'the great new generation that is being turned out by the Board schools, the young men and women who can just read, but are incapable of sustained attention'.[5]

We know now that the 1870 Act was only one of many significant advances in the history of education and literacy as well as of publishing. It did not make elementary education mandatory or free: in 1880 it was made compulsory for children to the age of 10, but school fees were not abolished until 1891. Literacy levels, moreover, had been increasing throughout the nineteenth century. By 1870, the formal literacy rate in England and Wales (measured as the ability to sign one's name) was estimated at 80 per cent, and in Scotland 90 per cent. By 1900 these figures had increased to 97 and 98 per cent. According to Lawrence Stone, by the late nineteenth century 'the ratios between name-signing and an adequate reading capacity, and between reading capacity and writing capacity, tended rapidly to converge'. Indeed, R. K. Webb has suggested that, as early as the 1840s, between two-thirds and three-quarters of the working class were 'fully literate', or able to read.[6]

Other factors of an economic and social nature nurtured the growth of popular fiction for the Unknown Public. In fact, by 1870 conditions were favourable for publishing of *any* kind. The elimination of stamp duties on newspapers, for example, was an encouragement not only to that genre but to all types of reading matter. In 1853 the duty on newspaper advertisements was repealed, and by 1861 all such 'taxes on knowledge' were abolished, allowing the sale of reading matter at a much lower price, in most cases one penny. The growth of the railways and extension of the telegraph afforded better distribution and communication. Increased rail travel also created a market for light reading to while away the journey. Improved methods of lighting, in the home and in public areas, encouraged reading. In the 1850s better paper-making machinery was developed, and the price of paper was cheapened with the use of woodpulp. The invention of the rotary printing press, which printed on continuous rolls of paper, speeded production considerably, and made possible larger editions.[7]

---

[5] George Gissing, *New Grub Street* (Penguin edn., Harmondsworth, 1987), 54, 497.

[6] Lawrence Stone, 'Literacy and Education in England, 1640–1900', *Past and Present*, 42 (Feb. 1969), 120; R. K. Webb, 'Working Class Readers in Early Victorian England', *English Historical Review*, 65 (1950), 333–51; see also Webb, *The British Working Class Reader 1790–1848: Literacy and Social Tension* (London, 1955).

[7] Herbert Tracey (ed.), *The British Press: A Survey, A Newspaper Directory, and a Who's Who in Journalism* (London, 1929), 15–16.

Booksellers saw the possibilities of this new market and moved to exploit it. In 1848 the first W. H. Smith railway bookstall, at Euston Station, was opened, the beginning of a network of stalls and bookshops throughout England and Wales. In early years this firm prided itself on stocking a 'better' selection of reading matter than the vulgar penny papers in great demand; in later years it carried the full range of popular fiction. W. H. Smith's Scottish counterpart, John Menzies, opened his first bookstalls at Perth and Stirling in 1857. In 1860 the W. H. Smith Circulating Library was founded, operating through each bookstall, in competition with Mudie's Library (1842). Both libraries were the principal purchasers of the first, three-volume editions of novels (or 'three-deckers'). Given the cost of an annual subscription (at least £1 per year, per volume), patrons of these libraries were largely from the middle class. In 1899 the main competitor of Mudie's and W. H. Smith, Boots Booklovers Library, was founded. John Menzies did not operate a library service.

Simultaneous with the expansion of subscription libraries was the growth of similar facilities for the working class. These included libraries of Mechanics' Institutes (610 in England in 1850, containing some 700,000 volumes), and, principally, the free or public libraries. The Public Libraries Act of 1850 empowered councils of towns with populations of 10,000 or more to levy a halfpenny rate for the building and maintenance of a museum or a library. The intention was to provide workers with a wholesome and edifying alternative to the public house during their spare time. The rate was increased to one penny in 1855, and in 1866 restrictions on population size were abolished. Library growth remained slow, however, until the end of the century. Opposition stemmed from the dislike of increased rates and an innate fear of the consequences of edifying the masses. The public library movement was spurred by the 1870 Education Act, the 1889 Technical Instruction Act (which increased demand for non-fiction holdings), and private benefactions from philanthropists such as Andrew Carnegie, who endowed 380 libraries throughout Britain.[8]

Prior to 1870, as Collins had argued, a thriving market existed for popular fiction. In general there were two types of reading matter catering to this market: these may conveniently be called 'classic' and 'sensational'. Sensational fiction was itself of two kinds: 'penny dreadfuls' and 'yellow-backs'. Penny dreadfuls, so named for their price and

[8] See esp. Thomas Kelly, *Books for the People: An Illustrated History of the British Public Library* (London, 1977).

poor quality, catered largely to a young working-class audience. The pejorative was used to describe both magazines issued in parts (such as *Sweeney Todd*) and bloodthirsty weeklies such as *The Boys of England* (1866) with its legendary hero, Jack Harkaway. Popular penny dreadfuls included *Seduction, or the Perils of a Woman's Life*; *Wild Will, or the Pirates of the Thames*; and two well-known thrillers, *The Blue Dwarf* and *Dick Turpin*.[9] Yellow-backs, so named for the colour of their lurid covers, contained complete stories of a similar type, although with more 'adult' themes. Reminiscent of the American 'dime novels', they are an early example of inexpensive popular fiction, bound in stiff or paper covers. The tone of the yellow-backs is suggested by two of G. W. M. Reynolds's publications: *Loves of the Harem* and *Bronze Statue, or the Virgin's Kiss*. Edition sizes for both types of publications varied between 1,000 and 10,000 copies; one can assume that copies were passed around and that the actual readership was much higher.[10]

Given their low price and sensational subject-matter, penny dreadfuls and yellow-backs were obviously aimed at readers from the working classes. They were sold through traditional bookstalls and, on a more personal level, by hand outside factory gates and through tobacconists, sweets vendors, and corner-shop grocers. Discounts of more than double the customary 25 per cent were offered by publishers to shopkeepers who gave these papers prominent display in their windows.[11] Edward Lloyd, one of the most prolific of this kind of publisher (known in the trade as the 'Salisbury Square School'), perhaps best characterized the presumed status of his patrons:

You see, our publications circulate amongst a class so different in education and social position to the readers of three-volume novels, that we sometimes distrust our own judgement, and place the manuscript in the hands of an illiterate person—a servant or a machine boy, for instance. If they pronounce favourably upon it, we think it will do.[12]

Richard Altick claimed that by the 1850s the first truly mass reading public in Britain had been established, largely due to such publishers as Lloyd and Reynolds. 'It was only around the fifties that the familiar

---

[9] According to E. S. Turner, *Black Bess, or The Knight of the Road*, published by E. Harrison, is, at 254 weekly parts, 2,028 pages, and over 2.5 million words, the longest penny dreadful by one author on record (*Boys Will be Boys* (London, 1975), 48).

[10] See 'The Literature of Vice', *B* (28 Feb. 1867), 121–3; Michael Sadleir, 'Yellow-Backs', in John Carter (ed.), *New Paths in Book Collecting* (London, 1934), 150.

[11] James Greenwood, *The Wilds of London* (London, 1874), 159–60.

[12] Quoted in Thomas Frost, *Forty Years' Recollections: Literary and Political* (London, 1880), 90.

phrase of "literature for the millions" ceased to be mere hyperbole and came to have a basis in sober fact.'[13]

In spite of the absence of circulation figures, there is no reason to doubt that this fiction was read in large numbers. The literary 'establishment', including Wilkie Collins, certainly thought so, and considered that it had harmful effects, particularly for younger readers. Thomas Wright, for example, regarded penny dreadfuls as 'such utter, unredeemed rot ... we are more inclined to believe that their "pull" must lie, not in interesting boys, but in flattering them, pandering to their weaknesses and want of sense'.[14] The *Quarterly Review* even blamed them for the increase in juvenile crime. 'The story is always the same. An errand boy or an office lad is caught in the act of robbing his master ... In his desk are found sundry numbers of these romances of the road.'[15] George Humphery claimed that such literature filled young people's heads with grand and unattainable dreams, such as how to become a duke or a countess. 'The effect of this is seen', he claimed, 'in the exalted opinions the young people entertain of themselves, even to the disuse of ordinary politeness. Out of ten boys who applied for work, only one said "Please" or "Thank you".'[16]

'Classic' popular fiction was also of two kinds: quality literature, which was distributed and sold at a cheaper price than new books, and the crop of second-rank novels ('sensation novels') which filled the shelves of the subscription libraries. The latter may be considered 'classic' in the sense that they were conceived and marketed like traditional novels. Before 1870 book publishing in Britain was dominated by a handful of large houses, including Chapman and Hall, Blackwood, and Macmillan. These firms produced new novels in the standard three-volume first edition, at a price of more than 31 shillings. But there did exist other opportunities for publishing quality literature which reached a wider audience at a cheaper price. These included part-publication of first novels; serialization in fiction magazines including *All the Year Round*; and the reprinting of novels in 'Collected Editions', such as the successful 'Railway Library' novels published by Routledge.[17]

[13] Richard Altick, 'English Publishing and the Mass Audience in 1852', *Studies in Bibliography*, vi (1954), 4–5.

[14] Thomas Wright, 'On a Possible Popular Culture', *Contemporary Review*, 49 (July 1881), 35.

[15] 'Penny Fiction', *Quarterly Review*, 151 (July 1890), 154–5.

[16] George R. Humphery, 'The Reading of the Working Classes', *The Nineteenth Century*, 33 (Jan.–June 1893), 692–3.

[17] See esp. John Sutherland, *Victorian Novelists and Publishers* (London, 1976), 9–40.

If penny dreadfuls and yellow-backs characterized much of the retail trade prior to the 1870s, sensation novels were the mainstays of the circulating libraries. In essence, these were similar in style and content to the penny publications but extended to three volumes. The prime exponents of this genre were Mrs Henry Wood (*East Lynne*, 1861), Mary Elizabeth Braddon (*Lady Audley's Secret*, 1862),[18] and 'Ouida' (*Under Two Flags*, 1867). Charles Knight described well the typical elements in such novels:

> In a sensation novel of the genuine sort, are to be found a pleasant distillation of the topics that daily present themselves in the records of the criminal courts and police offices, all so softened down and made easy to juvenile capacities, that murders, forgeries, burglaries, arson, breach of trust, adulteries, seductions, elopements, appear the common incidents of an English household.[19]

The greatest sensation these novels caused was the fact that the criminals were seemingly moral and upright people. None the less, good always triumphed over evil, and despite the strong overtones of sex and violence these were essentially morality tales, structured around a love story. As these novels were published in three volumes, obtainable mainly at the subscription libraries and serialized in the more expensive (6*d.*) magazines, it is unlikely that these authors at this time attracted a large working-class audience, though their sales demonstrate just how big the reading public was among the other classes. Their later popularity and influence, when cheaper editions became available, is, however, evident. In 1880 Thomas Frost claimed that 'the authors whose works are most in demand among the subscribers to Mudie's are also those which stand highest in favour of the readers of the penny periodicals, so far at least as they have been brought within their reach'.[20] In *Lark Rise to Candleford*, Laura described 'the more daring and up to date' girls in Candleford town 'who liked a thrill in their reading, devoured the novels of Ouida in secret, hiding the book beneath the mattresses of their beds between whiles. For their public reading they had the *Girl's Own Paper*.'[21] Mrs Henry Wood was the

[18] Braddon said that her intention in writing *Lady Audley's Secret* was 'to combine, as far as my powers allowed, the human interest and genial humour of Dickens with the plot-weaving of G. W. M. Reynolds' (Robert Lee Wolff, *Sensational Victorian: The Life and Fiction of Mary Elizabeth Braddon* (London, 1979), 81).

[19] Charles Knight, *Passages of a Working Life During Half a Century*, vol. iii (London, 1873), 180–1.

[20] Frost, *Forty Years' Recollections*, 323.

[21] Flora Thompson, *Lark Rise to Candleford* (Penguin edn., Harmondsworth, 1987), 497.

author most favoured by working-class men and women in Lady Bell's 1901 survey of Middlesbrough.[22]

II

The period from 1870 to the First World War is distinctive for the rapid acceleration of the trends outlined above. It was the recognition of both the size and the potential—commercial and educational—of the 'new' reading public, fuelled by the Education Act, which encouraged new publishing ventures. In particular, there were three landmarks in the development of the mass market in popular fiction. These were: the founding of the pioneering magazines *The Boy's Own Paper* (1879) and *Tit-Bits* (1881); the achievements of Alfred Harmsworth, Lord Northcliffe; and the boom in new publishing houses which precipitated the fall of the 'three-decker', paving the way towards cheaper fiction for the mass of the reading public. Through such commercial success the demarcations between 'Literature' and 'Fiction', and 'Popular' and 'Mass' (described so well in *New Grub Street*), became clearly drawn, as did publishing intentions. The 'improving' or optimistic publishers sought to replace the penny dreadfuls with more 'wholesome' publications. Their intention was less commercial than missionary. The other approach was unashamedly profit-minded. These publishers seized the emerging market to produce 'better' but no less thrilling publications.

The 1870 Education Act, if not the milestone contemporaries claimed it was, was used, none the less, by some publishers as an excuse to launch a kind of quality control movement to combat low-grade fiction and its apparent excesses. The weekly magazine trade was the first to be reorganized and 'sanitized' in this fashion. The same kind of reform was taking place in pubs, music halls, and at sporting events, as the middle classes increasingly attempted to regulate and 'control' leisure and recreation.[23] The concern of these literary reformers was motivated by the expanding number of young readers whose minds and futures, they felt, were at risk. In 1887 the *Edinburgh Review* issued an appeal to the publishing industry:

---

[22] Bell, *At the Works*, 165–6.
[23] See esp. Peter Bailey, *Leisure and Class in Victorian Britain: Rational Recreation and the Contest for Control, 1830–1885* (London, 1987); and W. Hamilton Fraser, *The Coming of the Mass Market 1850–1914* (London, 1981).

Carry the war into the enemy's camp; flood the market with good, wholesome literature instead of the poisonous stuff to which hapless purchasers are now condemned. The battle must be fought out by the purveyors of fiction, and it must be made as easy and profitable to provide a dainty, harmless, and well-seasoned repast as a dish of poison.[24]

Helen Bosanquet in 1901 recognized the improving trend in popular literature and gave credit where it was due. 'We have to thank the business man rather than the philanthropist. Publishers of some standing are finding out that it is profitable to cater for the million, and they are learning also that the million prefers good to bad, when good implies some positive merit and is not merely goody'.[25]

Leading the crusade against the penny dreadfuls was the Religious Tract Society, publishers of *The Boy's Own Paper* (1879) and *The Girl's Own Paper* (1880). The success of these publications (each achieved an initial weekly sale of 200,000 copies, equal to the most popular of the dreadfuls) was a revelation to the industry, demonstrating both the attractions of high-quality production and the seeming size of the market for 'wholesome' fiction. But the *BOP* was not founded without much deliberation within the Religious Tract Society about publishing a 'secular' paper which, in some respects, was only a much tamer version of a penny dreadful. In 1900 the chairman of the Society, responding perhaps to dissension, defended the magazines for confronting the 'terrible literature' of the competition (which, he claimed, encouraged gambling and suicides) on common ground. 'We have tried to face and counteract . . . That is really the ground-work of our publications, which are not strictly religious ones, such as the *BOP* and the *GOP*; we feel justified in meeting this difficulty in that way.'[26]

New journals, especially those for children, followed the lead of the Religious Tract Society in distinguishing themselves from the older dreadfuls, sometimes driving the point home through advertisements. In the 1880s *The Garfield Library* ('Full of Glorious Fun! Adventure! Exploration! And Exploit!') carried an endorsement from a Reverend School-master: 'They make bad boys into good boys, and good boys into better boys, and we all thank you heartily.' In an 'Address to Our Readers' in the first issue (1890), *The Boys' Guide* wrote: 'Our principal aim has been to produce a journal of which no boy need be ashamed . . .

[24] 'The Literature of the Streets', *Edinburgh Review*, 165 (Jan. 1887), 63.
[25] Helen Bosanquet, 'Cheap Literature', *Contemporary Review*, 79 (May 1901), 681.
[26] Quoted in *The Religious Tract Society Record* (June 1900), 44. The Religious Tract Society is discussed in Ch. 7.

There will be no occasion for any surreptitious indulgence in the luxury of poring over these columns, for THE BOYS' GUIDE may be introduced into any home or school.' Similarly, the first number of *Every Boy's Favorite [sic] Journal* in 1892 contained the following notice:

THE SERIAL STORIES are written by men well trained to the task of providing the young with a wholesome sensation which shall leave no taint of evil on their minds, and if in the course of any of the novels it is necessary to introduce a blackened character, a villain, be sure that villain will be served as he was in the good old days, that is, his bad life will end badly for him, right will triumph over might, virtue and innocence will be triumphant in the end.[27]

Blackie & Son received much critical praise for its wholesome books for children, a list which included G. A. Henty. This blurb, from the *Anti-Jacobin*, was printed in Blackie & Son's general catalogue for 1892/3:

Ninety-nine boy readers out of every hundred will acquire from these books enlarged conceptions of duty, of chivalry, of courage, of honesty, and of true manliness, and be quite unaware that to inculcate such ideas was the purpose of the author.

Clearly, such notices were intended as much for their parents as for the boys. They are the first signs of what was to be an important assumption of post-1914 publishing: that parents effectively determined what their children read, and that publishers could not alienate them by departing from conventional moral standards. Morality 'improved', therefore, simultaneously with technical quality.

   The public library movement was an important part of this reformist attitude towards publishing and reading. The most vocal and active crusader for public libraries was Thomas Greenwood.[28] Writing in 1886, Greenwood addressed himself to 'the book-hunger which pervades so universally the middle and lower classes especially', a demand which was 'as clear, as definite, as the cry for good drainage and good water'. His plea was prompted by the poor growth of public libraries in Britain: in thirty-six years only 133 towns had taken advantage of the Public Library Act. A public library, Greenwood claimed, was a 'centre of light' and 'sweetness': 'Free libraries not only feed, but they create a taste for reading, and unquestionably, whatever does this is of benefit

[27] *Every Boy's Favorite [sic] Journal* (7 Jan. 1892), 16.
[28] See Thomas Greenwood, *Free Public Libraries: Their Organisation, Uses and Management*, 1st edn. (London, 1886), 4th edn. (London, 1894); *Greenwood's Library Year Book 1897* (London, 1897).

to the community, and aids materially in the repressing and taming of the rougher and baser parts of men's nature.' These kinds of libraries, moreover, were open to all classes, 'from the professional man to the humblest working man. In a large Midland town there are two chimney sweeps and two members of Parliament among borrowers.' Greenwood solicited support from an array of prominent members of society. 'How far better it is to spend our money on libraries and schools than on prisons', Sir John Lubbock, MP ('a true lover of books'), said. 'To no other cause, I think, can we attribute the gratifying diminution in crime which has taken place, and is taking place.' If libraries could not offer bread or clothing to the working man, according to the (unidentified) President of the Statistical Society, they did 'make life sweeter and better, and so open out careers even to the poorest'. But it was Greenwood himself who talked toughest, making the spread of public libraries a national imperative. Britain was lagging perilously behind Germany and America, he warned in 1894:

The national need is that we be not placed at any disadvantage in the neck-and-neck race of competition with the Germans and Americans which has become inevitable, as the existence of libraries generally in the midst of these nations has given the people an advantage which has been lacking in English life, and it will take us years to overtake the drawbacks, on this account, which have inevitably accrued. National sentiment alone should lead every town and large rural district where a Public Library does not already exist, to at once set about the adoption of the Acts.

By 1918 there were 566 library authorities, representing 60 per cent of the population. But the great hopes of reformers such as Greenwood were not realized. Borrowers, for one, were predominantly not from the working classes, and the majority of issues—in some cases as high as four-fifths—were of works of fiction. Greenwood was undeterred in 1897 when forced to reply to what had become known as 'The Great Fiction Question'. While he had to admit that the public was using the libraries for borrowing fiction, he considered this, as did Wilkie Collins, natural and a good start, a kind of springboard to better things. Fiction reading was 'as much a habit and necessity of the age as church-going or money making', and was a useful way for men and women of all classes 'to induce *forgetfulness of the past day's labours*'. But fiction, he added, was the road to non-fiction. 'The refining, stimulating and refreshing influences of the novel are being positively swallowed in the feverish anxiety of young people to equip themselves in technical and other subjects to enable them to fight competing Germans.' There is no evidence that they did so, although non-fiction issues did tend to rise in wartime.

George Newnes was the first of a new breed of publishing tycoons who brought a change in style and direction to the industry. If these tycoons were sympathetic to the aims of the reformers, their primary goal, as businessmen, was the greatest return on investment. Their success initiated the trend towards a quasi-middle-class domination of popular publishing in Britain as well as the monopolizing of the market by a handful of large firms. In 1881 George Newnes founded *Tit-Bits*, the first 'snippet' paper, filled with easy-to-read trivia and useless information. The editor described the paper's intentions in the first issue:

The business of the conductors of *Tit-Bits* will be like that of the dentist—an organized system of extracting . . . Any person who takes in *Tit-Bits* for three months will at the end of that time be an entertaining companion, as he will then have at his command a stock of smart sayings and a fund of anecdotes which will make his society agreeable.

Here, then, was a simple way to be accepted by all classes. Flora Thompson noted how *Tit-Bits* was taken by 'almost every family', and how people delighted in the trivial knowledge dispensed by these 'Yellow Books'.[29] *Tit-Bits* was both praised as a unique path towards edifying the masses and derided as the beginning of the decline of English journalism. None the less, by 1888 it was selling an average of 350,000 copies per week,[30] an astonishing number, making it one of the first truly 'mass' publications in Britain. Its success, like that of the *Boy's Own Paper*, prompted a host of imitations: other publishing magnates, such as C. Arthur Pearson and Alfred Harmsworth (later Lord Northcliffe), achieved their initial successes with similar papers: *Pearson's Weekly* (1890) and *Answers to Correspondents* (1888). Competition between rival papers was great, and ingenious prize competitions served to boost circulation. *Answers* offered a macabre insurance scheme for their readers: if injured in a railway accident while bearing a copy of the publication, the victim would be paid £1,000; by 1892 the payment had risen to £2,600. During an influenza epidemic, eucalyptus oil, considered a preventative, was sprayed on copies of *Pearson's Weekly*.

[29] Thompson, *Lark Rise to Candleford*, 498–9.
[30] Thomas Smith and J. H. Osborne (eds.), *Successful Advertising: Its Secrets Explained*, 9th edn. (London, 1888), 414.

Alfred Harmsworth was the most prolific and innovative of this new generation of popular publishers. His achievements in magazine journalism stand beside his landmark newspaper foundations, the *Daily Mail* (1896) and the *Daily Mirror* (1903). By 1909 he was publishing nearly 50 titles that sold 8.5 million copies weekly.[31] His firm, the Amalgamated Press, founded boys' papers such as the *Wonder* (1892), *Marvel* (1893, which introduced Sexton Blake, Detective), *Union Jack* (1894), and *The Magnet* (1908), and established a magazine market for women with such titles as *Forget-Me-Not* (1891), *Home Chat* (1895), and *Woman's Weekly* (1911).[32] *Forget-Me-Not* was one of the first weekly penny magazines targeted specifically at women. With a pale blue wrapper and perfumed paper, it promised to be 'as bright and pure as the flower from which it gets its name'. Subtitled 'A Pictorial Journal for Ladies', among its features were romantic fiction ('Diary of a Professional Beauty' and 'Confession of a Wallflower'), and aicles on etiquette, fashion, and household management. The editors flattered the largely lower-middle-class readership by always using the term of address, 'Ladies'. Harmsworth's women's magazines inspired many imitations, all designed for wives and mothers with limited means who required domestic and maternal guidance, as well as 'wholesome' entertainment. One of his many innovations, opposed by newsagents, was starting a serial story in one paper, and continuing it in another, thereby boosting sales—but also increasing customer complaints.[33]

Harmsworth's 'targeting' of papers to specific audiences represents one of the more lasting innovations of this period, contributing to what Peter Keating has described as 'the relentless fragmentation and categorisation of fiction'.[34] A changing occupational structure persuaded many proprietors to develop storypapers featuring characters that would appeal to certain workers, such as mill girls, shop-assistants, and domestic help. Advertising was used to a degree not seen before as papers were marketed like any consumer product. Publicity gimmicks and superlatives were common. In the 1890s the Aldine Publishing Company produced several 'libraries' of thrilling stories

[31] *Souvenir of Banquet, Held at The Fleetway House* (London, 7 Nov. 1912), unpaginated.
[32] Circulation figures, July 1894: *Marvel*, 144,000; *Union Jack*, 132,000; *Wonder*, 184,000; *Answers*, 335,000; *Comic Cuts*, 425,000; *Chips*, 282,000; *Forget-Me-Not*, 141,000. The boys' papers were described as selling 'in the hundreds of thousands and yielded their quota of profits' (Reginald Pound and Geoffrey Harmsworth, *Northcliffe* (London, 1959), 165).
[33] Pound and Harmsworth, *Northcliffe*, 117.
[34] Peter Keating, *The Haunted Study* (London, 1989), 340.

for boys, priced between 1*d*. and 6*d*., depending on the length. *The Aldine O'er Land and Sea Library*, sixty-four pages for 2*d*., was described as 'the largest (containing more good reading), the Cheapest, and Best Twopenny Library in the World'. Newnes's *British Boys* (1896) was heralded as 'The Best and Biggest Halfpenny Boys' Paper in the World'. *The Grand Magazine* (1905), also by Newnes, was even more straightforward, announcing, 'Every Page in this Magazine is Interesting.' For women, Pearson's *Home Notes*, which was 'Profusely Illustrated', was subtitled 'The Hand that Rocks the Cradle Rules the World'. Horace Marshall's oddly titled *Ladies' Bits* (1892) and *Book-Bits* (1896) obviously preyed upon Newnes's success. Some popular authors edited their own papers: W. H. G. Kingston and G. A. Henty edited·the first *Union Jack* (1880), and Captain Mayne Reid *The Boy's Illustrated News*. Sharp advertising techniques which nurtured cults of personality around best-selling authors were satirized by one critic: 'a well-known and much-esteemed author of to-day "with the proceeds of some *blueberries*, sold to the mother of her future husband, bought the pencil with which her first story was written." This is the *fabulous* and *vulgar* trash which takes the place of history and criticism.'[35] But advertising did work: Nat Gould attributed sales of one million in Britain, his largest market, to publicity. 'My publisher, Mr John Long, pushes them vigorously and advertises them effectively here. You have, no doubt, seen the very taking posters and bills that he puts up at the railway stations and elsewhere.'[36]

The decades before the First World War witnessed a furious expansion of publishing houses and publications. The magazine market grew prodigiously along with the reading public: an estimated 50,000 periodicals were published in Britain by 1900.[37] In 1881 Francis Hitchman claimed that between five and six million penny publications—weeklies and monthlies—circulated in London alone every week, in what he described as 'a remarkable phenomenon of modern times'. He added that 'some 14 or 15 papers' for boys were published each week, with a total circulation 'of at least a million and a half'.[38] In 1898 *Blackwood's Magazine* counted over thirty weekly fiction publications costing a penny or less, each containing at least 20,000 words of

[35] 'The Literature of Snippets', *Saturday Review*, 87 (15 Apr. 1899), 456.
[36] *B* (5 Apr. 1912), 462–3.
[37] Keating, *The Haunted Study*, 36.
[38] Francis Hitchman, 'The Penny Press', *Macmillan's Magazine*, 43 (1881), 396. 'It is somewhat melancholy to have to add that, with few exceptions, these papers are silly and vulgar in the extreme, and that two or three are positively vicious', he concluded.

romance and adventure.[39] By 1914 there were some 200 publishers of weekly and monthly periodicals in Britain.

Book publishing also expanded. Many of the new publishing houses were, as in the magazine trade, family foundations run by a strong, influential proprietor. Often a publisher achieved great success with an individual author or a particular series, such as the 'Sixpenny Blacks', classic literature issued by Hutchinson (founded 1887). In format and price this series pre-dated the success of Penguin Books by some fifty years. Cassell (1883) was launched with a string of juvenile successes including *Treasure Island* (1883) and *King Solomon's Mines* (1885). Heinemann established an author and an imprint simultaneously with the publication of Hall Caine's *The Bondman* (1890), which had been turned down by Cassell. Similarly, Methuen published Marie Corelli's *The Sorrows of Satan* (1895), which had an initial sale greater than any previous novel, bestowing upon it the (largely symbolic) title of the first best-seller in English history. By 1919 202,000 copies had been sold.[40] Several book firms also published magazines, including the Religious Tract Society and Cassell (*Chums*).

Perhaps mirroring developments in the magazine trade, the existing trend towards cheaper-priced fiction continued, although not all of it was of high quality. T. Harrison Roberts's Gainsborough Novels, one halfpenny, were described as the 'Sensation of the Century', with such titles as *A Passionate Wooing*. Like yellow-backs, pocket-sized 'Complete Novelettes' were a common publication at this time, often published in connection with weekly magazines such as *Bow Bells* or *The Family Herald*. Laura's grandmother in *Lark Rise* was an avid reader of novelettes, including *His Ice Queen*. 'Except when engaged in housework, she was never seen without a book in her hand. It was always a novelette, and she had a large assortment of these which she kept tied up in flat parcels, ready to exchange with other novelette readers.'[41] The marketing of series of books, or 'libraries', was common: Methuen's 1/- Library (featuring Marie Corelli), Everyman's Library, and Nelson's Library, for example, as well as groups of sevenpenny fiction offered by Hutchinson, Hurst and Blackett, Macmillan, and Ward, Lock. Cassell's People's Library, which included in its list *Wuthering*

---

[39] See 'Penny Fiction', *Blackwood's Edinburgh Magazine*, 164 (Dec. 1898), 801–11. Such popular titles as *Tit-Bits* and *Home Notes* were excluded from the list, as these were not exclusively fiction-orientated.

[40] Brian Masters, *Now Barabbas Was a Rotter: The Extraordinary Life of Marie Corelli* (London, 1978), 3.

[41] Thompson, *Lark Rise to Candleford*, 94.

Heights, was offered at 1*s*. 6*d*. leather and 8*d*. cloth; the list had sold 850,000 copies by 1909.[42] The promotion of publishing imprints rather than individual authors in this fashion would be put to best use by Mills & Boon, founded in 1908.

It was the fall of the 'three-decker' in the 1890s, however, which had the greatest impact on the future of the publishing industry. The displacement of the costly three-volume novel by a one-volume, six-shilling edition, which was followed by even cheaper editions if demand warranted, encouraged the distribution of literature among all classes. The collapse occurred in the mid-1890s, under the pressure of increasing public demand for cheaper first editions, and from the circulating libraries, which were faced with rising storage costs and budget restraints. Heinemann published one of the first new one-volume novels, Hall Caine's *The Manxman*, at six shillings in 1894. Although cheaper editions were now established, the Net Book Agreement, introduced in 1900, prevented pricing wars between booksellers and publishers by forbidding the sale of any new book at less than the fixed price.[43]

With publishing increasingly in the hands of accountants and marketing men, and overtly aiming at a 'mass' market, writing became a profession, and 'fiction' was detached from 'literature' as each attracted different publics. In *New Grub Street* Gissing traced these separate paths in his study of two young writers, Jasper Milvain and Edwin Reardon. Milvain, ambitious and of the new school, is wedded to popular fiction, while the dreamer Reardon is determined to write a 'great' novel. 'Literature nowadays is a trade', Milvain declares:

Putting aside men of genius, who may succeed by mere cosmic force, your successful man of letters is your skilful tradesman. He thinks first and foremost of the markets; when one kind of goods begins to go off slackly, he is ready with something new and appetising.[44]

Milvain maintains, moreover, that 'we people of brains are justified in supplying the mob with the food it likes', to the author's financial gain. The novel chronicles the rise of Milvain and the decline of Reardon, who is both unwilling and unable to write 'in a popular way'—to his ultimate ruin.

Unsurprisingly, a number of 'how-to' books, some by important

[42] *PC* (13 Feb. 1909), 220.
[43] Guinevere L. Griest, *Mudie's Circulating Library and the Victorian Novel* (Newton Abbot, 1970), 182.
[44] Gissing, *New Grub Street*, 38.

authors, were published for aspiring writers of the Milvain tendency. In *How to Publish a Book or Article, and How to Produce a Play* (1898), Leopold Wagner neatly divided the book publishing industry into three types. The 'Manufacturing or Popular Publisher' maintained a large and varied list of titles, from 'shilling shockers' and cookery books to collected editions, publishing whatever was in vogue. The 'Editorial Publisher' was more respectable and up-market, catering to the small bookbuying public. Lastly, the 'Speculative or "Up-to-Date" Publisher' would publish anything, especially from 'proven' authors, so long as a good return was assured. In 1903 Arnold Bennett, in *How to Become an Author*, elaborated further. He suggested that successful writers were now concerned not with what readers *ought* to read but with what they actually *wanted* to read. He admitted that, although such a line of thought could lead to excesses, the writer of popular fiction was, after all, concerned with financial gain and not with literary merit: to be successful he had to understand his audience. To the writer of novelettes, for example, Bennett wrote:

The aspirant will perceive that these amiable inventions appeal to an extremely virtuous order of intelligence, and that they consist of what the superior person would call sheer drivel. But what is one woman's drivel is another woman's George Eliot. All literary excellence is comparative.[45]

Bennett did not condone such 'drivel': he recognized a need in society and offered financial hope to young writers, who might then proceed to better things. Ralph Rollington, himself a former publisher of boys' papers, observed in 1913 how this market had grown since the appearance of Edwin J. Brett's *The Boys of England* in 1866. Whereas writing for boys used to be an adventure and a lark, now writers could earn between £500 and £1,000 annually.[46] Market forces had indeed taken control of the publishing industry.

III

In looking at the state of the publishing industry, the market for popular fiction, and the reading habits of the lower-middle and working classes before and after 1914, it is possible to discern both continuities and discontinuities. Several of the developments outlined above, including the movement towards cheaper-priced fiction, the

---

[45] Arnold Bennett, *How to Become an Author* (London, 1903), 124.
[46] Ralph Rollington, *A Brief History of Boys' Journals* (Leicester, 1913), 85.

categorization and targeting of periodicals and series of books, and the use of lending libraries, reached their fullest expression between the First and Second World Wars. Equally, the reasons why people read (where we can determine them) do not seem to change: 'escapism' appears to have remained the principal motive. The types of fiction which were popular in these periods, however, were significantly different.

According to Victorians and Edwardians, the lower-middle and working classes read as a means of 'escape', and popular fiction was soon labelled 'escapist'—as it was after 1914. The legacy of the penny dreadfuls is apparent in the quest for thrills. Edward Salmon noted that crime and love were essential ingredients in popular fiction: 'The same dish is served up again and again, and the surprising thing is that the readers do not tire of the ceaseless record of wrong-doing on the part of the wealthy which forms the staple of these nonsensical, if not nauseating, stories.'[47] Helen Bosanquet found that while boys' papers were concerned largely with violence and sport, 'The girls are satisfied with one or two good murders, a rescue, and a deathbed, so long as hero and heroine are married or reconciled in the last chapter.'[48] Similarly, Margaret Loane noted that descriptions of crime, in newspapers or magazines, appealed to the working class in particular; the poor would spend a much-needed penny on a paper with a 'good murder' in it.[49] Lady Bell quoted one Middlesbrough woman as favouring penny dreadfuls, which she found 'thrilling, as they give such a good account of high life and elopements'.[50] James Haslam interviewed a working-class woman in Ancoats who admitted, 'It is the chief pleasure of my life . . . to read these tales—they're lovely!'[51]

In 1897 *The Academy* surveyed readers in a style reminiscent of Mass-Observation, and its conclusions, indeed, are similar to those gathered by Mass-Observation during the Second World War.[52] One woman, a waitress, preferred love stories with happy endings. 'She looks upon a story, I suppose, not from the outside, as a work of art, a presentment of another life than her own, but rather as a suggestion of what her own life might be with a little more money and the requisite hero', the reporter observed. A publisher scorned novels, which were

---

[47] Edward Salmon, 'What the Working Classes Read', *The Nineteenth Century*, 20 (July–Dec. 1886), 113.
[48] Bosanquet, 'Cheap Literature', 673, 675.
[49] Margaret Loane, *An Englishman's Castle* (London, 1909), 32–3.
[50] Bell, *At the Works*, 144, 147.   [51] Haslam, *The Press and the People*, 7.
[52] Mass-Observation's findings are discussed in Ch. 3.

read by 'only half-educated women' and then as 'a form of opium taking'. A seafaring man, described as an 'Ambassador of Commerce', offset his boredom at sea with the annual collected volumes of such women's papers as the *Family Herald*. 'Oh, don't you make any mistake! I always lend them, when I've done with them, to other men on board, and they like 'em better than anything. They're the most popular things on the ship,' he said, adding, 'I read to prevent myself thinking. That's the difference.'[53]

Several critics identified restorative, instructional, and politically conservative qualities in 'escapist' fiction. The happy ending, a fixture of romantic fiction, was praised in *Blackwood's Magazine* in 1898: 'So long as to be happily married and to "get on in the world" are the secret or avowed ideals of ... the working classes, so long will any dangerous and far-reaching scheme of communism remain an impossibility.'[54] Flora Thompson noted that the 'mental fare' of 'most of the younger women and some of the older ones' consisted almost exclusively of the romantic novelette, stories of the poor governess who married the duke, much in the *Jane Eyre* mould. These were passed around constantly, a large library in perpetual circulation, but were regarded as a vice and kept from public view. 'They did the women good, for, as they said, they took them out of themselves', she wrote.[55] Others were tolerant of light fiction as a type of safety-valve, a harmless method of improving the temper of the working class. Bosanquet, for example, while critical of the genre, recognized that it had, for the young in particular, a restorative quality:

The cashier-boy relieves the monotony of counting out other people's change by snatches of breathless excitement; the shop-girl soothes away the irritation of the long day's toil by soaring with a heroine (in whom she finds a glorified self) into a heaven of luxury and sentimentality; and the author, if he has reaped neither glory nor money, has, at any rate, made difficult lives a little easier.[56]

Similarly, Charles Dickens, personally reconciled to the new literature by writing a mystery novel at the time of his death, defended such reading habits: 'The English are, so far as I know, the hardest worked people on whom the sun shines. Be content if in their wretched intervals of leisure they read for amusement and do no worse.'[57] Lord

---

[53] C. R., 'What the People Read', *The Academy*, 52 (16 Oct. 1897), 303; 52 (4 Dec. 1897), 499; 53 (19 Feb. 1898), 209.

[54] 'Penny Fiction', *Blackwood's Edinburgh Magazine*, 811.

[55] Thompson, *Lark Rise to Candleford*, 109–10.

[56] Bosanquet, 'Cheap Literature', 674.   [57] Quoted in Knight, *Passages*, iii.17.

Randolph Churchill praised Harmsworth's work as instructive for boys, even inspiring. 'There is no reason at all why he should not go from your pages to the pages of the monthly magazines, from those to the quarterlies, and again from those all through the English classics.'[58] Indeed, Wilkie Collins's optimism was still present.

Some also recognized 'cross-over' kinds of reading which remained common after 1914. Bosanquet, for example, discovered that women enjoyed papers intended for girls: 'There are probably as many adults as juveniles amongst the readers; and, indeed, the "Girls' Friend" is careful to state in its title that it is a paper for readers of all ages.'[59] Girls were also enthusiastic readers of boys' papers. In 1886 Salmon commented on surveys which revealed that nearly as many girls as boys read *Robinson Crusoe*, *Tom Brown's Schooldays*, *Sandford and Merton*, and other 'long-lived "boys'" stories'. Girls, he believed, sought in such books the adventure and insight lacking in their own literature, and these preferences should not be discouraged. 'It ought to impart vigour and breadth to a girl's nature, and to give sisters a sympathetic knowledge of the scenes wherein their brothers live and work.'[60] G. A. Henty, in fact, valued the many letters he received from girls more than those from boys. 'Where there is a girl in the same family the brothers' books are generally common stock, and are carefully read, appreciated, and judged', he observed.[61] During the First World War *The Times*, noting that 'the tastes of the working-girl reader incline to the adventurous and the romantic', claimed that she possessed, 'like other little girls of her age, a keen appreciation of boys' books, and it is she who reads the volumes of adventures given by the soldier'.[62] *Everybody's Weekly*, another Amalgamated Press title, founded in 1911, proclaimed its universal interest in the first number. 'Though masculine in tone, *Everybody's* will make an equal appeal to men and women.'

Who were the most popular authors before the First World War? Among children, an 1884 survey of 2,000 boys and girls aged 11–19 ('from the ordinary Board schoolboy to the young collegian') is a rare source of information, although its conclusions have to be handled

[58] Quoted in G. A. Cranfield, *The Press and Society: From Caxton to Northcliffe* (London, 1978), 219.

[59] Bosanquet, 'Cheap Literature', 675.

[60] Edward Salmon, 'What Girls Read', *The Nineteenth Century*, 20 (July–Dec. 1886), 524.

[61] Quoted in G. Manville Fenn, 'Henty and His Books', in Lance Salway (ed.), *A Peculiar Gift* (London, 1976), 431.

[62] 'Working Girls' Reading: The Queen's Gift of Books', *The Times* (7 Aug. 1917), 9.

with care. Traditional children's authors ranked alongside sensation novelists. The most popular authors among 790 boys polled were Dickens (223 votes), W. H. G. Kingston (179), Sir Walter Scott (128), Jules Verne (114) and Captain Marryat (102). *Robinson Crusoe* was cited as most popular book, and the *Boy's Own Paper*, with 404 votes, was the runaway favourite among magazines, with *Tit-Bits* (27) a distant second. Girls also preferred Dickens (355 votes) and Scott (248), followed by Charles Kingsley (103) and Charlotte M. Yonge (100). Mrs Henry Wood ranked sixth (58) and Miss Braddon twenty-fifth (13). *Westward Ho!* was the most favoured book, and the *Girl's Own Paper*, with 315 votes, the best magazine, followed by the *Boy's Own Paper* (88).[63] The results of this survey, on the whole, support what we know about the sales of children's literature, but probably do not provide precise information, since it is unlikely that the sample was gathered with much exactness.[64] In any event, none of the authors mentioned, nor any of the periodicals, was very popular with children, particularly working-class children, after the First World War. Authors such as Kingston, Marryat, and Yonge were considered dated and boring; the *Boy's Own Paper* and *Girl's Own Paper* too tame.

Among adults, there were four documented 'best-sellers', to use the American term just coming into use in Britain. These were Marie Corelli, Hall Caine, Charles Garvice, and Nat Gould. Each author benefited from reprintings of cheaper editions and from serializations in popular magazines. Corelli's sales averaged 100,000 copies per year, and over one million copies were sold of Caine's 1901 blockbuster, *The Eternal City*. Both authors combined a passionate romantic plot with wider social issues. Garvice, author of *Just a Girl* and other light romances, sold more than seven million books between 1899 and 1920. In 1914 alone his sales reached 1,750,000.[65] Similarly, Gould's novels of the turf had sold in the 'millions' by 1912. His output averaged

[63] Edward Salmon, *Juvenile Literature As It Is* (London, 1888), 14–16, 21–4.

[64] It is impossible to know, for example, whether boys and girls were presented with a list of authors from which to choose, or whether prompting was received from schoolmasters and mistresses. Salmon admitted that, as the questionnaires were completed in school, some children—notably girls—may have given the 'expected' or 'best' answer. 'Even, therefore, though we assume that voting is not in all particulars quite sincere, there is at least the satisfaction of knowing that girls recognise the propriety of accepting, as entitled to in the first place, only books and periodicals of an irreproachable kind' (p. 27).

[65] *B* (Mar. 1920), 156; Douglas Sladen, *My Long Life: Anecdotes and Adventures* (London, 1939), 281. In 1911 *The Bookseller*, writing on 'The Making of a Popular Novel', deplored Garvice's books and their readers, 'a public that so readily surrenders its reasoning powers to the romancer who will touch its emotions' (30 June 1911, p. 867).

between four and five books and one annual per year.[66] The use of the term 'best-seller' by publishers in marketing books was much criticized by the literary establishment. In 1898 H. G. Wells complained bitterly to George Gissing of Hall Caine's latest success, *The Christian*: 'His damned infernal . . . book has sold 100,000 (one hundred thousand) copies . . . Otherwise he has no claim upon our attention.'[67] Similarly, as Peter Keating has observed: 'For a James, Conrad, Gissing or Joyce, the adulation given to the best-seller was a final confirmation of Britain's cultural decadence, damning evidence that the majority could not be trusted and that hope for the future lay with the sensitive few.'[68] None the less, some sort of debt is perhaps owed to these writers. As Amy Cruse has written:

> They immensely strengthened the taste for a literature superficial, flashy and untrue, yet presenting itself as the exponent of high moral ideals . . . they enforced the lesson that the reader's part was simply to listen and be thrilled without making any effort to understand . . . Yet it would be unfair to say that the work they did was entirely unfortunate in its tendency. They gave a vast amount of pleasure to a large number of people, many of them people whose sources of pleasure were few.[69]

Certainly the publishers owe them a debt, for, just as the popular pre-war magazines did, they helped to establish the trend towards the 'light' yet apparently 'wholesome' reading which has characterized mass-market publishing in the twentieth century.

In establishing the next rank of popular authors, the recollections of booksellers during this period provide some help. The manager of the W. H. Smith bookshop in Berkhamsted from 1906 until 1945 said that with the advent of the six-shilling novel 'we were never short of a best seller'. Stanley Weyman, Conan Doyle, Rider Haggard, Corelli, Kipling, and Caine were most popular.[70] Another newsagent recalled the favourite 'holiday reading' with people at Morecambe, Blackpool, Bridlington, and Scarborough. 'It seems to me, as I look back, that every other person I met was reading a book by Charles Garvice . . . Those who weren't were probably reading Effie Adelaide Rowlands or a "thriller" by Fred M. White, Headon Hill or Richard Marsh.'[71] In 1912 W. H. Smith surveyed sixty-four of its railway bookstalls to

---

[66] *B* (5 Apr. 1912), 462–3.

[67] J. A. Stewart, 'Sir Hall Caine: Our Most Popular Novelist', *PC* (4 June 1921), 571.

[68] Keating, *The Haunted Study*, 445.

[69] Amy Cruse, *After the Victorians* (London, 1938), 186.

[70] *TheNewsbasket*(W.H.Smith)(Mar.1948),47.   [71] *TC*(16Oct.1943),8.

determine the favourites among the book-reading public. 'Firm favourites' included John Masefield, Arnold Bennett (*Matador of the Five Towns*), and Harold Begbie (*Broken Earthenware*). Romantic fiction by Baroness Orczy (*Fire in Stubble*), Mrs Belloc Lowndes (*Chink in the Armour*), and Elinor Glyn (*Halcyone*) also sold well, as did new editions of Bram Stoker's *Dracula*. In fact, the large number of new editions of popular works, selling from 7*d.* to 2*s.* 6*d.*, illustrate the wider and cheaper distribution of fiction. Florence Barclay's emergence in 1912 as the pre-eminent romantic novelist was also recognized: 'Florence Barclay's books are now more popular than the well-known authoress Marie Corelli.'[72] Her first novel, *The Rosary*, published in 1909, sold over one million copies; *The Publishers' Circular* estimated in 1921 (the year of Barclay's death) that twenty million people had read it.[73]

Of the authors mentioned above, with the possible exception of Charles Garvice and Nat Gould, none was very popular after the First World War. Although these authors were indeed popular in their day, and editions of their novels sold in the thousands, they necessarily had a readership confined to those who could afford the (still somewhat costly) sixpenny edition. But in many respects it was the subject-matter of popular fiction, tied to the late Victorian and Edwardian era, which did not translate well after the First World War. An example can be found in romantic fiction. Modern authors such as Barbara Cartland and Mary Burchell have admitted the debt owed to such 'literary' pioneers as Mrs Henry Wood and Elinor Glyn. Burchell, one of the most successful authors for Mills & Boon, acknowledged that Wood 'worked exactly as I did. She was not of course of the Austen or Brontë standard, she was a talespinner . . . she always had a story to tell; you must read on.'[74] Cartland, who by 1950 was on the verge of her current fame, frankly admitted her inspiration came from two best-selling romantic novelists of this period: Elinor Glyn and Ethel M. Dell. She gave their kinds of stories the credit for turning her into a passionate romantic. Of Dell, who wrote over forty novels, Cartland said, 'I have copied her formula all my life . . . She believed, and I believed, that a woman, in order to be a good woman, was pure and innocent, and that God answered her prayers, sooner or later.'[75]

But although authors such as Cartland and Burchell claimed to have

[72] *The Newsbasket* (Mar. 1912), 67.
[73] 'Mrs Florence Barclay', *PC* (19 Mar. 1921), 309. The surprising title was taken from a popular song of the period.
[74] Mary Burchell was interviewed in 1986. See Ch. 4.
[75] Henry Cloud, *Barbara Cartland: Crusader in Pink* (London, 1979), 23–4.

been influenced by their predecessors, their styles are actually much tamer, as are the contents of their novels, and it is here, and perhaps only here, that the period before 1914 differs significantly from that after the First World War. Marie Corelli, for example, mixed escapist romance and adventure with heavy-handed sermons on contemporary issues. In *The Mighty Atom* (1896) she weaves her love story around the evils of cramming for examinations, recitation by rote, and other tenets of secular education. The central theme of *Ziska* (1897) is reincarnation. Other authors wrote about sex and love with a remarkable frankness, often considered obscene, which is lacking in both Cartland and Burchell. Glyn achieved notoriety as the author of *Three Weeks* (1907), a sensual story of an illicit affair between a Balkan princess and a young Englishman which sold two million copies.[76] This excerpt is typical:

Then a madness of tender caressing seized her. She purred as a tiger might have done, while she undulated like a snake. She touched him with her finger-tips, she kissed his throat, his wrists, the palms of his hands, his eyelids, his hair. And often, between her purrings, she murmured love-words in some strange fierce language of her own, brushing his ears and his eyes with her lips the while.[77]

Barbara Cartland never wrote anything like that. Dell, too, wrote a bolder fiction than the average Mills & Boon author. In *The Knave of Diamonds* (1912), the American rogue/hero takes advantage of the unhappily married heroine:

His quick breath scorched her face, and in a moment almost before she knew what was happening, his lips were on her own. He kissed her as she had never been kissed before—a single fiery kiss that sent all the blood in tumult to her heart. She shrank and quivered under it, but she was powerless to escape. There was sheer unshackled savagery in the holding of his arms, and dismay thrilled her through and through.[78]

The 'romance' in penny dreadfuls and yellow-backs would also have been considered unacceptable in Britain after the First World War. Their mixture of eroticism and violence was in the tradition of the Gothic novel. Scantily clad heroines with enormous breasts abounded: 'Her white bosom rose and fell in tremulous pulsations, and Ned

[76] Anthony Glyn, *Elinor Glyn* (London, 1956), 126. Glyn's reputation for frankness gave rise to a popular verse: 'Would you care to sin | With Elinor Glyn | On a leopard skin? Or would you prefer | To err | With her | On some other fur?'

[77] Elinor Glyn, *Three Weeks* (Duckworth edn., London, 1974), 134.

[78] Ethel M. Dell, *The Knave of Diamonds* (1912), 180.

Wilmot observing it, leered hideously'; 'In appearance she was of a great beauty—tall, with long, sweeping limbs, broad, rounded shoulders, and an exquisitely-developed and voluptuous bust.'[79] After the First World War, in spite of greater degrees of permissiveness in society, the romantic novel adopted more domestic, more austere features. Above all, authors were guided more by the editorial policy of the publishing house than by their own fantasies.

Romantic serial stories, on the other hand, had more enduring characteristics. *Blackwood's Magazine* in 1898 attempted to summarize these. There were two types of heroine: one shapely, divine, gorgeous, and dreamy ('A notable race of women, in good sooth . . . true to the core'), the other a long-haired schoolgirl in a short skirt. Female villains had to be 'the most abandoned hussies. You can tell them from a distance by their hair of raven blackness, and by their dusty cheeks tinted with vivid carmine. They look like beautiful demons.' These characters would become familiar in such publications as *Red Letter* from the D. C. Thomson stable. Heroes were 'pleasant and presentable specimens of English manhood' and 'splendid types of the true-born English gentleman'. Typical names, which could have come from a Mills & Boon or a Barbara Cartland novel, were Lord Straithland, Captain Carton, Pierrepoint Pinion, Herbert Hardress, and Rosslyn Cheyne.[80]

Continuities between boys' fiction from this period, and from 1914 to 1950, are actually more striking. In this case the crusade against penny dreadfuls initiated by the Religious Tract Society and Alfred Harmsworth had lasting effects. The boys' papers of D. C. Thomson were inspired more by the Amalgamated Press titles and the *Boy's Own Paper*, not to mention novels such as *Tom Brown's Schooldays* and *Robinson Crusoe*, than by the penny dreadfuls. The spirit of the latter was retained in the form of daring adventure and larger-than-life characterizations, but the gore was discarded and the morals enhanced. Perhaps this is why the epithet 'dreadful' continued to be applied to boys' papers by the literary establishment after 1914.[81] Bosanquet identified 'the detective interest, the school interest, the supernatural interest, the theatrical interest, the fighting interest, and even the historical inter-

[79] *Spring-Heeled Jack, the Terror of London, by the Author of Turnpike Dick* (London, [*c.* 1870s]), 6, 8.

[80] 'Penny Fiction', *Blackwood's Edinburgh Magazine*, 811.

[81] 'It was Lord Northcliffe who killed the "penny dreadful" by the simple process of producing a "ha'penny dreadfuller"', A. A. Milne wrote (quoted in Turner, *Boys Will Be Boys*, 115).

est', within the pages of a typical boys' paper; all of these were also passed down to the next century.[82] One legacy of the *Boy's Own Paper*, for example, was the public school story, of the type created by such masters as Talbot Baines Reed. The Harmsworth papers, although designed 'for office boys', none the less used the school story with great success, particularly in the *Gem* and *Magnet*. In this case, as in the penny dreadfuls, working-class readers seemed happy to read about what were thought to be upper-class life and traditions.

There is also evidence of the strong hand of editorial control which was displayed after 1914 by such successful publishers as D. C. Thomson. Often the proprietor's interests and values were only thinly disguised. Harmsworth's papers for boys, for example, embodied an extreme form of patriotism. His editorial directives included 'the cultivation of physical fitness in the young, the encouragement of adventure abroad and enterprise at home. In all of them the bugle-call of patriotism was loudly sounded, pride in Great Britain and the Empire.'[83] Harmsworth's ascendancy coincided with the 1897 jubilee, the Boer War, and Anglo-German rivalry, and his own politics were heavily impressed on the boys' papers. The reminiscences of a London newsagent suggest how effectively he did this:

From back there in 1911 or 1912, I recall a specially rousing *Boy's Friend* feature serial. This yarn, entitled 'Kaiser or King?' was grimly prophetic of the Great War that was to break out in August 1914—although William II's spike-helmeted legions did not (as they did in the story) manage to land on the beaches of Norfolk, Lincolnshire and Yorkshire.[84]

Indeed, the firm itself never concealed its intentions:

These journals aimed from the first at the encouragement of physical strength, of patriotism, of interest in travel and exploration, and of pride in our Empire. It has been said that the boys' papers of The Amalgamated Press have done more to provide recruits for our Navy and Army and to keep up the estimation of the sister Services in the eyes of our people, than anything else.[85]

An amusing article in *The Anglo-Saxon*, on 'How I Drew for a Boys' Paper', recounted the author's frustrations in his attempts to illustrate for an unnamed adventure weekly according to the strict editorial rules then in use. Pirates were to be armed with no less than fifteen weapons; the bully was to be fat and mean-faced, in perfect contrast to the hero:

[82] Bosanquet, 'Cheap Literature', 678.
[83] Pound and Harmsworth, *Northcliffe*, 160.
[84] *TC* (11 Sept. 1943), 3.   [85] *Souvenir of Banquet*, 9.

I had to depict the hero being wrecked. My younger brother patiently submitted to lying on the floor with a horror-stricken expression on his face, whilst I sketched him. The hero was shown utterly crushed. Nevertheless, my drawing came back with the curt message that I must obey the office rules—'Whenever a hero is wrecked he must always safely reach shore—usually a desert island—with a cheerful face, a peak-cap, and immaculate, unwrinkled trousers. He must bear the outward and visible sign of a hero'. The peak-cap and pressed trousers seemed to be his trade-mark. How could one be original under these circumstances?[86]

This attitude can be contrasted with that held by the editors of the more bloodthirsty Brett journals, including *The Boys of England*. One artist recalled receiving some firm advice from his editor: 'In future, we must beg of you to be good enough to make your scimitars more curly and your drops of blood bigger!'[87] *The Anglo-Saxon*, like most popular papers, took comments from readers very seriously, issuing rebukes to writers and artists when necessary. 'Whenever I saw a butcher-boy reading a paper I used to groan aloud. "Little beast," I thought, "He is concocting another letter to the editor." Sometimes I wondered whether there would be a loss in dignity in asking him for opinion and advice.'

Indeed, these nameless writers and illustrators of serial stories and popular novels at this time represent the precursors of the twentieth-century authors of popular fiction. After 1914, as we will see in the next chapter, the commercialization of popular fiction promoted the genre and even the imprint over the particular author. Successful magazines, for example, rarely listed story bylines. Furthermore, best-selling 'popular' authors such as Marie Corelli and Hall Caine retained links with the literary establishment which popular twentieth-century authors were denied: the gulf between the publics became more pronounced. Among Corelli's admirers was Gladstone; Florence Barclay included among hers the last Tsar and Tsaritsa of Russia.[88]

Florence Barclay (1862–1921) is an important case, an example of a popular author who bridged our two periods, combining qualities of

[86] 'How I Drew for a Boys' Paper', *The Anglo-Saxon* (27 May 1899), 18.

[87] Quoted in *PC* (4 Dec. 1920), 670.

[88] The Tsar was especially enamoured of *Through the Postern Gate* (1912), and was called by his wife 'Boy Blue' after the protagonist. 'I had to resort to my handkerchief several times. I like to re-read some of the parts separately, although I know them practically by heart. I find them so pretty and true!' he wrote to the Tsaritsa on 31 Mar. 1916. (C. E. Vulliamy (ed.), *The Letters of the Tsar to the Tsaritsa 1914–1917* (London, 1929), 162. According to Vulliamy, 'This book seems to have appealed profoundly to the Tsar and Tsaritsa, and there are several pathetic and playful allusions to it in their correspondence' (p. 164).)

both. Although she is often described as the natural successor of Marie Corelli, she was in fact a much more transitional figure in popular fiction. Barclay's purpose in writing, according to her daughter (and biographer), was 'the joy of helping humble people along the road to heaven'.[89] The sympathy imparted through her characters and their world was, apparently, infectious:

> She sympathised so truly with each of her characters that the reader could not but sympathise too; could not but get deeply engrossed, and feel that the characters really lived. People said that to read her books was *to live*, for the time, in the world they portrayed; to make friends with the people of that world; to share with them their joys and sorrows and anxieties and loves. The world she portrayed was a very sunny world; its people charming, amusing, true and brave. Hence it was a delight for the reader to live therein, for a while; to forget, perchance, the dull or sad world of his own life, the disappointing people of his acquaintance.

The desire to 'escape' among readers, so prevalent after the First World War, is evident here. Barclay's role, her daughter continued, was 'to supply her fellow men with joy, refreshment, inspiration'. Her 'ordinary' readers comprised 'the busy men and women who form the majority of the reading public, and who read fiction by way of relaxation and enjoyment . . . ask merely to be pleased, rested, interested, amused, inspired to a more living faith in the beauty of human affection and the goodness of God'.

Florence Barclay's unprecedented success, however, was not a matter of chance. Both she and her publisher were aggressive, ambitious business people, as were the most successful publishers and writers of this century. Barclay welcomed letters from readers,[90] greeted crowds at book-signing sessions, and courted the booksellers. 'She had a very tender corner in her heart for the booksellers; for the men who actually dealt out the books to the public, who displayed them so artistically in their windows, recommended them so warmly to their customers, and shared with her the pecuniary reward of her success', according to her daughter. Whether genuine or not, such affection marked the sign of a shrewd businesswoman. In 1911, with sales of *The Rosary* already

---

[89] See *The Life of Florence Barclay: A Study in Personality, by One of Her Daughters* (London, 1921), an obviously biased but none the less revealing work.

[90] Some of the letters quoted in the biography are of an incredibly florid and dramatic nature. One, 'written in the shaky hand of an invalid', thanked Barclay for the 'enormous pleasure' given through *The Broken Halo*. 'I am ill—hopelessly, I know. I feel if I do live a few weeks more I ought and shall try to be a better woman for having read it. I only wish I had read it thirty years ago.'

exceeding 300,000 copies, Barclay's publisher, G. P. Putnam's, announced there were no plans for a new edition cheaper than the existing, six-shilling one. 'It is sufficiently obvious that there is no reason why they should, and the large sale is an eloquent corroboration of Mr Heinemann's opinion that six shillings is and is likely to remain the proper price for a new novel', *The Bookseller* noted.[91] Barclay's fans would have to queue at the libraries and wait their turn: business was too good.

Barclay wrote for the people, and not, as her daughter pointedly remarked, for the critics. 'Crabbing' and 'spiteful' reviews (more common than not) 'hurt her very much, and cast her momentarily into deep gloom'. Her books remained pure, beautiful, devoid of sin, 'moral' and 'decent', governed by an editorial policy apparently self-imposed and refined by success.

Another ever-present aim of my mother's was never to write anything that might hurt any of her readers through seeming to slight their walk in life or their religious views, or any other matter upon which the human heart is naturally susceptible. To her there were no class barriers. From duchess to dustman she loved her kind.

She regarded her readers as personal friends; 'to have written anything that seemed to sneer at or ridicule any one of them would have been to wound her friends'. The more powerful of the popular publishers of this century would mirror Barclay's strategies. They selected fiction for publication not solely for financial gain, but also for what they took to be the better moral 'good'. The Amalgamated Press, D. C. Thomson, Hutchinson, and Mills & Boon are examples of these. Annie S. Swan, like Barclay, took pride in the fact that her books were praiseworthy. 'I had always been regarded as a "safe" writer, whose books could be put into the hands of young persons without any fear of deleterious consequences to the readers.'[92]

IV

Before the First World War, a thriving and increasingly 'mass' market in publishing and reading existed—as Wilkie Collins and others noticed. In fact, the major legacy of this period was the organization of such a market in a refined and sophisticated manner, supported by a readership accustomed to light, 'escapist' fiction ('fiction' as opposed to

[91] *B* (20 Oct. 1911), 1447.
[92] Annie S. Swan, *My Life: An Autobiography* (London, 1934), p. 281.

'literature'). Yet fiction in Victorian and Edwardian Britain is distinctive for its sometimes rigid divisions along 'popular' and 'mass' lines, classifications which become blurred after 1914. Mass reading matter included penny dreadfuls and yellow-backs, produced cheaply in the thousands and written by legions of unknown writers. They are, as such, the precursors of the modern, mass-produced fiction magazines. After 1870 a reaction against their 'racy' prose prompted publishers such as the Religious Tract Society to lead a middle-class reform campaign for a more 'wholesome', but no less entertaining or more expensive, equivalent. 'Popular' fiction included sensation novels by such authors as Marie Corelli and Mrs Henry Wood. Although these books in their day reached a largely middle-class audience, their authors established the pattern of women novelists writing prolifically for an extensive readership, made possible later by the introduction of the one-volume novel and cheaper editions. And it was they who began the process whereby the distinction between 'popular' and 'mass' literature became blurred. Thus, the commercialization of fiction publishing in the twentieth century, and the evolution of the market into 'low-brow' and 'high-brow' camps—made possible by developments before 1914— makes it harder to draw the line between popular and mass fiction. The twopenny magazines—often called tuppenny dreadfuls—were both popular and intended for mass consumption, as were the works of romantic novelists such as Ruby M. Ayres and Ethel M. Dell.

Both continuities and discontinuities can be established between fiction of this period and after the First World War. In terms of boys' papers, among the more lasting contributions were quality production values, superior fiction, new advertising techniques, fervent patriotism, and a paternalistic approach to the readership—all adopted by modern publishers such as D. C. Thomson. With romantic fiction, while the concepts of wholesome morals and the happy ending at the church door remained standard, sensational sub-plots and specific allusions to contemporary social issues did not, for the most part, survive the war. After 1914, styles *do* change, with fiction in women's novels becoming more domestic, realistic, and less violent. Contemporary drama replaced Gothic romance—although there were exceptions, notably in letterpress magazines. The significant link between pre-war and post-war fiction publishing, especially in the case of romantic fiction, is the aggressive commercial push personified in Florence Barclay, and used later to maximum effect by such successful publishers as Mills & Boon and D. C. Thomson.

2

'BOOKS *ARE* A COMMODITY': THE COMMERCIALIZATION OF POPULAR FICTION

IN the present century, despite two world wars and an economic depression, publishing, like most service industries, has displayed a remarkable resilience. Factors which should have deflated the market—paper rationing, almost prohibitive production costs, mass unemployment, and the expansion of the cinema and wireless—seem to have had the opposite effect: they unexpectedly promoted the reading habit and thereby preserved demand. This continued demand of all classes for light fiction, coupled with the necessity to restore revenues drained during the First World War, accelerated the process of commercialization initiated by the Victorians and allowed a more intense exploitation of the market. Record levels of production and the introduction of 'commodity-style' publishing techniques gave popular fiction an exposure to such a degree that it was woven into the cultural fabric of the nation. In a leading article in 1930, *The Publishers' Circular* ranked books with the 'indispensable necessities of life', and condemned the 'intellectual snobbery' of booksellers and publishers who still regarded the trade as a sacred luxury—in spite of declining sales. 'Books *are* a commodity, and we cannot get away from that fundamental fact', the journal claimed. 'Author, publisher and bookseller alike are engaged in business, the business of selling, or trying to sell, something that may bring them a reasonable profit.'[1] But commercialization was also a matter of financial necessity, to cope with and exploit burgeoning demand. Within the context of a broad overview of the period 1914–50, I will attempt here to show how the mass commercialization of popular publishing, the turning of books into 'commodities', occurred, and why it occurred. The genuine paradox of publishing at this time—the depression of the magazine market between the wars—will also be examined.

---

[1] '"Books *are* a Commodity"', *PC* (11 Oct. 1930), 513–14. Significantly, these views were also endorsed by the National Book Council.

I

The reading 'boom' in Britain after 1870 was hardly diminished by the First World War. Rather, as during the Second World War, restrictions on leisure activities and expenditure, and the reduction in reading matter forced by paper rationing, only served to intensify the demand for reading, the least expensive and most adaptable of leisure activities. This demand was sustained in peacetime, nurtured by the depression, the cinema, and the growth in cheap facilities for borrowing books. There is a good deal of statistical evidence which supports this. In Figures 2.1 and 2.2 the annual production totals of works of 'adult' fiction and of children's fiction, both new and reprinted, are presented for the years 1911–50. Figures for 1911–38 are from *The Publishers'*

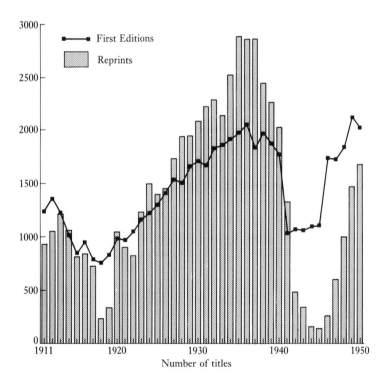

FIGURE 2.1. Annual Production of Adult Fiction, 1911–1950
Sources: The Publishers' Circular, 1911–37; The Bookseller, 1938–50.

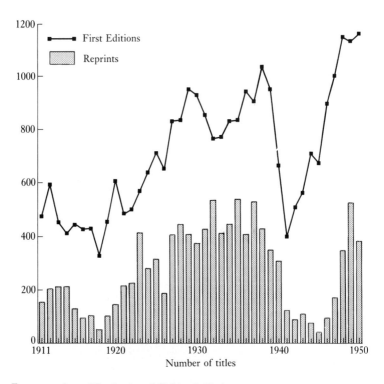

FIGURE 2.2 Annual Production of Children's Fiction, 1911–1950
Sources: The Publishers' Circular, 1911–37; The Bookseller, 1938–50.

Circular, thereafter from *The Bookseller*.[2] 'Fiction' was consistently the highest total in the detailed list of categories, which included 'Educational', 'History', 'Biography and Memoirs', even 'Veterinary Science, Farming and Stockkeeping'. These figures should be viewed in the context of the list of totals for production of all kinds of books contained in Figure 2.3. It should be noted that these figures are not an

[2] Only *The Publishers' Circular* contains an uninterrupted series of annual publications lists prior to 1929, when *The Bookseller*, in conjunction with *Whittaker's Cumulative Book List*, established its own list, which had been published infrequently before this date. Unfortunately, the *PC* lists were discontinued during the Second World War. Their figures are perhaps the more precise, as they listed 'Fiction' totals separately from 'Literature' and 'Poetry and Drama'. *The Bookseller*, on the other hand, did not list 'Literature' separately from 'Fiction'. Similarly, the *B* lists contained two categories for children, 'Children's Books and Minor Fiction' (included here) and 'Annuals and Serials'; *PC* included everything under 'Juvenile'.

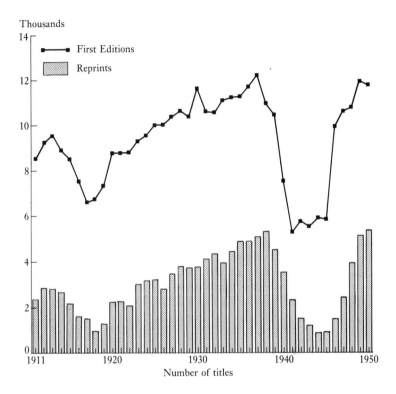

FIGURE 2.3. Annual Production, All Classes of Books, 1911–1950
Sources: The Publishers' Circular, 1911–37; The Bookseller, 1938–50.

indication of sales but of industrial output; low production in wartime, for example, is not an indication of low demand. There is evidence that personal expenditure on books, newspapers, and magazines had considerably increased by the end of the Second World War:[3]

---

[3] Central Statistical Office, *Annual Abstract of Statistics*, no. 86 (1938–48), 246. All figures revalued at 1938 prices. Robert Hewison, in *Under Siege: Literary Life in London 1939–45* (Methuen edn., London, 1988), commented on the inherent difficulty in using statistics of book production as a measure of consumer expenditure. 'These statistics relate only to the production and *sale* of books; there was an overall increase in reading simply as an activity. Librarians reported a much greater demand, but it is impossible to calculate how often a book might be read, or by how many people' (p. 86). The *PC* would agree: 'Naturally, it does not follow that because more books were published, more books were *sold*, but in the long run sales do govern production, and our tables for many years, with occasional lapses, show a continuous increase' (27 Dec. 1930, p. 877).

1938 £64 million   1944 £73 million
1940 £59 million   1946 £89 million
1942 £63 million   1948 £105 million

A comparison of Figures 2.1 and 2.2 reveal two striking features of book production and market differentiation. First, the significant but not spectacular decline in the production of fiction in general during the First World War, as opposed to the Second, is evident. This was largely due to the different degrees of wartime restrictions on paper and printing. Recovery after the First World War was immediate, and throughout the 1920s production in all categories of books attained record levels, only briefly interrupted by strikes. New editions of adult fiction rose from 1,051 in 1920 to 2,081 in 1930, and maintained their highest level, over 2,800, between 1935 and 1937. The maintenance of these levels during the depression proves that the consumption-based industries in Britain were comparatively unaffected by the slump. Presumably, but for the Second World War, production would have proceeded along these lines at least until the ascendancy of television during the early 1950s. It is also evident from Figure 2.2 that juvenile demand was more stable than the fluctuating adult market, but at a generally lower level. Consequently, production of children's books during the Second World War did not suffer as great a relative fall as other lines.

The second significant feature concerns the role of 'reprints' in both categories. Reprints were new and cheaper editions of (already published) popular novels or of revived classic works. In children's books these were consistently fewer than new and original books, which seemed in accordance with the apparent tastes of children, whose craving for 'up-to-date' works served such prolific authors as Captain W. E. Johns and Enid Blyton. But in adult fiction new editions consistently outsold new works. This was due in large part to restrictive financial conditions, which encouraged the publication of cheaper editions of proven books over the considerable financial risks involved in launching a new work by an unestablished author.

While there was a considerable increase in book publication during this period, the level of magazine publication remained steady. According to *The Writers' and Artists' Year Book*, magazines containing 'Serial or Long Stories' or 'Feminine' interest totalled 76 in 1914, 82 in 1925, 107 in 1935, and 88 in 1939. Production declined before the Second World War due to competition from other leisure activities, and during the war as a result of paper rationing. By 1951 there were 77 titles. Titles for 'Boys and Girls' also remained at a more or less constant level throughout this period: 38 in both 1919 and 1935, and 33 in 1951, another indication of the stable (if stagnant) publishing market for children.

The number of British publishing houses also remained fairly stable until the Second World War. *The Writers' and Artists' Year Book* lists 335 British and Irish publishers in 1914, 263 in 1930, and 320 in 1939. After the war this figure increased considerably: 412 in 1945, and 572 in 1950. As in the newspaper industry, a main feature of the publishing trade was the concentration of ownership of houses and publications, and the endurance of nineteenth-century foundations, although some in altered forms. In magazine publishing, this period was still dominated by firms established before the war, including the Amalgamated Press. Harmsworth's foundation was the largest publisher of periodicals in Britain, with a list of some 90 titles, which by 1931 had a combined circulation of more than 8,000,000 copies per week.[4] A 1931 advertisement touted the dominance of the Amalgamated Press, 'The Greatest Self-contained PUBLICITY MACHINE in Great Britain':

Through the widely read publications of the Amalgamated Press, you can appeal to every section of the community without waste and with a certainty that you are reaching your own particular public. Through the various groups you can APPEAL DIRECTLY TO WOMEN OR MEN, WIRELESS ENTHUSIASTS, CINEMA PATRONS, HOME and GARDEN LOVERS, BOYS or GIRLS. There are MONTHLY JOURNALS FOR WOMEN, MONTHLY MAGAZINES FOR MEN, FASHION PAPERS, WEEKLY PERIODICALS FOR MEN, WOMEN and CHILDREN.

Increased popular interest in other leisure activities is also apparent here. Other publishers' lists paled in comparison, despite containing some of the best-selling periodicals. In 1932, for example, Newnes published seventeen titles, including *Radio Times* (the best-selling periodical, over two million weekly), *John O'London's Weekly*, the new *Woman's Own*, and (still) *Tit-Bits*. Pearson published *Home Notes* and *Peg's Paper* among fifteen titles; D. C. Thomson twelve. In 1937 Odhams Press introduced the best-selling woman's paper, *Woman*, the first women's magazine printed in colour gravure. During the Second World War the *Picture Post*, the flagship of the Hulton Press, outsold most weeklies. Hulton also introduced the *Eagle* picture-story paper in

---

[4] *Advertising Weekly*, 59 (June 1931), 445.

1950, with its unprecedented print run (for a boys' paper) of one million copies.

The major publishers of popular fiction included some of the most respectable 'quality' houses. During this period Hutchinson expanded prodigiously, acquiring such firms as Jarrolds, John S. Shaw, Hurst and Blackett, and Stanley Paul. The figure of Walter Hutchinson, in fact, loomed as large as Harmsworth's did before the First World War. Hutchinson's 'Shilling Novels' series included works by Ethel M. Dell, Sydney Horler, and E. M. Savi. A Mass-Observer lurking about London bookshops in 1941 noticed 'a veering towards Penguins and, especially, Hutchinson's shilling "horribles"'. The principal series of the age, and envy of most publishers, was the two-shilling 'Yellow Jacket' list published by Hodder and Stoughton. 'Wise librarians place a standing order for all Hodder and Stoughton novels as issued', a John Menzies trade publication advised in 1935. According to John Boon, the success and wide distribution of this series led to a common conception that all fiction in England was published by Hodder and Stoughton. Mills & Boon and Collins were the principal publishers of romantic fiction. Methuen published Sax Rohmer's adventures of Dr Fu Manchu, as well as the series featuring the most popular fictional character in Britain in the 1920s, Edgar Rice Burroughs's *Tarzan*.[5]

The remarkable growth in lending libraries, which most of these publishers supplied with popular fiction, is an excellent barometer of reading activity. Both the public and subscription libraries expanded rapidly. A marked increase in patrons during the First World War, coupled with the abolition of the penny rate in England and Wales in 1919 and benefactions from the Carnegie and J. Passmore Edwards foundations, encouraged at last the spread of public libraries through-

---

[5] The most popular books, magazines, and authors during this period can be discovered from a variety of sources, including advertisements, sales figures, bookshop reports, and library surveys. Best-seller lists are rare. An American invention (begun in *The Bookman* in 1895 and, as such, criticized as 'unEnglish'), these were introduced in Britain by the wholesale suppliers Simpkin Marshall in 1931, with much controversy. J. B. Priestley led the campaign against misuse of the term 'best-seller' in advertisements, calling for a minimum requirement of sales of 25,000 copies (an enormous number for the time) in the first three months (*B*, 2 Mar. 1934, p. 146). Priestley's suggestions were not adopted, and the lack of standard rules means that reliable 'best-seller lists' are few. Sources of magazine circulations are also rare. Although the Audit Bureau of Circulations was founded in 1931, registration was voluntary and low. Few children's papers were registered; by nature these did not carry the significant percentage of advertising that the women's magazines did, so demand for audited figures was minimal. Advertising yearbooks, including *The Advertisers' A.B.C.* and *The Newspaper Press Directory*, contain some figures.

out the country. In 1920 there were 551 library authorities with 5,730 service points; the number of books in stock by 1924 totalled 15 million. In 1949 590 library authorities provided 23,000 service points with 42 million books in stock. Over 12 million readers borrowed nearly 300 million books a year, as compared with seven million readers and 208 million books in 1935. It was estimated that by 1949 only 60,000 people in Great Britain were *not* provided with library service, and that nearly 25 per cent of the population were registered borrowers, amounting to an average stock of 5.98 books per head of population. The largest number of issues from public libraries remained within the 'Fiction' category. With the exception of Mudie's, which closed in 1937, the principal subscription libraries also thrived. Subscribers to the Boots Booklovers Library, for example, increased from 116,224 in 1922 to 362,032 in 1932, 440,234 in 1940, and 893,956 in 1946. Average issues per *month* rose from 453,326 in 1932 to 901,493 in 1946.[6]

One of the more accurate indicators of reading activity among the lower-middle and working classes was the expansion of 'Pay-as-you-read', 'No Deposit', or 'tuppenny' libraries during the 1930s. These libraries were mostly run as adjuncts to newsagencies, tobacconists, or department stores. The principal motive in opening a library in a shop was to attract potential customers—Jesse Boot founded the Boots Booklovers Library in 1899 for just this reason. 'Books appear to have a fatal attraction as "loss-leaders," to use the American term', W. G. Taylor observed in 1935.[7] The tuppenny libraries offered a greater selection of light fiction than the public libraries for as little as twopence per volume per week (no deposit), or the cost of a weekly magazine; as such they were suited to accommodate the demands of the 'new reading public'. Books were purchased or swapped by either the owner of the particular shop or (more commonly) a wholesale library supplier. The first of this aggressive, seemingly omnipresent generation of commercial lending libraries was opened in Harlesden (London) by Ray Smith in 1930. Among the larger wholesale library suppliers were Argosy and Sundial Libraries (London and Liverpool; 2,217 branches and 1,350,000 books in circulation in 1934), and Foyle's Libraries (London; 747 branches with an average supply of 200 books in 1934). Argosy and Sundial Libraries was the union of two

[6] Sources: The Library Association, *A Century of Public Library Service: Where Do We Stand Today?* (London, 1949); Subscriber and Volume Statistics, The Boots Co. archives, Nottingham.

[7] W. G. Taylor, 'Publishing', in John Hampden (ed.), *The Book World* (London, 1935), 79.

companies founded at the turn of the century. Their service, which supplied 'everything but the shelves', was administered by shopkeepers who acted as agents for the firm throughout the country. Foyle's, in addition to supplying 'several hundred' newsagents, stationers, and tobacconists, also serviced London branches of Co-operative Stores, factories (J. Wellwork and Son, Manchester; Ellison and Co., Birmingham), and military vessels (HMS *Eagle* and *Cormorant*).[8] The Commercial Libraries' Association, founded in 1937 as a watchdog for the myriad of tuppenny organizations, could boast by 1938 that in 'practically every town in England there is now a well run commercial library'.[9]

The activity of the tuppenny libraries was sufficient to force re-organizations at both Boots and W. H. Smith during the 1930s. In a confidential report, the W. H. Smith management in 1933 admitted that the competition was formidable: 'There seems every reason to believe that the "Twopenny Library" has come to stay: some are of considerable size and well organized, and much thought has accordingly been given to this branch of the Library work.' Consequently, the W. H. Smith Library subscription rates were made more competitive, in line with the tuppennies; 2*d.* per volume for five days became the basic charge, and the customary half-crown (2*s.* 6*d.*) deposit was eliminated. There is no evidence to suggest, however, that the number of working-class subscribers increased.[10]

The Second World War rationalized library usage in Britain. The shortage of books, propaganda against unwise spending, difficulties of supply, and an increase in non-fiction interests (such as current affairs) all worked in the public libraries' favour. As during the First World War, public libraries across the country recorded peak levels of usage. Issues at Halifax Public Libraries, for example, increased from 716,000 in 1938 to 1,070,000 in 1945; in West Ham (London), 990,000 and 1,280,000.[11] In Bristol, three million volumes were lent during

---

[8] *B* (20 Feb. 1935), 182; Prospectus, Foyle's Libraries Limited (June 1934), John Johnson Collection, Bodleian Library.

[9] E. J. Olson (Secretary, The Commercial Libraries' Association), *B* (24 Mar. 1938), 342. The poor relations of the organized tuppenny libraries were the 'perambulating libraries on street barrows' which also lent and exchanged books at 1*d.* or 2*d.* per volume. These were a common sight in the poorer districts of east London (Terence Young, *Becontree and Dagenham: The Story of the Growth of a Housing Estate* (London, 1934), 176; Sir Hubert Llewellyn Smith, director, *Life and Leisure*, vol. ix, *The New Survey of London Life and Labour* (London, 1935), 119).

[10] Report, PA.182, W. H. Smith archives (Milton Hill), 20.

[11] *TC* (2 Mar. 1946), 14.

1944, a record. Even in bombed-out Coventry, one commentator noted, 'the distribution of reading matter to the people has become almost as necessary as the distribution of food'; mobile libraries served most of the affected areas of the city.[12]

Economic circumstances during this period enabled a more dense exploitation of the publishing market. This was in part obviously due to rising living standards. The average working week was reduced in 1919 to 48 hours, allowing more leisure time. Average real wages in 1938 were one-third higher than in 1913, and consumer expenditure increased. The growth of commercial libraries during the 1930s is one indication that the lower-middle and working classes were now able to spend something on reading, although they did not progress to the book-buying stage. In addition to the expansion of chains such as W. H. Smith and John Menzies, there was a considerable rise in the number of local newsagents. In 1919 the National Federation of Retail Newsagents, Booksellers and Stationers was founded, the amalgamation of several regional unions. Significantly, this body reflected the varied trade of the newsagent, which increasingly involved the sale of cheap fiction and the administration of a lending library in addition to the purveyance of newspapers and magazines. Membership grew rapidly, from 4,797 in 1919 to 26,117 in 1950. It was estimated that there were more than 50,000 newsagents in Great Britain by 1947.[13]

II

The impressive statistical evidence, however, conceals the fact that the publishing industry won its prosperity only at the expense of considerable restructuring. Although wartime encouraged reading as a leisure activity and boosted sales, it was an easily-won artificial prosperity that did not long survive the peace. Dramatic increases in production costs and lower profits forced publishers after the First World War to accelerate the movement towards cheaper-priced books, and to accommodate more closely the tastes of the lower-middle and working classes, the ever-expanding 'new reading public'.

Restrictions which affected the publishing industry were of varying degrees during each war. The major question was one of supply, and

[12] Frederick Cowles (Chief Librarian, Swinton and Pendlebury Public Libraries), 'Libraries in Wartime', *PC* (24 May 1941), 221.

[13] Sources: *The National Federation Year Book*, 1921–51 edns.; 'The Future of the Newsagent-Bookseller', *B* (1 Feb. 1947), 114–16.

the rationing of paper. The ramifications of reduced paper supply and increased production costs were far-reaching, influencing the trade between the wars and after 1945. A comparison of figures representing the number of individual works of fiction published during selected years in Britain illustrates this point. Totals for 1913 and 1936 are pre-war apogees.[14]

	1913	1918	1924	1936	1944	1950
New fiction (adult)	1226	755	1220	2046	1095	2018
Reprints (adult)	1220	237	1499	2862	160	1679
New fiction (children)	452	328	638	943	709	1159
Reprints (children)	212	50	283	408	76	384

Hence, it took the book trade eleven years to recover from the First World War, and at least fourteen from the Second World War. The decline in book production (as, indeed, in magazines and newspapers) which was precipitated by paper rationing did not, however, correspondingly depress the market; in most cases sales were stronger than ever. During the Second World War, for example, the publishing industry enjoyed a 'curious bonanza', according to Michael Foxell of the Lutterworth Press. Paper rationing certainly limited supply and therefore output, but in so doing it significantly increased demand for *any* output. 'You just sold out', Foxell recalled. 'You didn't have to do anything in fact—people *begged* you for them, the suppliers, the booksellers, the wholesalers.'[15]

Paper rationing during the First World War was not as severe or as extensive as it was during the Second. Unlike in 1940, the principal concern in 1916 was not the diminishing sources of paper materials but the need to economize in order to release all available shipping tonnage for military use. In March 1916 the Royal Commission on Paper was appointed to reduce imports of paper and paper-making materials by one-third of their 1914 levels. Additional edicts further restricted supply, authorized the collection of waste paper, and encouraged the manufacture of paper from home-produced materials. By 1918 the Board of Trade reported that imports had been successfully reduced by more than two-thirds.[16]

[14] Sources: *B, PC.*

[15] Michael Foxell was interviewed in 1988. Lutterworth Press was the book publishing arm of the Religious Tract Society, and sister firm to Lutterworth Periodicals Ltd. See Ch. 7.

[16] *Board of Trade Journal* (11 Apr. 1918), 430–2.

	1914 (tons)	*1916–17 (tons)*	*1917–18 (tons)*	*Decrease over 1914 (%)*
Papermaking materials	1,207,478	737,253	456,901	62.0
Paper and board	590,871	409,471	126,261	78.5
Total	1,798,349	1,146,724	583,162	67.5

The Commission was dissolved in 1918, but paper rationing was not lifted until May 1919. In spite of these restrictions, both publishers and retailers thrived during the war. Sales of weekly magazines in particular increased, partly due to more efficient methods of purchase. The Prohibition of Returns Order of May 1918 was designed to protect the newsagent as well as to save paper by reducing the number of unsold copies of magazines at the end of the week. By urging readers to arrange standing orders, this act not only promoted the newsagent's business but nurtured a regular habit of reading by subscription.

Publishing profits, however, were kept in check. Advertising revenues (still regarded as the life-blood of any publication) declined, a result of financial restrictions during the war. In 1916 one of the largest periodical publishers, Newnes, announced reduced profits due to a fall in revenues, higher costs of paper and printing, and restricted cash flow—all despite 'exceptionally large' sales of 6*d.*, 7*d.*, and one-shilling novels, and the maintenance of its magazine circulations.[17] Hence, although most publishers emerged from the war with expanded readerships, depleted financial reserves hindered development for some time.

Social and demographic changes created by the First World War served indirectly to promote the market in popular fiction for women. Women achieved a degree of economic independence through participation in the work-force during the war. Spending power increased; weekly wages for women of over two pounds were not uncommon by 1919, compared with the average pre-war salary of nine shillings. This fact, coupled with the post-war surplus of single women (unmarried or widowed), presented a large and captive market ready to be exploited by advertisers and by publishers dispensing romance and adventure. In promoting three of its magazines (*Woman's World*, *Woman's Weekly*, and *Home Companion*) in 1915, the Amalgamated Press reminded potential advertisers that 'each woman holds the purse strings of a whole family'.[18] Cynthia White has suggested that two new reading publics emerged from the First World War: the 'New Rich', middle-

[17] *PC* (9 Sept. 1916), 252.
[18] Advertisement, *The Advertisers' A.B.C.* (1915), 455.

and working-class women whose spending power had increased; and the 'New Poor', mainly single working women in the factories. New weekly magazines such as *Woman's Illustrated* (Amalgamated Press) catered to the former with cheery journals offering domestic advice and plenty of romantic fiction. At the opposite end of the market, the so-called 'blood-and-thunder' papers were designed to appeal to poorer women who wanted thrilling fiction to enliven an apparently mundane existence. *Peg's Paper* (Pearson), *Secrets* (Thomson), and *Oracle* (Amalgamated Press) were among the most popular.[19] At twopence these papers, moreover, were affordable to women in all classes.

The First World War accelerated the existing trend towards lower-priced 'inferior' fiction. Commercialization of publishing was a direct result of the need to increase revenues dramatically after the war in order to meet steep rises in production costs. By 1919 binding costs alone had risen to 11*d*. per book, compared to 3*d*. before the war.[19] *The Bookseller* reported that while it was standard practice before the war for a publisher to issue a first edition of 1,000 copies, only half of which had to be sold to avoid a loss, after the war 1,800 of 2,000 copies had to be sold to ensure a reasonable return. Consequently, commercial concerns were paramount in a struggle to remain in business. Two groups in particular were badly affected by these financial considerations: small publishers and new authors. Larger houses could absorb losses more easily, relying on sales of cheap popular editions of previously published works. Many publishers, moreover, were reluctant to risk precious revenues on untested, first-time writers.[21] 'In short, all the best books are in trouble', the *Manchester Guardian* reported in 1921. 'The lack of what is called "popular appeal"—meaning more often than not some element of trashiness or, at least, flimsiness—has become such a bar to publication as it never has been before.'[22]

Publishing between the wars, therefore, was characterized by the introduction of new styles of production and marketing along commercial lines. These included 'commodity-style' techniques: fiction had to be carefully planned and packaged, often as series, all with an eye on potential sales. Hence, books and magazines became commodities to be marketed and sold like soapflakes. Novels grew shorter;

---

[19] Cynthia L. White, *Women's Magazines 1693–1968* (London, 1970), 93.
[20] *PC* (29 Nov. 1919), 499.
[21] *B* (Dec. 1919), 688.
[22] 'A Bad Time for Good Books', *Manchester Guardian* (14 Sept. 1921), quoted in *PC* (15 Oct. 1921), 397.

the word limit was reduced, on average, from 200,000 words to 130,000, a length which the author Michael Sadleir said was hardly enough for plot development or adequate characterizations.[23] A 1924 textbook, *How to Write Saleable Fiction*, suggested the following plot guidelines:

Mystery, perhaps, appeals to the largest public. A love interest is essential until, at any rate, an author has made his name. Comfortable sentiment is absolutely necessary for popular success. Your work should also bear the stamp of sincerity. You cannot treat yourself and your reader too seriously. Flippant novels are seldom found amongst the 'best-sellers.'[24]

The author added that '*to make money*' it was advisable to write novels 'suitable for serial publication'. The long-running serial in weekly or monthly magazines became an attractive alternative again. Publicity costs increased; on average £100 was spent per 2,000 copies, or one shilling per copy. Advertising techniques, such as posters on buses and newspaper advertisements containing thrilling illustrations and story excerpts, were adopted. Popular weekly magazines were grouped together in advertisements and marketed as series. The Amalgamated Press, for example, promoted *Fashions for All, Horner's Penny Stories, Forget-Me-Not, Woman's Weekly, Home Circle*, and *Mother and Home* as 'The Essential Six' in 1915, and *Woman's World, Home Companion, Woman's Companion*, and *Family Journal* as 'The Reliable Four' in 1930; each group had a guaranteed cumulative circulation of one million copies weekly.[25] Convenience of price and size in addition to quality were also important factors in a bid to encourage book-buying among lower-middle-and working-class readers. In 1929, for example, the Leisure Library Company emphasized in advertisements the 'clear type … blue bindings … good paper … 4 colour picture jackets' of its sixpenny reprints. Hutchinson's new 'Sevenpenny' series in 1934 was advertised as 'a beautiful book for *any* shelf'.

Ernest A. Savage, writing in 1935, blamed publishers for adopting the bad habits of tabloid newspapers in marketing light fiction. Whereas 'the older type of publisher' desired large profits but none the less looked to publish 'good' books,

The newer publisher sought larger sales, whether of good books or bad did not much matter so that he offset the higher cost of advertising … Just as 'yellow' editors spotlighted the daily shock, so the publisher, reluctantly, began to

---

[23] *PC* (4 Mar. 1922), 219.
[24] George G. Magnus, *How to Write Saleable Fiction*, 14th edn. (London, 1924), 9.
[25] Advertisements in *The Advertisers' A.B.C.*, 1915 edn., 400; 1930 edn., 276.

spotlight the daily book, that which he believed to be a best 'seller'. The method was quite simple; the result usually odd and sometimes bad and sad.[26]

Splashy advertisements created the 'book of the hour', which was given a prominent showing in the tuppenny libraries. The 'block-buster' book was also a common fixture: *Gone With the Wind* (1936) and *The Citadel* (1937) were named after the Bible in a 1948 Gallup Poll which asked, 'What's the best book you've ever read?' A. J. Cronin's novel, in fact, sold 40,083 copies in nine days in 1937, a bookselling record.[27] 'Readers were maneuvered in mass formation towards spotlight books, whether literature or not', Savage added. 'So publishing became less a profession and more a job of selling factory goods.' One consequence, however, was an encouragement to borrow and not to buy, once a reader discovered just how unspectacular the title actually was; Savage claimed that this borrowing habit was eventually the public librarians' gain.

Similarly, magazine publishers capitalized on the renewed interest in cheap fiction. Cassell pioneered a new type of story magazine in 1912 with *Cassell's Magazine of Fiction and Popular Literature*, which undercut novels by offering 264 pages of fiction at 5*d*. It featured one complete 30,000-word novel and twenty short stories by such best-selling authors as the Baroness Orczy. Hutchinson's *Story Magazine*, a 9*d*. monthly with a circulation of 300,000 ('record value'), counted Orczy, H. Rider Haggard, and Charles Garvice among its popular contributors. Its sister paper, the *Family Reader*, made history in 1919 with the first Ethel M. Dell publication in a twopenny weekly magazine.

Although much criticized, given its concessions to low quality and novelty, commodity-style publishing was very successful between the wars. 'The habit of novel-reading has much increased since the war among the middle and lower classes', McMahon Trevor, a bookseller, wrote in 1921. 'They have no taste in literature, but the sale of cheap editions (of recent novels) to them is enormous.'[28] So enormous, in fact, that a lively debate ensued on whether too many novels were being published. In 1920 alone over one million copies of Hutchinson's and Hurst and Blackett's new 3*s*. 6*d*. series (hard-cover) were sold, by such authors as Dell, Arnold Bennett, Cosmo Hamilton, and Dolf Wyllarde. Edgar Wallace's thrillers were published by thirty different

[26] Ernest A. Savage, 'Rakes' Progress', *Library Association Record*, vol. 2 (Dec. 1935), 549.
[27] *PC* (20 Oct. 1937), 418.
[28] McMahon Trevor, 'Who Buys Novels?', *PC* (28 May 1921), 555.

houses. According to some, he was the most prolific writer of popular fiction the world has ever known; his exact output is uncertain. Unhappy the bookseller who failed to keep pace with fast-changing stock and a public ravenous for the latest books. Charles Young, of Lamley & Company, booksellers, echoed the old-fashioned feelings of many of his peers in complaining that an 'impossible' number of re-prints at too many prices (1s. 6d., 2s., 2s. 6d., 3s. 6d., 5s.) were being published; the bookseller could not afford to stock them all. He criticized the obvious profit motive behind such production:

It is often said: 'Well, I keep what the public wants,' and in so doing, of course, a public need is met; but that is not bookselling. We are not to be entirely concerned with a quick turnover, ignoring meanwhile the books which move men and influence their minds, the product of brains which really matter.[29]

But in fact the publishing industry had no other choice than to encour-age the 'quick turnover'. Even W. H. Smith issued a clarion call of sorts to its newsagent clients: 'With the remarkable growth of the de-mand for Sixpenny novels it has become very patent to most newsagents that to stick to newsagency alone and hold aloof from selling books is undoubtedly a mistake.'[30] Between September and November, 1929, book production in Britain exceeded the unprecedented total of 60 titles per day (a majority of them novels), prompting many to complain of an 'over-production' of books.

Through such restructuring, the publishing industry was able to acquire and retain a good deal of prosperity in spite of the economic depression. The year 1930 was, in fact, the most productive until then in the history of British publishing: 11,603 new books and 3,790 re-prints (in all categories) were published. 'The "ill wind" of financial stringency has a stimulating effect on reading, as can be proved from the statistics of our public libraries', *The Publishers' Circular* reported. 'When money is scarce for the theatre or the talkies, then the joys of the armchair and the book are discovered.'[31] Publishing was among those light service industries which displayed flexibility and resilience dur-ing the depression, when 'escapist' activities such as reading were regarded as necessities rather than luxuries. Similarly, the largest in-crease in radio licences in a single year was between March 1930 and March 1931, at a rate of more than one thousand each day; by Novem-ber 1932 the BBC had acquired its five-millionth licence holder.[32] In

---

[29] *PC* (21, 28 Nov. 1925), 720–1, 741.   [30] *TC* (31 May 1930), 6.
[31] *PC* (27 Dec. 1930), 877.
[32] Asa Briggs, *The B.B.C.: The First Fifty Years* (London, 1985), 110.

the case of book publishing, sales were further boosted during the
1930s by two additional developments: a dramatic increase in orders
from the commercial libraries, and the unprecedented success of the
paperback series Penguin Books.

So strong was the growth of the tuppenny libraries by 1938 that W. C.
Berwick Sayers, President of the Library Association, remarked, 'We
have the almost spontaneous appearance in thousands of shops of departments for lending light literature; so much so that it would seem the
lending of reading matter is becoming an auxiliary of every business.'[33]
The impact of the 'tuppenny' libraries on the publishing industry was
considerable. Their success galvanized sales by providing a guaranteed market for light fiction. In response to such demand, many publishers became 'library houses', tailoring publication lists to the
demands of the commercial libraries. Among these were Mills & Boon,
Herbert Jenkins, Wright and Brown, and Ward, Lock. More up-
market publishers added a 'cheap line' to their lists, light fiction which,
if not enhancing the reputation of the firm, certainly helped cash flow
during difficult times. Collins, for example, published the 'Crime Club'
series; Hodder and Stoughton the successful Yellow Jackets line; and
Oxford University Press was the first of many houses which published
Captain W. E. Johns's 'Biggles' books.

The publishing industry was divided on the merits of the tuppenny
libraries and their encouragement of the reading of light fiction. Traditional booksellers may have lamented the lowering of standards and
the 'over-production' of 'trashy' novels, but A. C. Hannay offered some
praise for publishers who exploited new markets and were sensitive to
changing tastes—all of which displayed sound business sense: 'Publishers, in spite of their theoretical objections, have been quicker to
adapt themselves to the needs of the day. Wisely, and rightly, they are
prepared to produce the books the libraries want. The novels are produced to meet a real and definite demand.'[34] A lending library was
regarded by many as a source of revenue and potential customers.
W. H. Smith warned its newsagent clients not to scorn 'the "Edgar
Wallace type" of reader'; if he entered their shops, then he was a
potential customer.[35] *The Publishers' Circular* was excited by reports of a
tuppenny library in South London which turned an average weekly

[33] *PC* (18 June 1938), 802.
[34] A. C. Hannay, 'Are the Lending Libraries Really a "Menace"?', *B* (11 Apr. 1934),
200.
[35] 'Books and the Public', *The Newsbasket* (May 1930), 104.

profit of £28 in 1936. 'That passer-by is your possible customer. He will not notice your dull front and dusty, ill-lighted window! He *will* notice the brightly-lighted 2*d.* library!'[36] The libraries were also seen by some as beneficial for the public libraries, which did not have to stock such 'worthless books ... these tuppenny libraries will drain away a weeping abscess'.[37]

Although Penguin Books, founded in 1935, did not appreciably attract readers from the working class, their success did serve to promote reading in general and new marketing ideas. Allen Lane pioneered the introduction of inexpensive quality paperbacks with Penguin Books. His success captivated the book trade: in the first year three million copies of 50 titles were sold, sixpence each, a turnover for the trade of £75,000. The firm's innovative marketing techniques changed the traditional nature of bookselling, for Penguins were also sold by newsagents and such chain stores as Woolworths and Marks and Spencer. A Penguin vending machine was installed in Charing Cross Road. If booksellers did not approve of the sale of sixpenny paperbacks in this way, publishers did, and many copied the Penguin format, producing 'books' with the same disposable qualities as magazines. Among these were Chevron Books (Queensway Press), Pearson's Sixpennies ('Romance'—'Western'—'Detective'—'Adventure'), and Selwyn and Blount's 'Not at Night' thriller series, which sold 250,000 copies. Hutchinson cheekily labelled its sixpenny series 'Toucan' and 'Jackdaw'. While these series could claim a healthy sale among working-class readers, Penguin Books could not, despite Lane's desire to direct such readers towards 'better' books. A Mass-Observation study commissioned by Penguin Books after the Second World War concluded that Penguins were bought by only 9 per cent of the total reading public. Working-class readers were few, a result both of the quality of fiction published and of the ingrained resistance among these classes to book-buying, even at sixpence a copy.[38] Paperback publishing on a mass scale in Britain was not introduced until after the Second World War, and only then after the creation of consortia which could underwrite the considerable costs of production

[36] *PC* (1 Feb. 1936), 101. Given such profits, the tuppenny libraries were accused in 1935 of violating the Shops Act; tuppenny libraries were exempt as they did not offer books for sale, and remained open, in some cases, to 11 p.m. ('Twopenny Libraries and the Shops Act', *PC* (10 Aug. 1935), 219.)

[37] Geoffrey Grigson, 'Novels, Twopenny Libraries and the Reviewer', *B* (20 Mar. 1935), 286.

[38] Mass-Observation, *A Report on Penguin World* (File Report 2545, M-O, Dec. 1947).

and marketing. In 1947 Penguin signed an exclusive contract with five publishers (Chatto and Windus, Faber and Faber, Hamish Hamilton, Heinemann, and Michael Joseph) to provide the first cheap two-shilling edition of their books. Also in 1947, Pocket Books, an American venture, was launched at 1s. 9d., and Pan Books, the paperback arm of Collins, Hodder and Stoughton, and Macmillan, at 1s. 6d.[39]

The relative prosperity of the book trade was naturally interrupted by the outbreak of war in 1939. The sudden and severe disruption imposed by the implementation of paper rationing in 1940 was, however, temporary. Given the restrictions placed on other leisure activities during the war, the demand for reading—and light 'escapist' fiction in particular—far exceeded supply. A buyer was found for every publication produced, but, as during the First World War, lack of paper dampened profits. Restrictions also hindered expansion. Even though it created a kind of 'captive' market, John Boon claimed that his firm might have performed much better if there had not been a war. Although the expanded wartime market consolidated Mills & Boon's market position, it impeded the firm's ability to exploit the situation. 'I mean, we were doing very well in the thirties, and we were developing the whole time. As soon as the austerity regulations came in, we were in a straitjacket.'

Paper rationing, which was enforced from 1940 until 1949, was the dominant influence at this time. Rationing was implemented by the Control of Paper Order of February 1940, which restricted publishers to 60 per cent of their annual supply of paper in 1939. A common complaint among publishers was that allocation judged on 1939, a relatively bad year in the industry (given the outbreak of war), was unfair. After the German invasion of Norway, the principal supplier of wood and pulp, allocations were steadily reduced, initially to 30 per cent, and by 1943 to as low as 6.5 per cent. Further acts prohibited publication of new titles and forbade the more frequent issue of those already on sale. When allocations were increased in small increments beginning in November 1943, this was done only to meet the demands of the armed forces, liberated territories, colonies, and overseas markets—not the home front. The severity of wartime restrictions on the publishing industry can be illustrated by a comparison of pre-war

[39] See also Hans Schmoller, 'The Paperback Revolution', in Asa Briggs (ed.), *Essays in the History of Publishing in Celebration of the 250th Anniversary of the House of Longman 1724–1974* (London, 1974), 285–318.

and wartime paper consumption. In 1939 consumption, in tons per year, was estimated by the Board of Trade as follows:

Newspapers (incl. weeklies)	1,110,000
Magazines and periodicals	300,000
Books	63,000

With rationing restrictions, for the major part of the war the Ministry of Supply allocated paper, in tons per year, according to the following averages:

Newspapers and magazines	250,000
HM Stationery Office	100,000
Books	20,000

Hence, the combined consumption of newspapers and magazines was limited to 18 per cent of pre-war supply; of books, 32 per cent. The War Office alone used 25,000 tons of paper, more than the entire book allocation. Book publishers used only 1.5 per cent of the total paper consumption; an increase of just one per cent, it was claimed, would have solved all supply problems.[40] Stanley L. Unwin estimated that as 1,000 tons of paper generated five million books, annual wartime production was in excess of 100 million books. This supply, however, had to satisfy the production of all technical, scientific, and educational books in addition to best-sellers and light fiction.[41]

Hardship caused by the shortage of paper was compounded by the Blitz. The raid of 29 December 1940 on Paternoster Square destroyed five million volumes in the warehouse of the wholesale distributors Simpkin Marshall, and the offices of Hutchinson, Collins, and Longman, among other publishers, were destroyed. Complaints of 'unavailable' or out-of-print books were commonplace: in 1941 the Publishers' Association announced that 37,000 titles were 'unavailable', a reduction since 1939 of 46 per cent for children's books and 36 per cent for adult fiction in print.[42] Some popular series, including the Yellow Jackets, were suspended until paper was available again to meet the expected huge demand. 'Nine new books out of ten are oversubscribed before publication,' the Publishers' Association reported in

---

[40] Hewison, *Under Siege*, 87. 'Magazines' included non-fiction titles, 'Books' all types including textbooks.
[41] Stanley L. Unwin, 'The Status of Books' (London, 1946), 9–10.
[42] *B* (27 Nov. 1941), 471.

1944, 'and it is not uncommon for the orders for new books and reprints to exceed the number printed by four or five times.'[43]

The magazine houses adjusted somewhat more easily. At the outset of the war, rationing restrictions forced the closure of many titles, and the larger firms were hardest hit, as can be seen from a comparison of the number of titles published at the beginning and the end of the war.

	1939	*1945*
Amalgamated Press	91	42
Odhams	25	17
Pearson	24	9
D. C. Thomson	22	17
George Newnes	19	8

Hence, the Amalgamated Press's list was cut by 54 per cent; D. C. Thomson's by 23 per cent. Most weeklies became fortnightlies or even monthlies in an effort to extend paper rations. In all, 916 periodicals and newspapers were suspended at the outbreak of the war. Children's papers were especially hard hit; many long-running titles such as *Gem*, *Magnet*, and *Chums* were stopped. But those magazines which did survive managed to maintain their pre-war prices, unlike books, and their readerships, despite reduced circulations. The most popular titles included *Picture Post*, *Everybody's*, and *Woman's Own*. One newsagent in Lansdowne Road, London, complained, 'I am so hardpressed for magazines that I ask people to return them when they are read so as to supply other customers.'[44] In 1940 W. H. Smith cited the case of the most popular woman's weekly, *Woman*:

This magazine's editorial department received in January and February of this year the astonishing number of over 85,000 letters—nearly 20,000 more than in the last 2 pre-war months, July and August. During 1939 close on a million readers wrote to *Woman* for something they wanted or wanted to know. No sign of a shrinking market here, and doubtless the same reassuring story could be told by other publishers.[45]

Indeed, despite supply problems, reading thrived during the war. In 1941 eighty-six new bookshops were opened; the number of issues from the public libraries increased by 15 per cent; and Hutchinson recorded book sales, including juvenile titles, of over 10 million copies.[46] Personal expenditure on 'Books, Newspapers and Maga-

[43] The Publishers' Association, 'Book Publishing in Britain Today', *B* (8 June 1944), 495.

[44] M-O 'Reading' Box 5 File B (26 June 1942).   [45] *TC* (23 Mar. 1940), 6.

[46] *PC* (4 Oct. 1941), 170; *B* (26 Feb. 1942), 185.

zines', as recorded by the Central Statistical Office, increased from £64 million in 1938 to £67 million in 1943 and £77 million in 1945.[47] To meet this demand, the number of book publishers actually increased during the war, despite the scarcity of paper. Although output was regulated by control of supply, there were no restrictions on the creation of new publishing houses. The market was invaded by 'mushroom' firms, small publishers of light fiction whose output exacerbated the critical paper situation. 'Their sources of supply were probably threefold—paper stolen somehow or other, black market paper (if distinction can be made here), and their own printers' ration for jobbing work', F. K. Foat, Book Manager of W. H. Smith, said in 1947. 'Much of the material published by the new, wartime firms was of little value. A great many children's books of poor quality were produced and sold well because of the shortage of toys.'[48] One such 'mushroom' firm was the United Anglo-American Book Company Ltd., which offered a line of mystery, romantic, thriller, and gangster novels, including *It's Only Saps That Die* by Buck Toler and *They Rubbed Him Out* by John Lacey Cora. Fortunately for these firms, the demand for such 'trash' intensified in wartime. 'I think a lot of publishers are just unloading rubbish on the public', noted a W. H. Smith employee in the Sloane Square branch in 1943. 'They know they'll be able to sell the classics and really good books after the war. *Anything* will sell at present. And rubbish will do while the war is on; that seems to be the attitude.'[49] In this way paper rationing may have influenced public choice by limiting the supply of certain types of fiction, such as the classics or the up-market literary periodicals, while expanding the supply of light novels and magazines. Occasionally even 'trash' had difficulty getting published, however. After the war the publication of *Forever Amber*, the 1944 American best-seller by Kathleen Winsor, was delayed in Britain due to lack of paper; one publisher commented that because of its length (800 pages) and the expected huge demand it would exhaust his paper quota for an entire year.[50]

III

During the 1920s and 1930s the leisure industries in Britain expanded significantly. Coincidental with the commercialization of popular

---

[47] *Annual Abstract of Statistics* (London, 1938–48), 246. All figures revalued at 1938 prices. The inclusion of newspaper sales in the total may distort figures.
[48] M-O 'Reading' Box 10 File F (5 Aug. 1947), 2.
[49] M-O 'Reading' Box 8 File K (7 Dec. 1943).
[50] 'A Best-Seller in Search of a Publisher', *B* (5 Apr. 1945), 406–7.

publishing along commodity lines, the cinema, wireless, organized sport, dancing, holidays, and (later) television expanded and were organized in a professional way. The popularity of these activities did not detract from reading but encouraged it, through tie-ins ('the book of the film', and circulating libraries in seaside resorts) or magazines relating to broadcasting (*Popular Wireless*, *Picturegoer*) and sport (*Topical Times*). Where the expansion of leisure activities did have an impact, however, was on retail sales. With more leisure opportunities on which to spend pocket money (and with an increase in real wages to do so), purchases of magazines in particular slumped, and public propensity to borrow novels instead of buying them increased considerably.

The cinema and the wireless were most important in promoting reading. The cinema was 'the essential social habit of the age' which 'slaughtered all competitors', A. J. P. Taylor observed.[51] There were 3,500 cinemas in 1914, 4,597 in 1951. Annual admissions increased from 903 million in 1934 to a peak of over 1.6 billion in 1946. As some 20 million tickets were sold each week, it was estimated that 40 per cent of the population went to the pictures once a week, and 25 per cent went twice a week or more. The publishing industry greeted this new form of entertainment with mixed feelings. In 1919 *The Bookseller* dismissed fears of the cinema eclipsing books. 'Surely the kind of people who are content to accept 'the pictures' as a substitute for books are so unsophisticated, and the sort of novels they would otherwise read are of such a quality, that there is nothing at all to worry about.'[52] None the less, the cinema did attract the interest of some 'quality' authors, perhaps mindful of financial gain. Jeffery Farnol (*The Broad Highway*) considered it a privilege for any author to have his work filmed, and A. E. W. Mason (*The Four Feathers*) regarded the cinema as a great new art form.[53] The publisher T. Fisher Unwin saw in film adaptations new life for older books, and anything which helped to sell books was welcomed. 'The film has produced a new and larger public, though of a lower grade', he wrote. 'Whatever happens, I think there is bound to be in the future an increase of the number of book readers.'[54]

Indeed there was. Given a shared interest in thrills, romance, and melodrama, a strong relationship was forged early between the film and publishing industries, and both book and magazine houses turned the

[51] A. J. P. Taylor, *English History 1914–1945* (Oxford, 1965), 313.
[52] *B* (Dec. 1919), 701.
[53] *PC* (23 Apr. 1920), 427.   [54] *PC* (5 Jan. 1924), 10.

new medium to their advantage. The Stoll Film Company announced in 1920 adaptations of novels by Edgar Wallace, Ethel M. Dell, and E. Phillips Oppenheim. Zane Grey's 'astonishing' popularity among 'all classes of the reading public' was further enhanced through filming of his Western novels.[55] In 1921 the National Federation of Retail News-agents and Booksellers condemned the practice of publishers who bypassed bookshops and sold 'books of the film' directly in cinema houses; Hutchinson was one of many firms which marketed sixpenny 'Film Editions' of such titles as *Queen of Atlantis* by Pierre Benoit (1933).[56] The book of the animated Walt Disney cartoon 'The Three Little Pigs' sold 188,000 copies in three months.[57] Bryce MacNab in 1935 observed that some authors were writing in 'film style' to attract the interest of Hollywood, although the movie moguls seemed inter-ested only in best-sellers. 'If there is any chance of exploiting a name, of trading on an author's popularity, of buying up the film rights of a "best-seller" and publicising it into success even before it has been made, the film factors will do it.'[58] Retailers were encouraged to retain stocks of best-selling books until film versions appeared. *The Bookseller* reported in 1947 that there had been a continuous waiting list for *Jane Eyre* in Derbyshire Public Libraries since 1940; the film version starring Joan Fontaine appeared in 1944, the radio serial much earlier.[59]

The popularity of the cinema was also reflected within magazines. Women's weeklies included features on the latest films and gossip on the glamorous stars. Publishers often boosted sales with free gifts, known in the trade as 'pushes'. In 1925, for instance, *Peg's Companion* offered readers 'Gloria Swanson's Shampoo Powder'; in 1932 a 'Beautiful Signed Portrait of Garbo' was inserted in *Britannia and Eve*. The cinema also spawned a number of film and photographic maga-zines, including the popular *Picturegoer*, and *Mickey Mouse Weekly*, introduced in 1936 as 'The Children's Paper that Grown-Ups will find Excuses for Buying'.

Similarly, the wireless benefited publishing. The publisher George H. Doran predicted in 1923 that the radio would help to sell books: 'It

---

[55] A. G. Cheverton, 'The Vogue of Zane Grey', *PC* (27 Mar. 1920), 345. Grey wrote over 50 novels, including his most famous, *Riders of the Purple Sage*, in 1912.
[56] *PC* (2 Apr. 1921), 345.   [57] *B* (1 May 1935).
[58] Bryce MacNab, 'Searching for a Film Story: The Type of Novel Which Film Producers Want', *B* (3 July 1935), 646.
[59] *B* (18 Oct. 1947), 730. Charlotte Brontë's novel is mentioned most often during this period on the subject of the influence of the film on reading.

is a tremendously multiplied lecturing platform; it is a new and more fascinating phonograph; it is the telephone in a million homes.' He added that the possibilities for serial stories were endless.[60] The Amalgamated Press's super sleuth Sexton Blake was one character who made a very successful transition from print to radio. Indeed, the radio drama had the same positive effect upon reading as the film drama. In 1950, amid 'an age of more reading than ever before in history', *The Publishers' Circular* praised the influence of the wireless and adaptations of such novels as *Jane Eyre*, *South Riding*, and *Tom Sawyer*. 'This serialising by the B.B.C. is one of the most useful and most acceptable efforts of the wireless. It is pretty safe to say that it has turned many listeners to the printed page as most libraries and booksellers would readily agree.'[61]

Given the close relations between publishing and broadcasting, and the record level of book production between the wars, it is surprising to record the slump in sales of magazines. The main explanation for this would appear to be the redistribution of consumer expenditure to other leisure activities. In addition to the cinema and wireless, expenditure on smoking, gambling, holidays, and sporting matches all increased, as it did on book borrowing. Weekly magazines did not have access to an alternative outlet for frequent and inexpensive distribution, as novels did with the tuppenny libraries. However, as there were some bestselling exceptions, which included special-interest magazines and those printed in colour, it is clear that the magazine trade also suffered from outdated technology and a rather tired look. A Gallup Poll in January 1938 concluded that only 21 per cent of the public read magazines 'regularly'.[62]

The depression in the magazine trade is evident from a number of sources. According to the Census of Production, the net output in the 'Printing [and] publishing of magazines and periodicals' reached a plateau between the wars, as did the sales of 'magazines and periodicals . . . by larger establishments'.[63]

---

[60] *PC* (10 Feb. 1923), 115.   [61] *PC* (19 Aug. 1950), 983.

[62] Multiple responses were common. Unfortunately, only five titles were identified: *Woman's Own* (6%), *Woman* (6%), *Strand* (6%), *John Bull* (5%), and *Chambers* (5%). 'All others' received 72% and 'No answer' 53%.

[63] Stephen K. Jones, *Workers at Play: A Social and Economic History of Leisure 1918–1939* (London, 1986), 48. Jones claims, however, that the main reason for the apparent stagnation and decline was 'the downward trend in prices which the crude Census data does not take into account' (p. 47).

	Net output per person employed (£)	Total net industry output (£m)	Sales of magazines and periodicals (£m)
1924	542	32.2	10.1
1930	518	37.0	10.0
1935	476	38.4	10.7

Declining circulations recorded by some publishing houses could account for this stagnation. In 1938 there were 234 weekly 'general interest' periodicals published in Britain, with a recorded weekly circulation of 18,635,000, a decrease from 21 million in 1935.[64] Sales of D. C Thomson's 'Big 5' papers for boys, the best-selling titles in this market, slumped before the Second World War; similar falls were recorded in the firm's popular weeklies for women, including *Secrets* and *Red Star Weekly*.[65] Notices of excess returns of unsold copies were common in the trade publications throughout the 1930s. The Amalgamated Press was a frequent advertiser, with papers for children (*Gem, Magnet, Schoolgirl's Own*) and for women (*Home Companion, Eve's Own Stories*) among the more seriously affected. In a somewhat desperate move, the firm's circulation manager addressed W. H. Smith's wholesale clients in 1931 with this anxious request:

We have 65 periodicals and there are approximately 40,000 agents in Great Britain and Ireland. *If every agent carries one unsold copy of all our weeklies, the returns would amount to 2,600,000 copies every week.*

What, then, is the solution? *We think that every agent should cut from his sheet each week half the 'overs' of the preceding week.* Thus, if an agent ordered 18 copies of *Answers* and had 2 left, his next order should be 17 copies. If 2 are left again, then 16, and so on. In this way, the returns problem would solve itself.[66]

Actually, only the tremendous demand created by the reading boom during the Second World War would solve the returns problem.

Both publishers and retailers laid the blame for the depressed magazine market on increased expenditure on other leisure activities. John Masefield, the Poet Laureate, was struck by how much less people were reading in 1939 than in 1909. He blamed 'amusements', claiming it was fruitless 'to expect the people of to-day to abandon their new toys for the toys which delighted the last generation'.[67] Similarly, Odhams

---

[64] Nicholas Kaldor and Rodney Silverman, *A Statistical Analysis of Advertising Expenditure and of the Revenue of the Press* (Cambridge, 1948), 86, 96.

[65] Source: Circulation statistics, D. C. Thomson & Co. Ltd.

[66] *TC* (6 June 1931), 14.

[67] 'Wanton Blemish Cut from Shakespeare', *The Times* (15 May 1939), 19.

Press, publishers of *John Bull* and *Woman*, noticed that increased ownership of cars and motorcycles had two adverse effects on reading: weekends were often spent motoring and not reading at home, and owners usually sacrificed both magazines and the Sunday newspapers ('luxury' reading matter, perhaps) to meet instalment payments on their new machines.[68] In 1933 the beleaguered Religious Tract Society, admitting in its Annual Report that 'things are different since the war', blamed the 'new inventions' which 'seem to attack that quiet reading hour—the gramophone, wireless, cinema, motor cars, cheap motor-bus and coach rides'. Daily newspapers, with their serial stories and magazine-type feature articles, were also accused of detracting from the sales of general magazines.[69]

In a comprehensive shop survey in England and Wales in 1927, W. H. Smith solicited from its employees both causes and remedies for the depression in magazine sales.[68] In addition to the attraction of new entertainments, workers mentioned an increase in participation in out-door activities, namely sport: 'The long light evenings, due to the "Daylight Savings Bill", tend to use up all the leisure time the public had for light reading in the shape of magazines.' Alternatives to the weekly magazine, including the sixpenny novel, and the growing presence of the commercial libraries were also mentioned. Among the suggested remedies, which were applied to some benefit before the Second World War, were more 'pushes'. A frenzied 'gift war' in weekly magazines ensued, reminiscent of competitions between early issues of *Tit-Bits* and *Answers* (and common among popular newspapers in the early 1930s). One working-class London woman, aged 60, was asked in 1940 why she was a regular reader of *Family Journal*. 'Well I just happened to see it advertised one day and I took it and I've been taking it ever since for 3 years. I think the attraction was 3 saucepans. They were giving 3 saucepans away with it.'[71]

It is also possible that weekly magazines could not retain their readers because they were, quite simply, looking tired and out-of-date:

---

[68] R. J. Minney, *Viscount Southwood* (London, 1954), 207.

[69] *134th Annual Report of the Religious Tract Society*, USCL 338 (1932–33), 112.

[70] 'The Decline in Magazine Sales', *The Newsbasket* (July–Oct. 1927), 157–61, 181–5, 209–11, 229–30. The amount of attention given to this subject is an indication of the severity of the situation.

[71] F/60/D, M-O 'Newspaper Reading' Box 2 File D (33 Coomer Road, London, 4 Mar. 1940).

the Religious Tract Society's titles, for example, suffered from this. 'If the contents of magazines are kept at a high level and a lot of the nonsense and hot air cut out, sales should not decrease much', one W. H. Smith employee said in 1927. This would explain the success of those magazines which *did* enjoy significant growth during the 1930s. Letterpress production of poor quality, and formulaic fiction—which characterized countless weekly magazines—looked feeble beside such bright, new, unorthodox titles as Odhams's *Woman* (1937), the first weekly magazine to be produced by photogravure and in colour (along the lines of the glossy American magazines), and D. C. Thomson's comics *The Dandy* and *The Beano*. 'Hobbies' magazines on such subjects as gardening (*The Smallholder*), aviation (*Popular Flying*), and photography were also popular, and the influence of broadcasting was apparent in the enduring popularity of *Radio Times* and illustrated magazines such as *Picture Post*. 'By far and away the most popular periodical, other than *Radio Times*, is *Picture Post*', a newsagent in Mill Hill, London, remarked in 1940. 'This is universally popular— working, middle and upper classes alike buy it. Nobody has to look through it to consider whether they want it or not.' *Everybody's* was also mentioned as a popular magazine, but only among the working classes.[72] *Picture Post*, *Everybody's*, *Illustrated*, *John Bull*, and *Radio Times*—all associated closely with the visual media—were identified in 1949 as 'mass-circulation' magazines. It was estimated that the number of copies of these titles per 100 families was 110.1 in London and the South-East, 115.0 in Wales, and 92.0 in Scotland.[73]

Finally, in the case of children's magazines, stagnation of sales may also may have been due to the falling proportion of children in the population. In England and Wales, children up to the age of 14 comprised 32.4 per cent of the population (10,545,000) in 1901; 23.8 per cent in 1931 (9,520,000); and 22.1 per cent in 1951 (9,692,000). In Scotland, figures were comparable: 33.4 per cent (1,494,000) in 1901; 26.9 per cent (1,305,000) in 1931; 24.6 per cent (1,255,000) in 1951.[74] With a declining juvenile population, saturation of the market was almost certainly achieved by the late 1920s. Indeed, D. C. Thomson blamed the failure of one of its boys' papers, *The Vanguard* (1924–6), on such market saturation.

---

[72] M-O 'Reading' Box 3 File D (104 Devonshire Road, NW7, 8 Feb. 1940).
[73] Major G. Harrison and F. C. Mitchell, *The Home Market* (London, 1950), 79.
[74] A. H. Halsey, *Trends in British Society since 1900* (London, 1972), 33.

IV

The strong demand in Britain for light fiction before the First World War was sustained and indeed increased in the twentieth century, in wartime and in peace. In fact, it was difficult to resist reading something, so wide and accessible was the variety of reading matter for all classes. Wartime increased the demand for escapist fiction; the post-war decline in retail prices of books and the ensuing competition by publishers led to a surplus of novels. During the 1930s, public and private facilities which permitted the borrowing of books cheaply and conveniently expanded across the country. Leisure activities, including the cinema and the wireless, promoted the reading habit. Reading levels increased, however, at the expense of retail sales and to the benefit of libraries, and magazine publishers suffered in particular. Of the latter, the successful firms, such as D. C. Thomson, Odhams, and the Hulton Press, prospered through innovation.

These developments, while sustaining the demand for reading, provoked major restructuring within the publishing industry. Publishers were forced to cater to the tastes of a specific audience (in this case, the lower-middle and working classes) more closely than before in order to ensure the maximum sale and to cover rising production costs. Commodity-style techniques were introduced, and some houses (including, with great success, Mills & Boon) tied all of their books to one readership, such as the women who patronized the tuppenny libraries. Such market-targeting was a strategy previously confined to magazines. Fortunately, the demand for cheap low-brow fiction produced by the thousand was great; reprinted works of adult fiction far exceeded new works. The Second World War served to institutionalize these new publishing techniques while intensifying the demand for reading even further, thereby preparing the market for the 'mass-circulation' magazines and paperbacks characteristic of the present day.

3

'THE QUICKEST WAY OUT OF GLASGOW': ADULT READING HABITS

WHY did light fiction sell so well between 1914 and 1950? What motivated members of the lower-middle and working classes to read what they apparently did? In 1944 a postman in Scotland was approached by a 'Mass-Observer' (a seemingly ubiquitous figure in the 1930s and 1940s) and asked just that. 'As the Cockney said: "Getting drunk is the nearest way out of London",' he explained, 'so reading is the quickest way out of Glasgow.'[1] Indeed, 'escapism' appears to be the principal motive in reading during this period, particularly among the working classes. When one considers the book stock of the tuppenny libraries or the magazines which sold best, this is not surprising. Reading as a means of escape—in fact, reading of *any* kind—intensified in times of adversity such as the war and the depression. It was also encouraged by the peculiar attitudes towards books and patterns of selection held by the new reading public. In general, working-class readers did not distinguish between books and magazines in looking for something to read (often confusing the two), and were more susceptible to the 'look' of a book or a sensational title. One consequence was that the best-selling authors, novels, and magazines preferred by this public were increasingly of the same style and genre. In this chapter I will examine the reading habits of lower-middle- and working-class adults, considering how much and how often they read, and why they read what they did.

I

Generally speaking, the reading habit was either maintained or increased during this period. The principal influence was war, in two respects. First, war increased the temptation of all classes, and espe-

---

[1] Mass-Observation, *Books and the Public: A Report for the National Book Council* (File Report 2018, 11 Feb. 1944, M-O), 85.

cially women, to continue to seek escapist fiction in book and magazine
form. Reading and the distraction it provided were identified as 'a
tower of strength' in 1915 and 'our safest refuge in the mental torment
of war' in 1939.[2] This habit, moreover, was sustained in peacetime;
after the First World War, for example, popular fiction was easier to
obtain because of increased competition, lower prices, and the saturation of the commercial libraries. Secondly, wartime not only served
to perpetuate existing reading habits but appeared to encourage new
readers. Among those introduced to lighter forms of reading were war
workers, either in the Forces or on civilian duty. This was the principal
growth area in the reading public.

To contemporaries, the First World War plainly encouraged
reading, especially of the 'lighter' kind. In 1915 the *Daily Mirror*
surveyed publishers and booksellers and reported that fiction, poetry,
and detective stories were 'in great demand'; books were selling 'remarkably well' in spite of the war, but war stories were no longer
popular.[3] According to the publisher Herbert Jenkins, people had
grown tired of war books. 'Indeed, they now asked for something to
make them forget how far it is to Tipperary, or that Piccadilly is being
kept as dark as the plans of the War Office ... something that will, for a
time at least, take them out of themselves.'[4] Jenkins crusaded against
those who criticized the number of novels, many by female writers,
which were being published. 'What a boon new novels are to the man at
the Front, the wounded, the bereaved. I have received many very touching testimonies of the gratitude of those who want to forget things
occasionally for an hour or so.'[5] Increases in fiction borrowing were
recorded by public librarians. In Leeds, the librarian cited escapism
for the growth of fiction issues during 1916, and the librarian at the
Guildford Institute said that 'light' literature never sat on his shelves
more than a few hours, such was the demand. *The Times*, surveying
public libraries nation-wide in 1917, attributed the reading 'boom' to
'the fact that people seek distraction from the worry of the times in the
reading of works of imagination'.[6] The paper also cited restrictions
imposed on other leisure activities during the war as a reason for the
'distinct revival in reading':

[2] 'Reading in the Time of War', *The Times* (13 Apr. 1915), 6; Compton Mackenzie,
quoted in 1939, M-O 'Reading' Box 3 File D.
[3] Quoted in *PC* (2 Oct. 1915), 317.   [4] *B* (19 Feb. 1915), 169.
[5] *PC* (20 Jan. 1917), 50.
[6] *PC* (23 Mar. 1918), 267; 'Reading and War Worry', *The Times* (12 Apr. 1917), 8.

The civilian population at home have had much more money to spend than before and fewer ways of spending it. There were no longer any cheap tickets to tempt people to travel, and the dark streets made them disinclined to venture out again after they had once found their way home. The result was that the new quietness of the evenings and the Sundays provided a harvest for the book-sellers.[7]

This was probably important in promoting reading during both world wars. 'The war has increased reading among the English public 40 per cent', John Buchan wrote in 1927. 'Lots of the new reading class started the habits in hospitals, others because they found books cheap and plentiful when other entertainments were dear and scarce.'[8] Fifteen years later, *The Publishers' Circular* gave a similar explanation for the unprecedented growth of reading at the height of the depression. 'In recent years there has been an amazing increase in the amount of reading done by the general public. It may be said with truth that the ordinary man or woman is now discovering that books are one of the cheapest and most satisfying forms of interest and amusement', the journal reported in 1931. 'If the economic blizzard has caused much evil, it may be put to its credit that it has driven thousands of potential readers indoors to the fireside and the book.'[9]

The Second World War encouraged a similar boom in reading, and one that is better documented.[10] The strong participation in reading by the lower-middle and working classes, illustrated by the success of the tuppenny libraries during the 1930s, was intensified after 1939 for the same reasons as during the First World War: escapism, and a lack of alternative leisure activities. The trade journals documented the surge in popularity of light fiction. In 1939 *The Publishers' Circular* surveyed publishing houses, concluding that 'the great British book-buying public are ... choosing the lighter books these dark days, and leaving the heavier ones for future happier times and occasions'.[11] *The*

[7] Quoted in *PC* (12 Aug. 1916), 147.
[8] Quoted in *The Book Window* (W. H. Smith), Christmas 1927, p. 97.
[9] *PC* (26 Dec. 1931), 793.
[10] Thanks mainly to the efforts of Mass-Observation, which in 1938 embarked on an ambitious investigation of reading habits, including interviews with librarians, news-agents, and readers of all classes around the country. The London evidence from the boroughs of Fulham, Chelsea, and Tottenham is particularly full. The material is invaluable for its impressionistic quality, rather than its scientific nature. From other sources it is easy to conclude that light fiction sold well, but only through Mass-Observation is it possible to assess how it was regarded by its readers, and what impression it made on them.
[11] *PC* (9 Dec. 1939), 577.

Bookseller was less pleased, describing the public taste by 1940 as 'mere drunk and disorderly novel reading'. Christina Foyle, of the London booksellers, was impressed by the active book market in 1942:

There's been a tremendous boom in books . . . There's been nothing like it, even in the last war. It's easily explainable of course—books aren't rationed, there's no purchase tax, and they don't require coupons, and then people have so much more time for reading than they used to have, with troops stationed in lonely places where books are the only things to amuse themselves with, with people unable to go away for holidays or to travel much locally, and with the black-out evenings.[12]

She added that the boom was not confined to one type of book, but that 'everything under the sun' was selling well. The weekly magazines which survived paper rationing also sold well, shrugging off the gradual decline in this market between the wars—and showing that *anything* would sell.

Surveys conducted by Gallup and by Mass-Observation indicate that measured percentage levels of reading were either maintained or increased during and after the Second World War. A 1942 inquiry by Mass-Observation involving over 10,000 people across the country found that 40 per cent of men and 40 per cent of women said they read 'much'; two years later these figures had increased to 59 and 56 per cent, respectively. Figures referred to the reading of books, magazines, and newspapers.[13] A Gallup Poll published in February 1940 determined that 62 per cent of the adult public (an estimated 19,840,000 people) was reading books; 38 per cent (12,160,000) was not.[14] Four later Gallup Polls illustrate that the level of reading declined after the war, then recovered. To the question, 'Do you happen to be reading a novel or other book at the moment?', the response was as follows:

	Jan. 1941	*Sept. 1946*	*Nov. 1947*	*Dec. 1949*
Yes (%)	51	45	45	55
No (%)	49	55	55	45

[12] M-O 'Reading' Box 6 File C (12 June 1942).

[13] Mass-Observation, *Report on Books and the Public: A Study of Buying, Borrowing, Keeping, Selecting, Remembering, Giving, and Reading* BOOKS (File Report 1332, 2 July 1942, M-O), 8, 11; Mass-Observation, *Books and the Public*, 1.

[14] It is interesting to compare the Gallup population totals with those announced in an address to the Library Association annual conference in 1931. As reported by *The Times*, 'This was, of course, a reading age. It had been estimated that 17,000,000 persons read on an average twelve novels each a year. Some read at least 150, thus bringing up the average' (1 Sept. 1931, p. 14).

The recovery shown by 1949 was probably caused by the end of paper rationing and the appearance of greater numbers of books and magazines. One reason for the evident decline in reading after the war is suggested by the deputy public librarian in Portsmouth in 1941. Reading habits, she claimed, though strengthened by war, could be disrupted by peace:

All figures point to the fact that reading is not only well maintained in war-time, but actually increases while population and libraries remain intact. When the population are no longer there, then, and only then, do figures decrease. This fact is important, since the figures of issue do not alone reveal it.[15]

Disruption could also explain why Gallup's measured reading levels declined between February 1940 and January 1941; as the public librarian in Stepney said, 'The public simply isn't reading. That's all. They don't want to make themselves responsible for the books, I think . . . Not since the trouble—there's been some very heavy bombing in this district, you see.'[16] Once the general public adjusted to the situation, however, borrowing was brisk again. The librarian in Canterbury, in recording a 20 per cent increase in fiction borrowing early in 1940, commented on how borrowing habits had changed:

Formerly, we were fairly slack in the day-time, and very busy from 5–7 p.m. (we closed at 7 p.m. even before the war). Now it is the other way round. We get slight queues early in the morning, decided congestion in the afternoon, and immediately the black-out screens go up, miraculous peace and quiet.[17]

Black-outs, in fact, served to promote reading during the war. 'ONE BLACK-OUT BENEFIT! More time for READING! Long winter evenings at home means lots more leisure for reading. Join Boots BOOKLOVERS LIBRARY', ran one wartime advertisement. In a leading article in 1940 *The Publishers' Circular* observed that reading had supplanted the wireless in most homes as the principal leisure activity. 'The wireless is often in use only for news, being switched off at other times so that the wailing of the sirens cannot be missed. Then a book provides just the relaxation required, and if it becomes necessary to take cover, the enforced inactivity can be profitably employed.'[18] One working-class man in Fulham, London, admitted that the black-out had had an effect upon his reading tastes and reading time:

[15] M-O 'Town and District' Box 17 File D (Aug. 1941), 18.
[16] M/50/B, M-O 'Reading' Box 3 File G (14 Sept. 1940).
[17] M-O 'Reading' Box 3 File D (30 Jan. 1940).   [18] *PC* (5 Oct. 1940), 185.

I like Crime, Murder stories. Stories with excitement in them. *The Madonna of the Sleeping Cars* (by) M. Dekobra; *The Crooked Hinge* (by) J. D. Carr. Looks as if there'd be a murder—it would be gripping . . . I got used to being awake when the blitz was on—I've kept it on. I read in bed a lot.[19]

The size and complexion of the reading public in general did not change appreciably during this period. Evidence suggests that reading buffs read at least as much, possibly more. Conversely, those less interested probably continued to avoid reading. But where change is noticeable is in the addition of the new 'leisured class'. This group, drawn largely from the lower-middle and working classes, was composed of men and women who were compelled, either by war or the depression, to accept a larger amount of leisure time than normal. These included the mass of the unemployed, who made good use of the public libraries, and (in wartime) men and women in the Forces, evacuees in the provinces, and Civil Defence workers. Of the latter, for example, Mass-Observation recorded during the Second World War that voluntary workers 'have plenty of spare time, but cannot use it in peace-time ways because they have to stay at their posts. Reading is the most unobtrusive, most easily-put-away method of using their spare time.'[20] Long hours spent in underground shelters also encouraged reading:

Librarians have often been asked lately for something to read in the shelter. They think people are settling down to their nocturnal dwellings and are providing light good enough to read or work by instead of just enough to see what they were doing. At least one librarian attributes this only (to) the speed with which people return books.[21]

The increased reading activity of the new leisured class undoubtedly enhanced the market for popular fiction in wartime, and probably promoted its continuance in peace.

Reading in the Armed Forces during each war was predictably light, with books passed around eagerly. Demand was high; according to one observer, soldiers read 'insatiably' and prisoners-of-war were as grateful for books as for food.[22] Light fiction was, as ever, in great demand.

---

[19] M/25/D, M-O 'Reading' Box 4 File A (29 Apr. 1942).
[20] Mass-Observation, *Books and the Public*, 3.
[21] M-O 'Air Raids' Box 7 File D (18 Oct. 1940).
[22] Wilson Midgeley, 'Reading in Wartime', *John O'London's Weekly* (4 June 1943), 81–2.

In 1917 the novelist Beatrice Harraden surveyed wounded 'Tommies' and discovered that their favourite authors were Nat Gould, Charles Garvice, and E. Phillips Oppenheim. She defended what were criticized in the press as low-brow tastes: 'Our wounded warriors have surely earned the right to amuse themselves with the books that please them most, and to be free from the kind of officious pedantry that would seek to thrust upon them literature of a class and type for which they have, as they themselves would say, "no use".'[23] Reports filed during the Second World War indicate that detective novels and sex stories, especially the quasi-pornographic magazines from America, were most popular among troops, although Oppenheim, William Le Queux, and H. G. Wells were cited as favourites in one survey. 'Soldiers are at times escapist, like anyone else. Some read because it is their life's habit, others to forget the war', according to one critic.[24] The *Daily Express* reported that soldiers wanted only thrillers: 'The gorier the better, the highest-browed being about the level of, say, Agatha Christie.'[25] Romantic novels were also popular: a sergeant stationed with the army in Italy got 'the surprise of my life' when he discovered the demand among his men for the soppy love stories of Annie S. Swan. 'I suppose it means the lads out here have their weak moments. But Annie S. Swan, I ask you!'[26]

There is some evidence as to what people spent on their reading matter during this period. Surveys suggest that in the 1930s as much as two shillings was spent each week by the 'average' family. In 1934, for example, the average expenditure per week, per family, on leisure activities was 4s. on smoking, 2s. 6d. on 'entertainments', and 2s. on reading matter—quite an amount as a magazine could be purchased or

[23] *B* (June 1917), 251. In the *Life of Florence Barclay: A Study in Personality, by One of Her Daughters* (London, 1921), Barclay's daughter recounted how much the Tommies loved her mother's books. Barclay often visited Red Cross hospitals, and on one occasion encountered a man, 'screened off because his wounds were so severe', reading *The Following of the Star*. 'She asked him gently if he liked it. "Yes," he said, "it makes me forget my pain." She always treasured that remark as her very highest reward.'

[24] Frank Buckland, 'What We Read in the Army', *John O'London's Weekly* (31 Dec. 1943), 121–2.

[25] *B* (7 Mar. 1940), 307.

[26] *PC* (17 June 1944), 347–8. 'Classics'—e.g. Jane Austen and Charles Dickens—were also popular among troops in both wars. J. M. Dent reported in 1941 that sales of Everyman novels to the Forces had increased, an indication, according to the publisher, that men liked to vary their reading among humour, thrillers, and the classics. But as in wartime everything which was printed was sold, soldiers may have read Dickens and Austen as they did Gould and Swan simply because they were available.

a novel borrowed for only twopence.[27] The 1938 Ministry of Labour inquiry into the cost of living concluded that of working-class families with an income of £250 per annum or less, the average weekly expenditure per head on books, stationery, pens, and pencils was 2½d. per week, and on newspapers and periodicals one shilling. The latter amount, if spent exclusively on library borrowing or at the newsagent, could have bought, for example, three twopenny library books and three twopenny magazines (or six twopenny newspapers) in a given week. *The Publishers' Circular*, faced with a sluggish retail market for books, was encouraged by these last figures. 'The information does provide conclusive evidence that the working classes *do read*, and that in pennies and tuppennies they spend millions a year in satisfying their hunger for knowledge and relaxation.'[28]

There is also some evidence about the level of reading activity and the actual number of readers. In the 1930s the popularity of reading among the working classes was measured in the Merseyside social survey, which concluded that 64 per cent of Class 'C' men and 70 per cent of Class 'C' women read fiction in any particular week.[29] In 1947 the Hulton Readership Survey estimated that 68.5 per cent of working-class men read at least one magazine a week; 19.8 per cent read three or more. Among working-class women, 61.9 per cent read general weekly magazines, 51.1 per cent women's magazines, and 33.2 per cent monthlies.[30] Similar conclusions were also reached in the 1940s by Gallup and Mass-Observation. A Gallup Poll in February 1940 found that 75 per cent of 'higher income' groups read books, and 58 per cent of 'lower incomes' (magazines as well as books).

Perhaps predictably, reading was popular among the unemployed. In 1938 the Pilgrim Trust, in noting the prevalence of reading among jobless men, discovered that the newsagent's shop was the chief source of escapist reading matter, rather than the public library. 'They escape

---

[27] Major G. Harrison and F. C. Mitchell, *The Home Market* (London, 1936), 90–1. The average annual budget per family was set at £330, described as typical of 'an average small lower middle class family'.

[28] Cecil Palmer, 'The Working Classes and Books', *PC* (15 Feb. 1941), 93–4. Palmer added that 'the £5 a week wage-earner is a rarer bird than the one who earns fifty shillings a week', and wondered what his weekly spending was.

[29] D. Caradog Jones (ed.), *The Social Survey of Merseyside* (London, 1934), iii. 275. Oddly, 'Newspapers' were included under 'Fiction'. The survey cited the Sunday newspaper and magazines (including American ones) as very popular among poorer families.

[30] J. W. Hobson and H. Henry (comp.) *The Hulton Readership Survey* (London, 1947), 22. Statistics for the reading of newspapers were higher, with the tabloid papers *News of the World*, *Daily Express*, and the *People* most popular.

into an imaginary world by buying, as a Deptford newsagent said, "magazines to forget their troubles . . . twopenny magazines with stories, bad of their kind, of schoolboy adventures, pirates, buffalo ranches and highwaymen", and sport and betting', the report concluded.[31] Like children, unemployed adults probably bought and swapped magazines. Similarly, the Carnegie UK Trust's survey of jobless men aged 18–21 in Glasgow, Cardiff, and Liverpool in 1943 found that, although the cinema was the most popular leisure activity (80 per cent), reading was recognized as the 'main interest' (45 per cent).[32]

Those outside the working classes, to the extent that their evidence is reliable, were confident that there was a 'new reading public'. One of the results of the First World War, according to *The Publishers' Circular*, was the marked increase in novel-reading by both the middle and working classes. 'They have no taste in literature, but the sale of cheap editions to them is enormous', the journal reported, adding that ultimately the librarian and not the bookseller would reap the benefits.[33] In 1932 Q. D. Leavis was struck by the activity of what she called 'tuppenny dram shops':

In suburban side-streets and even village shops it is common to find a stock of worn and greasy novels let out at 2*d.* or 3*d.* a volume; and it is surprising that a clientele drawn from the poorest class can afford to change the books several times a week, or even daily; but so strong is the reading habit that they do.[34]

Geoffrey Grigson in *The Bookseller* characterized tuppenny library users as 'a public which I think we shall all agree does not consist of people who were reading books before but of those whose reading had been confined chiefly to newspapers and magazines', i.e. the working class.[35] Reading habits were indeed often divided along class lines. In 1942 Mass-Observation investigated public library usage in the Swansea area. Whereas readers in Sketty, Mumbles, and Dystimouth ('middle-class suburbs') preferred travel books, novels (high-brow), and non-fiction, readers in St Thomas (a 'dock and industrial working class district') preferred 'nearly all fiction. Cowboy stuff, thrillers, love

[31] Pilgrim Trust, *Men Without Work* (Cambridge, 1938), 294–6.
[32] *Disinherited Youth: A Report on the 18+ Age Group Enquiry Prepared for the Trustees of the Carnegie U.K. Trust* (Edinburgh, 1943), 100.
[33] McMahon Trevor, 'Who Buys Novels?', *PC* (28 May 1921), 555.
[34] Q. D. Leavis, *Fiction and the Reading Public* (London, 1932), 7.
[35] Geoffrey Grigson, 'Novels, Twopenny Libraries and the Reviewer', *B* (20 Mar. 1935), 286–7.

stories, adventure. Nothing else goes there.'[36] Another Mass-
Observer, upon completing an exhaustive (and exhausting) series of
interviews in 1943, divided up the reading public as follows:

> A class doesn't read at all (or else it reads *Das Kapital*)
> B class: highbrow, technical
> C class hasn't got the leisure
> D class reads, and lives, for pleasure
> (The higher you are the harder you fall).[37]

According to contemporaries, interest in romantic and detective fiction remained high. In 1921 the *Daily Telegraph*, accounting for the
'phenomenon' of increased novel publishing in Britain, identified the
romantic novel as a boom industry: 'One thing must be true—there
must exist a very large body of readers who swallow down anything in
the shape of romance, however badly it is written and faultily con-
structed.'[38] W. Pett Ridge defended romantic fiction in an address
before the London Master Printers' Association in 1920. 'Love was like
drink—it made the world go round', he said. 'The whole excuse for
fiction was that most people lived monotonous lives, and they were
extremely glad to read about people who lived lives of a different
kind.'[39] Reports from retailers and librarians agreed; an assistant in the
Boots Library branch in Hammersmith commented in 1947, 'The
majority like a thriller and light novels, you know, love stuff. It's surprising how many people do read the light stuff: it's the times—they
don't want anything deep.'[40] It is not surprising, then, to record the
great success of publishers like Mills & Boon at this time. On the other
hand, the reception given by all classes to detective fiction was a more
unusual and intriguing phenomenon. C. Day Lewis, a prolific detective writer as 'Nicholas Blake', claimed that all classes and political
views 'join hands over a corpse. One touch of bloodshed, it seems,
makes the whole world kin.'[41] The popularity of detective novels remained high even after the Second World War, perhaps as a result of
the cinema. A Gallup Poll in October 1950 found that 48 per cent of
respondents had read detective fiction; of these, nearly a quarter con-

[36] M-O 'Reading' Box 5 File E (1 June 1942).
[37] M-O 'Reading' Box 8 File C (1943).
[38] *Daily Telegraph* (7 Jan. 1921), quoted in *PC* (15 Jan. 1921), 41.
[39] 'The Cost of Printing: Mr. Pett Ridge on Love in Fiction', *The Times* (17 Mar.
1920), 14.
[40] M-O 'Reading' Box 10 File F (20 Feb. 1947).
[41] Nicholas Blake, 'Detective Stories and Happy Families', *B* (13 Mar. 1935), 268.

fessed to reading such fiction frequently. Favourite authors included Edgar Wallace (14 per cent), Conan Doyle (10 per cent), and Agatha Christie (7 per cent).

Three readership surveys suggest that the large majority of readers of popular magazines came from the lower-middle and working classes. *Press Circulations Analysed* (1928), *Investigated Press Circulations* (1932), and the Hulton Readership Surveys (1947–53) were each conducted to provide the advertiser with information, during a period when market research was still in its infancy and audited circulation figures were even rarer. Given the small amount of advertising in magazines for boys and girls, none was included in these analyses. In each case, the estimated readership of a periodical was displayed in terms of class and region. Weekly magazines with the highest percentages of lower-middle and working-class readers (amounting to at least 50 per cent of the total number) were as follows (listed in order of popularity):

	General Interest	Women
1928	*John Bull*	*Home Notes*
	Answers	*Home Chat*
	Pearson's Weekly	*Woman's Weekly*
1932	*John Bull*	*Woman's Weekly*
	Radio Times	*Woman's World*
	Tit-Bits	*Red Letter*
1947	*Radio Times*	*Woman's Own*
	Picture Post	*Woman*
	Everybody's	*Woman's Weekly*

With the exception of *Red Letter*, *John Bull*, *Tit-Bits*, and *Answers*, all these magazines were 'middle-class' publications, and yet the core of their readership was not from this class. This suggests a kind of escapism among working-class readers towards a middle-class ideal, which was encouraged by publishers like Mills & Boon. The shift in interests and advances in technology are also significant: by 1932 the popularity of the cinema and wireless is evident, as is the decline of the traditional letter-press magazine by 1947.

II

With the commercialization of literature and the introduction of commodity-style publishing techniques after the First World War, greater attention was paid to the 'look' and marketing of a publication, as in colourful dust wrappers and more aggressive advertising. To what extent were members of the 'new reading public' particularly suscept- ible to such stimuli in the selection of a novel or magazine? During the 1940s, Mass-Observation identified factors of selection which were deemed 'unique' to working-class readers. It was estimated, for example, that only one-tenth of these readers attached importance to the author's name in selecting a book; a majority would commonly read several books by the same author without realizing it. Most were conser- vative, uncomfortable in experimenting with different genres. 'People stick to their own type, and have prejudices in some cases against other types. If you give people short stories, said a librarian,—"they look at you as though you had given them margarine instead of butter".'[42]

Often a reader left the choice of a new book or magazine to the librarian or newsagent, who was trusted to be familiar with the reader's tastes. Stephen Mogridge, who ran a lending library in a southern English village after the Second World War, remarked, '80% of my customers are incapable of choosing a book for themselves. I suppose this reflects a lack of interest in life. They suffer from boredom.'[43] In the 1930s the playwright John Osborne's grandmother shunned the public library, dispatching her husband regularly to the local tuppenny library. Although the implication was that her tastes were special, even refined, '[the] truth was that she thought her husband incapable of even choosing a book for her whereas at the twopenny library they know, of course: Ethel M. Dell, Netta Muskett and, that pre-war Dickens of them all, read and re-read again, Warwick Deeping'.[44] The average time spent in choosing a book from a tuppenny library, according to Mass-Observation, was five minutes, which was 'far lower' than for public library users.[45]

Production values were an important influence. In 1942, Mass-Observation asked 400 people if they were affected by the 'look' of a book. Of Class B readers, 32 per cent said they were; Class C, 47 per cent; and Class D, a remarkable 73 per cent. The look of a book usually meant the type of jacket; blue was the most popular colour. 'I'd go for a

---

[42] Kathleen Box, 'Selection and Taste in Book Reading', M-O File Report 48 (Mar. 1940), 31.
[43] Stephen Mogridge, *Talking Shop* (London, 1949), 85.
[44] John Osborne, *A Better Class of Person* (London, 1981), 46.
[45] Mass-Observation, *Report on Books*, 70 f. Although books were chosen quickly, working-class women tended to spend more time chatting with each other and the assistants. '2d. libraries are thus much more of a social centre than any other type', M-O concluded.

nice blue or red cover; it looks more attractive than the duller ones', said one woman.[46] An interesting drawing, preferably depicting a romantic or amusing scene, was also a plus:

Best laugh I ever had was a thing I got in Woolworths, no I don't remember its name but it had a girl with legs on the cover and a bloke looking through a window. I thought, that's a bit of all right, and it was. I never finished it though, had to hide it from the missus, and never found it again, oh but it was funny. (M/45/C)[47]

'It's very strange', the proprietor of Mitchell's 2d. Library in Fulham commented in 1940. 'The person who is a reader selects often according to the author. The person who isn't selects according to the lurid-ness of the jacket. It needn't indicate anything about the contents of the book.'[48] Good printing was also a concern, as was cleanliness:

I've no fads, yet all the same I don't like a shabby book—one that looks as if the bacon fat was poured over it.   (M/50/C)

I always look at a book; and it must be clean—very strongly; if I pick up a book and find a grub in it I drop it like a red hot brick.   (F/50/B)[49]

The physical weight of books was taken into account (too heavy to carry home, or hold while reading in bed) as well as size; shorter novels that could be read quickly were preferred to longer ones.

I hate a book about a lot of people—I always forget which one I've to think of. I never choose a big book, it's much too heavy to carry around with you. I like books what I call easy reading—that is, big print, and not too crowded looking on the page.   (F/25/C)[50]

Some readers would rely upon the frequency of issues of a book from the library as a guide in choosing a novel (the tuppenny libraries usually date-stamped books on the inside front covers). 'I just look at the front page where the date stamps are marked and if there's a lot of dates on it, then a lot of people must have read it, and so it must be a good book', said one woman from Marylebone.[51] Mills & Boon's novels were notorious for being covered in date stamps. 'Book of the Month' selections, introduced in daily newspapers in the 1930s, also

---

[46] Ibid., 140; F/50/D.
[47] M-O 'Reading' Box 8 File C (Notting Hill Gate, 9/10 Sept. 1943).
[48] M-O 'Reading' Box 3 File A (Fulham Road, 8 Feb. 1940).
[49] Mass-Observation, *Report on Books*, 156; M-O 'Reading' Box 4 File A (Marylebone, 17 May 1942).
[50] 'Pretty typist type', M-O 'Reading' Box 8 File C (14 July 1943).
[51] F/70/D, M-O 'Reading' Box 4 File A (8 Apr. 1942).

directed readers' attention to the 'best' in light reading. Although these were probably based not on critical acclaim but on the suggestion of publishers, they nevertheless generated important publicity. Finally, there was also the lure of novelty. Mogridge claimed that many of his customers had a hankering for the newest and the latest. 'Whatever the customer wants—crime, romance, cowboy, highbrow novels, biographies—the demand is for a *new* book. There is an obsession that anything over six months old is out of date and not worth reading.' His average reader took two books a week, although the book-a-day customer was quite common:

The fashion in reading now is quick and superficial. Fostered by the libraries, the habit of reading a book as fast as possible and then discarding it for ever is firmly established. Time is now so crowded. The quiet lawns of literature are trampled by impatient feet.[52]

Susceptibility to these stimuli was probably engendered by the way these classes regarded the care and possession of books and magazines. According to Mass-Observation, working-class readers (Class D) had a unique attitude towards books: 'D's have on the whole no feeling of acquisitiveness, pleasure in possessing books. They share and pass round their magazines and "real" books, without expecting their return, or worrying very much where they came from or whence they go.'[53] Among reasons cited for such behaviour were the reluctance (or, indeed, inability) to spend money to buy good quality books, high usage of lending libraries, and the extensive reading of magazines and light romances. One reader, a postal worker, remarked: 'I don't buy many books. Occasionally we buy the sixpenny ones, and after it's read, it goes to the Forces reading.'[54] The omnivorous readers of an industrial town surveyed by *The Bookseller* in 1941 were not book buyers but active borrowers: 'People buy few books because they consider them luxuries: when it is a choice between books and butter, between Shakespeare and bacon, necessity becomes the mother of abstention.'[55] But when books *were* bought by the working class, these were generally reference and picture books which were highly prized and passed down, as revealed by a 1947 investigation conducted for Penguin

---

[52] Mogridge, *Talking Shop*, 90, 183.
[53] Mass-Observation, *Report on Books*, 115.
[54] F/45/D, M-O 'Reading' Box 6 File B (London W10, 20 May 1942).
[55] Bernard Lennon, 'Books in an Industrial Town', *B* (9 Jan. 1941), 26–8. The 'industrial town' was not identified but was described as 'large enough to return one Member of Parliament'.

Books by Mass-Observation of libraries in working-class homes. 'Cloth books have far more prestige attached to them than paper books among people who have not acquired the reading habit and who are therefore impressed by contents rather than appearance.'[56] In Osborne's Fulham home in the 1930s, the only 'permanent' books (magazines and 'books', presumably novels, were discarded when read) were *The Doctor's Book*, *Angel Pavement* by J. B. Priestley, *Contraception* by Marie Stopes, and *The Boy's Own Annual*, 1908–15, collected and reread by Osborne's father.[57] A housewife in Muswell Hill, London, in 1942, showed the contents of the one bookshelf in the home to a Mass-Observer:

These leather books were given to my husband at school. We've filled the others up here and there. Mostly in Smith's bookshops and usually at bargain prices ... (Cooper's *The Deerslayer*)—I picked that up at a bookstall—I thought it was going to be interesting, but it's not. I like thrillers—*Not at Night* is lovely—all about horrors.[58]

In the author Alan Bennett's Leeds home during the war, the only books, apart from those picked up at the library, were reference books, mostly bought by subscription, such as *Enquire Within*.

No book whether from the library or otherwise was ever on view. Anthony Powell's 'Books do furnish a room' was not my mother's way of thinking. 'Books untidy a room' more like or, as she would have said, 'Books upset'. So if there were any books being read they would be kept out of sight, generally in the cabinet that once held a wind-up gramophone, bought when they were first married and setting up house.[59]

This 'bookless' character of working-class homes was often blamed by critics for the popularity of 'inferior' fiction. In 1929 Stanley L. Unwin claimed that 'the *real* problem' in the book trade was not over-production but underconsumption and insufficient sales. 'Most people have not yet learned to regard books as a necessity. They will beg them, they will borrow them, they will do everything, in fact, but buy them.' In Unwin's opinion, dynamic efforts were needed to encourage the new reading public which was expanding daily.[60] Similarly, Fred Easton in 1935 urged retailers to embark on a national campaign with teachers

[56] Mass-Observation, *A Report on Penguin World* (File Report 2545, M-O, Dec. 1947), 130.
[57] Osborne, *A Better Class of Person*, 65.
[58] F/25/C (married to a building tradesman), M-O 'Reading' Box 6 File B (17 May 1942).
[59] Alan Bennett, 'Alan Bennett Remembers the Treachery of Books', *The Independent on Sunday Review* (28 Jan. 1990), 9.
[60] Stanley L. Unwin, *The Truth about Publishing* (London, 1929), 57–8.

and education authorities with the message, 'A bookshelf is as essential as a cupboard'.[61] But 'commodity' publishing, as we have seen, did not encourage this, as it highlighted the disposable quality of cheap books. According to Raymond Irwin, director of the School of Librarianship and Archives at London University, the decline of the domestic library was a twentieth-century phenomenon:

Those who go about with their eyes open must surely have noted how many homes today are apparently bookless. Moreover, the word 'book' itself is commonly misused for things that are not books at all, but popular magazines that are never regarded as permanent possessions, and are discarded when the next number arrives.

Good or bad, such things are not the stuff of which the domestic library is built. One Friday recently I stood for a few moments in a newsagent's shop in a small Midland town, watching one woman after another come in with her weekly order of 'books' for the family—eight or ten titles scribbled on a sheet of paper. This particular town had no true bookshop, nor had it a very satisfactory library, though I am doubtful whether this would have made much difference.[62]

It was also partly because of the way that many working people read that the type of fiction published and reading matter selected were simple. Working women in factories, for example, were fond of the 'blood-and-thunder' pulp magazines published by D. C. Thomson which were exciting to read and, more importantly, easy to pick up and put down. 'The tastes of the working-girl reader incline to the adventurous and romantic. She wants something that is not wordy and will hold her attention', *The Times* reported in 1917.[63] Mass-Observation recorded the 'phenomenon' of 'scattered reading' before and during the Second World War. Regular times for reading, it was claimed, were rarely set aside. Rather, reading was recorded in public transport, at work, during mealtimes, in bed—whenever there were a few spare moments. Reading at mealtimes was especially common; many instances were observed in Lyons Teashops in London.[64] 'The newspaper serial is good for "scattered" reading but for most people the comic strip is even better', Mass-Observation noted. 'Eyes and mind

---

[61] Fred Easton, 'Capture the Book Trade! Don't Blame Others—Act Yourself', *National Newsagent, Bookseller, Stationer and Fancy Trades' Journal* (23 Mar. 1935), 1.

[62] Raymond Irwin, 'The English Domestic Library in the Nineteenth Century', *Library Association Record*, 56 (Oct. 1954), 388.

[63] 'Working Girls' Reading: The Queen's Gift of Books', *The Times* (7 Aug. 1917), 9.

[64] See esp. M-O 'Reading' Box 5 File B (1942). These accounts are minutely detailed and wonderfully evocative ('. . . 3 pm looked up at clock—gazed at reflection in wall mirror—fiddles with hair and scarf—back to book . . .').

must be occupied but not strained.'[65] One reader during the Second
World War justified her choice of *The Way of an Eagle* by Ethel M. Dell
in this way: 'I like something like—you know—something you can get
into quickly—especially these days—when you couldn't possibly be a
long while getting to the point.'[66] Scattered reading may have declined
during the Second World War, when black-outs encouraged more
reading at home. In 1944 Mass-Observation concluded that 73 per cent
of people did their reading at home in the evening, and only 12 per cent
while travelling. Hence, housewives were probably the most dedicated
and consistent section of the reading public, as they could vary reading
times to suit their work.[67]

Finally, selection of fiction was influenced by the cinema. The growing popularity of film and the frequent treatment of the thriller and the
love story did not detract from the reading market but enhanced it. In
fact, in Bournemouth the *Daily Echo* placed the cinema next to black-
out regulations as responsible for the city's visible revival of reading
during the Second World War.[68] In 1935 Grigson noted the strong
influence of the cinema upon tuppenny library users:

A new public, a cinema-going public, wants to read nothing but novels, and
only those which are 'hot huddles of sensation'. The huddle that is hottest and
most sensational, providing that such qualities are effective but decently
draped, will be this or that Book of the Month or 'recommendation'; and this
mass public without traditions of book-buying or book-owning will at once
swarm into the libraries in search of it.[69]

Similarly, Mass-Observation noted that the 'book of the film' was
particularly coveted by the lower-middle and working classes:

The most frequently *bought* fiction books, especially by C and D class people,
are definitely those which have been filmed, like 'Hatter's Castle', 'The Grapes
of Wrath', 'Love on the Dole', 'Rebecca', 'North West Passage', 'Gone with the
Wind', etc. Here again we come to the souvenir and permanent value of the
book. Having seen a film, people like to keep it in some permanent form by
buying the book.[70]

However, at least one reader was not happy with her 'souvenir'; having

---

[65] M-O 'Reading' Box 1 File A (1937), 3.
[66] F/50/C, M-O 'Reading' Box 3 File A (Fulham, 1940).
[67] Mass-Observation, *Books and the Public*, 20.
[68] *The Daily Echo* (Bournemouth), 2 Mar. 1940, quoted in M-O 'Reading' Box 3
File A.
[69] Grigson, 'Novels, Twopenny Libraries', 286.
[70] Mass-Observation, *Report on Books*, 59.

TABLE 3.1. Authors in Demand at Tuppenny Libraries, 1933–1935

	Tuppenny libraries		Mudie's
	1933	1935	1934
Ruby M. Ayres	24	21–5	59
Charlotte M. Brame		31	0
Edgar Rice Burroughs	24	16–20	23
Marie Corelli	9	16–20	27
Richmal Crompton	14*	16–20	15
Warwick Deeping	41	46	46
Ethel M. Dell	23	26–30	31
Jeffery Farnol	14	21–5	15
J. S. Fletcher		56	97
Charles Garvice		0–8	5
Elinor Glyn	13	10–15	12
Nat Gould		0–8	35
Zane Grey		26–30	35
H. Rider Haggard		26–30	46
A. G. Hales	28	38	43
Sydney Horler		45	47
W. J. Locke	24	26–30	29
Kathleen Norris		34	35
E. P. Oppenheim	38	75	84
Margaret Peterson	26	26–30	28
Denise Robins		36	36
Sax Rohmer	18	21–5	20
E. Adelaide Rowlands		26–30	40
Rafael Sabatini		26–30	30
'Sapper'		16–20	32
E. M. Savi		56	51
Joan Sutherland	25	26–30	34
Paul Trent		31	47
Edgar Wallace	100	101	116
P. G. Wodehouse	32	40	43
F. E. Mills Young		33	42

*All 'William' books.

Sources: *1933*: T. E. Callender, 'The Twopenny Library', *Library Association Record*, 3rd ser. 3 (Mar. 1933), 88–90. The library surveyed contained 2,500 titles; according to Callender, 'The predominant flavour of the list is definitely lowbrow' but representative. *1935*: Garfield Howe, 'What the Public Likes', *B*, 19 June 1935, pp. 580, 583. Howe examined 'one of the largest and newest' tuppenny libraries. Exact figures for the most popular authors were given; those with less than 31 titles (but 'definitely in the "best-seller" class') were placed in groups of five. Howe's list is more extensive than Callender's. *Mudie's*: *Mudie's Catalogue of the Principal Works of Fiction in Circulation at the Library*, sect. 1: 'Works of Fiction Under Authors' Names' (London, May 1934).

seen *Gone With the Wind*, she 'rushed straight out and bought it afterwards. I was rather disappointed in the book to tell you the truth ...'[71]

III

Which books did the 'new reading public' choose most often? Who emerged as favourite authors? Given the uniquely 'popular' nature of the tuppenny libraries, analyses of their book stocks can help to answer these questions. Table 3.1 compares the findings of two such surveys of 'busy' establishments with the contemporary catalogue for Mudie's Library. Only the authors listed were mentioned in the tuppenny library surveys. The preference for thrillers (notably Edgar Wallace) and romantic novels is especially evident. Somewhat surprisingly, Mudie's matched or exceeded the tuppenny library totals (notably with the works of Ruby M. Ayres). This is an indication of three things: the broad-based appeal of these authors; the automatic stocking of all titles by Mudie's; or the number of former tuppenny library users who now subscribed to Mudie's, which had lowered its rates (together with Boots and W. H. Smith) in the 1930s in a response to the competition.

A body of material related to the tuppenny libraries is also important here. In 1925 an employee of W. H. Smith wrote to *The Newsbasket* asking if a list could be provided of best-selling authors that branches could stock without fear of loss or remainders. The categorized list of such proven 'fairly safe stock', perhaps more representative and comprehensive than Table 3.1, is reproduced below.[72]

Light Fiction

Kathlyn Rhodes	Gertrude Page	Olive Wadsley
Cecil Adair	Dolf Wyllarde	Berta Ruck
Muriel Hine	Paul Trent	Maud Diver
Ruby M. Ayres	Margaret Peterson	

Detective and Exciting Stories

E. P. Oppenheim	Sax Rohmer	William Le Queux
H. Rider Haggard	Ottwell Binns	J. S. Fletcher
Rafael Sabatini	Edgar Wallace	P. B. Kyne

Western Stories

Clarence Mulford	Zane Grey	B. M. Bower
C. Zeltzer		

[71] F/25/B, M-O 'Reading' Box 8 File C (Notting Hill Gate, 9/10 Sept. 1943).
[72] *The Newsbasket* (Mar. 1925), 48.

Good Fiction

Stephen McKenna	H. G. Wells	Arnold Bennett
H. A. Vachell	A. E. W. Mason	Philip Gibbs
Hugh Walpole	W. J. Locke	J. M. Barrie
John Galsworthy	Robert Hichens	Gilbert Frankau
Sheila Kaye Smith		

Presumably either personal taste or the book trade itself determined which authors were classed as 'Good Fiction' and which merely 'Light Fiction'. Similarly, in the appendix to his 1938 book *How to Run a Twopenny Library*, Ronald F. Batty provided 'A Short Check List of the Most Popular Twopenny Library Authors', subdivided into categories. Notably, five authors listed in Table 3.1—Corelli, Gould, Rider Haggard, Savi, and Mills Young—are not offered by Batty. His additions include:

'Love and Romance'	Barbara Cartland, Maysie Greig
'Detective and Mystery'	Agatha Christie, G. D. H. and M. Cole
'Air and War Stories'	W. E. Johns, Ian Hay
'Western'	Max Brand, W. C. Tuttle
'Adventure'	Jack London, P. C. Wren
'Humorous'	W. W. Jacobs, Dornford Yates

Curiously, Batty provided separate listings for 'Novels' (Ursula Bloom, Baroness von Hutten, Compton Mackenzie) and 'Modern Novels' (Vera Brittain, Colette, Evelyn Waugh—and Mae West!).[73]

Mass-Observation also sought the opinions of tuppenny librarians and library assistants, though this evidence is probably more impressionistic. One tuppenny librarian in Fulham in 1940 observed, 'Some of these silly women like a lot of slop . . . But men will look for something really blood and thunderish, something like—oh—*Who Killed Oliver Cromwell?* sort of business.'[74] Similarly, in Chelsea in 1943 a library assistant commented on the state of the business:

I get in forty new books every four weeks for the twopenny library, but as you can see from the shelves, most of them are out, so there's never much of a choice. The men all choose those detective stories or the Wild West sort of

[73] Ronald F. Batty, *How to Run a Twopenny Library* (London, 1938), 91–6. Another useful source of popular fiction is contained in a pamphlet printed by John Menzies, 'A Selected List of Popular Fiction Suitable for Lending Libraries', Apr. 1935 and Mar. 1937 (John Menzies PLC archives, Edinburgh).

[74] Box, 'Selection and Taste', 23. *Who Killed Oliver Cromwell?*, by Leonard Gribble (1937), was a best-seller before and during the Second World War. An 'Inspector Slade Mystery', it concerns the murder of a man masquerading as Cromwell during a ball.

thing, but the women are always asking for a really nice novel: Vicki Baum or Daphne du Maurier—they've both been very popular.[75]

Mogridge was impressed by the huge adult readership of Westerns in his library. 'Authors' names mean nothing to the western fan; it is the story that is the thing, a fresh book every day the ideal.' One of his customers, a veteran of the First World War, chose his Westerns not by author but 'by whether they've got a woman in or not'. Soppy romance spoiled the story; this reader flipped through a novel in search of female names before deciding.[76]

Newsagents also assumed that there were marked sex differences in reading habits. An Aston newsagent said: 'They go in for short fiction stories the ladies do. And the murder books the men—the rough stuff.'[77] Similarly, a Fulham newsagent, commenting on magazine ('books') reading, stated, 'The young girls read the same they read before. Love stories'. He added, however, that interest in such fiction was variable:

The girl of about 17 or 18 will start buying books every week (points to *Miracle*—sex stuff). And then she goes courting and she gets saturated with it—with her young man and she ceases buying them. Then after six months when the young man's got sick of taking her out she'll come back for two pen'north of love again.[78]

One Manchester woman preferred *Illustrated* to *Picture Post*:

We used to get *Picture Post* too but my husband stopped it—he said it was too full of rude ladies—it wasn't fit to have where there's children. (*Illustrated*) hasn't any of that in, and I like those war pictures.[79]

In the case of popular books and magazines, sensation always sold, whether in the form of a racy novel or a weekly 'two pen'north' pulp paper. An amusing response from a working-class newly-wed on his wife's tuppenny reading is fitting here:

No, I don't read books, the paper's all I can do with . . . But you should have met my missus before we got married—read—why, she was always at it, morning

[75] F/60/C, M-O 'Reading' Box 8 File C (14 July 1943).

[76] Mogridge, *Talking Shop*, 33.

[77] F/50/C, M-O 'Town and District' Box 1 File B (23 Nov. 1946).

[78] Assistant, S. Hughes & Co., M-O 'Newspaper Reading' Box 2 File D (Estcourt Road, Fulham, 2 Mar. 1940).

[79] F/40/C, M-O 'Newspaper Reading' Box 2 File E (22 Jan. 1943).

noon and night. She was crazy on desert stuff and sheiks and all that. The chemist at the corner kept a twopenny library, and she used to go down every day for another book and say to him, 'Haven't you got anything *hotter*?' He thought she was a real bad lot, but she wasn't, she was just nuts about books. When we got married, he made sure it was because we had to; he was quite surprised we didn't have a kid in the first six months. But since she married me, she's quite different—she never opens a book now.[80]

The most notorious and widely read best-seller of the Second World War—among the working classes—was probably *No Orchids for Miss Blandish* by James Hadley Chase, published by Jarrolds (a division of Hutchinson) in 1939. This vicious story of the kidnapping of the 'Meat King's daughter' by the mob, her repeated rapings, torture, and ultimate suicide, is told at a furious pace. Why Chase's novel was not subject to prosecution is anyone's guess; Jarrolds, however, regarded its sensation as a marketing tool. The endpiece of the novel contained the following teaser:

The Publishers, Printers, and Readers of *No Orchids for Miss Blandish* are still convalescing from shock. They thought they could take it until they ran into Slim Grisson . . .
James Hadley Chase has another burst of electricity in store for them, and in store for YOU. Look out for THE DEAD STAY DUMB, the new James Hadley Chase novel to be published shortly. It is very tough indeed![81]

Contemporary critics were, on the whole, dismayed by the level of popular reading habits. 'Let people enjoy plenty of fiction—good fiction—by all means,' *The Bookseller* declared in 1919, 'but it is a thousand pities that so many should limit their reading entirely, or almost entirely, to "stories".'[82] Charles Masterman, recording the findings of a visitor to a soldiers' hospital, was more sympathetic. These men, he claimed, 'wanted forgetfulness, and surely they had earned the right to it'; the authors most in demand were Orczy, Garvice, Gould, and 'Sexton Blake'.[83] But Rebecca West, perplexed by the public adoration of florid romances by such authors as Garvice, Dell, Corelli, and Barclay, wrote, 'In trying to understand the appeal of best-sellers, it is well to remember that whistles can be made sounding certain notes which are clearly audible to dogs and other of the lower

---

[80] M/30/D, M-O 'Reading' Box 8 File C (SW1, 13 July 1943).
[81] Endpiece, *No Orchids for Miss Blandish* (1939), 256.
[82] *B* (Nov. 1919), 625.
[83] Charles F. G. Masterman, *England After War: A Study* (London, 1923), 113–14.

animals, though man is incapable of hearing them.'[84] Finally, Robert Graves and Alan Hodge claimed that 'pulp' fiction was a staple of the reading public between the wars:

What did people read, besides newspapers, in the period immediately following the war? The low-brow public . . . read monthly story-magazines and 'pulp' fiction—that is to say, the light amorous and melodramatic sort, printed on wood-pulp paper, like newspapers, and not intended to last. Most of these novelettes were written by hacks and sold by the title and cover-design rather than by the pull of the author's name.[85]

Nat Gould, William Le Queux, Sax Rohmer, J. S. Fletcher, and the stable of boys' magazines were all cited as examples. '"Tarzan of the Apes" was the most popular fictional character among the low-brow public of the Twenties; though the passionate Sheikh of Araby, as portrayed by E. M. Hull and her many imitators, ran him pretty close.'[86]

War themes do not appear to have been very popular among adults during either war. *The Bookseller* reported during the First World War that by 1917 interest in 'war books' had waned; readers wanted greater emphasis on the lighter and more human side of war. Similarly, most readers seemed to prefer to avoid war themes during the Second World War: 'I never read a war book, for that purpose I read the paper and hear the news on the wireless—it would only be the same old joint dished up with a different gravy.'[87] According to one Mass-Observer, 'I avoid any plays, fiction or films dealing with the war like the plague. Would run a mile from any film called "Wings over Anything" or "Somebody in the RAF". Absolutely sick of shots of planes flying in formation or having rather indistinct dogfights in the air.'[88] Presumably, scenes of combat and violence in literature were regarded as too uncomfortably familiar in wartime; the exception, of course, was evident in children's literature.

[84] Rebecca West, 'The Tosh Horse', in *The Strange Necessity* (Virago edn., London, 1987), 323. She added, perhaps with a touch of envy, that one sight 'which must fill the heart of any serious English writer with wistfulness ... is when he gazes across the esplanade of any watering-place and looks at the old ladies reading their Ethel Dells. Truly we are a strange nation.' Such was Dell's appeal that West estimated the readership of her novels as equivalent to the combined populations of Surbiton, Bournemouth, and Cheltenham.

[85] Robert Graves and Alan Hodge, *The Long Week-End: A Social History of Great Britain 1918–1939* (London, 1941), 50.

[86] Ibid. 51.

[87] F/45/D, M-O 'Reading' Box 6 File B (London, W10, 20 May 1942).

[88] Mass-Observation, 'War Themes in Entertainment', File Report 1380 (Aug. 1942), 1.

IV

Why did people read what they did? In 1944 Mass-Observation surveyed 10,000 readers to try to find the answer. The results indicate that the strongest desire among lower-middle- and working-class readers was for 'relaxation'.[89] (Figures are percentages: it can be seen that multiple responses were common.)

Reason	Men	Women	Class B	Class C	Class D
Relaxation	53	57	39	62	58
Knowledge/education	50	26	39	38	39
Rest	10	17	17	13	9
Stimulation	8	4	11	4	6
Technical knowledge	6	1	5	4	2
Others	2	7	14	1	2

Between the classes, if reading for educational purposes was consistent, the increase in the apparent need to unwind and be entertained is evident as one descends the social scale. Evidence from contemporaries and readers suggests that Class 'C' and 'D' readers read light fiction to 'relax' and to 'escape'. In 1922 *The Times* praised the fantasy elements in detective stories: fast cars, beautiful women, exotic locations. 'Perhaps in real life your purse may seldom, if ever, allow you these delights; all the more reason, then, for enjoying them in imagination. They are to you what the caves of diamonds and rubies and pearls were to the readers of the Arabian Nights.'[90] The novelist Jermyn March (*The Man Behind the Face*) believed that the average reader sought vicarious thrills from novels. 'They like to feel that the least little turn of fortune's wheel might have involved themselves in just such a throbbing romance, have headed straightaway on just such a reckless, joyous venture, or high enterprise, as the hero or heroine embarks on.'[91] Similarly, Ruby M. Ayres, the doyenne of romantic novelists, offered this advice to aspiring writers of the genre:

In novels there are two rules: men must be tall and strong, but not necessarily good-looking. You must have two men and a girl, or two girls and a man. If you

---

[89] Mass-Observation, *Books and the Public*, 75–6.
[90] *The Times* (8 Feb. 1922), 8.
[91] Jermyn March, 'The World of Fancy', *TC* (19 Feb. 1927), 3.

have not £20,000 a year you like to read about people who have. If you have not a handsome young man, you like to read about someone who has.[92]

George Magnus encouraged authors to set their sights high. 'The world is a snob, and the Editor must cater for the world. There is a much bigger demand for stories dealing with people who live in Mayfair than about "persons" who exist in Battersea Park. It is the latter people who read the stories.'[93]

Mass-Observation found that most readers during the Second World War described their tastes in reading as 'escapist'. While wartime did not profoundly influence the character of popular reading, it may nevertheless have encouraged 'light' reading by making the escapist motive something less to be ashamed of. A stenographer in 1944 regarded light fiction 'as I do cigarettes: nothing so potent as a drug, merely a harmless bromide', a frivolity she felt she could well afford during wartime.[94] Other readers agreed; some added that they found a kind of solace in such fiction:

At present I read them purely as a drug. I don't know who you are, but I don't see why I shouldn't tell you. I can't bear my job and I'm unhappy in my personal life, and I absolutely stupefy myself with reading ... I stay in bed the whole of Sunday and read. (F/35/B, Chelsea)

Well, my tastes have got very depraved since the war. I used to read like a reasonably intelligent human being, but now I read like a tired business man. I suppose it's because I *am* tired. A book worth reading gives you a great deal, but it makes an initial demand on you that I'm just too exhausted to comply with, nowadays. I just stupefy myself with detective fiction, all the time ... it's just a drug, anyway. (F/40/B, Chelsea)

I read more now than I ever did. My boy's away in the Middle East, and I don't go out much, I expect that's the reason. I like light fiction best, of the family story kind, and I prefer them to have a happy ending, even if it is highly improbable. There's enough tragedy in real life to want to read about it, and that's one of the reasons I *never* read a war book. (F/25/C, 'pretty typist type')

---

[92] 'Miss Ayres Shares her Ideas', *TC* (22 Apr. 1933), 10. In *Eggs, Beans and Crumpets* (1940) P. G. Wodehouse lampooned Ayres as Rosie M. Banks, Bingo Little's famous wife. '... authoress of *Only a Factory Girl, Merveyne Keene, Clubman, 'Twas Once in May*, and other works. You see her name everywhere. I understand she makes a packet with the pen' (Penguin edn., Harmondsworth, 1986, p. 8).

[93] George G. Magnus, *How to Write Saleable Fiction*, 14th edn. (London, 1924), 38.

[94] Mass-Observation, *Books and the Public*, 85.

My two sons are away, and I read a lot to stop me worrying and thinking about them. It takes my mind off things.   (F/50/D)[95]

Some readers—notably admirers of romantic fiction—were more conscious of the idea of an 'escape' from a disagreeable reality. Alan Bennett recalled the 'theme of escape' which 'tantalised' his parents in their choice of reading, especially Wells and Priestley. One of the few books his mother bought was *I Haven't Unpacked* by William Holt, 'the story of someone brought up as she had been in a mill town but who had bought a horse and gone off on his travels'.[96] Other readers would have sympathized:

I like Daphne du Maurier's books, especially *Frenchman's Creek* and also Baroness Orczy's. Books dealing with some costume period when smugglers had the rule of the seas. I like books to take me into another world far from the realities of this. I've only lately taken to reading. I've been engaged and we decided to break it off, and I wanted something to take it off my mind. (F/25/D, war worker)

I haven't much time for reading, but when I do I like to settle down to a nice love story—easy reading, one by Ethel M. Dell. I like books about people who go out to seek a fortune, and find it. Nice happy books.   (F/45/D, postman)[97]

The cinema had a similar effect, especially for the unemployed or the overworked housewife, who could forget their worries for a couple of hours in a palatial setting. But some sought a more realistic sort of 'escape' in their reading. In 1926 a library assistant in Manchester, when asked to recommend a book for a 'lady', produced a detective novel by J. S. Fletcher and a romantic adventure by W. J. Locke, for the following reasons:

If a woman is taken up with a house all day, she doesn't want tales about married problems or misunderstood wives—she knows enough about those already; she can't be bothered with dialect after a day's work, and historical novels aren't alive enough. What she enjoys is something that is possible but outside her experience.[98]

---

[95] M-O 'Reading' Box 8 File F (13 Oct. 1943); Box 8 File C (13 July 1943); Box 8 File C (14 July 1943); Mass-Observation, *Books and the Public*, 59.
[96] Bennett, 'Alan Bennett Remembers', 8–9.
[97] M-O 'Reading' Box 8 File C (14 July 1943); Box 6 File B (London W10, 20 May 1942).
[98] 'Mr Manchester', 'To-night's Diary: Book Psychology', *Manchester Evening News* (22 Feb. 1926), 3.

Certainly popular fiction of the period, with its emphasis on happy endings, supported this theory, as did the opinions of readers:

I've always liked Naomi Jacobs' books; I find them so interesting, and the theme of the story isn't exaggerated. The characters experience incidents likely to happen to any one of us, and that's part of the charm of her writing, it rings true. She usually writes a series of books dealing with one particular family, with the result that by the time you've finished the story, the characters come to life, and you follow them up in the next book. (F/30/C, aircraft factory inspector)

I like to read family books about plain Mr and Mrs, no lords and princes and dukes—people more in my way of living that I can understand. I like writers that don't exaggerate. If they're writing about a Cockney—they should give a true picture of one—not put the Cockney stuff on with a trowel—that makes me lose all confidence in the writer—and I just put the book down. (F/45/D, London)

I like novels about commonplace people and their little dilemmas—I suppose they come under romantic—my reason [is] the feeling of intimacy one gets with the characters, which combats the real loneliness of one's own life and is an antidote to the fact that one cannot get intimate with real people—every person is separate. (Housewife, aged 38)[99]

Finally, the intentions of some readers of thrillers and detective stories are less clear. These carried the reader into an exciting, if condemned, life of crime. C. Day Lewis ('Nicholas Blake') believed that, in addition to promoting the universal ideal of virtue triumphant,

the reading of crime fiction, like the playing of some violent physical game, enables us to let off steam, to get some of our natural pugnacity off our chest . . . It brings within the reach of every purse the alluring sparkle of wickedness and the riotous sensation of unleashed emotions, without any of the unpleasant consequences.[100]

Although a distinct fondness for gore is suggested by some of Mass-Observation's reports:

I read quite a few detective novels . . . in general, I prefer to have my murders good and gory. Not to have the whole book devoted to the putting right of just one murder, but to have horror piled up on horror, until the whole book is swimming in blood—and the characters whittled down, so that even I have a fair chance of discovering whodunit before the author is graciously pleased to let his customer into the secret. (M/35, insomniac, reads six books weekly)

---

[99] M-O 'Reading' Box 8 File C (14 July 1943); Box 8 File C (18 oct. 1943); Mass-Observation, *Books and the Public*, 96.

[100] Blake, 'Detective Stories', 268.

I like a good detective or crime story best of all. There's logic in it. The way it's all planned out, and the way it keeps you guessing all the time, and then unmasking the murder. Books like these make your blood curdle. I enjoy reading the gruesome methods people are killed by.   (M/35/D London; plumber, 'Looks quite a prosaic type')

(I'm reading) *Murder in the Bud*—Phyllis Bottome. Because it interests me. (M/20/D; Fulham)

It's all according to the mood. If I fancy a good bloody murder—I get one.   (no details)[101]

Sidney Dark, who coined the phrase 'new reading public', was one contemporary who could understand why light fiction was probably popular among tired workers. 'The trouble is most men begin their leisure so wearied by their work that they are naturally more inclined to take down from the shelf Edgar Wallace, who demands little from his reader, than to discover why Tolstoi's "War and Peace" is acclaimed as one of the world's great novels.'[102] He tried, however, to discourage such habits; books 'that are nothing but narcotics are, in the long run, as destructive of real life and real living as cocaine'.[103] Some higher-brow novelists agreed. In J. B. Priestley's 1942 novel *Blackout in Gretley*, shopkeepers turn a good profit by selling dreams and dope: druggists dispense 'miraculous cures', and the tuppenny libraries, 'bright with book jackets showing South Sea maidens and shop-girls marrying dukes, pure opium without a hangover at about a farthing an hour'.[104] In *Love on the Dole* (1933) Walter Greenwood wondered whether such literary escapes actually did more harm than good: here, Helen finds life in Hanky Park stifling and longs for a genuine escape:

Dully, insistently, crushing came the realization that there was no escape, save in dreams. All was a tangle; reality was too hideous to look upon: it could not be shrouded or titivated for long by the reading of cheap novelettes or the spectacle of films of spacious lives. They were only opiates and left a keener edge on hunger, made more loathsome reality's sores.[105]

---

[101] Mass-Observation, *Books and the Public* 88; 'Reading' Box 8 File C (14 July 1943); Box 3 File A (1940); Box 8 File E (n.d., *c.* Oct. 1943).
[102] Sidney Dark, *After Working Hours* (London, 1929), 41–2.
[103] Sidney Dark, *The New Reading Public* (London, 1922), 12.
[104] J. B. Priestley, *Blackout in Gretley* (Dent edn., London, 1987), 19.
[105] Walter Greenwood, *Love on the Dole* (Penguin edn., Harmondsworth, 1987), 65.

V

Documentary evidence from the Mass-Observation archive in particular demonstrates that reading habits among lower-middle- and working-class adults actually changed very little during this period. Reading patterns established before 1914 were preserved, even during war and the depression, when the recreational and 'escapist' qualities of light fiction were especially appealing. In fact, the opinions of contemporary critics and readers suggest that the principal motive in reading among the lower-middle and working classes was 'escapism'. In some cases, thrillers, detective stories, and romances were regarded as essential distractions from problems personal and public, particularly in wartime; in others, they were frivolous 'bromides'.

Significantly, Mass-Observation admitted that 'no cut and dried answer' can be given on the conscious motives of what constituted 'escapist' reading. In a 1944 report the firm concluded that 'at the conscious level, thriller-reading is widely considered as remote from reality; while most of the other types of fiction-reading are in one way or another felt to enlarge the reader's experience or knowledge'.[106] Indeed, it is apparent that these readers—some very omnivorous—were dependent upon popular literature to a degree unseen before or since. Consequently, given the non-confrontational quality of such fiction, it was possibly a significant instrument in maintaining morale and social cohesion, as well as in promoting conventional views of morality and society. Some publishers, including Mills & Boon and D. C. Thomson, were conscious of this and attempted (although only for as long as it was commercially successful) to lead their readership towards a 'better', 'wholesome' good. Others, such as the Religious Tract Society, accomplished this with less skill—and much less success.

[106] Mass-Observation, *Books and the Public*, 97–8.

4

'TAKE THE PLACE OF VALIUM': MILLS & BOON LTD.

MOST women who sought to lose themselves for a while in a romantic novel searched the shelves of Boots or the local tuppenny library for one name: Mills & Boon. From the 1930s, this firm exploited with great success the demand for light fiction, becoming one of the principal suppliers of the circulating libraries. Over the years an extensive list of titles, popular and prolific authors, and clever marketing techniques have achieved a unique status for Mills & Boon. 'It's always been said that there were only two publisher's imprints that the British public have been conscious of', Philothea Thompson, a former editor of *The Bookseller*, said. 'One was Mills & Boon, and the other was Penguin.'[1]

Before 1950 and the advent of the mass-market paperback, Mills & Boon was not the largest publishing house, nor was it the most successful (as it is today). But the firm exemplifies the major structural changes in the publishing industry between the wars and in this respect is of great importance. First and foremost a commercial enterprise, Mills & Boon was the pioneer in the promotion of books as commodities and in the rationalization of established publishers into 'library houses' in the 1930s. A politically conservative house, it also attempted to guide its readers to a vision of a higher moral ground—but only up to a point. With an eye on commercial success, Mills & Boon followed the changing tastes of the readership closely, even as it tried to influence them. The result was a spectacular success, a soothing combination of realistic instruction and escapist, almost sedative entertainment. According to Alan Boon, son of the co-founder of the firm and the acknowledged 'genius' behind the best-selling Mills & Boon romance, 'It has been said that [our books] could take the place of valium, so that women who take these drugs would get an equal effect from reading our novels.'[2]

---

[1] Philothea Thompson was interviewed in 1987.
[2] Alan Boon was interviewed on four occasions between 1986 and 1988.

I

Mills & Boon was founded in 1908 by two former employees of Methuen, perhaps best known then as Marie Corelli's publisher. Gerald Mills was educational manager, Charles Boon sales manager and general manager. The two men, in their early thirties, had very different backgrounds. Mills came from a well-to-do Stourbridge family and was a Cambridge graduate; Charles Boon grew up in a working-class family in Seven Dials, and his father had worked for a library before entering the publishing business. Both left Methuen unhappily; Charles Boon, according to his son John, 'had seen Methuen grow very well, and he thought that he had made a substantial contribution to it, and had not been, [as] all young men think, adequately rewarded'.[3] The new company was registered on 28 November 1908. *The Bookseller* was optimistic: 'The two partners have had ten years' experience with Messrs. Methuen and Co., and propose to throw their publishing net widely.'[4]

Mills & Boon was not founded as a romantic fiction publishing house, although its first book was, prophetically, a romance: *Arrows from the Dark*, by Sophie Cole. Early lists of its publications reveal the variety of the firm's interests. These included novels by Jack London, Cosmo Hamilton, Victor Bridges, Hugh Walpole and Horace W. C. Newte. A 1920 advertisement of 'Mills & Boon Gossip' revealed that Newte's novel *Sparrow* had attracted three million readers, and another edition of 20,000 copies had just been printed. The 'Thrilling Adventure Library' included *The Phantom of the Opera* by Gaston Leroux. Separate lists of books on humour, health, children, cookery, domestic improvement, and travel were also published. Early in its history Mills & Boon acquired an extensive educational list from a publisher called Whittaker (no connection with the *Almanack*); some of the first books were very successful, including *Nerves and the Nervous* by Edwin L. Ash. 'They did books on algebra and geometry by a man called Walker, who besides being a very good author was Examiner in the Liverpool area, so he always had a market', John Boon said. 'They were selling in the fifties.' Indeed, an early advertisement named Eton, Harrow, and Sandhurst in a 'List of Schools and Colleges in which Mills & Boon's books are used'.

[3] John Boon was interviewed on three occasions between 1986 and 1988. The younger brother of Alan, John joined his father's firm in 1938 and has worked on the financial side. He is presently Chairman.

[4] *B* (5 Feb. 1909), 183.

Before the First World War the new company made steady progress. During its first year 104 contracts were signed with authors, reviews were good, and, most importantly, sales were excellent. Mills & Boon published 'quality' six-shilling hardbacks, one-shilling reprints, and sixpenny paperbacks. Turnover rose from £16,500 at the end of 1909, to £22,127 in 1913; salaries were increased and £300 advances to authors were common.[5] John Boon thought that establishing a small publishing house early in the century was not difficult. 'In those days ... I don't think they were great accountants or anything like that. It was more sort of basic bookkeeping. I don't know whether we had a sales force.' The latter, for instance, was not necessary, given the sophisticated networks of wholesale suppliers and circulating libraries then accessible to even the smallest publisher.

Despite this, however, between the First World War and Gerald Mills's unexpected death in 1928 the firm fell upon hard times and nearly collapsed. John Boon attributed the young company's difficulties to two factors: lack of capital and the absence of a 'back list', books which consistently sold well. After the war sales declined by 45 per cent, as the firm was faced with a stock of 250,000 one-shilling hardbacks which it could not sell to a market demanding new editions and cheaper prices. Several strikes, culminating in the General Strike, added to the firm's financial difficulties. Struggling with large stocks but low financial reserves, Mills & Boon was unable to retain its top authors. Hugh Walpole, for instance, was poached by Macmillan. Victor Bridges's departure was heralded in an advertisement, 'The inevitable has happened! Victor Bridges has moved to Hodder and Stoughton!' Jack London, one of the leading authors under exclusive contract with Mills & Boon, died in 1916. The firm's crisis came to a head in 1928, when Mills died suddenly, with a considerable portion of the company left in his estate. J. W. Henley, a former office boy at Methuen, became joint managing director and acquired about a third of Mills's equity; the Boon family eventually bought the rest in the 1950s. Henley's shareholding solved the firm's financial problems, and enabled Mills & Boon to remain in private hands.

With the solution of the cash-flow problem, Mills & Boon prospered once more. The 1930s witnessed a major shift in the firm's direction which reflected changes in the market-place. As library sales increased between the wars, fiction displaced the general and educational lists. At the same time, Mills & Boon specialized in what was its most successful

[5] John Boon, 'The Early Years of Mills & Boon', *B* (2 May 1959), 1650.

type of novel, the romance. Romantic fiction had always been a strong element in the publication list, with Sophie Cole, Denise Robins, Joan Sutherland, Louise Gerard, and Dolf Wyllarde big sellers. In 1923 Mills & Boon published Georgette Heyer's first novel, under the pen-name Stella Martin.[6] Charles Boon, moreover, was an avid theatre-goer and encouraged light novels written in the style of shows at the Haymarket Theatre in London. His experience at Methuen may also have pushed him in this direction. According to John Boon, the founder, Sir Algernon Methuen, 'like all good publishers, was not averse to having a really popular low-to-middle-brow author like Marie Corelli' on his list, even though the seriousness with which he regarded her and her work amused his employees. Even if she was not a quality writer, Corelli would certainly have improved the cash flow.

John Boon believes his father's decision was a purely commercial one which corresponded with the contemporary trend towards the commercialization of popular fiction and the promotion of books as commodities, not to mention the spread of the tuppenny libraries. 'I think really he was essentially a commercial publisher, as you would expect from his background. I think he found that the ready market developed with the commercial libraries, particularly for romance. It was low-risk publishing, because you can compute the likely sales. It was low overhead, and promotion zero. You didn't advertise'—given the captive readership.

Mills & Boon responded not only to the demand for romantic fiction but also to changes in style. Several factors—the entry of women into the work-force, a greater domestic stability, tighter editorial control by publishers, possibly a reaction to the violence of the war—served to change the character of the romantic fiction published between the wars. Exotic styles established by such torrid writers as Ethel M. Dell and Elinor Glyn did not last long after 1919; an emphasis on 'middle-class' domesticity and realism took their place, apparent in the less sensational, socially narrower romances now produced by Mills & Boon. In the same way, magazine editors themselves also reflected the 'old school' and what was supposed to be its morality: two examples, both first appointed before the war, were Winifred 'Biddy' Johnson of *Woman's Weekly* (Amalgamated Press) and Flora Klickmann of *The Girl's Own Paper* and *Woman's Magazine* (Religious Tract Society).

In lieu of advertising, Mills & Boon developed some clever strategies

---

[6] *The Transformation of Philip Jettan*, later reprinted by another publisher as *Powder and Patch*.

to sell its commodity, the romantic novel. 'We had inherited a marketing technique, which I think dated back to the Methuen days', John Boon said. 'Even though we were selling almost a branded product in the books, that were so similar, each one was promoted individually, *if* it was promoted. We changed that, and promoted the list, with some heart-searchings from the older members of the establishment.' Although the firm did a small amount of advertising, it depended primarily upon four agents in marketing its product: word-of-mouth generated by the libraries; a mail-order catalogue system, through which readers were informed of future publications; a large list of titles; and a uniform physical appearance. Mills & Boon's books, in distinctive brown bindings with brightly coloured jackets, were fixtures on library shelves and the firm became known as a library house. 'The commercial libraries needed a tremendous amount of books to keep their customers happy. Some of them would read a book in, say, three days, so they needed many books', Alan Boon said. In fact, it is doubtful whether Mills & Boon would have been as successful without the libraries, which became their life-blood—as the mass-market paperback is for the firm today.

All Mills & Boon titles published after the First World War were hardbacks; paperbacks on a mass scale were introduced only in the 1960s. Retail sales were mainly to the libraries. According to John Boon, given the nature of the books it was almost impossible to encourage booksellers or newsagents to stock them: the speed with which women read them, and the price of the books, made borrowing more attractive. For better authors the average print run was 8,000 copies in a 7s. 6d. edition; for lesser writers 3,000. Books were reprinted several times according to demand in cheaper editions. Mills & Boon promised to issue two to four new books every fortnight, and an astonishing number of books were produced: the exact number is uncertain. The publication list for January–June 1938, for example, contained 47 new novels (by 36 authors) and 37 reprints: a total of 84 publications, or 14 per month—and all romances. In 1939 Mills & Boon had more than 450 novels in print by over fifty authors. The firm relied heavily upon standing orders from public libraries; the largest circulating libraries, including Boots (which purchased between 300 and 500 copies of each title); and the wholesale library suppliers, such as the Argosy and Sundial Libraries (up to 700 copies), for distribution to their tuppenny clients.

The golden age for the hardback Mills & Boon novel was in the

1930s and 1940s. 'In the thirties, with the libraries [Mills & Boon] was doing extremely well in a period when most publishers were not doing well. It was a very profitable small firm then', John Boon said. So profitable, in fact, that Walter Hutchinson, director of Hutchinson and Co., attempted to buy the company to add to his list of publishing acquisitions. 'But my father was very independent, and he wasn't going to work for anybody else, and he very much disliked Walter Hutchinson', Boon explained. International sales of Mills & Boon novels, limited mainly to Europe, Australia, and New Zealand, were also good. Like most publishers, Mills & Boon thrived during the war, although paper rationing limited editions to 4,000 copies. 'Undoubtedly the war encouraged readership', John Boon said. 'If we had paper we would have sold probably ten times as many.' He added that his firm has not been given sufficient credit for maintaining morale during the war. On one occasion the Ministry of Supply refused to give Mills & Boon its paper allocation. 'The PA (Publishers' Association) protested on our behalf, saying quite rightly that these were the sort of books which were read by the women in factories and all that. They gave way.' Boon attributed the controversy to 'some Civil Servant whose literary views probably belonged to the Left Book Club'.

For several reasons Mills & Boon, recognized today as a paperback publisher, did not follow the Penguin lead in this direction during the 1930s. Of Allen Lane's venture, John Boon recalled, 'Publishers in those days were extraordinarily conservative. They thought at first it was gimmicky'. But Mills & Boon, although prosperous, could not have afforded the then substantial costs involved in publishing paperbacks. 'We were not big enough', Boon added. 'To launch mass paperbacks you require a fairly considerable investment, because you've got to print 20,000 copies. And a fair degree of advertising, and also the sales force which we didn't possess. We were running then I think on two or three salesmen. And we didn't feel that we could make the investment.' Instead, Mills & Boon wisely stuck to hardbacks and cornered the market. Ironically, Penguins were selling well in the very places Mills & Boon would have done, such as newsagents and Woolworths.[7]

---

[7] In 1958, Mills & Boon negotiated with a Canadian publisher, Harlequin, to publish paperback editions, initially for the North American market. In this way the firm experimented with the scheme without having to make the large initial investment. It was hugely successful, presaging the firm's movement away from the traditional hardback novel.

II

None the less, despite the early decision not to go into paperbacks, Mills & Boon's success and longevity in the romantic fiction market are legendary. 'We were dominant', John Boon recalled. 'Romance was synonymous with Mills & Boon.' Although before 1950 many firms, including Collins, Hutchinson, Herbert Jenkins, and Wright and Brown, published a romance list, Mills & Boon's specialization in this genre was unique, and served to establish a substantial and loyal readership which has sustained the firm to the present day.[8] In 1938 Mills & Boon's reputation was such as to prompt W. H. Smith into advising its wholesale clients: 'Lovers of romantic fiction have learned to rely on Mills & Boon titles, for these publishers specialize in popular romances. Their books are consequently favourites with women readers . . . Make your selection now!'[9] Similarly, in the early 1950s Thomas Joy, honorary treasurer of the Booksellers Association and librarian of the Army and Navy Stores, claimed of Mills & Boon's list: 'Any title, even new ones in the series may be confidently obtained and your buying problems simplified.'[10] How did Mills & Boon achieve such success and maintain its dominant position in a crowded and competitive market?

Mills & Boon were masters of the 'personal touch', a device which promoted sales by encouraging close contact with their readership. By the early 1930s, for example, the end-pages of each Mills & Boon romance, which usually featured the current publication list, opened with a full-page notice headed 'To the Reader: Why you should choose a Mills & Boon novel':

The Fiction Market is overburdened with new novels, and the ordinary reader finds it most difficult to choose the right type of story either to buy or to borrow . . . Really the only way to choose is to limit your reading to those publishers whose lists are carefully selected, and whose fiction imprint is a sure guarantee of good reading . . . Mills & Boon issue a strictly limited Fiction List, and the novels they publish all possess real story-telling qualities of an enduring nature.

---

[8] Mills & Boon is the largest publisher of romantic fiction in Britain today, with a market share of about 85%. International sales (in translation) are enormous, with representations on every continent. The firm remained in the Boon family until 1972, when it was purchased by Harlequin, although the British operation is still self-run.

[9] *TC* (9 July 1938), 8.

[10] *Year Book for the Scottish Newsagent, Bookseller and Stationer* (1st edn., 1954), 61.

This 'guarantee of good reading' was followed by an extensive publication list, usually running to sixteen pages, of new and reprinted novels: essentially, an inexpensive way of advertising the novels to a captive audience. Similarly, a common dustjacket blurb used in the 1940s read, 'When You Choose a Mills & Boon Novel . . . You are benefiting from over forty years' experience in publishing the best popular fiction. You are selecting a book from the largest and best-known list of romantic novels in the British Commonwealth.'

Each novel also featured 'the bait', an announcement that Mills & Boon would read every manuscript submitted for publication. This encouraged readers to send in their drafts, as new authors were always sought. Most publishers endorsed such a policy, but Mills & Boon were the only ones to put it in print. First novels by new authors were given prominence in publication lists: 'They represent authors likely to be extremely popular in the near future and can be read by everyone interested in first rate popular romance.' In fact, three of the firm's best-selling authors, Mary Burchell, Jean S. Macleod, and Sara Seale, were 'discovered' by Mills & Boon in this way in the 1930s.

Mills & Boon's prosperity was achieved through quantity as much as 'quality'. The firm concentrated on building a stable of popular authors, instead of pinning all its hopes on a single star of the Barbara Cartland or Denise Robins mould. In this way, the Mills & Boon imprint became better known than the authors, which offered a distinct advantage in promotion. 'Remember, we specialize in this type of story, and our imprint is a guarantee of good reading', one dustjacket blurb read in 1950. Another blurb, in the 1940s, ran under a photograph of an attractive smiling woman holding a Mills & Boon novel in one hand and pointing to the spine of the book with the other. 'I always look for the "Mills & Boon" when I want a pleasant book', she says. Shirley Russell, a London literary agent (whose most famous client is Barbara Cartland), emphasized how advantageous this recognition was to Mills & Boon. 'They published a brand of books and people never bought them by the author. They bought them because they were Mills & Boon novels. Ask an average Mills & Boon reader who had written the book, and they wouldn't be able to tell you.'[11] In 1949 Miss F. L. Belton, a Boots employee in Walsall,

[11] Shirley Russell was interviewed in 1988. She joined the firm of Rupert Crew, Ltd. in 1950. In addition to Cartland, her clients included Patience Strong, the poet, and Jean Marsh, a thriller writer.

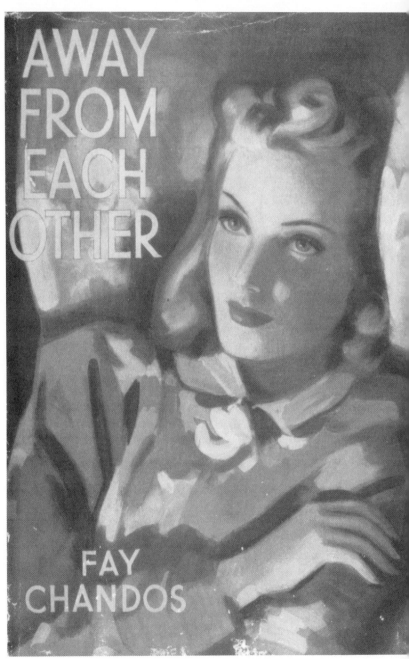

AWAY
FROM
EACH
OTHER

FAY
CHANDOS

Plate 1: Fay Chandos, *Away from Each Other* (1944). In a bow to Hollywood, the lonely soldier's wife
left behind was portrayed as wistful yet glamorous.

recalled her exasperation when an elderly lady requested a particular romantic book, and all she could remember was that it had a brown binding:

Desperately I clung to my only clue—a brown book—and prayed to heaven for inspiration.

I hadn't realised before just how many brown books there were in the Library, and silently I cursed Mills & Boon for choosing the colour for their publications.

'Was it "Meant for Each Other" or "Teach me to Love?"' I asked hopefully.[12]

The imprint was also encouraged by the extensive mail-order catalogue system introduced before the First World War. 'Our catalogue is a complete guide to our novels, and you ought to have it', one advertisement said. Readers wrote for a catalogue that presented the publishing list on a monthly basis, and could therefore pester librarians in advance to order new books: another low-cost but effective method of advertising. The catalogue system was the forerunner of the direct-mail subscription system that Mills & Boon has exploited so effectively since the early 1960s. Consequently, with such extensive networks of word-of-mouth recommendations and catalogues, the firm did not need to spend large sums on publicity. In a 1935 analysis of advertising expenditure by publishing houses, Mills & Boon ranked twenty-eighth in a field of 46, spending £345 over thirteen weeks (including £304 in the *Sunday Times* and £25 in the *Observer*—the principal newspapers for book advertisements). Mills & Boon's closest competitor, Wright and Brown (another 'library house'), was thirty-fifth with £267.[13]

Although it is clear that the core of Mills & Boon's readership was lower-middle- and working-class women, Q. D. Leavis's claim that there 'is no reason for supposing that novelettes are bought exclusively by the uneducated and the poor'[14] would probably have been true at this time. 'Our books were very successful in Harrods Library, and they were also very successful in the [commercial libraries] in the industrial areas. Everywhere, really', Alan Boon observed. Jean S. Macleod, one of the more successful Mills & Boon authors at this time, recalled that all types and classes of women read her books: 'Young girls, happily

[12] F. L. Belton, 'Library Episode', *The Bee*, 20 (Oct. 1949), 28. The book was *Forever Amber*—and had a green binding.

[13] *B* (3 Apr. 1935), 347. By way of comparison, Victor Gollancz ranked first, with £2,287, followed by Hutchinson (£2,285); Hodder & Stoughton was ranked sixth (£1,226) and Ward, Lock twenty-fifth (£354).

[14] Q. D. Leavis, *Fiction and the Reading Public* (London, 1932), 277–8.

married young women, *and* the dowagers.'[15] Similarly, another popular author, Sara Seale, claimed: 'Every kind of woman reads romantic novels. I know that the addresses on MILLS & BOON'S mailing file range from S.W.I, through country towns, industrial cities, North, South, East, West, to the Falkland Isles and back again.'[16] The novelist Mary Burchell received many letters in her heyday, from both sexes. An Indian girl, who had had an arranged marriage, once wrote that she and her husband read Mary Burchell books together. 'I trust *that* marriage worked out all right!' Burchell commented.[17]

Mills & Boon's prominence in the tuppenny libraries is illustrated in two surveys. In 1935 *The Bookseller* analysed the stock of 'one of the largest and newest' of the commercial libraries.[18] Among the Mills & Boon authors listed in 'the "best-seller" class' were Denise Robins (36 titles), Joan Sutherland and Sophie Cole (26–30 titles each), Louise Gerard (21–5), Elizabeth Carfrae (16–20), and Deirdre O'Brien and Marjorie M. Price (10–15 each). A comparison of these names with those in stock in Mudie's Library in 1935 reveals equal if not higher figures; Sophie Cole, for instance, had 38 titles in Mudie's. In another survey in 1950, Mills & Boon, in association with W. H. Smith, solicited library owners across the country in an attempt to determine the frequency of borrowing of Mills & Boon titles, calculated by the total number of date stamps inside a given volume. On average, a Mills & Boon novel was issued 165 times: the highest borrowing figures were recorded in Scotland, in English coastal towns, and in the West Country. Seaside places such as Portsmouth had especially high lending rates; Mills & Boon attributed this to the lonely sailors' wives 'left behind' who took up reading, and to the influx of holiday-makers during the summer months. Tone Libraries in Taunton reported the highest number of issues of any Mills & Boon novel, 740, for a 1935 title, *Anchor at Hazard* by Ray Dorien. Originally priced at 2s. 6d., over

---

[15] Jean S. Macleod was interviewed in 1986. A native of Scotland, Macleod has written over 160 novels for Mills & Boon, beginning with her first, *Life for Two*, in 1936. She was the co-founder, with Barbara Cartland, Denise Robins, and Vivian Stewart, of the Romantic Novelists Association in 1950.

[16] Sara Seale, 'Who Said Romantic Novel is Dying?' *TC* (29 July 1950), 13.

[17] Mary Burchell was interviewed in 1986. Her first novel, *Wife to Christopher*, was published by Mills & Boon in 1936. Burchell had written over 130 novels for the firm before her death in 1987. Mary Burchell is a pen-name; her real name was Ida Cook.

[18] Garfield Howe, 'What the Public Likes', *B* (19 June 1935), 580, 583. The name of the library was not given.

fifteen years this title had generated £9 in profits.[19] Another librarian, in Tottenham, recorded similar results: 'I have some MILLS & BOON books which have been going out since 1932, 60 times for the first year and 40 times for subsequent years. I do not, however, stamp my books, otherwise they would be covered with dates—and my customers would be as wise as I.'[20] The longevity of Mills & Boon novels in the tuppenny libraries was a problem, as it discouraged sales of replacement copies. '"We sometimes wish", say Mills & Boon, "that we could fit our novels with a self-destroying fuse to operate as the hundredth reader closes the book after the last page"', *The Bookseller* reported in 1950.[21]

Both Burchell and Macleod agreed that writing for Mills & Boon was a lucrative way of earning a living, especially for a woman in this period. 'If you were making a thousand a year then, that was very big money', Burchell said. She added that Charles Boon told her never to pass a Boots shop in Eastbourne, or wherever she happened to be, without popping in and chatting up the library customers, to encourage new readers.[22] Macleod said that successive reprints of her novels, at 3s. 6d., often sold, cumulatively, 30,000 copies. As there were no retail sales, selling serial rights to weekly magazines—often for as much as £500—was the chief source of revenue for the author. Mills & Boon retained a 10 per cent commission on such rights, which helped cash flow, according to John Boon.

Unfortunately, sales figures no longer exist for Mills & Boon titles for the 1930s and 1940s, and we must rely upon very general estimates from sources such as the Boon brothers. A 1949 advertisement, however, does give some important evidence:

406,473 copies of Mary Burchell's books have been sold, mostly to the Library Trade. On average each book is lent 100 times at 3d. a time, thus earning 25s. 25s. × 406,473—£508,091 5s., not a bad figure for one author.[23]

---

[19] At 2d. per loan, £9 in profits was the equivalent of 1,080 loans. The figure of 740 was perhaps due to the fact that during the war borrowing costs were often increased to 3d. or even 4d. It comes as no surprise that *Anchor at Hazard*, the saga of a lonely Navy Officer's wife, was popular in Somerset.

[20] 'One 2s. 6d. Novel: Library Profit—£9', *TC* (6 May 1950), 22.

[21] *B* (20 May 1950), 1078.

[22] Burchell recalled her thrill when her second novel, *Call—And I'll Come*, was chosen as the '*Daily Mirror* Romantic Book of the Month' during 1937. However, she understood the nature of the award. 'I did realize the *Daily Mirror* was not quite the top. And I remember Charles Boon said to me, "My boy Alan worked very hard for that". I was terribly impressed, you know.'

[23] *TC* (5 Nov. 1949), 22.

By 1949 Burchell had published forty-one novels; according to this information, each could have sold (with reprintings) an average of 10,000 copies, and so could have been read by as many as one million people. According to John Boon, these statistics were not exceptional for a Mills & Boon author during this period: Burchell was a popular but not a top author, and anyone writing for as many years as she had been (since 1936) would have achieved comparable figures by 1949, given frequent reprintings. Sara Seale, in fact, probably exceeded these. 'I think where we scored was that so many of our authors achieved these sort of figures. We had a very high general level, because the imprint was very well known', Boon said. The firm also managed to sell more books by encouraging the most prolific authors to publish under different names. This would circumvent restrictions at Boots Booklovers Library, for example, which would order only two titles from any one author per year. Hence, 'Molly Seymour', 'Guy Trent', and 'Barbara Hedworth' were the same person, as were 'Kathryn Blair', 'Rosalind Brett', and 'Seline Conway'. 'It was rather a sort of Gilbertian situation', Alan Boon said. 'They [the libraries] would take them.'[24]

III

'Romance is easy ... A safe answer for any romance reader is to thrust a new Mills & Boon book into his hands', Steven Mogridge advised Scottish librarians in the early 1950s.[25] The implication here, recognized by the trade, was that Mills & Boon had hit upon a successful 'formula'. What were its basic components? While Mills & Boon demanded a strong moral line in all of their romances, it is not the case that editorial policy was inflexible and averse to change: changes in the taste of their readership were followed closely. The primary concern, within reason, was commercial: to provide an entertaining, up-to-date, yet 'wholesome' product. It was a complicated combination of escapism and realism. 'Although we live in an age of escapism,' Sara Seale claimed, 'I think the English romantic novel manages to combine this

---

[24] However, one writer in *The Bookseller* seemed in on the secret. 'In the middle ranks an author can hardly consider himself a professional unless he has at least a couple of identities', the journal reported in 1937. 'This plurality seems most prevalent amongst the writers of romance—and by romance I don't mean High Histories of the Holy Grail, but Low Fictions for the Modern Girl.'

[25] *Year Book for the Scottish Newsagent, Bookseller and Stationer*, 1st edn. (1954), 61.

with a story which could conceivably apply to many of its reader's lives and this is the secret of its popularity.'[26] Guidelines prepared for Mills & Boon authors today confirm this important point:

We're in the business of providing entertainment, a short foray into the emotions. Our readers don't expect to read about the sort of petty worries they can encounter any day of their lives, such as an overdue library book, or the sort of serious problems which cause too much heartache or anguish. We're talking about escapism. But escapism must be based on reality.[27]

It is possible to identify three influences which together shaped Mills & Boon's editorial policy—the formula—during this period: the editorial staff; the editors of weekly women's magazines which serialized Mills & Boon novels; and the authors themselves.

According to Alan Boon, the special attraction which Mills & Boon novels held for women was their 'wholesomeness', that is, the lack of premarital sex and 'immorality'. Indeed, before 1950 the closest physical contact, before the marriage proposal, was hand-holding, or perhaps a peck on the cheek. However, whenever the heroine falls, hits her head, and is knocked out (as so often happens), she is usually revived when the shocked hero smothers her with frantic, anxious kisses. Such is the case with Randall in *Life for Two* (1936), who successfully resuscitates Claire when she is thrown from her horse. Boon claimed that Mills & Boon novels 'represented, as we thought it, morality at the time. Now people live together without the bat of an eyelid; then it was quite something, actually.' Towards this end, Mills & Boon editors imposed a carefully crafted set of guidelines on their authors. One aspect of the formula, which has remained essentially unchanged over the years, is that the Mills & Boon heroine is a virgin, aged between 18 and 27. A career-minded woman, often struggling, she meets a dashing man, aged 30–40, usually in a romantic setting. In the end, they marry or, if already husband and wife, settle their differences and make a new start.

The two main company guidelines for writers (still in use today) are called 'Lubbock's Law' and 'The Alphaman'. Lubbock's Law endorses the views of the literary critic Percy Lubbock, who argued that fiction should be written from the heroine's point of view, in order to promote

[26] Seale, 'Who Said Romantic Novel is Dying?', 23.
[27] Transcript, 'And Then He Kissed Her . . .', Mills & Boon promotional cassette (1986).

reader identification and increase interest and suspense. 'The Alpha-man', according to the Boon brothers, is based upon a 'law of nature': the female of any species will always be most intensely attracted to the strongest male of the species, the alpha. Translated in terms of fiction, the hero must be absolutely top-notch and unique. 'The wimp type doesn't work. Women don't want an honest Joe', Alan Boon said. But while the novels today tend to emphasize the physical characteristics of the hero, in the 1930s and 1940s Mills & Boon men did not have to be rich, famous, or even handsome. Dicky in *The Net Love Spread* (1935) is a struggling artist, and Lucian in *The Gentle Prisoner* (1949) is facially disfigured by a hideous scar. In all cases, however, the hero is recognized for his strength, integrity, and potential for providing a secure yet exciting future.

Mills & Boon believed that its readers were gullible, susceptible to suggestions made in the books. As a result, editors carried large responsibilities. 'We probably haven't had sufficient credit for our effect on readers at large', Alan Boon claimed. 'I've often thought if a dictator could edit our lists he could influence our readers' minds. I don't say sexually, but if he did it very subtly, saying "Communism is the solution to all our problems" or something like that.' Indeed, to this day, Mills & Boon editors excise from manuscripts all smutty or political references. French kissing, for example, is still forbidden (although Boon doubts whether this has had much effect), as are references to large families. Mills & Boon believes that readers would actually want to emulate the happy fictitious couple who said, 'Let's have three or four of each.'

The editors of women's magazines were an equally important source of suggestions—and directives. 'These editors were in a powerful position', Alan Boon explained. 'If the author could sell the serial, she was well paid for it. It meant a great deal to their income, so the editors really could use their clout to make the authors dance their tune.' The strong moral tone in Burchell's novels was reinforced by demanding editors at D. C. Thomson, publishers of the best-selling magazines *My Weekly* and *The People's Friend.* 'In those days a Scottish publisher wouldn't have had anything at all. I mean, if at the end of Chapter Three [the heroine] had had a second sherry, I would get a telegram saying, "Cut out the sherry".' Macleod recalled John Davidson, managing editor at D. C. Thomson, as 'a bit of a taskmaster. He would say, "What have you got?" and I would show him two ideas, and he would say, "Nonsense"', depositing his own ideas with her before she left

Dundee. Similarly, Jean Marsh, who wrote thrillers for the publisher John Long, also wrote romantic serials for Amalgamated Press magazines in the 1920s and 1930s. In her case frequent (and urgent) telegrams were used as the source of communication between herself and Mrs Henry St John Cooper, managing editor at the Amalgamated Press. 'PLEASE GO ON WITH INSTALMENT EIGHT', ran one message in 1936. 'WRITE IT UP IN HOMELY WAY. DON'T WANT IT SENSATIONAL'. Another, late that same year, was more specific:

LIKE BINNIE DARCH STORY VERY MUCH INDEED. PLEASE GO ON WITH FIRST INSTALMENT. WILL USE IT IN *ORACLE*. SHOW VERY CLEARLY BINNIE BEING AFRAID TO LOVE BECAUSE OF CURSE. SEND TELEPHONE NUMBER.[28]

Writing in serial form also influenced the way a novel was structured; a crisis or 'curtain' was required at the end of each instalment, or chapter, to maintain suspense—and circulation. Macleod regarded her training with *The People's Friend* as a kind of apprenticeship. 'A good book doesn't always make a good serial, but a good serial will *always* make a good book, because you've got these peaks all the time.'

One of the most influential magazine editors was Winifred 'Biddy' Johnson, a legendary figure in Fleet Street who edited such Amalgamated Press magazines as *Woman's Weekly* and *Woman and Home*. *Woman's Weekly* and Mills & Boon 'were sort of brother and sister at this time', Alan Boon explained. 'All their serials usually were published by ourselves.' Johnson crusaded for realistic yet morally conventional romantic serials. 'Mrs Johnson's idea doubtless was to have everything very cosy indeed, without any jarring. The characters wouldn't speak with any accent', Boon said, adding, 'She may in a way have effected a strong moral tone in our books, because she would not have any sort of sex or drink.' Johnson often battled with Mills & Boon authors, particularly Sara Seale. In one instance, Sara Seale had her heroine, a sales assistant, annoy the hero, her boss and owner of the department store, by daubing lipstick on the store mannequins. Johnson attacked this as unrealistic and unbelievable; she was convinced, according to Alan Boon, that girls 'wouldn't do things which would lose a job like that, in a tough time like the thirties'. Readers desired escapist romance with which they could identify, but the escapism had to be grounded in reality, not fantasy. Johnson's brand of

[28] Jean Marsh was interviewed in 1988. She joined the Amalgamated Press in 1922, with a contract for 9–10 serials per year at a salary of £500. She graduated to thrillers: her most famous, *Death Stalks the Bride*, was published in 1943.

'realism' was situational and unfantastic. She was the inventor, for example, of a plot situation, called 'MINO', which broadened story possibilities within the acceptable moral line. For example, a man and woman could live together in a contrived but unconsummated kind of marriage, such as shipwrecked on a desert island. This was a 'Marriage In Name Only', or MINO. This created a potentially (but *only* potentially) sexy situation, as the reader waited anxiously for the moment when love would blossom and thaw the frost between the characters. Similarly, a common plot device recommended by Mills & Boon was 'what Alan and his father used to call a sort of post-moral story', Macleod recalled. 'You could have a married couple [and] something came between them. It's awful trying to keep two people apart for 258 pages, let me tell you.' Within this context, both partners could face titillating temptation, but with the reader aware that marital love would triumph, sensibly, in the end.

Most of the women who wrote for Mills & Boon during the 1930s and 1940s were young; Burchell and Macleod, for example, were in their early thirties. These women were therefore likely to be fairly closely in touch with their potential readers and in tune with changes in mood and style. They were certainly sympathetic, for instance, with the single working life. Alan Boon admitted that during this period authors were given greater freedom and creativity than they are allowed today; the conformity required by mass production had not yet been imposed. If a 'bolder' novel was very successful, Mills & Boon, with one eye on commercial concerns, 'took it with the tide'. Burchell's first novel, *Wife to Christopher* (1936), had such an impact. 'I think Alan probably knew, as did his father, that a little early on I was already, without knowing it, exploiting a rather bolder form of romantic novel', she said. Indeed, *Wife to Christopher* represented something of a departure for Mills & Boon. Vicki and Margery are sisters who need money to get their widowed father medical treatment. Margery persuades convinces Vicki to compromise her rich and handsome boss, Christopher, and blackmail him into marrying her. Naturally, Vicki falls hopelessly in love with Chris—'There was a careless magnificence about him'—but he learns of her trickery and proceeds to bed her, in a sequence that resembles marital rape. Chris calls it 'settling his account with a cheating woman'. They separate; Vicki's baby is stillborn; she adopts her sister's love child; flees to Salzburg—but all turns out well with Christopher in the end. Clearly, this storyline was hardly the typical boy-meets-girl romance, but Burchell got away with it, as it was

WITH ALL MY WORLDLY GOODS

MARY BURCHELL

Plate 2: Mary Burchell, *With All My Worldly Goods* (1938). Companionate marriage and financial security were the goals of the Mills & Boon heroine, and, no doubt, reader.

a best-seller. 'Charles Boon, certainly, and Alan, were prepared to publish whatever I wrote. And so they must have believed in me', she said.

It should be noted that Mary Burchell was not the first writer to venture into 'bold' territory at Mills & Boon. Before they became a romantic fiction house, Mills & Boon had published Louise Gerard's novels with much success. Her lush adventures owed as much to E. M. Hull's *The Sheik* as to Elinor Glyn's *Three Weeks*. One of her most popular, *A Sultan's Slave* (1921), is a breathless tale of kidnapping, rape, murder, and passion. This was no penny dreadful, however: as in all of Gerard's works (including the earlier *The Witch-Child: A Romance of the Swamps*) the heroine, though bruised and battered, gains the high moral ground. Sultan Cassim Ammeh ('Women to me are only toys. Good to look upon, if beautiful, but not so good as horses') does not, in the end, force himself upon the fair Pansy Barclay. He marries her first, at her insistence, a victory in what is described as 'the last hopeless struggle for right against wrong'. It is the switch from these last vestiges of fantastic romance to the more identifiable, 'middle-class' love story which constitutes the significant change at Mills & Boon in the 1930s.

Although greater creativity and 'boldness' were in some cases permitted, 'immoral behaviour' in the novels was never tolerated. Mills & Boon probably screened the convictions of its authors carefully. Both Burchell and Macleod, for example, were unwavering in their support of such a stand, which at the time might have been regarded as slightly old-fashioned. They were scornful of the present crop of romantic fiction writers and their 'soft-porn' morality, which they considered offensive and unnecessary. 'But of course today so many people think that all they've got to do is to have them rolling about like dogs, although not quite so healthily', Burchell said. 'I reckon that you're not a really good writer of romance unless you can have the hero put his hand around [the heroine's] arm, and she's wearing a sleeve, and she has the sort of, the *frisson*. You must be able to do that.' The heroine's reactions were basically your own, she added, and thereby natural. Macleod, a Scot, argued that Scottish people were by nature more conservative: if you did not reflect that in your stories, you were of no use to a Scottish publisher like D. C. Thomson. 'For the time, for the age, there were things you just didn't write about.' She believed that her fiction reflected 'exactly' the morals of the day, and as she wrote for D. C. Thomson as well as for Mills & Boon, she did not think there was any difference in taste between English and Scottish readers. 'You couldn't write about sex, or people living together before marriage. Drinking was permitted, but discreetly and in moderation.' In all cases, a happy ending was essential; authors learned the lesson of tampering with this when they received bundles of hate mail from readers.

Mills & Boon's editorial policies were undoubtedly successful: the business prospered, and they were not troubled by censors either at home or abroad. During this time, censorship laws in Ireland and South Africa posed the greatest potential problems. 'We were astounded that our books could go into nunneries in Ireland, and [those were] our books which were getting a bit steamier', Alan Boon said. Similarly, Mills & Boon books in South Africa enjoyed a good reputation: 'any of our books were OK'.[29] Nevertheless, the firm did tread carefully; character names were always slightly exotic, primarily to protect the author against libel actions brought by real people with the same names, and each novel carried a disclaimer in the front of the book.

An interesting contrast to Mills & Boon's editorial policies are those held by Barbara Cartland, certainly the most famous and successful author of romantic fiction in Britain and, indeed, the world. Cartland has been publishing continuously since 1923, and currently has more than 500 titles to her credit—a record. She has never, in fact, been published by Mills & Boon. 'I didn't want to be published by Mills & Boon. I can't imagine anything worse', she said. 'They always had the doctor marrying the nurse. Some of them aren't bad, but they aren't very good.'[30] Shirley Russell claimed, quite rightly, that Cartland was too famous to have been included in Mills & Boon's list, where authors ranked lower than the imprint. 'The authors rated not at all. It was just another romance. And we never classed Barbara in that sort of writing. She was always above that.' Cartland maintained that her publishers, including Duckworth, Hutchinson, and Rich and Cowan, were more 'up-class' than Mills & Boon. But Alan Boon revealed that his firm did, at one point, consider Cartland's works for publication. 'To my knowledge, in the thirties we examined some of the modern Barbara Cartlands, and thought they were a bit too advanced for us, actually.'

---

[29] But the wholesome nature of Mills & Boon novels excluded them from the lucrative North American market. Until recently, US publishers took no notice of the novels because they were considered 'too tame'. Judging from the semi-pornographic nature of many American magazines and novelettes distributed in Britain in the 1930s and 1940s, this was probably true.

[30] Barbara Cartland was interviewed in 1988.

Although Cartland and Mills & Boon shared the same literary and moral planes, they differed sharply in their attitude to a changing readership and world. From her first novel, *Jig-saw* (1923), Cartland has been a moralizer, devoting long sections of narrative to the wicked consequences for a girl if she forsakes her innocence in a cruel world. Her personal crusade against premarital sex has inspired some graphic prose. She lacks the light, even witty, touch with which Mills & Boon authors wove such convictions seamlessly into a story. In *Jig-saw*, for example, the heroine weeps for her girlfriend Sally, jilted by a man with whom she has had a passionate affair. 'No nice man will want to marry me now', Sally confessed. Cartland expresses a moral outrage with an explicitness never found in a Mills & Boon novel:

Sally, the innocent, trusting child! It was not the physical injury that counted, it was the deliberate massacre of her ideals, the smashing of fairy-castles, the trampling of golden dreams. With the splendidness of youth her wounds would heal, the misery pass. But the scars would always remain, memorials of a crucifixion ... To the very few, the very favoured, perhaps only to one person in our lives, do we open the gates with the key of love. Too often do we find too late they are merely trespassers, ruthlessly picking the flowers, to leave them dying by the roadside, scoffing at the ambitious little buildings we have erected, destroying our temples with laughter. Then, when we are barren, they leave us to a desert of desolation.[31]

Cartland has remained confident in the ideal of womanhood—spiritual, physical, utterly feminine—which she promotes in her novels. Ian, the rugged hero of *Sawdust* (1925), meets his dream in Wanda, who has been raised, nymph-like, in the forest:

Every ideal of woman he had ever forgotten, half-formulated or imagined, came into his mind from some unknown store of memory. A radiant mother in jewels or laces kissing a child of four good-night; the fairy at his first pantomime; the sister of his school friend; Joan of Arc; the Blessed Virgin Mary; a nurse in the sanatorium at Eton; Lily Elsie; a little actress on the pier at Brighton.[32]

Significantly, unlike Mills & Boon, Cartland has refused to follow the changing tastes of readers and modernize her 'Victorian' values. Consequently she has lost many commercial opportunities, refusing, for example, to compromise with directors anxious to film her novels. During this period, Cartland said, her novels were never filmed

---

[31] Barbara Cartland, *Jig-saw* (London, 1923), 66–7.
[32] Id., *Sawdust* (London, 1925), 74.

'because I was pure. They wanted rather hot, steamy things, everybody kissing and mauling about. My people are not allowed to be touched.' She resisted attempts by publishers to pressure her into revising her moral views. 'They kept on saying, "Oh, come on Barbara, you must *really* be up to date", and I said, "*No*". That's why I write in the past. Everybody's a virgin in the past; it was all right.' Herein lay the compromise: in order to continue writing about virginal single women in a changing world, especially after the Second World War, Cartland had to abandon contemporary romance for historical romance. Since 1948, every one of her novels has been set in the period 1790–1914. Ironically, the past, which used to be the source for bawdier plotlines (*Forever Amber* is one example), has been used by Cartland as a kind of distant Eden.

Mills & Boon, on the other hand, were not averse to change, if it meant commercial success—which it did. In one sense, Cartland has provided the reading matter for the small minority of former Mills & Boon readers who were dissatisfied with the firm's changes. 'In our books now there is an awareness of sex, and I'm afraid they sometimes get into bed without the benefit of a priest', Alan Boon said. 'But they should marry each other in the end.' Today, Mills & Boon believes readers would find a romantic novel boring without sex. 'I hope we don't do it in a way that is titillating, but [in a way] which is natural', Boon added.

IV

What, then, did the editorial policies of Mills & Boon look like in practice? A close reading of several Mills & Boon novels published before 1950 reveals some surprising characteristics. Naturally, the writing style is often tedious and verbose, the action predictable, sometimes incredible. But the Mills & Boon heroine is wholeheartedly a representation of the contemporary woman, rooted in the time and often struggling with such matters as money, managing a household, and holding down a job. She is either a single working woman, supporting herself and/or her parent(s), or a housewife facing a crisis (usually financial, *never* adulterous) in her marriage. Although the unmarried heroines dream of finding Mr Right and settling down, they do not waste time worrying about it, but are out and about on their own. If the heroine, moreover, does not necessarily do the chasing in the novel, the reason is not that she lacks strong feelings concerning love and romance, but that she is not obsessed with finding a husband. Indeed, a detectable undercurrent of quasi-feminism runs through most of the novels, and it is arguable that the Mills & Boon heroine of the 1930 and 1940s was more advanced for her time than she is today. Admittedly, it is true that every Mills & Boon novel ends with the marriage proposal and/or the ceremony, or a reconciliation between spouses, and the heroine probably goes on in life as a housewife—but this is left to the reader's imagination. Companionate marriage and a sense of security are deemed more essential than a good lover, which was probably the dream of most readers from the middle and working classes.[33]

Among the issues raised and decided upon in Mills & Boon novels is virginity. In all cases the firm toed the Barbara Cartland line. Despite great temptation, the heroines remain pure before marriage. Virginity, however, is never equated with prudishness; rather, the heroine takes a moral stand and gains the respect, not the laughter, of the reader. In *The Net Love Spread*, for example, Roseen is abducted by deceitful Gerald, who plans to marry and spirit her away. Their car breaks down *en route*, much to Gerald's glee:

'What can we do? Why not camp out in the forest for the night? It's gloriously warm, and there will be a full moon later. I've lots of rugs, and plenty of food. Darling, it would be heaven.'

'I'm afraid I don't agree. You seem to forget that we are not married yet. And what will happen in the morning? . . . I may be old-fashioned, but I object to spending a night out alone with a man who is not my husband.'

'You're being absurd, sweetheart.' The smile died out of his eyes. She saw

---

[33] In selecting novels for review among the vast Mills & Boon canon, an attempt has been made to examine those which were most popular. The lack of best-seller lists and sales figures can be circumvented. Some books have been chosen at random based on the acclaim, inside and outside the firm, of the author: Mary Burchell and Louise Gerard, for example. Other books were cited in surveys as being very popular: *Anchor at Hazard*, *Be Patient with Love*, and *Anne Finds Reality* in the 1950 commercial library survey; *Lady by Marriage* and *The Net Love Spread*, which outsold Agatha Christie and E. Phillips Oppenheim in a 1935 W. H. Smith shop survey (W. H. Smith & Son, Ltd., 'Books in Great Demand' (London, Library Dept., 12 Jan–15 June 1935, WHS PA.167)). Some of the books won awards: *Call—And I'll Come* was the *Daily Mirror* 'Romantic Book of the Month' in 1937; *The Gentle Prisoner* (which Alan Boon called 'one of the great classic books we published') was judged 'Romantic Novel of the Year' by *Woman and Home* magazine in 1949. Such distinctions may appear dubious but would probably have swayed loyal readers of romances. Finally, novels published after 1930 have been given precedence over earlier works. By 1930 the transformation to a romantic fiction publishing house had begun, and with it the careful crafting and marketing of the Mills & Boon imprint and house style.

them harden. 'What does it matter staying out together, if we're going to be married tomorrow? If you loved me you would want to stay here with me.'

'No, I shouldn't, Gerald. Loving has nothing to do with it. I should lose my self-respect. Surely my wishes count for something?' she added pleadingly.[34]

One can suppose how often this discussion took place among real-life couples. But Mills & Boon authors were hardly naïve; they appreciated that resisting temptation was never easy. Faith, in *Secret Love*, fights for control while bidding her beau farewell at the railway station:

He just looked at her, as a starving man might at a wonderful feast whose delicious odours and dishes he was allowed to smell and see but forbidden to taste.

With a wave of her hand Faith turned quickly away.

If she watched that hungry, pleading look on his face she might forget she was going to be a wise virgin. She might throw discretion to the winds, get into his carriage, creep into his arms, and let him love her.[35]

Significantly, Faith does not do these things. She therefore embodies an ideal of social behaviour, even if an unrealistic one. But those who do give in, and become pregnant, are treated with compassion. In *The Net Love Spread* Corinna, an unwed mother (as the result of a brief spell of 'free love' with 'a young portrait painter with more than a touch of genius'), is applauded for her devotion and respect for motherhood, despite all adversity. Corinna is the ideal mother, and Oonagh the perfect child. But single parenthood, although tolerated, is not endorsed. Corinna's plight in failing to attract the hero of the novel, Dicky, as a husband and stepfather is crucial. 'Corinna and Oonagh, another man's child, could never come to mean to him what Roseen had and still meant to him. He was better alone, ploughing his solitary furrow', Dicky muses.[36]

Mills & Boon novels generally endorsed old-fashioned methods of courtship, although a few concessions were made to changing times. 'Lovemaking' throughout these novels is kissing. In most cases 'modern' practices and 'modern' girls are prone to disaster. The generation gap is displayed in this exchange from *The Net Love Spread*: Nan and Phyllida are stepsisters, Nan in her thirties, 'Phyl' 18:

'Love?' scoffed Phyllida, with curling lip, looking at Nan with pitying contempt. 'You talk like a Victorian spinster—which of course you are, my dear, in spirit. I've done with love. It's an overrated commodity. No, let the men do the

[34] Nina Bradshaw, *The Net Love Spread* (1935), 221–2.
[35] Louise Gerard, *Secret Love* (1932), 84.
[36] Bradshaw, *The Net Love Spread*, 227–8.

loving in future. I'm fond of Tommy, of course. I like him, and I think we shall get on well together. But it's what he can give me—a position, a comfortable home, money—that counts.'

Nan supposed that this was the aim of at least half the women who married, so perhaps Phyllida was not so much worse than the others, after all.[37]

But in the end Phyllida becomes pregnant, loses Tommy, attempts suicide, gives up her child, and runs away. Elizabeth Carfrae, on the other hand, made some allowances for changes in courtship: in her novel *Lady by Marriage*, she sympathizes with the 18-year-old heroine, rather than with her 47-year-old overprotective stepfather.

'I don't want you to be cheap,' he said. 'And in my day a girl who let men kiss her indiscriminately was cheap. In, at all events, the eyes of the men who kissed her. In these days I know things have changed—and not for the better—'

'Perhaps,' Sheila said, interrupting him, 'that's true. They mayn't have changed for the better, but they *have* changed, Uncle John. In our lot . . . kisses don't count. It's part of the game. A girl who doesn't let a man make love to her—well, she's just out of it, that's all. There's nothing really to any of the things we do—'

'No,' John Ambrose said briefly. 'And yet, only this afternoon, I've been to see a girl of sixteen, a girl of your lot, as you call them, who's going to have a baby as the result of the things that mean nothing.'[38]

Sheila does realize, however, that her fun-loving generation 'isn't trained for marriage', and follows her dreams of marriage, a home, and children, in choosing to marry John.

Away from Each Other was one of many Mills & Boon novels published during the Second World War which warned the lonely wives left behind to remain faithful to their fighting husbands. Maive, in charge of the newsagency while her husband, Clifford, joins the Fire Service, is seduced by Shaun, a married army captain billeted in her home. Shaun's advances were initially repelled by Maive in a strongly worded exchange:

'Oh, don't start that again! We haven't time for prolonged discussions in ethics and conventions.'

'We haven't time?'

'Haven't you heard that there's a war on, darling? And I may be sent out East any day now.'

Her brain cleared a little at that. She thought coldly and dispassionately. The old, old story. That's what my father said to my mother in 1916. 'I may be sent to France any day now. Why should we wait? We can't afford to wait for

[37] Ibid. 251–2.   [38] Elizabeth Carfrae, *Lady by Marriage* (1935), 59.

Plate 3: Jean S. Macleod, *Reluctant Folly* (1942). Mills & Boon went to war in this 'story of our times', set in an A.T.S. unit 'somewhere in Scotland'.

each other. There's a war on—let's seize our happiness while we can. We may never have another chance.' And now it's I and Shaun ... 'I may be sent out East any day' . . . Only a romantic little fool falls for that old plea.[39]

Maive does succumb in the end, but Shaun is exposed as a rogue and a bounder in time for her to rekindle her 'indestructible' love for Cliff.

Some Mills & Boon courtships were fantastic, even shocking. The reasoning here was simple: as long as lovemaking was 'honourable' and ended in marriage, any kind of relationship was allowed, even between 'relatives'. The two Mills & Boon best-sellers of 1935, *The Net Love Spread* and *Lady by Marriage*, contained similar plots about romances between relatives. They are, in retrospect, early examples of the 'bolder' novels published by Mills & Boon. In *The Net Love Spread* Dicky Bannister, a struggling artist, is forced to raise his stepsister, Roseen, alone after his father's death. Roseen is an orphan rumoured to be from 'grand stock'. Eleven years pass, and Dicky, 38, falls in love with his 17-year-old sister and former playmate, although he does try to suppress his feelings:

But if he had made love to her, as a lover—and if they had gone on together he couldn't have helped it—what then? Would it all have been spoiled, ended, their perfect love as brother and sister, or would it have grown into a greater and closer love as husband and wife?[40]

Roseen, claimed by her heiress aunt, is spirited away as she is under age, to avoid the stigma of appearing to be a mistress. In the end, of course, they admit their true feelings for each other. The novel concludes with Roseen and Dicky spending 'a happy afternoon together in the studio, rearranging things to suit their future life together as husband and wife, instead of brother and sister'.[41]

The scenario in *Lady by Marriage* is slightly different but even less credible. Eminent physician John Ambrose grants a dying circus woman's wish and adopts her daughter, Sheila. Sheila grows into a beauty; John's fatherly affection turns into love. Sheila is 18, John 47.

---

[39] Fay Chandos, *Away From Each Other* (1944), 20. Charles Boon initially encouraged writers to leave the Second World War out of the romances, because it dated the story and prevented reprints. 'We couldn't really publish a reprint of a book [in which] guns and bombs were falling all over the place', John Boon said. Macleod recalled that this reluctance was part of the common belief at first that the war would not last very long. 'But then of course after two years, three, four—they realized they had to acknowledge the fact that boy was meeting girl during the war, just as anything else.'

[40] Bradshaw, *The Net Love Spread*, 155.   [41] Ibid. 248.

John suppresses his feelings until he is struck by a lorry, lapses into a coma, and confesses his love, deliriously, to a horrified Sheila. She refuses to tell her friends about her stepfather's love for her. 'It's the sort of idiotic thing that happens in women's novels, and I couldn't bear any one to laugh at Uncle John',[42] she says, and the reader is meant to share her shock at the situation. But, surprisingly, Sheila sacrifices young and exciting love with Jimmy for a lonely life as John's wife, out of a sense of duty and a desire for a secure home and children. She is thoroughly miserable, trapped in a barren marriage to an inattentive husband. She contemplates divorce, but is determined to honour her vows in the end.

Indeed, in all circumstances the primacy of marriage and marital vows was asserted, and fashionable practices such as adulterous affairs and divorce, which the reader might expect in a 'society' (or a sensa-tion) novel, were discredited. Even when the heroine is mistreated, or is tempted by a more noble suitor, her vows remain sacred and inviol-able. In *Be Patient with Love*, Joan risks a sudden marriage with her friend Phil for the security that is lacking in her lonely single life in the city. Although he turns out to be a gambler and a poor provider, Joan sticks with Phil, resisting her feelings for his swarthy and nobler brother Tom. She is never tempted to end the unhappy marriage:

> 'There's nothing to be done except try to forget. I'm married to Phil . . .'
> 'Joan, Joan.' Josie's tone was one of affectionate impatience. 'Haven't you heard the word divorce . . .? Darling, this is 1937, you know . . .'
> Joan's smile was a tragic flickering thing.
> 'That's some people's way out,' she admitted, 'but it wouldn't do for Tom and me . . . we've vowed never to let Phil down' . . .
> How do you explain to a young 'modern' like Josie that divorce was nothing in your life. Now, no matter what Phil did to you, he remained your husband and that for you there could be no other man?[43]

Joan does eventually reform her husband through love and under-standing. However, this being escapist romantic entertainment, Phil dies honourably while saving a lost sheep, and one month later Joan marries Tom, her conscience clear.

Sexual love between husband and wife was not only encouraged but often described in vaguely mystical terms. In one sense, ardent passion was presented as a kind of wonderful prize obtainable only through marriage. Here especially the influence of the Hollywood film is

[42] Carfrae, *Lady by Marriage*, 67.
[43] Guy Trent, *Be Patient with love* (1937), 176–7, 194.

Plate 4: Cicely Colpitts (who also wrote as Frances Braybrooke), *She Lied for Love* (1942). Motherhood was depicted as fulfilment of womanhood and as salvation for rocky marriages.

apparent. In *Once to Every Woman*, Jon and Gail experience marital bliss as newly-weds:

Jon lifted her in his arms and carried her to the couch. Gail lay back, her eyes closed, her whole being flooded with joy and tenderness. She felt Jon loosen her dress, slip it from her shoulders, felt his lips on her throat and breast. My husband, my lover, her heart said, but her lips were silent. In this sweet, wild moment neither of them had need of speech. Their love flowered swiftly, more passionate, more searching than it had ever been before.[44]

Predictably, motherhood was also frequently and fervently endorsed alongside marriage. Children were regarded in one sense as a panacea: motherhood provided fulfilment of womanhood, and also served as salvation for rocky marriages (although, as we have seen, large families were *not* endorsed). Manora, in *Call—And I'll Come*, tells Anna that 'No woman worth the name would value a voice above a child who would look at her with the eyes of the man she loved'.[45] So Anna freely sacrifices her career as an international opera singer to have a baby. Gail, the star actress in *Once to Every Woman*, also chooses motherhood:

'You've given up so much,' he said again. 'Do you realise how much? What can I give you in return?'

'Your son,' Gail whispered.

They stood heart to heart in the small, quiet room. Jon did not speak. There was no longer need of words between them.[46]

The hardships of pregnancy and birth were strongly noted by Mills & Boon. In *Secret Love*, for example, quasi-feminist undertones are apparent as the hero sees his wife in the hospital:

'My God, I shall be glad when it's over,' he said hoarsely. 'It's so beastly unfair. You have to suffer, and a great hulking chap like me gets off scot-free.'

There was a gurgle of weak laughter.

Then Faith lifted a corner of the silk coverlet. His amazed eyes saw a tiny, red-faced object asleep in a soft, white shawl.

At the sight his heart seemed to swell to the bursting-point. The room and all in it vanished in a sort of mist. Quite well he knew why he had been sent—to save him hours of anguish whilst the girl went, alone, through the Valley of Death . . .

Stooping, he peered closely at the red-faced object.

---

[44] Sylvia Sark, *Once to Every Woman* (1940), 20. The cinema was indeed an important influence. 'I'd have thought a lot of our authors owed something to the films', Alan Boon said. 'I'd have thought they'd enhanced it. Sometimes I'd read one and I'd say, "Oh, God, here's Clark Gable talking again". It was the Metro-Goldwyn-Mayer type of love story.'

[45] Burchell, *Call—And I'll Come*, 252–3.   [46] Sark, *Once to Every Woman*, 251.

'Hello, what's this?' he asked, his voice trembling.
'The son and heir. He arrived yesterday afternoon.'[47]

Similarly, in *Anchor at Hazard* childbirth is described as 'this crisis of a woman's life'.[48] The heroine in *Wife to Christopher* pleads with her husband to see her stillborn baby. '"Can't you tell me *anything* to comfort me?" she begged in sudden piteousness. "Don't you see that I've nothing but pain and terror to remember—and I meant it all to be so beautiful." '[49]

In an attempt to encourage reader identification, heroines in Mills & Boon novels were portrayed as proud of their class and status, defending their backgrounds and careers when confronted by the upper class. The value system normally associated with the middle classes was championed; unlike sensation novels, where the rich were admired and the poor despised, the less fortunate heroine in Mills & Boon is proud, rising to the occasion to defend herself—and winning the respect of all in the end. There was no substitute for good, hard, honest work and an independent life before marriage. Shop-girl Kitty in *Anchor at Hazard* is repelled by her greedy upper-class mother-in-law:

'You were in a shop?' gasped Mrs Lewis.
'I was in the office. I didn't stand behind the counter, not that it makes any difference,' said Kitty, amused at the other woman's prejudice.
She did not think it necessary to explain that the girls had to present a high standard of education and appearance to be considered at all by the firm ...
Although she had always earned her own living, she had discovered that her attitude to it was very different from that of people who in her opinion had not worked for money, and yet seemed to expect it as a matter of course. She felt the chill of this self-absorbed nature.[50]

Other characters in this novel agree. Rose is amazed that Kitty's marriage is viewed as a come-down by her husband's family: 'Nonsense! Hasn't the world moved since then?'[51] Similarly, Joan in *Be Patient with Love* resents her husband Phil's contented unemployment and their subsequent dependence upon his family. When accused of indolence, she reacts with passion:

Joan's colour leaped to her cheeks.
'I don't ask anyone to keep me,' she flared. 'I've earned my own living before, and I can do so again' ...

[47] Gerard, *Secret Love*, 252.   [48] Ray Dorien, *Anchor at Hazard* (1935), 247.
[49] Mary Burchell, *Wife to Christopher* (1936), 167.
[50] Dorien, *Anchor at Hazard*, 18, 50.   [51] Ibid. 10.

She was Joan Thomas who had earned her own living since her seventeenth birthday. She wasn't used to being dependent, and she resented owing her bread and butter to comparative strangers.[52]

In *Anne Finds Reality*, Anne is offended by her rich fiancé's snobbish opinions of her own, lower-class friends:

The colour flamed in Anne's cheeks. She sensed the fact that Roland did not approve of her friends and resented it. Vera, in her cheap washing dress, and stolid George, whose grey flannels compared so unfavourably with those Roland wore, were a part of her old life—the nicest part.[53]

When Anne receives an unexpected inheritance, she is determined to become a philanthropist and help the needy: 'Suddenly Anne realised the power of the wealth that was now hers.'[54] This promotion of middle-class ideals was often (not surprisingly) coupled with an attention to the value of money and material goods. For instance, when Anne is knocked down by a car, the driver of which becomes her roguish lover, her immediate concern is not her physical condition but the costly clothes she is wearing and cannot afford to spoil: 'She was hatless and dishevelled. Her hand was cut, but mercifully her dress was not torn.'[55]

V

One of the principal publishers of light fiction, Mills & Boon's success and longevity can be attributed to two factors. First, the rapid development of the commercial libraries during the 1930s supplemented the traditional outlets for Mills & Boon novels and provided a unique opportunity for exploitation, sizeable expansion, and financial gain. Had it not become a 'library house', Mills & Boon would probably not have survived for as long as it has. Second, one of the long-term advantages of the promotion of its single brand of fiction has been unequalled recognition of the imprint rather than the author, then (but perhaps not now) a distinct advantage in sales.

Mills & Boon's editorial policies were also governed by commercial concerns, and as such were flexible and receptive to change. In this respect, the firm closely resembles its rival and associate, D. C. Thomson. Relying to a large degree on its authors, its editors, and the

---

[52] Trent, *Be Patient with Love*, 48, 51.
[53] Francis Braybrooke, *Anne Finds Reality* (1940), 48.
[54] Ibid. 166.   [55] Ibid. 15.

popular women's magazines, Mills & Boon stayed in close contact with its readers, monitoring changes in attitudes and adjusting its views accordingly, though always within a conventionally 'moral' frame-work. The firm was conscious of a responsibility to provide morally acceptable fiction to an audience which it deemed to be gullible and impressionable: the identification of the Mills & Boon reader with the heroine was considered to be very strong. While some important con-cessions were made to 'modern' practices of wage-earning and court-ship—if only for commercial reasons—marriage and motherhood were treated as sacred. The firm embraced the significant changes in romantic fiction favoured by readers after the First World War. It was this flexibility and flair which evaded such Victorian publishers as the Religious Tract Society in the twentieth century, to their ruin.

5

'WE MUST PREVENT THE LEAKAGE': CHILDREN'S READING HABITS

A LEADING article in *The Times* in 1921 called attention to the significant expansion of reading among children. The modern child, it was
claimed, read ten times as much as his grandparents had done when
young. Hence, a golden opportunity now existed for all those trades
involved in children's publishing.[1] Although these claims were certainly exaggerated, the period from the First World War until 1950 was
indeed one of rapid growth in children's reading and publishing, as it
was for adults. What the young were reading, however, was the source
of some concern, even controversy. Sidney W. Anderson, writing in
the *Library Assistant* in 1934, expressed a common worry about the
reading habits of children, especially those reaching the 'crucial age of
14', the school-leaving age. These readers were, it seemed, reflecting
too closely the low-brow tastes of their parents:

Such children will, in nine cases out of ten, lose the reading habit which the
Junior Library has been at pains to inculcate, and subsist for the rest of their
lives on Sunday newspapers (*not* the *Observer*) and magazines of the more
sensational (or more sensual) kind ...
    The point is that we must prevent the leakage. Unless our libraries see that
the right books get into the hands of the rising generations at this crucial age,
they are jeopardizing their own chances of future survival.[2]

In terms of reading habits, the cliché, 'The child makes the man', often
rang true. I will consider here the reading habits of children and
adolescents between (roughly) the ages of 10 and 16, which has been
called 'the period of a child's greatest reading'.[3] I will examine what

---

[1] 'What Children Read', leading article, *The Times* (26 Nov. 1921), 11.
[2] Sidney W. Anderson, 'Catering for the Adolescent', *Library Assistant*, 420 (Sept.
1934), 194.
[3] 'Favourite Books of Children: "Treasure Island" A First Choice', *The Times* (8
Sept. 1932), 12. Given our age restriction, some well-known children's authors whose
principal readership was younger than 10 will not be mentioned: Enid Blyton is the most
famous example.

they read, how far what they read was determined by social class, and why—to the extent we can discover—they read it. Two curious and somewhat neglected phenomena will also be examined: the marked inclination of girls to read boys' literature, and for children and adolescents to read adult literature. The latter point is vital in establishing a possible link between the tastes of the young and the old among the lower-middle and working classes.

I

Just as the women's market was targeted by publishers of novels and weekly magazines after the First World War, so was the ever-expanding market for children. During the 1920s the Amalgamated Press presented its list of ten titles for boys (with a combined circulation of 'over one million' weekly, including *Union Jack*, *Magnet*, and *Boys' Friend*) as 'a unique and extremely powerful selling medium' for all advertisers:

THE SPENDING POWER OF YOUTH is Greater than it has ever been before. No Advertiser of any article appealing to boys and young men of any age from ten to twenty can afford to neglect the Amalgamated Press Group of BOYS' PUBLICATIONS ...[4]

At twopence, the weekly letterpress papers were within the reach of boys and girls of every class. They were, moreover, freely passed around and swapped, particularly in working-class neighbourhoods; each copy sold, therefore, was probably read by two or three children. As the *Advertising World* observed:

These periodicals are pondered over, as a rule, longer and often more seriously than the adult takes her reading, and copies remain treasures for some time. Then, too, the boy's paper acquires what amounts to a 'club circulation' when it goes round to his classmates in exchange for others.[5]

Stanley L. Unwin urged booksellers to tap this active readership. 'Think of the thousands of copies of the *Magnet*, *Rainbow*, *Gem* etc. you regularly sell. Are you making the best of the opportunity this gives to start the readers of these many children's papers as book-buyers?'[6] One of the fastest-growing sections of juvenile publishing was in Sunday

---

[4] Advertisement, *The Advertisers' A.B.C.* (1921 edn.), 401.
[5] Penrose Hunter, 'Selling though the Schoolboy: How National Advertisers Can Make Use of the Magazines of Youth', *Advertising World*, 60 (Sept. 1931), 196.
[6] Quoted in *The Newsbasket* (Jan. 1929), 8.

School 'Rewards', hard-cover books given as prizes to worthy students. Many authors of rewards were also contributors to the weekly magazines, including Percy Westerman, Talbot Baines Reed, and Angela Brazil.

Generally speaking, 'the vast reading public of children is becoming vocal', Eileen Colwell, a veteran children's librarian and frequent commentator on reading habits, wrote in 1937. 'The publishers are awakening to the importance of that public.'[7] Colwell attributed the continued growth in reading among children to three factors: improved educational facilities; 'broadening influences' such as the cinema and the wireless; and the gradual development of separate sections for children within the public libraries. By 1950 most public libraries in Britain contained a children's library, and some, like Walthamstow, also had 'intermediate' sections for adolescents. Most library authorities permitted borrowing at the age of 10, although there was no law on a minimum age.[8] The children's shelves, however, were often stocked with 'better' books than, for example, the best-selling 'Biggles' series. Alan Bennett, recalling his childhood in Leeds during the war, contrasted the bright, cheerful, and inviting Adult Library in Wesley Road with the section for children:

The Junior Library was in a room of its own and an institution more intended to discourage children reading could not have been designed. It was presided over by a fierce British Legion commissionaire, a relic of the Boer War, who, with his medals and walrus moustache, was the image of Hindenburg as pictured on the German stamps in my brother's album. The books were uniformly bound in stout black or maroon covers so whether they were Henty, Captain Marryat or (my favourite) Hugh Lofting, they looked a pretty unenticing read.[9]

None the less, the war and the shortage of books boosted juvenile usage of public libraries considerably. Issues to children in Sheffield public libraries, for example, increased from 629,608 in 1937–8 to 981,715 in 1947–8.[10] A 'dramatic' increase of 40,000 issues, or 28 per cent, was recorded in the children's library in Margate during 1943–4.[11]

[7] Eileen Colwell, 'Some Trends in Children's Books', *B* (1 Sept. 1937), 195.
[8] 'Encouraging Young Readers: Book-Borrowers Aged Five', *The Times* (16 Jan. 1937), 9. The Glasgow Corporation lowered its minimum age to 5, but this was the exception.
[9] Alan Bennett, 'Alan Bennett Remembers the Treachery of Books', *The Independent on Sunday Review* (28 Jan. 1990), 8.
[10] F. J. Gordon, letter, *The Times* (25 Jan. 1949), 5. Gordon was confident that other public libraries could show equally 'encouraging' figures.
[11] *PC* (27 Jan. 1945), 37.

Judging from formal surveys of children's leisure activities conducted during this period, 'reading' was either the preferred spare-
time activity, or a strong second or third choice. In their tastes children
reflected those of their parents. Table 5.1 displays the leisure activities
of boys and girls, aged 12–15, documented in two extensive surveys.
The Merseyside investigation used a largely working-class sample,
while the 1949 Social Survey was more representative. Nevertheless,
the similarities are striking. On Merseyside, reading competed in
popularity with sport among schoolboys, but was first choice among
schoolgirls. The decline in reading after leaving school, particularly
among girls, was a phenomenon noted by many observers; in this case,
it should be balanced by the fact that reading, the cheapest and most
manageable leisure activity to fit around a job, was now most popular
among both sexes.[12] By 1949, according to the Social Survey, broadcasting had surpassed reading in popularity, but the reading of
'comics' ('bloods' as well as *The Beano*) and other books was still strong,
particularly among schoolboys and schoolgirls. Other surveys confirm
this apparent decline in the popularity of reading after the war. A 1945
questionnaire sent to 4,000 Liverpool Youth Organization members
ranked reading in third place, after the cinema and dancing, while the
1950 survey of 1,000 adolescents aged 14–19 in Birmingham placed the
cinema and youth organizations ahead of reading.[13]

The seeming decline in reading suggested by these surveys can be
contrasted, however, with evidence of great activity. A. J. Jenkinson's
1940 survey, for example, examined the reading habits of secondary
(advanced) and senior schoolboys and schoolgirls aged 12–15.
Reading, he concluded, was popular among all ages; few did not parti-
cipate. On average, boys and girls read between three and four magazines and four and six books each month.[14] The war, moreover,
intensified reading among children; given paper rationing and limited
supply, demand was high. A Fulham newsagent in 1943 reported that
children's 'comics' were in very short supply:

---

[12] Although cinema attendance increased with age (and wage-earning) on Merseyside, it was still more expensive (and thereby less accessible) than reading for a
working-class adolescent, which probably accounts for the surprisingly low cinema
figures here.
[13] *PC* (13 Jan. 1945), 16; Bryan H. Reed, *Eighty Thousand Adolescents* (London, 1950),
23–47.
[14] A. J. Jenkinson, *What Do Boys and Girls Read?* (London, 1940); also, 'Children and
their Books: New Methods of Education are needed', *B* (19 Sept. 1940), 310–14. Jenkinson surveyed 1,570 boys and 1,330 girls, about evenly divided by school and by age.

TABLE 5.1 Leisure Activities of Young People, 1934 and 1949

| | 1934. Merseyside Social Survey | | | | 1949. Social Survey, nationwide | | | |
| | Boys (%) | | Girls (%) | | Boys (%) | | Girls (%) | |
	School age	At 15+	School age	At 15+	12–13 years	14–15 years	12–13 years	14–15 years
Outdoor sport or games excluding cycling and walking	57.8	49.8	36.4	22.9	69	56	68	35
Reading:								
General	53.0	51.9	57.0	44.7				
Comics					75	55	71	49
Library, other books					54	58	79	83
Cinema:								
Less than once a week	24.7	32.5	15.6	28.4	29	32	34	30
Once a week	2.9	7.6	1.5	6.8	30	34	39	37
Twice a week or more	37.2	37.3	–	–	39	34	25	32
Watching football					74	69	18	25
Listening to wireless					76	80	88	91
Needlework, knitting, dressmaking	–	–	26.7	19.0	–	–	73	74
Cycling	5.9	14.5	0.7	4.0	56	54	45	44
Dancing	5.3	1.4	13.4	5.4	9	12	15	31

Sources: D. Caradog Jones (ed.), *The Social Survey of Merseyside*, iii (London, 1934) 219–20; J. C. Ward, 'Children and the Cinema', Social Survey, NS 131 (London, Apr. 1949), 42.

If more were printed a lot more could be sold ... Why should the children suffer in particular? ... It's the boy that reads comics today who'll be the man of tomorrow. If they'd cut down some of this trash (he indicates sixpenny thrillers) and put a few more comics out it would be fairer.[15]

Similarly, *The Publishers' Circular* in the same year reported that more children than ever were reading, and reading more at that. 'Judging from experience after the last war, it is not unlikely that this extension of the reading habit will survive the peace.'[16] Two additional post-war investigations suggest that it did. Pearl Jephcott's study of working-class adolescent girls revealed that between four and six 'books' each *week* was not unusual reading for a girl by the age of 18. 'The number of girls of about 14 and 15 who, during a lunch hour, examine the exhibits of a "popular" bookstall in a place like a market hall is an indication that reading is a genuine enough interest.'[17] Similarly, a diminished if still regular reading habit was recorded in Birmingham, where of boys and girls aged 14–19, over 75 per cent admitted reading their last 'book' one week ago.[18] In both cases, 'books' and magazines were frequently synonymous.

Children from lower-middle- and working-class families were undoubtedly active readers, though what they read may have differed from the middle class. The reading of 'bloods' among both sexes was especially popular, particularly among readers who had not been shaped by the middle-class tradition of proper book reading.[19] Robert Roberts, for example, recalled the 'addiction' of working-class boys in Salford to public-school tales in the *Gem* and *Magnet*,[20] as did John Osborne, 'with grown-up encouragement'.[21] Bill Naughton remembered his childhood friend's weekly desperation to see the *Magnet*: 'I don't care if tha 'as to scour the town an' beyond. I mun 'ave my *Magnet*—I mun find

[15] M/40/C, M-O 'Newspaper Reading' Box 2 File E (Hughes, Estcourt Road, Fulham SW6; 18 Mar. 1943).

[16] C. M. J., 'Young People and the Reading Habit During Wartime', *PC* (18 Dec. 1943), 678–9.

[17] Pearl Jephcott, *Rising Twenty: Notes on Some Ordinary Girls* (London, 1948), 112. Jephcott interviewed 103 girls aged 14–18 from three areas: London, Needham, and Dowden Colliery.

[18] Reed, *Eighty Thousand Adolescents*, 45.

[19] Kirsten Drotner, 'Schoolgirls, Madcaps, and Air Aces: English Girls and their Magazine Reading Between the Wars', *Feminist Studies*, 9 (Spring 1983), 37.

[20] Robert Roberts, *The Classic Slum* (Penguin edn., Harmondsworth, 1987), 160; *A Ragged Schooling* (Manchester, 1987), 168.

[21] John Osborne, *A Better Class of Person* (London, 1981), 81.

out what Billy Bunter's been up to this week.'[22] The author of the 'Greyfriars' series, Frank Richards, confirmed that 'every paper desiring a wide circulation must circulate, for the greater part, among the working classes, for the simple reason that they form nine-tenths of the population'.[23] George Orwell observed that working-class boys clung to these papers longer than public-school boys, well past the age of 12:

They are certainly read by working-class boys . . . They are generally on sale in the poorest quarters of big towns, and I have known them to be read by boys whom one might expect to be completely immune from public school 'glamour'. I have seen a young coal miner, for instance, a lad who had already worked a year or two underground, eagerly reading the *Gem*.[24]

Of 1,850 boys and girls aged 11–15 surveyed in St Pancras in the early 1930s, over 50 per cent read three or more magazines (principally bloods) each week; of this number, about 30 per cent read *six* or more. Among girls, 'Reading' was the 'Principal Out-of-School Hobby or Pastime', followed by 'Knitting, Dressmaking, etc.'; among boys, it was placed a close second to 'Fretwork and Carpentry'.[25] In 1944 Mass-Observation found that in Blaina, a mining town, 99 per cent of the children read 'books' regularly, and 88 per cent had between 6*d*. and 2*s*. 6*d*. in pocket money to spend on reading, among other treats.[26] Again, it must be concluded that 'books' almost certainly meant for many, if not for most, bloods.

II

Which publications for boys and girls were most popular, quickest off the newsagent's or the library's shelves? Which types of fiction (school,

[22] Bill Naughton, *On the Pig's Back* (Oxford, 1988), 124.
[23] Frank Richards, 'Frank Richards Replies to George Orwell', in Sonia Orwell and Ian Angus (eds.), *The Collected Essays, Journalism and Letters of George Orwell*, vol. i (Penguin edn., Harmondsworth, 1987), 536.
[24] George Orwell, 'Boys' Weeklies', in Orwell and Angus (eds.), *Collected Essays, Journalism and Letters*, i. 512. For other reminiscences of working-class childhood reading of the Amalgamated Press papers, see Jeffrey Richards, *Happiest Days: The Public Schools in English Fiction* (Manchester, 1988), 291–4.
[25] J. H. Engledow and W. C. Farr, 'The Reading and Other Interests of School Children in St. Pancras', *Passmore Edwards Research Series*, no. 2 (London, 1933), 12–13, 17–18.
[26] Leonard Woolf, 'Mining Town—1942', M-O File Report 1498 (8 Apr. 1944), 190–2. Blaina was especially prosperous during the war, with busy munitions and silk factories.

adventure, etc.) were sought, and who emerged as the favourite children's authors? In terms of weekly magazines, the period after the First World War was dominated by two firms: D. C. Thomson and (to a much lesser extent) the Amalgamated Press. The arrival of the Thomson 'Big 5' boys' papers, beginning with *Adventure* in 1921, was as sensational, and as successful, as the début of the *Boy's Own Paper* in 1879. Each Thomson paper was read by between 600,000 and 1,500,000 boys (and girls) *per week* between the wars.[27] *Adventure*, *The Rover*, *The Wizard*, *The Skipper*, and *The Hotspur* were usually cited as favourites in reading surveys. St Pancras schoolboys, for example, preferred these titles to the *Gem* and *Magnet* by 1,575 votes to 127, as did boys of all ages and schools in Jenkinson's investigation.[28] D. C. Thomson's success, however, was confined to boys' papers. The girls' paper market was dominated by Amalgamated Press titles, including *School Friend* (1919, a sister paper of the *Gem*), *Schoolgirl's Own* (1921), and *Schoolgirl's Weekly* (1922), the latter two the firm favourites in 1933 and 1940.[29] These papers, unlike the multifaceted 'Big 5' titles, featured mainly school stories.

As children tended to find a favourite magazine and stick with it over long periods (given the consistency of favourite choices in surveys over the years), they were also loyal to particular authors. The interwar period witnessed the rise of several popular authors whose works, in series, resembled bloods in book form, with formulaic plots and stock characters. Notable among these were Captain W. E. Johns ('Biggles'), Richmal Crompton ('William'), and the doyenne of school-story writers, Angela Brazil. It is reasonable to assume, moreover, that bonding with fictional heroes was more intense among children than adults, which would have encouraged sales of series of books. In Table 5.2 three surveys of favourite authors, two in 1926 and one in 1949, are compared. Stepney and Manchester are probably representative of general tastes, including lower-middle- and working-class children, while Croydon provides an interesting

---

[27] Source: Circulation figures provided by D. C. Thomson & Co., Ltd. There were 10,823,000 children aged 14 and under in Britain in 1931; a Thomson paper, therefore, could have reached at the very least 14% of the population. See Ch. 6.

[28] Engledow and Farr, 'Reading and Other Interests', 12; Jenkinson, *What Do Boys and Girls Read?*, 68–70. Interestingly, *The Wizard*, *The Hotspur*, and *The Rover* also ranked very high in popularity among girls in both surveys.

[29] Engledow and Farr, 'Reading and Other Interests', 13; Jenkinson, *What Do Boys and Girls Read?*, 214–15.

TABLE 5.2. Favourite Authors in Children's Sections of Public Libraries, 1926 and 1949

	1926. Croydon public libraries		1926. Stepney public libraries		1949. Manchester city libraries	
					Number of copies	
	750 boys	750 girls	% boys	% girls	in use	left on shelves
Percy Westerman	220	–	27	–	334	518
Herbert Strang	213	–	–	–	–	–
G. A. Henty	198	–	7	–	6	60
Charles Dickens	101	90	2	3	–	–
John Finnemore	–	–	–	11	–	–
Angela Brazil	–	303	–	43	205	94
Andrew Lang	–	–	2	7	–	–
Enid Blyton					943	38
W. E. Johns					559	123
Richmal Crompton					398	21
Alison Uttley					344	146
Arthur Ransome					100	148
T. H. Burgess					129	69
C. B. Rutley					117	131
Louisa May Alcott					83	90

Sources: 'An Analysis of Child Reading', *The Publishers' Circular*, 20 Nov. 1926, p. 759; 'What East End Children Read', *The Times*, 23 Sept. 1926, p. 14; 'By Favour of the Public', *The Bookseller*, 10 Dec. 1949, p. 1488.

contrast.[30] The decline in popularity of boys' authors, such as Henty and Strang, whose heyday was the period before 1914, was noted, often with regret, by many observers. Children considered these old-fashioned or, in the terminology of the 1930s, 'unmodern' and 'not "live"'. Harry Blackwood, president of the Educational Institute of Scotland, observed that it was useless to try to encourage children to read books which were regarded as 'antediluvian'; young readers considered anything written before 1914 as ancient history.[31] The two exceptions were, of course, Percy Westerman and Angela Brazil, whose respective outputs were remarkable.[32] Both authors were cited, along with Arthur Ransome, by *The Bookseller* in 1933 in a list of 'Juvenile Best-Sellers'.[33] The Manchester survey also illustrates the later dominance of the market, beginning in the 1930s, by three equally prolific authors: Captain W. E. Johns, Richmal Crompton, and Enid Blyton.[34] In 1948 Eileen Colwell, when asked which books were best-sellers among children, replied: 'Every bookseller and librarian knows the answer—Enid Blyton, Richmal Crompton and W. E. Johns, of course. The demand for Enid Blyton's books is almost insatiable; William provides slap-stick comedy; Biggles is the Superman of this generation.'[35] The basic appeal lay in their timely, 'up-to-date' nature: Blyton's fast-paced adventures; Crompton's satirizing of 'middle-class' life and values (through the anarchic behaviour of her hero, William Brown) and Johns's appeal to youthful interest in aviation, the Forces, and the war. A 1935 advertisement for Oxford University Press's 3*s*. 6*d*. 'Biggles' series proclaimed Biggles as 'a "live" character: he stands for the spirit of the air-arm and typifies the modern age of invention'.[36]

[30] Stepney was largely working class, Croydon middle class. Hence, similarities between the two indicate the broad-based popularity of some children's authors. The Manchester results are undoubtedly representative, as they are post-war, when usage of public libraries had increased among all classes of children.

[31] *The Times* (29 Dec. 1937), 6.

[32] Westerman began writing in 1907 and was a regular contributor to boys' papers. He had a life contract with Blackie & Son for three books a year, and by 1950, at the age of 74, had written 170 books for boys. Angela Brazil, who died in 1946, was also published by Blackie, and wrote over sixty books. Such was her popularity that in 1923 Blackie offered her a lucrative 6% royalty deal to try to dissuade her from leaving (*PC* (19 July 1950), 911–12; Mary Cadogan and Patricia Craig, *You're a Brick, Angela!: The Girls' Story 1839–1985* (London, 1976), 111–24).

[33] 'Juvenile Best-Sellers', *B* (3 Nov. 1933), 10.

[34] Although Blyton claimed to write for all children between the ages of 3 and 15, it is doubtful that she was read much by children older than 10 or 11; certainly there is little evidence to the contrary from this period.

[35] Eileen H. Colwell, 'Which Books Delight Children?', *TC* (28 Aug. 1948), 9.

[36] *B* (4 Sept. 1935), 854.

It would appear that the types of stories preferred by children also remained rather constant. In Table 5.3 the favourite types of reading by young people, from the lower-middle and working classes, in three areas (two urban, one rural) are compared. The similarities are impressive, particularly between East Ham and Blaina, as the ages surveyed there were closer. Among boys, adventure and mystery stories were as popular as school stories were among girls. The 'distressingly high' preference for 'War' stories, recorded by the East Ham children's librarian, referred to tales of the Great War; anything earlier was rejected as 'ancient history'.[37] Although there is no such category in the 1942 survey, war-related themes in fiction, especially popular among boys, were probably categorized under 'Adventure'. 'There are not enough good stories devoted to the Army and Navy to go around',[38] *The Publishers' Circular* claimed in 1943. By 1950 school stories and 'thrillers' were still popular among both sexes in Birmingham. We should also note the popularity of fiction (books), both 'modern' (including *Gone with the Wind, Rebecca, Forever Amber*, and *No Orchids for Miss Blandish*) and 'classical' (*Great Expectations, Oliver Twist, Jane Eyre*), each type encouraged by film and radio adaptations. One reason, perhaps, why the percentages for fiction reading decline among 'attached' boys and girls is the amount of time consumed by membership of a club, which might otherwise be devoted to a long book.

TABLE 5.3. Preferred Reading by Young People: 1932, 1942, 1950

(i) East Ham, London: Central Junior Library (Average age = 11)

904 Girls: Most enjoyed 'book'		853 Boys: Most enjoyed 'book'	
School Tales	377	Adventure	200
Fairy tales	232	School life	142
Adventure	105	War	134
Guide stories	61	Sea and ships	81
History	40	History	66
Home life	37	Animal stories	44
Mysteries	18	Cowboys and Indians	43
Animal stories	18	Travel	38
Nature stories	9	About machinery	30
Poetry	3	Scouting	28
Humour	3	Air stories	24
Plays	1	Fairy stories	23

[37] 'What Children Read', *PC* (12 Nov. 1932), 561. [38] C. M. J., ibid.

TABLE 5.3 (*cont.*)

(ii) Blaina, South Wales: Social Survey, 1942 (Average age = 14)

	Favourite books	
	Among boys (%)	Among girls (%)
Mystery stories	77	40
Adventure stories	70	58
Love stories	6	34
Hobbies	38	8
School stories	20	43
Scientific books	20	12
Classics	0	16
Historical stories	0	11

(iii) Birmingham: Adolescent Survey, 1950 (Ages 14–20)*

	Books read by young people			
	Unattached boys (%)	Unattached girls (%)	Attached boys (%)	Attached girls (%)
Classical fiction	14	14	9	14
Modern fiction	15	27	8	19
Adventure and school stories	10	15	20	14
'Thrillers'	14	4	15	11
Paper-covered romances, etc.	9	19	6	21
Sport	7	–	8	–
Technical subjects	3	–	5	–
Other non-fiction	9	6	7	5
'Do not read'	19	15	22	16

*The sample consisted of about 1,000 children, divided by sex, and by attachment to a youth organization, such as church clubs, the Scouts, the Guides, or political units.

Sources: 'What Children Read', *The Publishers' Circular*, 12 Nov. 1932, p. 561; Leonard Woolf, 'Mining Town—1942' (M-O File Report 1498, 8 Apr. 1944), 191–2; Bryan H. Reed, *Eighty Thousand Adolescents* (London, 1950), 46.

Significantly, differences in percentages for the other, 'lighter' types of reading are mostly negligible between attached and unattached children.

Rather like some of their peers in the adult market, including Mills & Boon, publishers of popular fiction for children embraced their readership in a paternalistic fashion. This was, of course, the legacy of such publishers as the Religious Tract Society and Lord Northcliffe. Both authors and publishers of the best-selling children's books and magazines during this period were remarkably conscious, even proud, of acting *in loco parentis*. Underlying such 'responsibility' was a desire not to offend children or—perhaps more importantly—their parents. The parent, in fact, was the unknown yet omniscient quantity that had to be considered by any ambitious publisher or author. D. C. Thomson, for example, carefully screened all contents of its papers for boys, for fear that a parent might object and ban them from the house. Lawrence Cotterell, of Harrap publishers, claimed that the first question his firm asked when considering a manuscript of a new children's book was, 'Will the children, and the adults responsible for their upbringing and education, like this book?'[39]

Captain W. E. Johns epitomized this new breed of conscientious writers for children. He maintained that authors bore a great responsibility in protecting vulnerable young minds. In some respects Johns picked up the baton passed by Frank Richards of *Gem* and *Magnet* fame. 'If the child be the father to the man,' Richards wrote, 'it is surely worthwhile for an author to give his attention to the fathers of men.'[40] He believed that the duty of a boys' author, whose largest audience was from the working class, was ameliorative:

to entertain his readers, make them as happy as possible, give them a feeling of cheerful security, turn their thoughts to healthy pursuits, and above all to keep them away from unhealthy introspection, which in early youth can do only harm. If there is a Chekhov among my readers, I fervently hope that the effect of the *Magnet* will be to turn him into a Bob Cherry![41]

Johns's series of air adventures featuring 'Biggles' and 'Worrals' offered a generation of boys and girls lessons in patriotism and duty to one's country. The first Biggles novel was published in 1935. During the Second World War the Air Ministry, impressed by the popularity of Johns's hero among boys, and the value of Biggles as a recruiting aid for the flying corps, persuaded Johns to create a female counterpart. *Worrals of the W.A.A.F.* was published in 1941. Both series were also serialized in such magazines as the *Boy's Own Paper* and the *Girl's Own Paper*, and were throw-backs of sorts to the intensely patriotic themes of

[39] Lawrence Cotterell, 'Before the "Juvenile" Reaches the Shop Window', *TC* (25 Sept. 1948), 5.
[40] Frank Richards, *The Autobiography of Frank Richards* (London, 1952), 172.
[41] Id. 'Frank Richards Replies', 540.

the late nineteenth-century boys' papers. Johns, like many, initially wrote for an adult audience; his style changed when faced with an increasing army of young admirers:

Success was due I think, to the fact that I never wrote *down* to boys. At first the stories were adult. But soon perceiving that with a growing juvenile readership I had certain responsibilities I toned down the expletives, cut out hard drink, and shaped the character to my own idea of what sort of man a boy should strive to become ... If, by his exploits, he can produce men like himself, the country should be well served.[42]

Among the principles that Johns tried to instil in his readers—both boys and girls—were decent behaviour, sportsmanship, unselfish team-work, and loyalty to Crown, parents, and rightful authority. 'I teach a boy to be a man, for without that essential qualification he'll never be anything', he said, adding:

Today, more than ever before, the training of the juvenile mind is important. The adult author has little hope of changing the outlook, politics, or way of life of a reader, whose ideas are fixed. The brain of a boy is flexible. It can be twisted in any direction. A born hero-worshipper, he adores his heroes, and what they do he will do, so by the actions of his heroes will his own character be formed.[43]

It is difficult to ascertain whether this moral stuff had any appreciable effect upon the young reader. But as the series continued to sell well into the 1950s, Johns saw no reason to change his style. The Worrals books, moreover, have been particularly praised: 'For thousands of girls growing up during the 1940s and 1950s, it can be said that the Worrals books influenced them in challenging the old sexist assumptions',[44] for example, although this is not the kind of praise Johns would necessarily have appreciated.

III

Why did children choose to read what they apparently did? As might be expected, the reasons given by librarians, retailers, adults, and the children themselves are varied and often inconsistent. There are, however, some common characteristics, many of which are reminiscent of

[42] Quoted in *TC* (2 July 1949), 10–11.
[43] Captain W. E. Johns, 'What the Modern Boy Expects of his Hero, Biggles', *TC* (20 Aug. 1949), 15.
[44] Peter Berresford Ellis and Piers Williams, *By Jove, Biggles!: The Life of Captain W. E. Johns* (London, 1981), 190.

adult reading habits. Children, for example, craved escapism, seeking excitement and adventure in their reading to complement the action and immediacy of the cinema, and also as a release from a dull existence at home and at school. They also turned to fiction for information, and to satisfy a natural curiosity of such exotic matters as public-school life and affairs of the heart.

In 1937 Mass-Observation solicited essays from Middlesbrough children aged 13–16 on the title, 'Why I read books' (or, better, maga-zines).[45] Thomas (L/5/A) read for self-improvement: 'The books about adventure have more grip than books about love but I read them to increase my vocabulary and for the spelling of the words.' Indeed, pub-lishers pride themselves on correct grammar and spelling in children's papers. But some children read simply for reading's sake, as in the case of another boy (U/5/B):

My favourite books are detective or school stories or some other exciting kind of book. I do not read for the sake of perfecting my English grammar or any other kind of thing like that but only because it is a kind of hobby.

This distinction was also mentioned by Edward (U/5/C). 'I get much pleasure in reading twopenny books better known as twopenny bloods. I also read books in order to gain knowledge.' But often, among boys, particularly in the case of a series like 'Biggles', the two reasons con-verged:

I read more Navy and Army books than any other kind. This is because I am going to join the army or the navy.   (L/5/A)

Books which I prefer most are books of air stories by 'Johns' usually thrilling episodes of 'Biggles and Co'. This gives me a lot of knowledge concerning air-planes.   (U/4/A)

Flying stories often tell of the difficulties of the pioneers of flying or of the difficulties in the war when at first machine guns could not fire through the air-screw ... War stories are sometimes very far-fetched but most of them show the grim horrors of war and many dangers which have to be endured.   (U/4/A)

'In books sometimes classed as "trash" "nonsense" or some other term', another boy (L/5/A) wrote, 'there is often some knowledge to be gained by reading them.' But other Middlesbrough schoolchildren said they

[45] Mass-Observation, predictably, did not specify what kind of school these children attended, only the age range and level. Given the region, and the fact that Mass-Observation would not have been interested in replies from public-school children, it can be assumed that these were state-school children from the working classes. (M-O 'Reading' Box 1 File B (9 Sept. 1937); 160 essays in total.)

from a depressing reality. 'I read to pass the time away for it is better than lying about the house doing nothing', Charles (U/5/B) wrote. 'I read also to take my mind off some regrettable incident.' Andrew (L/4/B) wrote, 'My greatest pleasure is to sit down with a book of pirates . . . when you are frightened a book of interesting stories will take your mind of(f) your loneliness.' Lastly, the popularity of bloods is evident from a number of replies from boys and girls. In nearly every case bloods are called 'books'. 'There are books like the "Wizard" and "Hotspur" which a great number of boys read', one girl (U/5/A) wrote. 'I like to read these but some of the stories are silly and are not worth reading.' But another girl (U/4/A) stated simply, 'The best books are the Wizard, Rover, Etc. which are published each week.' A classmate, John (U/4/A), agreed: 'Most boys like reading twopenny books because of the exciting tales. Of course I am one of these kind.' Robert (U/4/A) admitted reading bloods to obtain the free football and cricket cards, showing how useful 'pushes' could be.

It is difficult today to appreciate the hold which weekly magazines in particular had upon children, let alone their effect on tastes in reading. 'I find it hard to understand what influences made us cast out our cultural nets so haphazardly', John Osborne, an avid reader of *Gem*, *Magnet*, *Hotspur*, and *Wizard* when young, recalled.[46] Mass-Observation blamed the longevity of the children's magazine market, which by the Second World War had conditioned three generations of children to the reading of bloods. In its 1947 survey for Penguin Books, intended to explore the market potential for the new 'Puffin' series of quality children's books, Mass-Observation concluded that the tuppenny blood trade militated against the sale of books in general, not to mention well-produced ones:

Puffins obviously try and attract by quality, but the effects of quality production on children are unknown and virtually unexamined. For decades children have been reading with enthusiasm badly produced magazines, badly printed on bad paper, and it seems as things are, the rival to the Puffin is not primarily the cloth bound book at all but the paper magazine. This was stressed by many school teachers and particularly by teachers in elementary schools. A typical schoolteacher comment was something like this:

'Paper backed books are not used in the schools. Some of the girls have those: *Woman's Own* and *Home and Beauty*—sometimes they have them with them—I expect they borrow them from their mothers. And the boys read the ordinary weekly comics.'[47]

[46] Osborne, *A Better Class of Person*, 81.
[47] Mass-Observation, *A Report on Penguin World* (File Report 2545, M-O, Dec. 1947), 203–4; 205–6.

Indeed, the popularity of some book series, such as 'Biggles' and 'William', could be explained by the fact that they resembled bloods in book form, rather than conventional books, which the typical schoolchild would have regarded with dread. When asked in 1926 what boys read by choice, the chief librarian in Edinburgh answered quite simply: any thriller or a *Robinson Crusoe*-type novel was not refused. 'The typical sort was that in which going out of bounds, drinking, smoking, betting, money-lending, petty thieving were recurring themes', he said. 'No book written to this pattern seemed stale to boys, so that there was little inducement for authors to write more original or better books.'[48] Here again the influence of the blood is apparent.

Another factor, particularly important among the lower-middle and working classes (as with adult readers), was the lack of home libraries, which tended to discourage respect for real books among children. In the St Pancras study, over 50 per cent of the children surveyed came from homes which contained fewer than fifty books; of these 'libraries', half contained fewer than twenty-five volumes, and most were books of verse.[49] Osborne admitted that his generation was the product of homes 'where books and music were almost completely disregarded. Although no one said as much, people who went out to work every day had no time for such luxuries.'[50] They did, however, eagerly devour other 'books', namely novelettes and bloods, which were disposed of or swapped when read. Mass-Observation noted how indifferent, even hostile, to children's reading working-class parents could be. One Chelsea woman in 1943, when asked about her son's reading habits, replied, 'Well, my younger boy always used to have his nose in a book—I had to stop him—he was getting round-shouldered. I don't think it's healthy for children to read too much.'[51] The recollections of Annie Wilson of Nottingham are appropriate here. Born in 1898 and one of nine children, her father was employed in the hosiery trade. Although the time spoken of is Edwardian, the attitudes probably prevailed among a good section of the working classes:

Father thought all book learning was piffle ...

I read a lot of books on the sly I did—I will tell you that. I borrowed them from school. I remember one and I shall never forget it. It was about a farm and

---

[48] *PC* (3 July 1926), 7.
[49] Engledow and Farr, 'Reading and Other Interests', 9.
[50] Osborne, *A Better Class of Person*, 81.
[51] F/50/C, M-O 'Reading' Box 8 File F (Chelsea, 13 Oct. 1943). This woman added that she liked 'a nice love-tale to read on a Sunday afternoon. Sometimes the girl says, "This is a nice one", and I take it.'

this family. I can't remember the title. And I had to hide it because you see reading was a vice. You've got something better to do than put your nose in a book. That was the expression you see. But I did love it ...

The only books in the house was the Bible. Mother and Dad's Bible that I told you about. They were on the sideboard. And she paid for one paper—*Home Companion* or something—or *Sunday Circle*. I forget exactly. And they had the *Evening Post*. But there was no proper reading. You see at first they could not read.[52]

The tuppenny bloods for boys and girls generated the most criticism and controversy among adults. Strong reactions for and against were reminiscent of Victorian discussions on the merits of the penny dreadfuls. Defenders of these papers praised their convenience, their encouragement of reading outside school, and their relatively harmless fiction which stimulated the imagination. L. Stanley Jast described bloods as 'a god-send to the errand-boy and to the maid-of-all-work': they could be purchased by the children themselves, were small enough to carry in a pocket and could be read anywhere, and were passed on or exchanged for others. He also praised the affinity between paper and reader, for the author wrote to the child, not over him, which could only serve to build the reading habit.[53] Similarly, Rodney Bennett condemned the tendency to look down on the boy with a magazine stuck in his pocket; it was better, in his opinion, to remember that 'these boys' lives are dull enough, and if the "penny dreadful" enlivens things a little for them, well, good luck to them'.[54] Jephcott noted that working-class girls enjoyed erotic bloods as much for the thrills as for their ease of reading amid distractions. 'It must be uphill work, in homes where there are rarely periods of complete silence, let alone absence of physical movement, for the girl to undertake any reading that demands much closer thought than the exploits of Raymond, or any other of *Crystal*'s characters, compel.'[55] But the only real harm done to children by bloods, according to Edgar Osborne, Derbyshire County Librarian, was in their shoddy style, slipshod thought, and poor production values, including ill-coloured paper. His conclusion, endorsed later by Jenkinson, was that the best remedy was to improve on these papers, not ban them, as the *Boy's Own Paper* had shown in 1879.[56]

Many critics, heartened by the activity of reading among children,

[52] Thea Thompson, *Edwardian Childhoods* (London, 1981), 93–4.
[53] L. Stanley Jast, *The Child as Reader* (London, 1927), 49.
[54] Quoted in *TC* (9 Aug. 1930), 9.   [55] Jephcott, *Rising Twenty*, 36.
[56] Quoted in *PC* (5 Nov. 1932), 527.

tempered their personal distaste for bloods. J. MacAlister Brew believed that, although children should read better fiction, it was an encouragement that they read at all, if only bloods. At least these were 'impregnated with a wholesome if elementary, but quite distinct moral code'.[57] But the danger was that children might grow tired of such reading, and therefore of reading in general:

> The tragedy would seem to be that many young people become the *victims* of their ability to read because when their taste for thrillers and the more luscious type of romance has been sated, they are unable to find a bridge to adult reading and they 'Give up reading' because 'all the tales are much the same with the names changed'—which after all is how most of us, if we are honest, graduated out of school stories through E. M. Dell to Conrad.[58]

Similarly, at the Library Association Conference in 1950, Dr R. G. Ralph, youth section librarian at the RAF Training College, Cranwell, urged librarians to be tolerant and patient. Morally bad, psychologically harmful, and poorly written fiction should be banned, but this was rarely found in children's books anyway. 'Remember that a child was unlikely to jump from comics to Conrad; but could go from comics to Edgar Rice Burroughs, from Burroughs to Buchan, from Buchan to Masefield, and from Masefield to Conrad.'[59] Both Margaret Phillips and Brew suggested simple yet persuasive substitutions for popular literature which had proved successful in their respective teaching experiences among young girls. 'Sexton Blake can be replaced by Conan Doyle, or by Chesterton. If school stories are wanted, *Tom Brown* and *The Hill* are better than *The Captain* and the *Boys' Friend*', Phillips said.[60] Brew recalled the 'intense interest' among young people when they discovered that *Treasure Island* was a blood and *Jane Eyre* a thriller, which encouraged them to read both classics.[61]

IV

Tastes in reading were considered to have been formed by the school-leaving age, or 14. Judging from evidence that many children as young

[57] J. MacAlister Brew, *Informal Education: Adventures and Reflections* (London, 1947), 131.

[58] Ibid. 130.

[59] 'From Comics to Conrad: The Librarian as Readers' Guide', *The Times* (21 Sept. 1950), 2.

[60] Margaret Phillips, *The Young Industrial Worker: A Study of his Educational Needs* (Oxford, 1922), 112.

[61] J. MacAlister Brew, *In the Service of Youth: A Practical Manual of Work among Adolescents* (London, 1943), 359.

as 12 were already enjoying 'adult' authors and weekly magazines, an important continuity can be established between the child reader and the adult reader. In fact, critics lamented the so-called 'gap': this apparent lack of a bridge between children's books and classic fiction, which encouraged so many young readers to take up adult light fiction. In 1930 *The Librarian and Book World* warned that 'children of all classes, not of the poor alone', were at risk:

Our children's books are amongst the best in the world. But it is in that transition stage from childhood to manhood and womanhood, from twelve or fourteen to eighteen or twenty that the fondness for tripe is to be found. Our literature for that stage is lamentable, poor both in numbers and quality.

It is because of that gap, bridged, if it is bridged at all, by the worst of both classes of literature that so many children who in their young days are intelligent and eager readers, become non-readers or avid devourers of the grown up story of action—the detective tale, or the romance which is but a poor variant of Cinderella, substituting the slime of the sex novel for the romance of the fairy tale.[62]

Indeed, evidence suggests that this 'gap' was barely bridged among child readers. Two significant features of the reading habits of boys and girls during this period are a preference of both sexes for 'adult fiction' over 'juvenile fiction', and a fondness for 'boys' fiction' among girl readers. Both are illustrated in an example from *The Bookseller* in 1935, which described the reading habits of 'Matilda', a 'normal 14 year old'. Matilda had read fifty-eight books over the past year, eleven by her favourite author, 'Sapper'. She was also fond of P. G. Wodehouse, Sir Arthur Conan Doyle, Ian Hay, and Dennis Wheatley—all authors with a traditionally male (and adult) appeal. Matilda obtained her books through her own library subscription, presumably one of the tuppenny libraries. Her peers, *The Bookseller* concluded, enjoyed thrillers and adventure books as much as boys; over half of her book list fell under these headings. An increasing number of children were imitating the reading tastes of their parents: 'It appears that fourteen-year-olds prefer the books meant for grown-ups rather than the literature specially written for children; that the "girls' school" story is not in universal demand; and, cheering news for authors, that the young are clamouring for their work and, in one case at least, getting it.'[63] While Matilda's tastes were perhaps not typical of most children, given

---

[62] 'Reading Rationally: the Adolescent's Choice', *The Librarian and Book World*, 19 (Mar. 1930), 243.
[63] *B* (9 Oct. 1935), 1024.

the wide popularity of such authors as Richmal Crompton and Captain W. E. Johns, there *is* evidence to suggest that this trend was growing, particularly among lower-middle- and working-class children. It is likely, therefore, that the prodigious adult demand for light fiction had its origins in the reading preferences of children and adolescents. Frederick Cowles was one of many contemporary observers who tried to bring this point to the attention of the public. By the age of 14, he claimed, the reading habit was firmly formed by the tuppenny bloods: girls were wallowing in 'sentimental rubbish', boys in mysteries, Westerns, and sea stories. Given the lack of guidance when they left school, by the age of 16, 'both boys and girls are reading adult literature. This is to be regretted, to a certain extent, but neither publishers nor librarians have solved the problems of catering for adolescent tastes.'[64]

Jenkinson's documentation of the extent of reading of boys' bloods among girls aged 12–15 did not come as a surprise, merely confirming long-held suspicions in the trade, some of which we have noted in the 1880s and 1890s. Among children, gender differentiation in reading tastes was less apparent than, say, for adult readers of romantic fiction. The popularity of the *Boy's Own Paper* among girls, for example, was well known, and Frank Richards noted that 'the *Magnet* is intended chiefly for readers up to sixteen; though I am proud to know that it has readers of sixty! It is read by girls as well as boys.'[65] In 1922 Phyllis Orgel, aged 11, of London claimed that girls choose from a larger number of books because 'they will not hesitate to read a book written exclusively for boys. I do not think there are many boys who would condescend to read a girl's book!' She added that she had 'read and re-read' *Treasure Island* and *Kidnapped*.[66] Jane Hardington, aged 14 in 1949, was one of many female fans of Arthur Ransome, Malcolm Saville, and, especially, 'Biggles'. 'Captain W. E. Johns seems to be the favourite author with all the boys I know', she wrote. 'They get very excited about the secret missions of Biggles, and I believe their sisters generally manage to read about Biggles.'[67] W. H. Smith reported in 1936 that another publishing 'myth' was shattered when Collins

---

[64] Frederick Cowles, 'Children's Reading in Wartime', *PC* (23 Aug. 1941), 92.

[65] Richards, 'Frank Richards Replies', 533.

[66] *PC* (22 Apr. 1922), 360. The Editor certainly agreed, noting that Phyllis's letter 'confirms what has so often been said in our columns for generations past, *viz.*, that most girls like books written for boys as much or even more than the books specially written for girls'.

[67] *TC* (27 Aug. 1949), 7.

received a letter from a Lancashire schoolgirl, asking to join their Wild West Club. 'We girls take as much interest in Westerns (or even more, as the case may be) than the boys', the girl wrote.[68]

There appear to be three reasons for this tendency of children to follow the tastes of their parents. First, a child's natural curiosity and imitation of adult ways and manners may have included investigating the literature which crammed the newsagent shops and the libraries, promoted by the latest films. Second, as provision in circulating libraries for school-leaving children was poor, most graduated to the logical successors of bloods: thrillers, love stories, and erotic bloods. Third, as libraries in lower-middle- and working-class homes were uncommon, 'books' in hand were freely passed around. As Jephcott described the family reading habits of one of her subjects, a working girl of 17, 'Her father, a pitman, reads the twopenny love novels that her mother brings home whenever she goes shopping. The house is full of *Women's Novels*, *The Moon Series*, and *True Love Stories*. Two other brothers who work at the pit enjoy *Randland Romances*.'[69]

Girls more than boys, in fact, preferred the works of 'adult' authors and 'adult' magazines. The principal attraction, it would seem, was the love and romance, often of an illicit kind. In 1913 Priscilla Moulder found that working girls displayed more 'adult' tastes than boys in their choice of Mrs Henry Wood, 'Ouida', Miss Braddon, and Marie Corelli. The weekly papers so beloved by these girls were taken 'mainly for the touching "to-be-continued" love stories which are kept running through its pages, stories that often contain records of quite impossible heroes and heroines'.[70] According to Jenkinson, girls from both senior and secondary schools displayed adult tastes in reading, although of a very different nature: the working-class senior girl preferred the so-called 'erotic' bloods, the middle-class secondary girl romantic novels. These tastes were probably shaped by different environments:

The Senior School girl goes out into a life which offers her little chance of growing beyond these values and standards. It is significant that the Senior School girls often described these magazines as 'books' . . . when they recognized the *Schoolgirl's Own* and *Wizard* as 'bloods'. For them literature tends to be such stuff as *Miracle* is made of.

The Secondary School girl seems to miss erotic magazines and moves on to

[68] *TC* (1 Feb. 1936), 12.
[69] Pearl Jephcott, *Girls Growing Up* (London, 1942), 100–1.
[70] Priscilla E. Moulder, 'The "Story Interest" Only: What Working Boys and Girls Read and What They Miss', *The Book Monthly* (May 1913), 544–5.

Dell, Orczy, Porter, and Gray, with the possibility of wider and deeper reading experiences before she is exhausted by 'the hard realities of life', by earning a living.[71]

Similarly, Jephcott found that working-class girls progressed naturally from 'girls' books' to their mothers' papers upon leaving school. On Tyneside, 'The girls go straight on from the comics of their childhood's reading to *Silver Star* and the other more suggestive magazines of that constellation.'[72] She estimated that the circulations of these semi-provocative magazines, mainly published by D. C. Thomson, 'must be very extensive because the magazines are universally known among young people'. An astonishing amount was consumed each week, Jephcott observed:

One not entirely untypical girl who gets a great deal of pleasure from the [cheaper women's magazines] bought the following magazines in a single week (November 1945): *Oracle, Miracle, Weekly Welcome, Woman's Own, Woman, Woman's Weekly, Home Chat, Red Letter, Red Star, Family Star, Picture Show* and *Glamour*.

She also borrowed, from her particular friend, *Lucky Star, Silver Star*, and *Melody Maker*. In the same week she read, too, a 4*d*. romance, *Love Tangle*, and a 1/3 book, *Unsuspected Witness*.

She paid less than the market price for these magazines because she deals at a shop which works on a 'take-two-old-ones-in-and-get-one-new-one-out' system; but even so her week's spending on reading was about 5/- out of her 65/- income.[73]

A 1950 investigation of working-class boys went further. Martin Parr spoke before the London Council of Social Services about his seven years' experience with boys aged 14–18 in his Shoreditch club. Parr could not interest his young charges in Dickens, Thackeray, or Anthony Hope; *Robinson Crusoe* was quite out of favour, but there was 'a regular, consistent demand' for Henty. In general, however, boys' tastes lay firmly in the adult sections:

Among the 'indispensable' books and authors for a boys' club were, he found, Zane Grey, Sydney Horler, Agatha Christie, Nevil Shute, *Poisoned Arrow*, *Tarzan* and *I Chose Freedom*.

The 'most beloved' were *Sherlock Holmes, William, Bulldog Drummond, Biggles*, Peter Cheyney and *The Saint*.[74]

[71] Jenkinson, *What Do Boys and Girls Read?*, 219.
[72] Jephcott, *Girls Growing Up*, 101.
[73] Id., *Rising Twenty*, 113.
[74] 'Reading in Youth Clubs', *B* (18 Feb. 1950), 224; also 'Why Boys Read: Decline of Robinson Crusoe', *The Times* (15 Feb. 1950), 8.

Clearly Johns and Crompton had much—if somewhat unexpected—competition. Some publishers were aware of the advanced tastes of boys, however; Hodder and Stoughton advertised the latest 'Bulldog Drummond' thriller in 1949 as, 'For the delight of a huge public—Man and Boy'.[75]

The influence of the cinema in promoting such authors among children should not be underestimated. Children maintained similar tastes in films as in reading. It is hardly surprising that the favourite types of films cited by children aged 11–15 in the 1948 Social Survey were in the 'Mystery, murder, thrillers' category: 48 per cent of boys and 33 per cent of girls preferred these. In 1949 boys were equally divided between 'Cowboy' and 'Gangster/Detective' films (25 per cent each) while girls chose 'Musicals' (22 per cent).[76] The 1950 Birmingham survey concluded that adolescents, like adults, were susceptible to reading books which had been filmed or mentioned on the wireless. Among favourite books listed were *Forever Amber*, *Gone With the Wind*, *No Orchids for Miss Blandish*, *Rebecca*, and *Jane Eyre*.[77] Eileen Colwell was one critic who blamed the cinema for a child's often 'perverse' taste in reading:

In a census taken recently among girls, fifty percent voted unreservedly for the mystery story. 'I like mystery and murder', said one. 'I like murders and kidnapping' said another, aged eleven!
    This seems a strange demand from a girl, but it is typical of many requests

---

[75] *B* (5 Feb. 1949), 190. Although Jenkinson did explore the popularity of 'adult' authors among boys, his analysis was limited to such authors as Buchan, Dickens, Sir Walter Scott, and Mark Twain. Oddly, he dismissed the appeal of lower-brow authors, blaming lack of space; this evidence would perhaps have been revealing: 'A few, but not many, authors who write for the adult market, but are quite widely read by boys, have been omitted, including Edgar Rice Burroughs, "Sapper," and Edgar Wallace. The reading of these authors by children has its significances, of course, and would not be neglected in a complete survey' (p. 48).

[76] J. C. Ward, 'Children Out of School', Social Survey, NS 110 (London, June 1948), 46; Ward, 'Children and the Cinema', Social Survey, NS 131 (London, Apr. 1949), 36.

[77] Reed, *Eighty Thousand Adolescents*, 45. Similarly, Hilde T. Himmelweit's 1958 study of the effects of television on children found that the most consistently popular type of programme among boys and girls aged 10–14 was the adult serial crime thriller, including 'Fabian of Scotland Yard' and 'Dixon of Dock Green'. In general, children preferred adult programmes to children's programmes and, as such, 'The child, though sharing the viewing with his parents, may be developing adult tastes earlier'. The study concluded, however, that television, like film, stimulated the reading habit and heightened curiosity in a wider range of books, including non-fiction (Hilde T. Himmelweit, A. N. Oppenheim, and Pamela Vince, *Television and the Child: An Empirical Study of the Effect of Television on the Young* (London, 1958), 24, 125–7).

in the children's library. I can only conclude that it results from the undue publicity given to the sensational, and to the prevalence of the 'gangster' film.[78]

The opinions of young readers themselves support these conclusions. Jane Shirley, aged 12 in 1949, liked Enid Blyton and Greek mythology but reserved her greatest praise for thrillers, 'especially the Sherlock Holmes and Bulldog Drummond books, which send lovely creeping thrills down my back. Agatha Christie writes gorgeous murder stories and you never can discover the murderer till right at the end.'[79] One would hardly expect a child of 12 to enjoy 'Sapper's' works. William, a Middlesbrough schoolboy (L/5/B, 1937), also admitted reading Bulldog Drummond, 'because I like the way that he expresses himself'. A classmate, Robert agreed. 'There are several interesting crime writers such as Sapper and Edgar Wallace whom I like because they know what they are writing about.'[80]

The principal attack on the 'advanced' reading tastes of children revolved round the harm which these sorts of books could inflict upon young undeveloped minds. This line of argument was similar to that launched against the penny dreadfuls in the 1870s, and the claims that reading tales of highwaymen encouraged juvenile delinquency. Although a 1938 survey of young offenders did reveal the prominence of 'Reading' among favourite leisure activities (it was either most popular, or a close second to 'Sport'), the type of books and magazines read was not specified, nor was any connection proposed between reading and crime.[81] If a child demanded 'adult' reading, Brew actually thought detective stories were preferable to bloods and thrillers. At least the former genre had attracted 'clever and conscientious' authors such as Dorothy L. Sayers, was rooted on the side of law and order, and encouraged the use of one's wits rather than deliberately trying to frighten one out of them.[82] Some children agreed. In 1934 Collins received another surprising letter, this time from a 14-year-old schoolgirl in Leeds, asking to join their Crime Club; she apparently did so despite great opposition from her 'Auntie':

---

[78] Eileen H. Colwell, 'What the Children Want From the Publishers', *B* (4 Sept. 1935), 841.

[79] 'Our Favourite Authors and Books', *TC* (20 Aug. 1949), 11.

[80] M-O 'Reading' Box 1 File B (9 Sept. 1937).

[81] A. M. Carr-Saunders, Hermann Mannheim, and E. C. Rhodes, *Young Offenders: An Enquiry into Juvenile Delinquency* (Cambridge, 1943), 93.

[82] Brew, *Informal Education*, 46. She added that detective stories flourished only in democratic countries; Germany and Italy had banned them in the 1930s.

When I was away at my Auntie's, my friend sent me a cutting out of a news-paper. This said that a boy in a Crime Club had hanged himself. My aunt was shocked when she heard that I was in one. I told her that I wasn't going to hang myself, and that the best authors wrote for the Crime Club and that it took a very clever person to write a first-class mystery.

She said something about 'putting ideas into children's heads!' But most children are not as inocent [sic] as most grown-ups fondly imagin [sic]. Besides I don't think that Crime Books make people want to go and do a few murders. Most crime books are just the opposite. They show how hard a life of crime really is. For however ingenious the murderer may be he is invariably found out in the last chapter or before. This should deter any would-be criminals.[83]

Similarly, in 1935 a 'Club Boy', R. H. Dixon, dismissed claims that gangs of small boys committed minor thefts as a result of reading 'Wizards, Rovers and what-not . . . In my opinion, adventure yarns have done no one any harm yet. I [have] read "penny dreadfuls" for years and I don't think I am a criminal.'[84]

On the subject of the reading of women's magazines and bloods by girls, opinion was also divided. George Orwell would have found an ally in Lucille Iremonger, an enemy in Madeleine Henrey. These two authors squared up in a series in the *Trade Circular* in 1950. Henrey extolled the virtues of magazine articles, 'seven out of ten' of which were instructional, dealing with cookery, sewing, and the like. Reading these, she claimed, was excellent preparation, as a girl's first thought 'is to get married and well it may be. That is our function in life.' In addition to educating their readers, she believed these publications also promoted the reading habit:

I gave up smoking without difficulty but I could not so easily give up *Woman*, *Woman's Journal*, *Everywoman* and the like. The teen-agers who read them like I do and who appear to be so blamed for it, develop by necessity an urge to read not only more magazines but also more books, and as they become married women they, *not* the men, borrow most often from the lending libraries and eventually, if they can afford it, buy books.[85]

---

[83] *B* (26 Sept. 1934), 636. The writer also claimed that 'good' literature such as Shakespeare was often just as 'horrible' as crime books.

[84] R. H. Dixon and G. K. Tattersall, 'Literature and Morals: A Boy's View and a Man's Reply', *The Boy*, viii. 3 (Winter 1935–6), 332. In his reply Tattersall agreed: 'I am quite convinced that if I robbed a till, it would not be because I wanted to imitate a film-villain who conducts a gigantic bank-robbery. It would be because I wanted the money' (pp. 334–5).

[85] Mrs Robert Henrey, 'Why Deride Teen-Ager and Her Magazines?' *TC* (27 May 1950), 19. Henrey was the author of 15 books, including *Matilda and the Chickens*.

But the novelist Lucille Iremonger challenged Henrey, noting that the comparison with smoking was an admission that women's weeklies were essentially 'mental drugs ... Glossy fiction does not lead anyone to better literature, any more than a taste for chocolates develops a fine palate.' The library books chosen would only be more of the same detrimental fiction, she maintained:

There is no humour in their love-stories, less wit, less realism. No understanding of what people are really like (or a determination to ignore it), and the plots are few, flimsy and unconvincing. Read one, and you have read them all. This is sickly stuff.

In moderation it does no harm. But a girl who (as one of the 80,000 adolescents did) reads 24 of these publications a week is living in a world of dangerous fantasy. Read in excess, I hold, these magazines could be a danger to society, certainly as much so to girls as gangster films to boys.

The glamour-struck girl goes into marriage in a spirit of fear, jealous possessiveness and bovaristic discontent. She is 'a natural' for suburban neurosis, and for making her husband miserable. The end of this road is one of the forty thousand squalid divorces a year.[86]

If Mills & Boon would hardly have agreed with Mrs Iremonger, Margaret Phillips and Pearl Jephcott would have done. Both women were alarmed by the extent to which working-class girls unconsciously absorbed ideas, values, and a distorted world-view from these publications. In 1922 Phillips found this was reflected in the writing styles of her continuation students, young wage-earners in special schools to further their education:

... essays, poems, and stories written in leisure time, sometimes of unmanageable length, were beginning to pour in. But the stories, alas, fell almost without exception into one of half a dozen classes. There was the story of slum life based on George R. Sims; the war melodrama with the German villain and the English hero; the sadly sentimental story recalling *Little Meg's Children*; the crude school-story; the 'strong' personal romance in which love is identified with jealousy; and the supernatural story, founded on Richard Marsh and the cinema serial.[87]

She admitted, moreover, her 'shock' at reading a violent short story, 'The Girl who Paid her Price', written by girl of 16 with an apparently misleading 'facial expression of childlike innocence'. Similarly, one of

---

[86] Lucille Iremonger, 'Our Girls Deserve Better', *TC* (10 June 1950), 26, 29. Iremonger was the author of the novel *Creole*. In his postscript the Editor of the *Trade Circular* wrote, 'We do not share all Mrs. Iremonger's explosive opinions.'
[87] Phillips, *Young Industrial Worker*, 104.

Jephcott's subjects in 1948, a Needham girl called Celia, had written a novel, *Greater Love*, in her spare time after working days in a factory. This, too, exhibited all the drama, frivolous love, and happy-ever-after endings contained in the pulp magazines so eagerly devoured. Jephcott was appalled by the emphasis on sex and romance, without a thought to the realities of marriage:

The same girl observes that lots of people get married without any such bother as having to pay for a house or knowing how to run it—just for pleasure. An older woman puts it bluntly, saying, 'They think "We can't do it in the street or the pictures, only in bed—so let's get married"'.[88]

In 1925 delegates to the United Conference of the Training College Association and the Association of Head Masters heard the belief that less emphasis should be placed in schools on 'the virtues of Scott and Dickens', as this discouraged children from reading. One speaker's experience had shown that 'usually boys who professed a keen love for Scott and Dickens were found to be not so good at composition as others who frankly said they preferred modern writers, Zane Grey, for example'.[89] Although this is perhaps unlikely, light fiction did, at the very least, encourage children to develop a reading habit, and publishers such as D. C. Thomson actually believed that an insistence on proper grammar and spelling within children's stories was beneficial. As a boy on Orkney, George Mackay Brown was an avid reader of the Thomson boys' papers, to, he believed, his betterment. 'The unfolding imagination must feed on what it finds nourishing—never on what it is told must be good for it. I still can't read Scott or Dickens with any joy; school, in early adolescence, destroyed them for me.'[90]

V

The Carnegie UK Trust, in presenting its report on unemployed young people in 1943, observed that 'the only activity of school-life carried into the post-school years to any appreciable extent was reading'.[91] Indeed, at this time children aged 10–16 were active readers, particularly of bloods, school stories, and adventures. In general, there was less differentiation in reading tastes among children of different classes than there was among adults. To a large degree,

[88] Jephcott, *Rising Twenty*, 80.   [89] *The Times* (9 Jan. 1925), 7.
[90] Quoted in 'George Mackay Brown', *Contemporary Authors Autobiography Series*, 6 (1988), 66.
[91] *Disinherited Youth, A Report on the 18+ Age Group Enquiry Prepared for the Trustees of the Carnegie U.K. Trust* (Edinburgh, 1943), 101.

girls, while retaining a strong interest in love and romance, also preferred 'books' (usually magazines or novelettes) normally associated
with boys and masculine tastes—notably, Westerns and thrillers, and
the 'William' and 'Biggles' series. Both boys and girls, moreover,
shared their parents' affection for light adult fiction. In some cases this
was a natural progression, from the boys' 'blood' to the 'Bulldog
Drummond' thriller, for example. The point is not so much the actual
books and authors which young people read, but the fact that the
inculcation of such reading tastes at a young age represents an important continuity between children and adults. For lower-middle- and
working-class children a 'bookless' environment at home, and a lack of
parental interest in 'quality' reading, may have encouraged their
marked preference for magazines over books; the cinema may have had
a similar effect. Children's magazines ('bloods') were shaped by these
tastes. A desire for new and exciting material favoured D. C.
Thomson's lively blend of science fiction and international settings,
while the sedate Religious Tract Society magazines, stuck in the nineteenth century, suffered the same 'antediluvian' fate as Henty, Baines
Reed, Marryat, and other authors of the same era did with young
readers in the twentieth century.

6

'GET ME THE BOY FROM THE AGE OF SIX':
D. C. THOMSON & CO., LTD.

THE most successful publisher of letterpress weekly papers for women and for boys during this period was D. C. Thomson & Co., Ltd. of Dundee. It has also been one of the more controversial. In his lifetime Mr D. C. Thomson, the founder, was branded a 'warlock', 'the newspaper Mussolini of Dundee', 'the Howard Hughes of publishing', and 'a man of reactionary views' who belonged to the 'Citizen Kane tradition'. The *Sunday Observer* in 1952 called him a legendary figure, a veritable 'Northcliffe of the North' whose influence extended far beyond the confines of his printing plant: 'The citizens of Dundee have for long been as conscious of his existence as Edinburgh people are of the Castle looming over them.'[1] On the other hand, in recognition of the firm's achievements in magazine journalism (including such titles as *The Beano* and *The People's Friend*), D.C. has been praised as 'a publishing phenomenon', 'a brilliant success story', and 'one of the most powerfully-entrenched and successful publishers in the country'. Yet in spite of such notoriety little is known about this reclusive firm; Orwell's 1940 essay provoked a strong reaction in Dundee and is a major reason why the firm to this day regards journalists and researchers with suspicion.[2] I will look here at the extraordinary success of the D. C. Thomson company by examining in turn the firm's history, the ways in which it entrenched itself as the dominant force in the market, and its editorial policies. As Jack Mackersie, an employee on the boys' papers recalled, 'I think whoever was thinking in the background was trying to shape the nation's thinking too. "Get me the boy

---

[1] 'Profile—D. C. Thomson', *Sunday Observer* (18 May 1952).

[2] As one Thomson employee said of Orwell in 1950: 'He wrote about our place once. Kicked the shit out of it, he did. They still haven't got over it. Naturally they'll do what they can to stop it happening again.' But Orwell's views were endorsed in later years by a number of writers, culminating in a scathing account of life at the firm by a former employee, George Rosie, in the *Sunday Times*. (See Benny Green, 'George Orwell, Great Wilson and the Tuppenny Bloods', *The Spectator* (26 Dec. 1970), 841; George Rosie, 'The Private Life of Lord Snooty', *Sunday Times Magazine* (29 July 1973), 8–16).

from the age of six", and working it from there.'[3] But ultimately, as with any successful publisher, this was a reciprocal relationship, with the readership dictating much of what was actually published.

I

W., D. C., & F. Thomson, the forerunner of D.C. Thomson & Co., Ltd., was founded in 1886 by a prominent Dundee family. In that year William Thomson II, a shipowner, rescued the *Dundee Courier* from financial trouble and acquired its publisher, Charles Alexander & Co. At the age of 23 his son, David Couper (D.C.) was placed in charge, soon joined by another son, Frederick. In later years D.C. would acknowledge his brother, who died in 1917, as the genius behind the firm's early success with such newspapers as the *Courier* and the *Weekly News*, and two papers for women, *Weekly Welcome* (1896–1960) and *Red Letter* (1899–1987). William Thomson died in 1896, and in 1905 the company name was changed to D. C. Thomson & Co., Ltd. The business has remained in the family's hands since. Twenty years of bitter competition with John Leng & Co., publishers of the *Dundee Advertiser* and the *Evening Telegraph*, ended in 1906 when a pooling arrangement of the two companies was reached. D. C. Thomson retained two-thirds interest in the new firm, and John Leng (three different families) one-third.[4] The companies continued to publish separately, however, until the 1930s. In time the management of both companies was assumed by D. C. Thomson. By 1939 separate advertising in trade journals ceased, replaced by listings of 'Thomson-Leng' publications, and by 1949 only one Leng family member remained on the board of directors. The Leng name, however, remains in use; it is one of several D. C. Thomson companies.

In retrospect, it is clear that the acquisition of John Leng was a shrewd investment which considerably strengthened D. C. Thomson. Leng was an established fixture in the Scottish magazine market, publishers of the most popular weekly, *The People's Friend* (1869–). They also published *The People's Journal* (1858–), a local-interest publica-

---

[3] Jack Mackersie was interviewed in 1986 and 1987. He joined the firm as a junior sub-editor on *The Skipper*. As editor of *The Hotspur* after the war, he engineered its redesign into a picture-story paper, *The New Hotspur*, in 1959.

[4] The exact reasons for this merger are unknown, but it may have been precipitated by the death, in 1906, of Sir John Leng. Leng, the founder of the publishing house, was the Liberal and Progressive MP for Dundee, and an active campaigner for the repeal of the taxes on knowledge.

tion known throughout Scotland as the 'Ploughman's Bible'. It was estimated in 1898 that the *Journal* was read by one million people every week.[5] These titles, along with *My Weekly* (1910–), *Secrets* (1932–90), and *Flame* (1935–40), were the most successful women's papers published by the firm, even after the Lengs were eclipsed on the management level. Hence, the company's statement, 'It has never been the policy to acquire outside papers (the exception being *The Scots Magazine* in 1927)', is hardly true.[6] The Leng papers, moreover, had their largest following in Scotland, thereby giving D. C. Thomson an assured market there while it concentrated on penetrating the market south of the Tweed.[7]

Thomson-Leng's letterpress weeklies for women and for boys exploited the demand for stories of romance, crime, and adventure created by light fiction and the cinema. The firm did not publish titles exclusively for men or for girls, possibly because the women's papers contained schoolgirl stories for all ages, while men were readers of two Thomson publications which attracted both sexes and all ages: the detective-thriller monthly *Dixon Hawke Library* (1919–41) and the football weekly *Topical Times* (1919–40).[8] An early attempt at entering the girls' paper market (*Blue Bird*, 1922–4) was not successful.

James Cameron remembered the Thomson women's papers as 'either unbearably sweet and wholesome, or diabolically bloodthirsty'.[9] They may indeed be divided into two categories: the romance papers

[5] Source: John Leng & Co., *How a Newspaper is Printed* (Dundee, 1898), 18. This in-house publication offers some rare information on the prosperous firm and its activities. *The People's Journal*, described as the 'mouthpiece of Scottish radicalism', interspersed serial stories, prize competitions, and a children's page with advice on legal matters, the rights of workers, and parliamentary campaigns.

[6] Source: from a brief history of D. C. Thomson & Co., Ltd., distributed by the firm today.

[7] *The People's Friend*, next to *Chambers's Journal*, 'is the most widely-circulated periodical north of the Tweed', Leopold Wagner noted in 1898 (*How to Publish a Book or Article, and How to Produce a Play* (London, 1898), 133). Arnold Bennett cited Leng among the principal publishers of novelettes (including *Aunt Kate's Penny Novels*) in 1903 (*How to Become an Author* (London, 1903), 124).

[8] The *Dixon Hawke Library* was published twice monthly, in novelette form, at 4d. This was D. C. Thomson's response to the successful Amalgamated Press detective series, *Sexton Blake*. The *Topical Times* featured pools tables, betting tips, the latest football, boxing, and automobile racing news, and stories with sporting and crime themes ('—And What a Fight!'). The correspondence columns advised readers on muscle-building and football trivia. The *Advertisers' A.B.C.* listed the circulation of the *Topical Times* as 257,386 per week between 1926 and 1930.

[9] James Cameron, *Point of Departure* (London, 1967), 31.

and the blood-and-thunder papers. The blood-and-thunder papers had exotic titles which suited their sensational brand of fiction: *Red Letter*, *Secrets*, *Flame* (merged with *Secrets* in 1940), and the oddly named *Family Star* (1934–77) and *Red Star Weekly* (1929–1983).[10] Conversely, the romance papers had a homely ring: *The People's Friend*, *My Weekly*, *Weekly Welcome*, and *Woman's Way* (1927–39, merged with *Weekly Welcome*). The longevity of most of these titles attests to the achievements of the firm in a very competitive and changing market. All the papers had in common the Thomson commitment to service features, including fashion patterns, gardening hints, recipes, picture competitions, crosswords, humour, a children's page, and the ubiquitous advice column. Here especially the knack of Thomson editors of embracing the reader and making her feel at home (the 'personal touch' used by Mills & Boon) was most apparent and effective. *Woman's Way*, for example, featured 'Secrets told to Leonora Eyles: When you come to a difficult crossroads in your life and don't know which way to turn, please confide in me.'

The average women's paper cost 2*d.*, was 32–6 pages and included between six and ten short stories and serials. The character of the fiction varied according to the class of publication. The blood-and-thunder papers, for example, featured 'daring' stories about forbidden loves, domestic violence, and crime:

'The True Story of Mary Ashford—Were These Letters from the Man who Killed Her?'

Red Letter, 20 May 1939.

'A Rogue for a Sweetheart'—He was a jailbird and a thief—but that was just the sort of man Jill Cook wanted to walk out with.

Flame, 27 May 1939.

'No Mercy in her Heart'—The Story of Joan Morgan, whose Mother-in Law stole her baby from her.

Family Star, 17 June 1939.

The romance papers, on the other hand, contained traditional, sentimental fiction, usually love stories with a little titillation:

'Someone Interested'—Just a gift of flowers, donor unknown, but they brought back youth and beauty and happiness to the lonely woman who received them.

My Weekly, 21 August 1937.

---

[10] Employees in Dundee are perplexed over the origin of the title for *Red Star Weekly*; according to one, 'Makes me think of the *Red Star Allied Weekly*'.

'A Stranger Steps In'—Janice was in love with handsome Hugh Wright, who could do everything. But that was before she taught a certain young man how to swim!

Weekly Welcome, 23 July 1938.

My Weekly and *The People's Friend* published serial stories by such popular romantic novelists as Annie S. Swan and Mary Burchell, the latter one of several Mills & Boon writers under contract. These papers incorporated a particularly large percentage of advertisements, perhaps to defray the costs of purchasing serial rights.

It is hardly surprising to discover that the readership of the Thomson women's papers varied according to the type. Most papers were designed with a specific readership profile in mind. For example, according to the firm, *Secrets*, *Red Star Weekly*, and *Flame* were founded for mill workers in Scotland and the industrial towns of Lancashire and Yorkshire. These contained the stories supposedly sought after by working-class women. 'They liked not the spicy thing in terms of sex, but the spicy thing in terms of somebody murdering somebody else, this kind of thing', David Doig, who joined D. C. Thomson in 1927, said. *Flame*, for instance, specialized in skullduggery stories: 'The heroes were baddies. This was slightly [what] we'd call downmarket.' Readers of *Red Letter* favoured a particular kind of serial story: 'a dastardly woman who schemed to get her way by murdering somebody cleverly. And then she got away with it. It was more or less a romantic detective story.'[11] In the 1940s both A. J. Jenkinson and Pearl Jephcott noted the popularity of such blood-and-thunder papers as *Red Letter* and *Red Star Weekly* among working-class adolescent girls in particular.[12]

The romance papers, on the other hand, were socially more 'exclusive', given the old-fashioned nature of the fiction. This was also reflected in the higher quality of production, more up-market advertisements, and the homely type of publicity and marketing. 'Sell to the Housewives of Britain', a Thomson advertisement proclaimed in 1931. 'The reader confidence which these papers enjoy ensures that your announcement will get a friendly hearing from a very large middle-

[11] David Doig was interviewed in 1986. He worked in turn on *The Rover*, the *Evening Telegraph*, *Topical Times*, *Weekly Welcome* and, as editor, *Woman's Way*. After the war Doig wrote feature stories for the Thomson newspapers, including the Glasgow *Sunday Post*. He retired in 1978 as general manager of the adult magazines.

[12] A. J. Jenkinson, *What Do Boys and Girls Read?* (London, 1940), 214–15; Pearl Jephcott, *Girls Growing Up* (London, 1942), 99–110; Jephcott, *Rising Twenty: Notes on Some Ordinary Girls* (London, 1948), 113.

class audience.' According to Doig, *Weekly Welcome* was for the 'business girl'. 'This magazine dealt with very romantic stories, where people travelled off. In those days there weren't so many people catching planes; it was quite a thing to go abroad, whether you went by ship or plane.' Maurice Paterson, who joined the firm in 1940, noted that *The People's Friend* in particular has enjoyed a healthy circulation over the years, especially in Scotland, because it always 'stuck to the same line of old-fashioned manners and standards and morals . . . I don't mean they're narrow-minded, but they do uphold family life.'[13] The two market-research surveys conducted for the advertising industry generally support the popularity of the women's papers, although they do call into doubt claims of a large middle-class readership.[14]

While Thomson-Leng shared the women's paper market with such strong competitors as Newnes-Pearson (*Peg's Paper, Home Notes*) and the Amalgamated Press (*Home Chat, Woman's Weekly*), it had no real competition in the boys' paper field. Here the firm's publications represent its most enduring and significant contribution to the popular press in Britain. As the Religious Tract Society set the standard for boys' periodicals in the late nineteenth century, so D. C. Thomson established the mode between the wars. Its secret involved a combination of creativity, spontaneity, and imagination which took boys out of the traditional school-story setting (unlike the Amalgamated Press[15]), confronting them with all sorts of adventures and inventions. There were boys who could disappear at will, consume wonder drugs and grow stronger, even defeat the Nazis singlehandedly, as in this example from *Adventure* (4 November 1939):

[13] Maurice Paterson was interviewed on three occasions in Dundee in 1986 and 1987. After the war he was chief sub-editor on *Secrets*, and in 1961 became editor of *My Weekly*. He retired in 1987 as managing editor of the women's magazines.
[14] In *Press Circulations Analysed* (London Research and Information Bureau, 1928), four Thomson–Leng papers, *The People's Friend, My Weekly, Weekly Welcome,* and *Red Letter* were examined. Of these, only *The People's Friend* had an appreciable middle-class readership; the others were read by the working class and the lower-middle class. *The People's Friend*, however, was only mentioned by those surveyed in Edinburgh and Glasgow. In addition to Scotland, the other papers were as popular in Newcastle, Derby, Bradford, Exeter, and Southampton. *The Hulton Readership Survey* in 1947 found that *The People's Friend* still had the greater middle-class following, but was much decreased in favour of working-class readers; *Red Letter*'s composition was unchanged. In terms of region, they were also unchanged from the 1928 survey.
[15] The *Gem* and *Magnet* were exclusively school-story papers, featuring such characters as Tom Merry and Billy Bunter. It is significant that by the later 1930s the Amalgamated Press solicited adventure stories for the *Magnet*, perhaps in a last-ditch attempt to compete with the 'Big 5' papers.

THE SCHOOL OF DEADLY SECRETS

Doomed to live in a concentration camp? Tony, Jules and Roger hear plans for their kidnapping by the Nazis! . . . Col. Gerhardt had stationed German soldiers in the Headmaster's summerhouse to kidnap the 3 pals. But the boys had heard of the plot—and bombarded the summerhouse with stinkbombs!

The Thomson boys' papers entered the market with a fresh approach, and the audience responded.

These letterpress weeklies, 2*d.* each, were known by boys and the industry alike as the 'Big 5' papers, attesting to their popularity and dominance. The Big 5 papers were *Adventure* (1921–63), *The Rover* (1922–73), *The Wizard* (1922–78), *The Skipper* (1930–41) and *The Hotspur* (1933–81). *The Skipper* was discontinued because of the paper shortage. Two other papers for boys were published but failed, victims of a saturated market: *The Vanguard* (1924–6) and *Red Arrow* (1932–3, merged with *Adventure*). The boys' papers catered for an audience aged 8–14 from all classes. As George Moonie, a Thomson veteran who worked on *The Rover*, *The Wizard*, and *The Hotspur* (and went on to found *The Beano* in 1938), claimed, 'I'm quite sure that Prince Charles read this sort of thing. I'm sure that when he came up to Glamis and stayed there as a boy, somehow our magazines would find their way to Glamis Castle.'[16] The papers were almost entirely composed of fiction, six or seven stories with a prize competition and a joke page. Each title also published an annual for the Christmas trade, usually 128 pages and an excellent seller. Physical appearance and layout were carefully planned, and even the papers' names were chosen to be evocative. 'Hotspur', for example, brought to mind thrilling adventure (Shakespeare's Harry Percy and the Border tales) as well as exciting sport (Tottenham Hotspur FC); 'Rover' recalled 'roving around'. Unlike some of the women's papers, D. C. Thomson aimed its boys' papers and comics squarely at the English market in a bid, no doubt, for both financial success and trade recognition. According to Moonie:

We really had to gear ... to the English market because that's where the large percentage of readership lay. If you look at the middle belt of England, the industrial belt—Birmingham, Wolverhampton, Manchester, Nottingham, Northampton—these big places, very heavily populated, [were] your first

---

[16] George Moonie was interviewed in 1986 and 1987. He joined the firm in 1930 as a sub-editor on *The Rover*. After the war Moonie founded two papers for girls, *Judy* and *Diana*. He retired in 1983.

target. Then the south coast of England, a great place. Scotland was only six million or so population; most of it was [in] London.

In time each boys' paper developed a unique flavour, featuring regular characters who entered folklore. Dixon Hawke, for example, was introduced in *Adventure*. The 'Wolf of Kabul', a British Secret Agent (whose faithful Himalayan companion Chung wielded a deadly cricket bat), resided in the pages of *The Wizard*, as did William 'Great' Wilson, the amazing 150-year-old athlete from Yorkshire. *The Hotspur* countered the *Gem* and *Magnet* with stories of public-school boys at the Red Circle School. Here lads from all over the world studied and played and got into all sorts of mishaps. *The Rover* followed 'Middle Wicket Mulligan', an American baseball star who became one of England's best bowlers, and Morgyn the Mighty, the Strongest Man in the World. Finally, *The Skipper* chronicled the adventures of Puck McLean, the schoolboy who possessed a 'Vanishometer' to disappear at will (particularly when threatened with a caning), and Vortz, the legendary Hooded Spy, elusive mastermind of the German Secret Service. The editors of the boys' papers concentrated on a number of popular subjects. 'You couldn't go wrong with football, or boxing, or racing; blood-and-thunder, adventure types. In those days King and Country was a great thing. Khyber Pass was a mysterious and dangerous place,' Moonie said.

By 1950 D. C. Thomson was the largest publisher of magazines outside London, with 30 titles, as compared with the London-based Amalgamated Press's 70 papers. Most of the Thomson publications, however, declined in popularity during the 1950s (the exceptions being *The Dandy* and *The Beano* comics, still very popular). In the case of the boys' papers, there were probably two reasons: the growth of television (Saturday serials which eroded demand for reading), and the appearance, not unexpectedly, of the picture-story paper, or comic. *The Eagle*, published by the Hulton Press, was an instant success in 1950, selling more than one million copies per week. As the market for its boys' papers declined, D. C. Thomson found new success in storypapers for girls, beginning with *Bunty* in 1958.

Similarly, the women's papers declined after the war, largely due to their technical inferiority to such glossy mass-market rivals as *Woman* and *Woman's Own*, both printed in colour. As a non-union house, D. C. Thomson had to train itself on the new gravure technology, a lengthy process but successful in the long run. *My Weekly*, for instance, is currently ranked eleventh in popularity among seventeen women's papers in Britain; in 1991 its average weekly sale was 475,000 copies. *The People's Friend*, still sustained by a loyal Scottish readership, has been even more successful: ninth in popularity with sales of 500,000. Somewhat surprisingly, *Red Letter* and *Secrets* continued to be published by the firm well into the 1980s. Their circulations averaged below 30,000, but as they were still printed by letterpress, D. C. Thomson could afford the production costs and keep a minority of readers satisfied.

Throughout its history the firm's provincial base, although unusual, nevertheless had its benefits. According to Moonie, D. C. Thomson had the advantage of watching over sales and distribution in the north of England and Scotland more closely and easily than its London-based competitors, which resulted in a stronger market share in those regions. Paterson added that Thomson editors were more in sympathy with the needs of the entire country, rather than simply those of London and the South. 'Up here, we work here, and then we all go to our own home, we have our own kind of friends—not journalists—and I think we're far more in touch with what goes on in the country. People in London can't see further north than Watford.'

But D. C. Thomson has had more than its share of controversies over the years. The most famous of these concerned the ban on trade unions, initiated by D.C. after a crippling strike in 1926, before the General Strike. A kind of 1920s Rupert Murdoch, D.C. required all his employees to sign a pledge agreeing never to join a union. None the less, underground unions in the Thomson offices and printing departments persisted, notably in Glasgow, where the sacking of a union sympathizer in 1952 precipitated a major industrial dispute. In the end a Ministry of Labour inquiry recommended that the firm reconsider its non-union pledge, which it did; employees were no longer obliged to sign. But D. C. Thomson remains essentially a non-union house, which is another reason why it is so secretive. As Paterson said, 'We don't want a lot of publicity. It's in a way grist to the unions.'

Relations with newsagents have also been less than cordial over the past eighty years. The firm often clashed with the National Federation of Retail Newsagents over unfair pricing, in addition to the union issue. Two retired Oxford newsagents recalled less than favourably their visits from Thomson 'reps'. Apparently, D. C. Thomson set strict limits on ordering, and refused to accept unsold copies. 'Whatever you didn't sell was your hard luck. They just didn't seem to care', H. R.

Wyatt recalled. 'The trouble was, the magazines and stuff they were selling were popular, and they got you. You had to sell it because people wanted it.' R. D. Cooper assumed that by keeping supplies low D. C. Thomson helped to increase demand. 'If you keep a thing tight, people have always got that impression that they'll [have to] have it. A lot of people would like to be one up on the neighbours: "I've got one". A system operated by Mercedes-Benz.'[17]

II

The best way to gauge the success of the D. C. Thomson papers for women and for boys is through circulation figures. Unfortunately, few independent sources for these exist, apart from a handful of advertising journals (which largely disregarded boys' papers). Although circulation figures are a closely guarded secret at D. C. Thomson, the firm has released some figures which do confirm its supremacy in the market. According to L. Murray Thomson, one of the present directors of the firm, these figures are an accurate representation of the trends in sales during our period of analysis, until 1950.[18] Figure 6.1 shows the circulation of the boys' papers for three dates: the first issue sale; January 1939; and January 1950. To place these in perspective, the following figures exist for 1924 Amalgamated Press titles.[19]

Boy's Friend	99,794
Boy's Herald	55,514
Boy's Realm	114,653
Nelson Lee Library	112,289
'Union Jack Series' (including *Union Jack*, *Marvel*, *Magnet*, *Gem*)	354,694

Certainly, given these lower figures, the launch of the Thomson papers in the early 1920s was impressive. In fact, judging from the reputation of

[17] H. R. Wyatt and R. D. Cooper were interviewed in 1988. Wyatt opened his newsagent's shop in Cowley Road in 1945; Cooper in Botley Road in 1955.

[18] There is no reason to doubt the accuracy of the figures released by D. C. Thomson. The 1939 figures, for example, correspond to claims made by Thomson–Leng in an advertisement in that year. The 'Big 5' papers were advertised as selling 'Over a Million Copies Weekly'; The 'Family Three' (*Family Star*, *Secrets*, and *Red Letter*) a 'combined circulation 600,000 copies weekly'; and the 'Feminine Five' (*Red Letter*, *Red Star Weekly*, *My Weekly*, *Woman's Way*, and *Woman's Welcome*) 'Over 1,250,000 Copies Weekly' (*The Newspaper Press Directory*, 1939 edn., 364). It is unfortunate, however, that annual circulation statistics, which would reveal sales fluctuations more precisely, were not released by the firm.

[19] *The Advertisers' A.B.C.*, 38th edn. (1924), 133–4.

Thousands

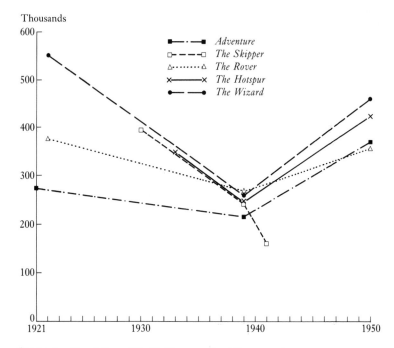

FIGURE 6.1. Circulations of D. C. Thomson Boys' Papers, 1921–1950
Source: D. C. Thomson & Co., Ltd. First figures are 'No. 1 sale'. The 1941 figure
for *The Skipper* is the last number sale.

the Big 5 papers, one can safely assume these sales were the top end of
the market. The Thomson circulation figures, moreover, confirm the
general downward trend for magazines in Britain before the Second
World War, and the dramatic recovery which the wartime reading
boom prompted.[20] Bearing in mind, as the trade did, that each copy
sold was read by at least three boys, in 1950, for example, *The Wizard*
was probably read by 1.5 million boys weekly.[21]

Figures 6.2 and 6.3 show sales information, on similar dates, for the

[20] Although Kevin Carpenter, in *Penny Dreadfuls and Comics: English Periodicals for
Children from Victorian Times to the Present Day* (London, 1983), claims that *The Wizard*
reached a peak circulation before the war of 800,000 copies per week, the Thomson
figures do not support this (p. 65).

[21] 'We couldn't afford to buy them all—*Wizard, Adventure, Rover, Hotspur, Skipper*—
but we managed to get hands on most of them by some complex form of barter', George
Mackay Brown recalled, adding that parents and teachers 'disapproved' ('George
Mackay Brown', *Contemporary Authors Autobiography Series*, 6 (1988), 65–6).

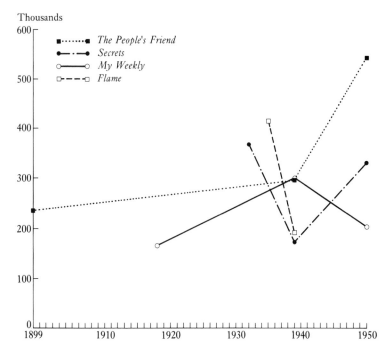

FIGURE 6.2. Circulations of John Leng Women's Papers, 1899–1950
Source: D. C. Thomson & Co., Ltd. *Flame* combined with *Secrets* in 1940.

women's papers.[22] Curiously, three titles, *The People's Friend, My Weekly* (both Leng), and *Red Letter*, seem to have resisted the market depression during the 1930s, perhaps attesting to the loyalty of their readers (Scottish women for the former two, and working-class women for the latter) and the skill with which D. C. Thomson picked its markets. The same specialized readerships, moreover, sustained *Secrets, Red Star Weekly*, and *Family Star* during their unusually long runs. The actual number of readers, it is worth repeating, would be much higher. The Hulton Readership Survey in 1947, for example, estimated the weekly readership of *Red Letter* at 970,000, and *The People's Friend* at 1.06 million.

As the women's papers contained more advertisements than the

[22] According to D. C. Thomson, the first issue sales figures for *The People's Friend, Weekly Welcome, Red Letter*, and *My Weekly* are unknown; the earliest available date for each title was provided instead.

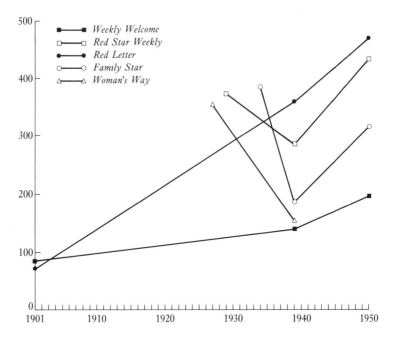

FIGURE 6.3. Circulations of D. C. Thomson Women's Papers, 1901–1950
Source: D. C. Thomson & Co., Ltd. *Woman's Way* combined with *Weekly Welcome* in 1939 and its title changed to *Woman's Welcome.*

children's publications, other sources of circulation and readership statistics exist, helping to place the Thomson statistics in perspective. In Figure 6.4 three papers are considered: *The People's Friend*, *Weekly Welcome*, and *Red Letter*. Circulation figures obtained independently of D. C. Thomson are plotted against the 'official' figures. As D. C. Thomson did not provide statistics for the First World War and the interwar years, these trade figures help to flesh out the broad outlines created by the Thomson figures and reveal fluctuations in the market. The strong and consistent demand for *Red Letter*[23] and *The People's Friend* is generally supported, while a large decline in sales for *Weekly*

[23] Throughout 1914, advertisements in *Red Letter* described the paper as having 'Over One Million Readers Weekly'. According to the available evidence, this was probably an exaggeration. However, some copies of *Red Letter*, which had a circulation of about 200,000 in 1914, could certainly have been passed round to five, or even more, people—in a factory, for instance.

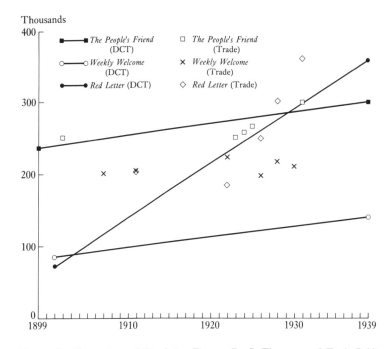

FIGURE 6.4. Comparison of Circulation Figures, D. C. Thomson and Trade Publications
Sources: 1899, 1901, 1939: D. C. Thomson & Co., Ltd.; 1902: Thomas Smith and J. H. Osborne (eds.), *Successful Advertising: Its Secrets Explained*, 21st edn.; 1907, 1911, 1922: *The Newspaper (Benn's) Press Directory*; others: *The Advertisers' A.B.C.*

Welcome between 1930 and 1939 is shown. According to the readership surveys conducted by *Investigated Press Circulations* in 1932, in England and Wales *Red Letter* was the fourth most popular 'Ladies Paper' (so labelled by *IPC*), with an estimated 595,000 readers, or 1.25 per cent of the population. The most popular titles were *Woman's Weekly* (1,093,000 readers); *Home Notes* (684,000), and *Home Chat* (601,000). *Red Letter* readers were about equally divided between the middle and working classes. In Scotland, *The People's Friend* outsold all other women's weeklies, with an estimated 1,520,000 readers, or 24.1 per cent of the population. Next most popular in Scotland were four other Thomson titles: *My Weekly* (203,000 readers; 3.2 per cent); *Red Letter* (184,000; 2.9 per cent); and *Red Star Weekly* (80,000; 1.3 per cent). Again, readership was divided among all classes. *Woman's*

Weekly in Scotland only attracted 45,000 readers, or 0.7 per cent. Audited figures for the average weekly circulation of a number of the leading papers also illustrate that the Thomson titles were matching or surpassing their competitors in the letterpress market, with some exceptions. *Woman's Own* and *Woman* were gravure-printed and in colour, and thus belonged to a separate stratum of the market:[24]

	1938	1950
Woman	750,000	2.2 million
Woman's Own	357,000	1.8 million
Woman's Weekly	498,000	1.6 million
Woman's Illustrated	148,000	559,000
Home Notes	151,000	349,000
Woman's Companion	176,000	221,000
Home Chat	127,000	323,000

The 'Big 5' boys' papers were frequently and prominently mentioned in reading surveys during this period, as noted in the last chapter. They were, for example, the most popular magazines among boys of all classes in the 1933 St Pancras survey and in Jenkinson's 1940 survey. Jenkinson also noted a strong interest among girls in these titles. Although they were well aware of girl readers, Thomson editors made no allowances for them, believing that these were papers for boys, and boys only. Girls were specifically addressed in the Thomson comics, and eventually in storypapers founded in the late 1950s. Jenkinson's survey also revealed the high percentage of schoolgirls aged 12–14 who were avid readers of the Thomson blood-and-thunder papers ('erotic bloods') including *Red Letter*. Similarly, Brew in 1943 announced that 'an astonishing number of *Wizards* and *Red Letters* are read' among adolescents of both sexes.[25]

Mass-Observation also measured the popularity of the Thomson papers. For example, one working-class man in 1942 stated, 'I never buy books, I only read the *The Wizard*.'[26] A Fulham newsagent, when asked in 1940 which magazines were generally most popular, replied, '*Red Star* and that sort of thing. You know they want just short stories

---

[24] Source: Cynthia L. White, *Woman's Magazines 1693–1968* (London, 1970), Appendices IV and V.

[25] J. MacAlister Brew, *In the Service of Youth: A Practical Manual of Work among Adolescents* (London, 1943), 129.

[26] M/25/D, Mass-Observation, *Report on Books and the Public: A Study of Buying, Borrowing, Keeping, Selecting, Remembering, Giving, and Reading* BOOKS (File Report 1332, M-O, 2 July 1942), 5.

and things like that.'[27] Another newsagent recorded the Thomson share of the market in his weekly sales report for the last week in February 1940. It is remarkable how many Thomson titles appear alongside the quality competition. Of 48 titles on his list, nine were Thomson papers, accounting for 17 per cent of total sales, although no paper sold more than six copies, as compared with twenty-six copies each of *Everybody's* and *Radio Times*.[28] Finally, the 1937 Middlesbrough inquiry revealed both fans and critics of the Big 5 papers. William (L/4/B) was critical: 'Some books such as the "Rover" and the "Skipper" are books which put fantastic ideas into boys' heads.' But another boy (U/4/A) found reading *The Hotspur* educational:

Many of the stories are about foreign countries; they are adventure stories and about two paragraphs tell us how foreigners live. Therefore they tell us about some geographical parts of that country.

Other stories tell us about things that happened years ago e.g. in 'The Hotspur' a story called 'The wearer of the Scarlet Acorn must not die'. While we read it, small pictures of historical nature are in our mind. This story is about 'Hadrian's Wall', therefore pictures of that kind come to our minds . . .

Most people like reading, and I think some stories are thrilling and yet help us in our educational life.[29]

D. C. Thomson's prominent position in the market was not achieved, nor maintained, by chance. Although editors are inclined to deny it, throughout its history D. C. Thomson has kept a firm finger on the national pulse by vigorously researching its readers and their changing tastes. Several methods, some of them novel, were used to identify and cater to the readership. A Thomson innovation, for example, was the editorial page, featuring a snappy, inviting title and a warm, friendly article which not only made the reader feel at home but encouraged him to write in with information. The editor of *The Skipper* addressed all his 'pals', 'What about sending me a postcard telling me all about yourself and your chums?' *The Wizard* featured a page headed, 'Step Right Up and Have a Chat with Your Editor!' In an early issue it proceeded:

My dear chums,
    See the heading? That's the spirit. No hanky-panky, get right down to bedrock and have a chat, you and I, like two pals . . .

[27] George's Newsagent, Dawes Road, Fulham, M-O 'Newspapers' Box 2 File D (1 Mar. 1940).

[28] S. Hughes & Co., Estcourt Road, Fulham, M-O 'Newspapers' Box 2 File D (2 Mar. 1940).

[29] M-O 'Reading' Box 1 File B (9 Sept. 1937).

You have as big a hand in the pie as I have. I've done a great deal of scouting around and have chatted away with hundreds of boys to find out what kind of yarns they like best . . .

I was pleased to discover that their tastes and mine were the same. I want stories of sports and stories of adventure, real go-ahead lively yarns with a kick in them . . .

> Signed, Your Pal, The Editor.

One issue alone of *The Wizard* featured letters from Wigan, Cardiff, Dover, Kingstown, Heysham, Barrow, Larne, Sheffield, Manchester, Nairn, Ealing, Cork, Wexford, and Inverness. The Big 5 papers also received letters from 'Old Boys', fathers who were still regular readers, and were now bringing up their children (as Mackersie put it) 'in the faith'.

The editors of the women's papers also promoted a warm and friendly attitude in their columns.[30] The first issue of *Woman's Way* in 1927 promised 'to give you a paper which will be a "complete chum" to you every week, and which will appeal to the wide and ever-growing interests of the modern woman and girl'. The first issue of *Flame* in 1935 asked its readers, 'When you write, please tell me all about your-selves. I want every one of us to be real friends, and the more I know about you—who you are, what you do, and everything else—the sooner we shall all be able to get to know each other.' A 1934 letters page in *Family Star* revealed that men enjoyed the paper; one, signed 'Old Soldier' from Cardiff, said: 'I'm ill in hospital with a bad leg, and my wife brought me your book to read yesterday. Believe me, it's made to-day fly, and I've hardly felt my leg at all, I've been so interested in the stories.'[31]

Another Thomson novelty was the frequent, sometimes lucrative, prize competitions and giveaways in each paper. These also generated response from readers, although often in an unwelcome volume. Doig lamented the occasions when a paper asked readers to send in their favourite stories, 'which were always a bane to everybody's existence because we'd get as many as 6,000 job stories, and somebody had to

---

[30] The editor of the Thomson women's papers was usually a man, who signed his weekly column 'Your Editress'. Thomson editors found nothing unusual in this, saying, 'a job was a job'.

[31] Similarly, Annie S. Swan, commenting on the craze for serial stores in *The People's Friend*, claimed that women 'no doubt, form the main body of readers, but a good many men, I have heard, do not despise the *People's Friend' (My Life: An Autobiography* (London, 1934), 284).

read them. We all took the stuff home, and we'd be up to our ears in stories. It took about six months to find a winner.' Twice-yearly the Thomson publications were 'pushed': the push usually coincided with the start of a new serial story. If successful, a push could influence weekly sales by as many as 70,000 copies. Among the more bizarre giveaways in the boys' papers, apart from the usual footballs, cricket bats, and sweets, were the electric shock machines offered with the first issue of *The Hotspur* in 1933: 'It's a great prize, absolutely harmless and will give hours of fun. Just watch your pal's face when you give him his first electric shock!' The women's papers, in addition to fashion patterns, recipes, and cosmetics, gave away a large number of love charms, fortune-telling guides and gypsy rings, usually tied in with the notorious murder of Maria Marten in the Red Barn. The public appetite for fortune-telling during this period was, apparently, insatiable; any giveaway of this kind was a guaranteed sell-out. In 1927 'The Gipsy Queen Book of Fortune Telling', presented free with *My Weekly*, contained such revelations as, 'If a baby cries a lot he will have great happiness in life, and make many friends' and 'When bread does not rise well the housewife should beware of meeting a red-haired man before seeing someone of her family, as bad luck is sure to follow the baking'. Similarly, the sequel publication on 'Dream Meanings' warned, 'To dream of varnish is a sign of unexpected distress' and 'You will talk to a foreigner if you dream of melons'.

Thomson representatives, or 'reps', were frequently dispatched to newsagents and schools throughout the country to eavesdrop on gossip about their publications. Jack Mackersie, one-time editor of *The Hotspur*, noted that during this period a newsagent was an excellent source of information as to why a boy bought a Big 5 paper every week, or decided not to one week, or stopped buying one altogether. 'A newsagent was on the ball, paying attention to customers' likes and dislikes. They would *know* what stories the kids liked and what stories they didn't like. Quite often a newsagent's kids themselves would tell them', he said. Reports from the reps were received in Dundee on a monthly basis, and sales were carefully monitored, particularly during push times. In the case of the boys' papers, Moonie explained that a common practice was to send reps to the major cities, such as London and Manchester, to stand outside school gates, both to ask departing boys about the papers and to inform them of any upcoming pushes or new features. This procedure was known in Dundee as 'speering'.[32] 'This, of course, was frowned upon by school authorities because confronting children at school gates was a dicey, touchy business', Moonie noted. 'So it had to be done with permission. We got a lot of information.'

Finally, editorial departments on each of the Big 5 papers were deliberately stocked with younger men, some just out of school. It was assumed (as Mills & Boon did, with their youngish authors) that such men would be more in touch with the current readership, resulting in a lively, up-to-date paper. The Amalgamated Press maintained the opposite policy, to its detriment, as W. O. G. Lofts noted after speaking to some of its editors:

Several have confessed to me that they were told by their Department chiefs to 'modernise' their papers, and this they were loth to do, mainly because of the old traditions and seemingly high standard of literature held at Fleetway House. The main trouble was that they were still producing papers appealing to boys of the twenties and did not move with the times.[33]

Moonie added that the Big 5 papers were as susceptible to changing tastes as were the women's papers. 'You don't want too foreign a background; you want a normal sort of background, with normal people. You've got to keep up-to-date, have your eye on the papers and your ear to what's going on in school. Kids have got to identify; if he doesn't understand it, it's finished.' He said that editors, in an effort to remain current and lively with boys, 'went to various things for story ideas: books, cinema, newspaper, other periodicals, the radio, and certainly television, which of course was coming into its own'.

III

Lofts, in praising D. C. Thomson and the Big 5 papers, also wrote, 'The great success of all their papers is simply that they (the editors) were brilliant psychologists, as they seemed to know what exactly boys wanted to read and prepared their papers accordingly.'[34] The same could be said for the editors of the women's papers, and the hallmark of D. C. Thomson throughout the period was editorial control. The presence of D.C., until his death in 1954, loomed large in all facets of

[32] 'Speering', according to the *Oxford English Dictionary* (2nd edn.) is derived from Scottish and northern dialect, meaning 'The action of questioning or inquiring; interrogation; inquiry' and 'Information obtained by inquiry'.

[33] W. O. G. Lofts and D. J. Adley, *The Men Behind Boys' Fiction* (London, 1970), 13.

[34] W. O. G. Lofts, letter, *The Spectator* (30 Jan. 1971), 169.

Plate 5: 'The Fiction Department', D. C. Thomson & Co., Ltd., Bank Street offices, Dundee, *c* 1925. Presumably this department commissioned and edited stories for the Thomson weeklies and newspapers.

production, and particularly editorial policy. Alfred Anderson, who joined the firm in 1925 and subsequently worked on *Adventure*, *The Vanguard*, and the *Dixon Hawke Library*, recalled the chairman as possessing a relentless, hard-as-nails personality: 'He was terribly strict. He was very much the leader of the band. He didn't like anything smutty in his papers at all. It's not so awfully long ago when you got a picture with a bit of cleavage in it, and you had to think.'[35] Company policy ensured close personal contact between employees at all levels. 'The team spirit has been well developed through the whole business. Every problem that arises is thoroughly discussed by directors, managers and editors concerned', D.C. wrote. 'I do not agree with the proprietors of other papers who leave all policy to the editors, for I hold that the proprietor is ultimately responsible for every word published.'[36] Mackersie recalled the fear among sub-editors of straying beyond set boundaries, of annoying 'Upstairs', from whence 'Policy' came. 'I only ventured in on tiptoe when I was sent [for by Upstairs]. You got the hell out of [there] as quick as possible, you know, because all the powers that be were up there.'

None the less, it is difficult to find any real signs of resentment of D. C. Thomson's strict ways and views among employees, despite the absence of unions. Morale was high, and the paternalistic nature of the firm guaranteed good wages and job security (even during the depression) for as long as an employee wished to work. When a paper failed, staff were not laid off, but transferred to other duties. Such reorganization was relatively painless at D. C. Thomson, given the numbers involved; only five or six people worked on the editorial side of each paper, for example, as compared with forty or fifty on each at the Amalgamated Press. Hence, it was not uncommon for employees to join the firm at the age of 16, and to stay in Dundee for fifty years or more; Doig, for instance, retired in 1978 after fifty-one years; Anderson in 1979 after fifty-four years.[37] The tribute paid by Glasgow

[35] Alfred Anderson was interviewed in 1986 and 1987. He later became editor of the *Topical Times*. He retired in 1979 as managing editor of the newspapers.

[36] D. C. Thomson, 'Memorandum by Mr. D. C. Thomson, Chairman and Senior Managing Director, D. C. Thomson & Co. Ltd. and John Leng & Co. Ltd.', published in Royal Commission on the Press, *Minutes of Evidence*, 27th day (31 Mar. 1948), 8.

[37] Whether such loyalty was unique to D. C. Thomson or common among Scottish firms is open to question. John Leng was apparently also known for friendly terms between employer and employees: the 1898 in-house publication testified to 'the goodwill' and 'most cordial' relations. 'There is a veteran who has, as boy and man, been 55 years in the service, and looks as if he was equal to another decade of service. Several

workers to D.C. on the occasion of his jubilee in 1934 was typical of the general good will: 'We have always looked up to him as the head of the family. He has won our confidence by his just, generous and fair-minded consideration of all matters affecting the welfare of his ever-growing household.'[38] And there was a certain egalitarian camaraderie: Paterson attributed his firm's eighty years of success to the cordial relations between employees:

The biggest reason for success in this firm comes from the top. Our directors are very approachable people. In a way, although you're never friends with them, you're friendly with them. I mean I've golfed with my directors at Gleneagles and Turnberry, I've drunk with them, I've argued with them. There comes a time when the argument has to stop, and if I haven't convinced them then I'm the one who has to give way. But that's very rarely.

Mackersie remembered his years at D. C. Thomson with great affection: 'Everything was a lovely golden haze.'[39]

Possibly one reason for such harmony was that employees appear to have been carefully screened so as to be compatible with the firm and its policies. Mackersie said that each applicant for a job at D. C. Thomson had to sit a test paper, 'to try and find out which way your imagination or your brain or your thoughts tended. On that, on your general knowledge as to the world about you, you either got a position or you didn't.' He added that no particular rules of behaviour or morality for employees were specified; it was taken for granted that you would know how to behave. 'You've got to be morally correct with children, and with yourself too. It was in you to be like that, otherwise you wouldn't be in that job. This is where your interview, your background and your test paper showed what you were made of.'[40]

members of the staff have served 45 years, others 40 and 30 years, and a large number have been upwards of 25 years in the office. The apprentices are almost without exception sons or other relatives of the employees' (p. 23).

[38] 'Jubilee Presentation to Mr. D. C. Thomson', *Dundee Courier and Advertiser* (18 Dec. 1934).

[39] But times, and attitudes, change. In 1987 Paterson claimed that the same spirit of dedication and hard work was diminishing at the firm. 'The generations behind us are completely different from what we worked with. Even the staffs are different; they don't have the same loyalty or dedication ... I don't mean that they slack, but their own personal lives are equally important. I can't argue with that, but in my day if we had a problem, or we were running late, the staff would come in and work in the evening without being asked. Nowadays if you ask them to come in the evening there's an awful lot of discontent.'

[40] Julie Davidson, who was employed at D. C. Thomson in the early 1960s, has described the firm's intelligence test in her article, 'Speak Softly and Say Yes Please', in a collection of critical essays, *The D. C. Thomson Bumper Fun Book* (Edinburgh, 1977).

The relationship between writer and editor at D. C. Thomson was exceptionally close, probably to ensure that stories were written to the firm's strict specifications. As Lofts noted of the boys' papers: 'On the question of which was the easiest firm to write for—D. C. Thomson or the Amalgamated Press—many authors have told me (in writing for both firms) that the former was the most difficult and their stories had to be right up to the highest standard every time.'[41] Perhaps this was the reason why D. C. Thomson never printed bylines above stories, except in the book-format Christmas annuals. 'The thing is, was it the writer's work entirely, or was it editorial and writer, in combination, producing it?' Moonie explained. All of the writers (and most of the artists for the few line illustrations) were freelance; none was kept on staff. Senior editors paid periodic visits to writers to give them a roster of story ideas for six months of work. Those writers who have been identified came from a variety of backgrounds and wrote for both the boys' papers and the women's papers. Their output was enormous. Dugald Matheson Cumming-Skinner of Dundee, one of the most prolific contributors, claimed to have written eight million words of fiction during his eight years as a freelance writer. Gilbert Dalton once wrote every short story in *The Hotspur* for eight consecutive weeks. Frank Howe wrote 150 *Dixon Hawke Libraries*.[42] Anderson noted that the writers themselves were 'moral' men who could be trusted not to breach company policy. One, Jimmy Watt, 'would never write a thing out of line—he was such a nice bloke, a fairly elderly fellow', Anderson said. 'Dugald Cumming-Skinner—his father was a minister. All was very right, you know—no great violence or anything like that.' None the less, the Thomson editorial grip on its writers was strong. As Norman Fowler, who joined the firm in 1934 and eventually became editor of *The Wizard*, explained, the writer 'would get on our wavelength. We would channel his way of thinking to our needs.'[43] Similar attention was paid

---

[41] Lofts and Adley, *The Men Behind Boys' Fiction*, 13.

[42] Ibid. 109–10, 111, 198–9. Cumming-Skinner started work for D. C. Thomson after winning a juvenile literary competition run by John Leng; he 'soon became their most prolific contributor'. Similarly, just after the First World War the romance-thriller writer Jean Marsh got her first job in journalism after winning £25 ('a fortune in those days') in a Christmas short-story competition run by *The People's Friend*. The editor contacted her afterwards asking if she would write a serial for them. James Cameron's father contributed stories to the Thomson blood-and-thunder papers; the rate of pay was 30*s.* per 1,000 words.

[43] Norman Fowler was interviewed in 1986. Fowler also worked on *The Hotspur* and *The Rover*, retiring in 1986 as director of the girls' papers.

by editors of the women's papers to authors of romantic fiction who contributed serials; Mary Burchell and Jean S. Macleod of Mills & Boon, for example. In 1934 Annie S. Swan was florid in her praise for John Leng and *The People's Friend*, in which she launched her career as a novelist:

Its public has been loyal and faithful to me for over fifty years, and there is no visible sign of waning enthusiasm even yet. The *People's Friend* has been ably edited by men who knew their public, its limitations, and its quality. I have fitted in—that is all: and much of my best work has appeared in its pages.[44]

The concern of both editor and writer, Doig added, was to tug at the reader's heart-strings. 'You know if you have this very great emotional ending—which is the "lump-in-the-throat" bit—you are going to have a saleable story', he said. Although he privately admitted, as Mills & Boon did, that most fiction was written to a perfected and marketable formula, Doig claimed that editors tried to make each story seem fresh and unique. 'You must try and put so much into the writing of it, that it seems you don't seem to have read the story before.'

D. C. Thomson did not mind serving up sensations in its women's magazines, if they sold papers—and they did. The morals, however, were under all circumstances proper and correct. According to Doig, Thomson editors were very strict indeed. Drinking and smoking were not allowed, nor was the mention of the unmarried man or the adulterous woman. 'Oh, no affairs. No, no, no. You weren't allowed to enter that at all', he said. Adultery, in fact, was regarded as as great a sin as robbery, even murder. Divorce was also forbidden, and nothing bad was ever said about the mother in a story. 'Crime does not pay' was a common theme. Doig accepted that writing with all these editorial restrictions in mind was difficult and challenging, 'except when you went straight for it. What you could do, you'd have a nasty woman who everybody was terribly amazed about, who killed the poor little girl who was going to marry the man she wanted. This was all right, because it was just a straightforward sin.'

According to Paterson, in Dundee there was always a way around being too smutty and explicit in romantic serials. 'You can take somebody up to the bedroom door, but once the door's closed you don't need the colourful details. That's the difference between us and other magazines', he said. In violent situations, as when a character had vitriol thrown in her face, 'we didn't dwell on the screams of agony or this or

[44] Swan, *My Life*, 283–4.

that. It was a sentence, and that was it. We got the effect we wanted.'
Paterson also gave the example of a story situation in which a man and
woman were snowbound in Canada, found shelter, and obviously had
to spend the night in the same room. What the Thomson editors decided was to have two beds, with a blanket hung between them—*and* to
reveal that the man was a doctor, which made everything all right.[45]
There are few things D. C. Thomson has not done, Paterson said—it
was simply the way it has done them.

James Cameron is illuminating on this question of just how far
editors would go, in terms of violence and sex. In the 1930s Cameron
worked on *Red Star Weekly*, 'which catered for a public of working girls
whose tastes must have verged on the sadistic, so heavily were our pages
soaked in gore'. But while D. C. Thomson allowed its readers 'good
clean violence', it never introduced a sexual dimension:

The most frightful things were encouraged to happen: stranglings, knifings,
shootings, disembowelings, burials alive, hauntings, drownings, suffocations,
torments of a rich and varied nature abounded, and each instalment was
obliged to end with a suspenseful promise of worse to come, but in no circumstances and at no point was permitted even the hint of sexual impropriety. This
was the ark of the covenant and the cornerstone of our editorial principles.

Cameron offered as an example the illustration ordered for one issue's
cover which depicted the body of a woman whose throat had just been
cut. When he showed it to David Donald, managing director of the
women's papers, he was soundly rebuked.

Accepting that I might possibly on this occasion have overdone it, I murmured:
'It is a bit strong, maybe.'
   'Strong, strong,' cried Mr Donald. 'It's no' a question o' strong; it's no' a bad
scene. But for God's sake, boy—look at the lassie's skirt; it's awa' above her
knees!'
   Abashed, I realized what rule I had broken. I took the drawing back and had
the hemline lowered a modest inch or two, and in the cover went, slit windpipe
and all.[46]

The parallel here between D. C. Thomson and Mills & Boon is significant. Both firms knew exactly what their distinctive readerships
wanted: in D. C. Thomson's case, good, clean violence; in Mills &

---

[45] Reminiscent of the Clark Gable–Claudette Colbert bedroom scene in the Frank
Capra film *It Happened One Night* (1934).
[46] Cameron, *Point of Departure*, 31–2.

Boon's, a realistic romance. Both also stretched these limits, often most creatively—but only to a point, that point being sexual propriety. Given their owner's staunch Presbyterian beliefs, this is not surprising in Dundee; as for Mills & Boon, it was to reflect, as we have seen, a kind of middle-class idealism.

On the Big 5 papers, company policy also kept morals and subject-matter in tight check. Correct spelling and grammar were essential; as an editor of *The Beano* once said, 'A high standard of English is strictly adhered to at all times nowadays with mis-spellings, abbreviations and slang carefully vetted.'[47] Expletives may have been acceptable in the pages of the *Gem* and *Magnet*,[48] but never in the Big 5. Moonie summarized the taboo subjects at D. C. Thomson as follows:

You see we never stepped into politics, we avoided religion, and we never took advantage of people who were crippled and hurt in some way. We never did that. We really kept it very straight, moral. If there was anything bad, it had to be rectified. If anybody did anything that was wrong, it had to be punished. It was editorial policy throughout all the papers to keep a very strict control over what went into publication.

In fact, not much has changed in the editorial policy governing the children's papers for some seventy years.

The overriding concern of editors on both the women's papers and the boys' weeklies was not to step out of line, and risk offending the readership, or the readership's parents—which could jeopardize circulations. Doig noted that the women's magazines, however sensational, were still regarded as 'family' papers. As such, there was 'always the fear that the mother in the family would say, "I'm not having that paper in the house", and that would be it'. This reasoning would explain ostentatious efforts to make the more obviously sensational papers, such as *Red Letter* and *Red Star Weekly*, acceptable by subtitling them 'For the Family Circle', and including such features as a children's page. Paterson said that it would have been foolish to have tried to be offensive: 'If you have a readership that's family-minded, that wouldn't like their son living with his girlfriend, and that was the

[47] From a confidential script on the history of the D. C. Thomson children's papers, prepared at Moonie's request; no date. When asked how he learned to write, Kingsley Amis thanked the boys' papers he had devoured as a child. 'Nowadays you'd think it was Graham Greene who invented beginning a story with dialogue, but people who'd read *Magnet* and *The Wizard* knew all about that' (Ray Connolly, 'A Childhood: Kingsley Amis', *The Times* (24 Mar. 1990), 35).

[48] In *The Magnet*, for example, Billy Bunter was often described as 'esteemed and idiotic', a 'fat chump', a 'howling ass', and a 'blithering bloater'.

core of your readership, there's no use starting to put in things that's going to offend them.' Moonie noted that even the choice of slang words in the boys' papers was carefully scrutinized, so as to avoid antagonizing the readership—in this case, the boys' parents. 'Some of the words that had been adapted, like "Gadzooks", is "Godsakes". You might get people mistaking it and objecting to this type of language. We did get rebukes now and then.' The purpose of the papers was to entertain and to inform, not to offend, and, judging from circulation figures, they were successful in this.

IV

According to Fowler, a good editor at D. C. Thomson 'will impose his ideas on the reader. The reader believes that this is the kind of story he wants to read. But really, the editor is saying, "This is the kind of story that I know you will want to read."' In this fashion D. C. Thomson passed on socially acceptable views on a number of issues to its readership. A selection of excerpts will illustrate how editorial policy was actually translated into fiction, and show the types of wish-pictures and symbols in use. The loyalty of thousands of readers each week to a particular publication is probably a fair indication that a kind of affinity did exist between editor and reader.

Two themes are prominent in the fiction in the Thomson women's papers during this period: the promotion of old-fashioned romance (without any sexual references) and the struggle, often violent, between the forces of good and evil (a staple in the blood-and-thunder papers). *My Weekly* and *The People's Friend* were the two women's papers which consistently promoted a notion of 'feel-good' romance. Stories were advertised as 'strong in heart interest'; the 'lump-in-the-throat' sensation which Doig described was omnipresent. Happy endings were essential:

'Babyclothes', by Gertrude Taylor
You'd think there could only be happiness at a baby linen counter—young mothers in the first pride of parenthood, little blushing mothers with dreams in their eyes, new-made grannies so bustling and important. And yet the girl who sold these little soft garments to those happy people had only sad, wistful dreams.

My Weekly, 3 December 1927.

Plate 6: 'The *Red Letter* Room', D. C. Thomson & Co., Ltd., Bank Street offices, Dundee, *c.*1925. Oddly, the staff is entirely female except for a male secretary; this may have been staged for publicity purposes.

'Follow Your Heart', by Netta Muskett
At last for Eve the Storm is over—and she finds Peace and Contentment in the
Haven of Jeremy's arms.

My Weekly, 21 August 1937.

'The Lovely Day'
Try it any way you like, it's still a plain, no-nonsense kind of name ... But she
needn't always be Jane Brown. One day she would marry—one lovely, lovely
day.

My Weekly, 2 December 1950.

The skill of both writers and editors in moulding the same formula into
different storylines is remarkable. The central character was usually a
shopgirl, secretary, or a poor farmer's daughter who was either unlucky
in love or suddenly met the man of her dreams—precisely the sort of
scenario that would appeal to the readership. In 'Beauty in Distress', a
serial which ran in *The People's Friend* in 1914, Freda meets Dick
during a difficult Channel crossing. Dick turns out to be the nephew of
Freda's horrible boss, who has just sacked her as his private secretary.
In one short paragraph Freda's fears of unemployment and a life alone
vanish:

'Be my wife,' he said softly. 'I've loved you for ever so long—I believe ever
since we first met on the Calais–Dover boat. I felt then that I wanted to take care
of you and kiss away that frightened look in your eyes and now I want to more
than ever.'
    He laid his hand on her shoulder with a sudden caressing movement. She
made no effort to release herself . . .[49]

Paterson admitted that writers during this period were greatly inspired by the cinema. There was an affinity between fiction and film. 'In
those days your films were love stories. A woman could sit in the cinema
and identify, just as she could sit at home and read a serial and
identify', he said. The cinema, in fact, was probably responsible for the
striking change in focus in the Thomson romance papers between the
wars (as it was at Mills & Boon). During the First World War, and
immediately afterwards, stories often had a gritty, realistic, and overtly
working-class edge to them. Settings, for instance, were harsher—
factories or the inner cities, probably where most of the readers worked
or lived. 'Molly King, The Mill-Girl Detective' ('Molly King was only
a worker in a great factory in Litchborough. But Molly was a clever
girl, and became a private detective') and 'Mollie Summerton: A

[49] *The People's Friend*, 9 Feb. 1914.

Romance of a Great Warehouse' ('Satan, who is always at hand to tempt people in their weakest moments . . .') are two examples from 1914; 'Molly' was a common name.[50] Towards the Second World War the outlook had become much rosier and certainly more 'middle-class'. *The Writers' and Artists' Year Book* chronicled the change in *My Weekly*. In its entry published in the 1923 edition, the paper solicited the following:

strong love stories of the novelette type, and all subjects of feminine interest: light, breezy schoolgirl stories; stories of the adventuress 'above her station' type . . . All contributions should make their appeal to the working classes.

By 1939, however, the *My Weekly* entry included the significant alteration: 'All contributions should make their appeal to the modern woman.'[51] Two excerpts from *My Weekly* illustrate this change. The heroine of the first story fights to survive, as do those around her; in the second, she is comfortable and amorously pursued.

Our Great Drama of Factory Life:
'A Daughter of the Mill', by Stuart Martin
The Characters.
Emily Kay, the heroine, a weaver at Palm Mill, Oldham, who is pursued by the evil intentions of Frank Booth, manager at the Mill.
John Hall, a young operative at Palm Mill, who rescues Emily from Booth's hands. A love springs up between them. His plans for a new and improved loom, deposited with Mr Livesey, late manager of the Mill, have been stolen by *Frank Booth*, now manager of Palm Mill.
Alice Hall, John Hall's sister, has been betrayed by Frank Booth. Overcome with shame, she flees from Oldham, is brutally repulsed by Booth, and commences to sing in the streets of Manchester. Two theatrical artistes, struck by her voice, engage her in a scene at the theatre . . .
(28 January 1911)

'It Happened That Way', by Dorothy Black
Barbara Tetley was peculiarly alone in the world. Four years before, not long after she had left school and started work in a Government office, her father and mother were killed in an air raid . . .
One thing, she had no financial worries. Her people had left her amply provided for, and she had a pleasant home in a pretty, modern flat.
And she was in love. In love with Derek Lancing, a squadron leader in the RAF. Derek was handsome and devil-may-care, and although he hadn't actually said so, she believed he returned her love.
(18 November 1944)

---

[50] *Red Letter*, 30 July 1914; *The People's Friend*, 9 Feb. 1914.
[51] Even more significantly, the *My Weekly* entry in the 1988 edn. is unchanged.

In practice, *My Weekly*'s claim to appeal to the 'modern' woman was unrealized: the happily-ever-after heroines depicted in storylines such as the one above were actually regressive stereotypes. Similarly, *The Annie Swan Annual*, published by D. C. Thomson in the 1930s, was filled with cheerful love stories featuring 'middle-class' heroines. In 'Love at Second Sight', Dick Harrington dreams of his ideal future: a business and a wife:

A vision rose before his excited eyes—the vision of a blue-eyed, pretty young wife helping at the petrol pumps when they were extra busy. He saw it all—Harrington's Garage and Filling Station, and the well-furnished rooms above, where Harrington's wife was waiting for him to come to dinner.[52]

The treatment of such issues as patriotism and the war also varied considerably over the years. First World War readers were exposed to more credible, socially conscious storylines, while by 1940 the influence of Hollywood was clearly apparent. Throughout the period, however, love of country and a woman's 'duty' were paramount in the papers:

'His Young Wife at Home'
Alice Langdale was one of those unknown heroines who, with a brave smile, sent their husbands out to fight for King and Country. Many were the trials she had to meet in the days that followed—days of sickening suspense, of fear for her loved one's safety, days made darker by the constant pinching and scraping to keep herself and her widowed mother on an all-too-meagre separation allowance. In trying to help those poorer even than herself she met Old Moll, a regular rough diamond, and this week is told how the pair visited some of the worst of London's slums.

Red Letter, 14 November 1914.

'The Big Thrill Came to Camp'
The A.T.S. girls just couldn't believe their luck when Terry Fraser, film star, arrived amongst them. Right from the first moment they had high hopes of hooking him!

Red Letter, 22 May 1943.

'Afraid to Marry in War-Time'
The little, tired-faced woman dabbed her eyes and smiled across to Phyllis—'In war a woman's job is to bear her troubles with a smile and keep her man's pecker up,' she said gently.

---

[52] Douglas Walshe, 'Love at Second Sight', *The Annie Swan Annual* (n.d., *c*.1935), 37. Not all of the stories were written by Swan, who died in 1943. Her name was probably used for its recognition value.

Phyllis flushed—she'd never looked at things in that light before.
Family Star, 3 May 1941.

Needless to say, all of the above stories ended happily, either with a proposal of marriage or the blissful reunion of spouses. The transition from wartime romance to florid peacetime romance was often immediate:

'Peggy in Peace Time—The Romance of a Farm'

Only a year ago Peggy had worn khaki with leggings and a soft peaked cap as she drove a motor ambulance backward and forward from a clearing station to a base hospital in France.

To-day she looked as smart in a short blue print frock, with a big white pinafore, as she milked cows, fed chickens, and made butter at her father's farm among the hills of Perthshire.

The People's Friend, 10 January 1919.

'His Pretty "Boss"—A Complete Short Story of How
a Plucky Shop-Girl Won Love'

She was one of the 'finds' of the war; the firm thought there was none like her. And Jim's heart was a bit bitter. He'd fought and suffered so that girls like Lil Carter could live in security. It was hard that they should keep the cushy jobs when the boys came home.

Lil never seemed quite at ease with Jim. When he wasn't looking her grey eyes had a way of watching him wistfully.

Red Letter, 4 January 1919.

The Thomson women's papers also exploited the 'struggle' between good and evil. No sensation, as James Cameron related, escaped the pens of Thomson writers. The criminal, in fact, was often a woman, which may have provided a vicarious thrill for female readers (and, indirectly, identification of a kind):

'Katherine Birch—He had married a murderess!'

'To-morrow you can go where you like—I'm finished with you!' Jim said scornfully.

Maddened by his words, Katherine hurled herself at him, pushing him against the rail. At the unexpected attack, Jim staggered back, and, clutching wildly in the air, stumbled and toppled over –

What she had done was terrible, but she was free. The menace had gone.

Flame, 18 May 1940.

'Her Brute of a Sister'

'Gee, it's a chest!'

'Maybe there's a body in it.'

'We'd better tell the police.'

Esther Tapley's secret lies in the hands of two boys.

Red Star Weekly, 3 October 1942.

The moral, however, was always clearly and repeatedly presented: crime does not pay. The villain gets his (or her) due, and the protagonists are reunited in the end. In style and content, the blood-and-thunder papers owed much inspiration to the nineteenth-century sensation novels. In most cases, an innocent girl is wronged by someone who is trying to steal her dashing fiancé or break up her happy marriage.

'But He Married Her Mother!'

Most mothers are quite pleased when their daughters get engaged. But not Mrs Leslie. She wanted Anne's sweetheart for herself!

Secrets, 5 February 1938.

'Rogue's Bride'

'Cancel Your Honeymoon—Get Back Home! He's Not Your Husband!'

Flame, 18 May 1940.

'Lady Norah's Secret'

John and Elsie gazed at one another in sudden fear. The door of the room was locked—and the house was on fire! Lady Norah had trapped them! . . .

'John', she said, 'kiss me, my darling!'

He held her close. The thrill of that kiss seemed to draw the soul out of her . . .

Family Star, 25 October 1941.

The bigamous marriage was a common scenario. Often the innocent engaged girl (or wife) is used by an evil fiancé (or husband), who is already married. Presumed-dead first spouses return in droves in the Thomson papers.

'The Girl They Both Married'

Trudging along the dark lane Joyce's heart was heavy. What sort of welcome would she get from her dead husband's family? Would they help her when they learned he had married her bigamously? What was to become of her and her unborn child?

Family Star, 8 November 1941.

'With His Next Bride Chosen!'

Desperately Nora clutched at the upturned boat. 'Help Roger! Help!' she cried.

In the darkness Roger Seaton smiled—and went on swimming steadily towards shore!

Flame, 13 April 1940.

In the end, Joyce marries her brother-in-law to save the family name, whereupon her 'dead' husband returns. Roger marries his mistress, but Nora does not drown as planned.

As Cameron recalled, violence in stories was often depicted quite graphically. Real-life sensational crimes were dramatized in several parts ('The Dr Reede Scandal—The Confession of a Woman who Stole a Dead Body'; 'Mary Sullivan's Wedding—Story of an Irish Poisoning Tragedy'). Then as now, people loved to read about a murder; one of the selling points of *Red Letter* in 1914 was, 'A famous Crime Investigator contributes each week the true story of a famous tragedy'. The scheming woman was a common character, instantly recognizable as wicked because of her dark features. Clarina Singlar, for example, a circus dancer who attacked her husband with a lion, 'wasn't like other women. The warm blood of the South ran in her veins.'[53] Robina Dawson, 'the woman with the face of an angel and the heart of a fiend', inherited from her Spanish mother 'eyes and hair as dark as night'. In 'The Woman Without Mercy', Robina tries to steal her saintly stepsister's fiancé through theft and blackmail, but is exposed by Grace. After a struggle ('Hate and passion swept over Robina Dawson like a red flood'), Grace is floored with a torch, and Robina makes plans:

A cold and cruel resolve took the place of the mad rage that had seized her. There was only one way. Grace Calvert must never recover consciousness to tell what she knew.

A knife? Yes, that would be best.

She remembered a Chinese dagger that hung on the wall of the landing just outside. She had seen it that afternoon.

Grace Calvert, lying on her side, moaned and put out a hand along the carpet as if seeking support.

A moment later, Robina Dawson had the dagger, sharp and deadly in her hand. With clenched teeth and eyes that blazed like burning coals, she crouched and plunged it into the back of the defenceless girl.

Red Letter, 16 September 1933.

Clearly, the Thomson papers exploited concurrent themes in published works of popular fiction, notably thrillers. But it seems that no one could be trusted in the Thomson papers, not even the saintly visiting priest in the parish church:

'Eastford Blamed the Girl!'

Mr Samson was away on a fortnight's holiday and Kenneth Turner was taking the evening service. He looked more like an athlete than a minister, with his

[53] *Red Star Weekly*, 10 June 1939.

Plate 7: Red Letter, 16 September 1933. 'Without one pang of remorse for her terrible deed, she fled.'

broad shoulders and his lean body. His eyes were blue and intense and his voice low and boyishly eager.

Listening to him Helen's heart hurt her, she loved him so much ...

Flame, 6 January 1940.

Actually, Mr Turner is a thief in disguise, and poor Helen escapes his clutches by becoming, of all things, a partner in a circus knife-throwing act. Ministers of religion were used so long as the denomination was never mentioned, and the evil ones were exposed as impostors.[54]

The 'Big 5' papers also had recurrent themes, of which foreigners, education, and patriotism were the most common. Predictably, the boys' papers promoted fashionable racial stereotypes. Caucasians, with the noted exception of Germans ('Huns'), were regarded with affection. In *The Hotspur*, for example, students from all over the world attended Red Circle School, including Denys van Berg (South Africa) and Kit Delaney (USA). Blacks and Orientals fared less well: *The Wizard* featured several racist cartoons, including one in colour on its front cover every week (and as late as 1950) which followed the slapstick adventures of the black natives on Spadger Island. *Adventure* had 'Ginger, Joe and Sambo—Three pals out for FUN—a darkey, a donkey and a Cockney'; *The Hotspur* lampooned the Coalblacks tribe, and Sing Small and his little yellow friends (it also, however, parodied Scots in a strip called 'The Clan McSporran').[55] Chinese characters were made extremely menacing; the elusive villain in the *Dixon Hawke Library* was Chao-Feng, who seemed to be forever hissing, 'The white race will learn one day the power of the Yellow Peril.'[56] Black people were often terrifying, especially in groups. In *Adventure*, for instance,

---

[54] In the romance papers, ministers were more virtuous and genuine. Bob Crampsey recalled a favourite storyline in *The People's Friend* in which the Scottish girl decided to leave her village for the excitement of Glasgow or London, leaving behind the handsome young minister. 'Of course the heroine . . . soon repented of her mad hankering for gaiety and returned to Auchmithie and quiet, handsome, glinting Keith or Ninian. If by some chance there was no handsome young minister in the story there was certain to be a wise, kindly older one very often called Ninian or Keith. The *People's Friend* took absolutely no notice of the hundreds of thousands of Catholics, Episcopalians, Jews and Nonconformists who dwelt in Scotland even then' (*The Young Civilian: A Glasgow Wartime Boyhood* (Edinburgh 1987), 71).

[55] Until recently, Dundee was also home to Robertson's Preserves, with their distinctive mascot 'Golly' the golliwog.

[56] Anderson, recalling his days on the *Dixon Hawke Library*, added, 'Oh yes the Chinamen. Oh, they were a doughty lot. Wasn't it amazing how "Limehouse" and "Chinamen" conjured up the sinisters? Always have. There's so many Chinamen around now in our times; probably that's destroyed some of that.'

Plate 8: 'The *Adventure* Room', D. C. Thomson & Co., Ltd., Bank Street offices, Dundee, c.1925. This sedate scene contrasted with the rowdy atmosphere among staffs of the Big 5 papers. The lighting fixtures, Alfred Anderson recalled, were smashed often by footballs and bunches of paper

Ju, 'The Black Giant' from Nigeria, is given a potion that makes him invisible; he escapes and proceeds on a mad rampage, terrorizing, of all places, Bedford and Leighton Buzzard.[57] A frequent storyline featured a white adventurer who is captured and tortured by natives. The debt owed to authors such as H. Rider Haggard, and to the cinema, is obvious:

'The Nigger of the Narwhal'
They were an ugly group, and Dick counted that two of them besides the leader carried guns.

They began to talk, volubly and incoherently as niggers do, but the big fellow cut them short, roared a few orders, and spread them out in line . . .

The big man's overalls were open at the chest, to reveal hair matted like a doormat. His face was one of the most hideous the boy had ever seen, his nose broken and crooked, his cheeks scarred by knife slashes, and his broken teeth giving his mouth a one-sided appearance. 'Dey ain't done dat, I'se swearin! Dey's hid away somewheres, an' when I done git 'em I'se gwine to carve de flesh from dere bones'.

The Rover, 17 August 1929.

'Rip Foster in the Dark Continent'
'You said, white dog, that you would bring the Ju-ju to-day,' snarled the witch-doctor. 'You lied!'

'That was your fault,' rasped Foster. 'If you'd left it alone I would have brought it.' 'If,' he continued in English, 'if I could get my fingers on you, you squinty-eyed little swab, I'd wipe the floor with you!'

Soka could not understand the words but he sensed the meaning, and he brought his face close to Foster's . . .

'My people demand a sacrifice, and I will make sure that you do not die too quickly. For you the death by ants!'

The Skipper, 4 April 1931.

A 1938 story in *The Skipper*, 'The One Man to Fight the Klan', even depicted the racist American organization as having once 'always been a great power for good, and Rhet had been very proud to be accepted as a member'. Ultimately, however, the Klansmen are exposed, not as a racist lynch mob, but as bank robbers in disguise.[58]

Underlying the hundreds of school stories in the Big 5 papers was a strong belief in Dundee in the importance of education and respect for authority. School was depicted as fun, interesting—and obligatory. 'Scrapper Corrigan—Kid Catcher' in *The Hotspur* dealt with truants in the Wild West town of Stovepipe. 'Scrapper was the only man who was

[57] *Adventure*, 4 Jan. 1936.   [58] *The Skipper*, 16 Apr. 1938.

able to hold down the job of School Attendance Officer. The Tombstone boys were tough, but Scrapper was tougher, and he made them attend.'[59] Similarly, a recurrent *Hotspur* character was the 'Big Stiff', the tough but amiable school inspector. Mr Smugg, the Red Circle School headmaster, though the victim of countless pranks, is obeyed in the end. Public-school stories were especially popular because most of the readers of the Big 5 papers were from lower-middle- and working-class families and did not attend such schools; hence curiosity about them was great. A popular serial in *The Wizard*, entitled 'Smith of the Lower Third', followed the adventures and discoveries of a poor boy who won a scholarship to Lipstone College, the most distinguished public school in England (Smith eventually graduates to the Fourth Form). Another story, 'Public Enemies Trained Here', was set in America. In a somewhat bizarre way, the British system of education earned high praise indeed:

Actually, Rockport was a school for crooks. Professor Derval, once of Sing-Sing Prison, was running it as a training ground for the sons of gangsters and members of the underworld. He encouraged a few honest pupils as a blind to fool the police, and Charlie was one of these . . .

All the fifty boys who turned out were expert gunmen. At Rockport they had a secret range where the pupils were taught to shoot at dummy policemen. Most of the boys had learned to be crackshots there.

Things of this kind would never have happened at the British schools he had attended.

The Hotspur, 27 April 1935.

Indeed, in the Big 5 papers school became a place of adventure as much as a seat of learning, which made the setting all the more appealing to a boy. 'The School of the Skull and Crossbones' in *The Skipper* (16 April 1938) followed Cornish master Roger Hawkins and his pupils as they defeated L'Olonais, the most dreaded pirate of Port Royal, somewhere in the South Seas. Another *Skipper* serial, 'Whoopee! We've all gotta Gold-Mine!', involved just that: 'They struck it rich at the back of their school! The Boys Who Dig Their Pocket-Money Out of the Ground!' (3 September 1938). And, of course, there were the sporting heroes, from *Adventure*'s Springy Jack, the lad who could leap any height, to Billy Bung in *The Rover* ('The Heaviest Centre-Half in Boys' Football! 14 years old, 14 stone in weight—How would *you* like to play centre against Billy Bung?').[60]

[59] *The Hotspur*, 5 Jan. 1935.
[60] *Adventure*, 12 July 1924; *The Rover*, 5 Jan. 1929.

Patriotism and war, popular subjects among boys, also featured prominently. Mass-Observation in 1940 surveyed the Big 5 papers to examine the influence of the war on boys' fiction. During the last week in 1940, for example, *Adventure* contained 244 references to the war, *The Wizard* 259, including 114 references to Germany.[61] Apart from urging boys to do their patriotic duty, such as collecting waste paper, Thomson editors cleverly made war approachable, interesting, and even fun for boys by introducing it into sport, school, and adventure stories. Football heroes became secret agents and cricket bats deadly weapons. In 1941, for example, the Wolf of Kabul and Chung were sent behind Italian lines in Libya to thwart enemy plans. In this way Chung stopped one Italian officer from torturing his prisoners:

'Pronto!' A corporal rasped the command. 'Una! Due——'
It was the last command that ever passed his lips. The foliage of a nearby tree rustled and a strange object flashed down. It landed with a thud on the soldier's helmet and even his steel helmet failed to protect his skull.

The object which had hurtled down was a cricket bat, much battered and ominously stained. The blade was split and bound in places with lengths of brass wire.

'Ho! I crack skulls!' howled a terrible voice. 'Tremble, little men who serve He-of-the-Chin! The Shadow of the Wolf falls upon you!'

The Wizard, 29 March 1941.

In the same year the football serial 'The Ninety Minute Nelsons' was published:

The 1938–1939 football season had just opened with a tremendous sensation. Captain Dick Nelson, the famous amateur centre-half of the Black Hawks, had been arrested as a traitor, accused of having gone to Berlin and sold Britain's secret defence plans to the Nazis . . .

But Dick Nelson was not a traitor. On the contrary, he had just made a tremendous sacrifice for his country. He was a member of the British Secret Service, and, though he really had sold plans to the Nazis, they were not the true plans of Britain's defences. They made out that Britain was far better prepared than she really was, and Dick had played the part of traitor to try and stop Germany's forcing war on Europe in 1938, when Britain was so unready that she might have been over-run by the mighty Nazi war machine.

The Wizard, 1 November 1941.

The Gestapo agents are portrayed as buffoons and—perhaps the worst insult of all—completely ignorant of football. One, called Schenk, watches a practice and grows suspicious. 'These men speak of rifle

---

[61] M-O 'Children and Education' Box 2 File E (22 Mar. 1940).

practice. We must note that carefully. Plainly the Englanders are prac-
tising shooting in large numbers. All these men can talk of is nothing
else.'

School stories were used to great effect by Thomson editors in promoting patriotism. The war entered stories often, resulting in heroic
acts by schoolboys, or by agents posing as schoolboys. This was a
dramatic departure from the tales of soldiers and battles which
featured in the nineteenth-century boys' papers. By putting the boys
themselves in the action (usually through the school setting), D. C.
Thomson guaranteed reader identification and an enthusiastic reception. In 'The Iron Teacher', a robot is enlisted by the Pahang School in
Burma, isolated since the war, to help sink Japanese submarines. During one battle the robot itself is sunk:

'He—He's gone!' groaned Jim Nesbett. 'He's wrecked the submarine and
saved the destroyer, but he—he's finished. Surely he—it can't swim. He's gone
to the bottom.'
    Even the sight of the Japs floundering in the harbour, yelling for help as the
submarine sank lower and lower, could not cheer the youngsters . . .

The Hotspur, 1 January 1944.

In 'Our School Files a Hurricane', Jimmy Douglas of the RAF aids
the Resistance while posing as a schoolboy (a mature student?) in
Remy, in south-east France:

Jimmy's guess was that the cars were rushing in the direction of the spot where
the parachutist must have landed.
    'Hope I've got enough ammo left,' he growled as he went down . . .
    Rat-a-tat, rat-a-tat! The eight guns poured their terrible blast of bullets
down on the highway, and when he looked back the trees were lit up by the
flames of shattered, burning cars. Crumpled figures sprawled on the ground. A
few staggered away.
    It was a grim sight, but this was war, and Jimmy had a stern feeling of
satisfaction as he roared away . . .

The Hotspur, 3 June 1944.

'Boys of the Bulldog Breed' chronicled the adventures of schoolboys
who sneaked into the Air Training Corps to assist the war effort. Ron's
father was a pilot killed in the war; Ron's grieving mother forbids Rob
to enlist, but he does so anyway and, singlehandedly, prevents a crash
during a German raid. This story is of particular interest because
mothers rarely graced the pages of the Big 5 papers:

locked themselves about the pirate chief's gun hand.

With an angry bellow, Sandy the Scot lunged at the sardonic Chinaman who had accompanied the Swede to the prisoners' cabin on the first day of their captivity.

He seized the astonished Oriental by the throat, and with his other hand plucked out the ugly knife at the Chink's waist.

Meanwhile Clem was scampering like a monkey up the mast. But Larry could not hold the Samson like Swede for long. One smash from the bear-like fist sent him reeling, and the Swede had levelled his revolver and was firing into the rigging.

Rage spoilt his aim, and the bellying sail hid the climbing boy from view. Now Clem was at the masthead. Once more the Swede's gun barked. Clem gave a shrill scream, threw up his hands, and toppled over into the sea.

"Dot hass feenished heem!" the pirate chief grunted, and then, swinging round, he covered Larry, Quartermaster Jim, and the Scot.

"Eef you move, I shoot!" he grated.

"You big brute!" rapped the quartermaster. "The boy's blood is on your hands!"

The American boy wound his legs about the thick waist.

49

late 9: An excerpt from 'Pirates of the Yellow Sea' by Henry Valentine, *Adventure Land* annual volume, 1925. 'The American boy wound his legs about the thick waist.'

'I know everything, Ron', she said. 'I've talked to Mr. Watson and to your Commanding Officer. And I realise now I've been a very selfish woman. Because you went up in that plane to-day you saved the lives of four others—and all of them have mothers, Ron. And if those mothers can give their sons to defend our country then I've no right to try and keep you from your duty. I'm proud of you Ron—more proud than I can say and—and your father is proud of you too'.

Adventure, 2 January 1943.

One wonders how many eager readers raced to show their Mums this story. After the war *The Wizard* ran a series called 'The Making of a British Soldier', which conveyed in story form 'in thrilling detail what happens when young men are called up to do their two years of military training'.[62]

V

D. C. Thomson & Co., Ltd. stands as the best example of the type of magazine publisher which dominated the popular press in Britain earlier this century: shrewd, paternalistic, conservative, and moralizing. The firm recognized the apparent needs of the reading public and perfected detailed formulas, repeated endlessly according to public demand. Editorial policy was aggressive and firm: D. C. Thomson kept its finger on the national pulse, testing all the time ('speering') in an effort to keep its publications 'current' and interesting. In presenting a conventionally moral, 'wholesome' product (on top of the violence), however, editors of both the women's papers and the Big 5 were governed by commercial concerns, and thereby were perhaps more flexible and receptive to socially acceptable changes than has been publicly admitted. Consequently, the Thomson boys' publications in particular enjoyed decades of supremacy and avoided the fate of more time-bound papers, notably the *Gem*, *Magnet*, and the *Boy's Own Paper*. In fact, in terms of style and skill, the contrast with the Religious Tract Society could not be more striking. The Society, despite pioneering these modern 'tuppenny dreadfuls', made no concessions to D. C. Thomson and the expanding competition: its unyielding editorial policy and inflexible approach to the market spelled commercial disaster in the long run.

[62] *The Wizard*, 16 Dec. 1950.

7

'THE PUBLIC MIND MIGHT BE DIVERTED': THE RELIGIOUS TRACT SOCIETY

D. C. THOMSON and the Religious Tract Society had much in common. Both firms enjoyed immediate success as publishers of popular magazines—a success that was sustained for decades, an unusual length of time in the publishing industry. In the field of boys' papers they were rivals to some extent; in fact, the *Boy's Own Paper* established the modern market for this schoolboy genre, just as the *Girl's Own Paper* did for the schoolgirl and, partly, for women in general. The Society and D. C. Thomson were both paternalistic employers who barred unions but enjoyed the loyalty of workers, many of whom remained for fifty years. Both firms, furthermore, were conservative in nature and regarded their publications, to varying degrees, as organs for moral propaganda. Anne Hepple, the new editor of the *Woman's Magazine*, expressed the Society's enduring campaign against 'dreadful' publications in a 1931 address:

The Society had now been engaged in its crusade of enlightenment for more than a century, but the need for its activities had never been more crying than at the present time. The sole appeal made by some of the cheap literature of to-day was an appeal to the lowest instincts of humanity. The films and their lurid posters were often very suggestive of evil. A vicious monster seemed to have been let loose on the community.

Direct opposition might strengthen rather than annihilate this monster, but there was a more effective treatment. The public mind might be diverted to more agreeable topics. This was the self-imposed duty of the Religious Tract Society, which, in this and other respects, was faithfully carrying out its purpose in this and every other country except Russia.[1]

---

[1] 'The New Editor of "The Woman's Magazine"', *PC* (4 Apr. 1931), 426. The Society's titles were among the few magazines mentioned in either *The Publishers' Circular* or *The Bookseller*. This publicity was perhaps as indicative of trade approval and support as it was a concession to one of the largest and oldest book publishers.

The fundamental differences between the two publishers, however, were in terms of experience, drive, and commercial considerations. The Religious Tract Society was, by nature, a publisher of books, not magazines. Consequently, it failed to grasp the intricacies of publishing within a mass market, displaying an ignorance of its readership and an amateur approach to the complexities of the situation. Editors were also crippled by the Society's evangelical concerns and 'reforming' aims, which inhibited success in an increasingly secular world. As one former employee said, 'All our magazines were *nice* magazines. That was why I suppose in a way it was a hard job to sell [them]. Parents bought [them] for their boys whether their boys wanted it or not, didn't they?' The decline of the once-mighty Religious Tract Society is the other side of the success of Mills & Boon and D. C. Thomson. An examination of its history provides an insight into the types of problems which beset all publishers of popular fiction during this period, but through the experience of one which, unlike Mills & Boon or D. C. Thomson, was not able to overcome them. It is also a witness to the ultimate failure of the lofty aims of one of the first Victorian reformers of the popular press.

I

The Religious Tract Society was founded in 1799 for the printing and distribution of tracts at home and abroad. An evangelical, anti-Catholic organization, the Society worked in sympathy with Established and Nonconformist Churches in Britain, and the Lutheran, Reformed (Calvinist), and Orthodox Churches on the Continent, acting as a kind of spiritual watchdog. By 1897 it had become an international publishing house with translations in 226 languages and dialects. Some sixty million items—a rate of 120–30 publications per minute—were issued from repositories around the world.[2] These included books (biblical, devotional, missionary, story), tracts (evangelical and evidential, narrative and biographical) and magazines, designed to appeal to every age and class. The scale and variety of its publications is staggering.[3] The Society paid special attention to supplying 'a pure and wholesome literature' to the young. It was a leading publisher of Sun-

---

[2] *Centenary of the Religious Tract Society* (London, 1898), 3.

[3] *The Invalid Library* (1896), for example, contained inspirational short stories of stricken heroes, printed on long strips of cloth. The 1929 publication list included *The Pilgrim's Progress* (a best-seller, available in 123 languages), a *Dictionary of the Nyanja Language* at 12s. 6d., and a *Russian Concordance to the Bible*, 1,127 pages in length, at 21s.

day School rewards, with a large list of juvenile fiction that was the envy of the book trade, featuring works by Talbot Baines Reed (a Society discovery), Elinor Brent-Dyer, Elsie J. Oxenham, and (in the 1940s) Captain W. E. Johns.

After the First World War the Society expanded and reorganized its operations. In 1932 the publishing imprint (books and magazines) was renamed the Lutterworth Press (after the village from which Wyclif's followers set forth). In 1935 the Society was amalgamated with the Christian Literature Society of India and Africa (founded in 1858) in a new firm, the United Society for Christian Literature, which exists today. The Christian Literature Society of China was incorporated into it in 1942. In 1941 the periodical business was established as a separate public company, Lutterworth Periodicals Ltd. It remained, however, under the jurisdiction of the United Society for Christian Literature, as did the Lutterworth Press.

Clearly, the Society's expertise lay in books, not magazines, which makes its initial success with the latter all the more interesting. Over the course of a century the Society published a number of weekly and monthly papers, the majority of these inspirational and of limited circulation, and mainly for Society members: *Friendly Greetings, Light in the Home, The Child's Companion, The Cottager and Artisan, True Catholic, The Leisure Hour, Our Little Dots*. Three of the Society's magazines, however, are remarkable for their longevity, initial 'mass' circulations, and contribution to the development of the market: *The Sunday at Home*, the *Boy's Own Paper*, and the *Girl's Own Paper*.

The Sunday at Home (*Sunday* for short), a monthly, was started in May 1854. It was a popular paper which contained a mixture of verse, inspirational articles, anti-Catholic tracts, and 'wholesome' fiction. One of its most beloved serials, 'Jessica's First Prayer' by Hesba Stratton, was published in book form by the Society in 1868 and proceeded to sell over 1.5 million copies.[4] Subtitled 'The oldest and best of the Sunday magazines', *Sunday* survived on a small but devoted subscription list, in spite of competition from weekly magazines such as the Amalgamated Press's *Sunday Companion* and, of course, the popular Sunday newspapers. The most purely religious of the Society's magazines, *Sunday* was the favourite of the Society's General Committee, and its demise in 1940 was widely mourned. As in all Society maga-

---

[4] See Brian Alderson, 'Tracts, Rewards and Fairies: The Victorian Contribution to Children's Literature', in Asa Briggs (ed.), *Essays in the History of Publishing in Celebration of the 250th Anniversary of the House of Longman 1724–1974* (London, 1974), 247–82.

TOM HERON OF SAX.

A STORY OF REVIVAL TIMES.

A MARK FOR THE BULLET.

CHAPTER XXVI.—FOUND AT HIS POST.

"TOM HERON, don't thee go to preach at the Quarries this even. There is mischief meant thee, if thee goes. If thee regards thy safety stay away. From, One who knows."

These words were scrawled, with many false spellings, upon a piece of dirty paper, and thrust beneath the door of Tom's cottage at Erncliff.

It was a Sunday morning, and he was eating his breakfast when blind Molly brought the scrap of paper she had found, and asked if it was anything of importance.

The young man cast his eyes over the words, and then folded the paper and slipped it into his pocket.

"Something about the preaching to-day," he answered quietly as he turned to his food again.

No. 1283.—APRIL 30, 1892.

PRICE ONE PENNY.

zines, moreover, the standard of printing was higher and the design more professional than the ubiquitous letterpress weekly papers on the market.

The *Boy's Own Paper* (1879) and the *Girl's Own Paper* (1880) were, we have seen, expressly designed as 'healthy' alternatives to the penny dreadfuls. The *Boy's Own Paper* ended in 1967 after eighty-eight years, the longest uninterrupted publishing run of any boys' paper. It was published weekly from January 1879 until September 1914 and monthly thereafter. The popular *Boy's Own Annual*, the bound collection of one year's issues, was published regularly until 1940, and then sporadically and in different formats until 1979. The *Boy's Own Paper* contained an assortment of exciting fiction, illustrations, articles on hobbies and current events, and an extensive correspondence page, all for one penny.[5] Some of the most popular authors of boys' fiction, including Talbot Baines Reed, G. A. Henty, and Jules Verne, serialized their work in it. The Society's first attempt at producing a quasi-secular, mass-market magazine, the *Boy's Own Paper* was an instant success, receiving the blessings of Church leaders, the trade, and—most significantly—parents. Its impressive circulation of 200,000 copies per week demonstrated that a quality paper with 'wholesome' stories was a viable concern. According to Patrick Dunae, the *Boy's Own Paper* did not kill the penny dreadful, as it had set out to do, 'but the large circulation which the paper commanded suggests that the *Boy's Own Paper* did win many readers from the old penny dreadfuls'.[6] This readership can be conservatively estimated at 600,000 boys (and girls, and their parents) before 1914, the golden age of the *Boy's Own Paper*. By 1899 it had published 35,251,200 words; by 1939, some 80 million.

The début of the *Girl's Own Paper* in January 1880 was also greeted

[5] The issue dated 4 Aug. 1906, for example, contained instalments of three serials, including 'The Voyage of the "Blue Vega": A Story of Arctic Adventure', by Gordon Stables; a 'Chat' with A. E. Relf, MCC and Sussex, with a page of photographs of 'Some Famous Cricketers'; a collection of school stories and school-related information called 'The Fourth Form Ferret'; and a correspondence page. The latter was a popular fixture of all Society papers, and the published replies to boys' queries make entertaining reading: 'No, Ferdinand, *don't* clean football boots with your tooth brush, and use it for its proper purpose afterwards.'

[6] Patrick Dunae, '*Boy's Own Paper*: Origins and Editorial Policies', *The Private Library*, 2nd ser. 9.4 (Winter 1976), 155. In 1888 Edward Salmon said that the 'best testimony' of the *BOP*'s successful campaign against penny dreadfuls 'is the fact that its enemies—the proprietors of penny dreadfuls—try to induce booksellers to insert advertisement slips of their own rubbish into copies sold of the *Boy's Own*' (*Juvenile Literature As It Is* (London, 1888) 186–7).

THE BOY'S OWN PAPER

No. 814.—Vol. XVI.　　　SATURDAY, AUGUST 18, 1894.　　　Price One Penny.
[ALL RIGHTS RESERVED.]

AN ADVENTURE WITH THE APACHES.

By Ascott R. Hope,

Author of "The Merry Swiss Boots," "An Amateur Dominie," etc.

(With Illustrations by H. M. Paget.)

"I tried my 'prentice hand at sign language."

Plate 11: Chapter 3, 'An Adventure with the Apaches' by Ascott R. Hope, *The Boy's Own Paper*, 1
August 1894. 'I tried my 'prentice hand at sign language.'

favourably by the trade and the public, with a weekly circulation of 250,000 copies. In fact, as we will see, the *Girl's Own Paper* was the most profitable Society title; it outsold the *Boy's Own Paper* consistently until 1950, six years before its demise. Initially a weekly, the *Girl's Own Paper* became a monthly in October 1908 and acquired a subtitle, 'and Woman's Magazine'. This was regarded as a natural progression for the *Girl's Own Paper*, which since its inception had attracted readers of all ages with articles on fashion, beauty, cookery, gardening, and sewing, in addition to its fiction.[7] *The Girl's Own Paper and Woman's Magazine* was retitled *The Woman's Magazine and Girl's Own Paper* in 1927. In 1930 the old *Girl's Own Paper* was revived as a magazine for girls and the *Woman's Magazine* was launched as a separate monthly. The *Woman's Magazine* ceased publication in 1951. The *Girl's Own Paper* was redesigned in 1947 as a 'teen-age' magazine called *The Girl's Own Paper–Heiress*, renamed simply *Heiress* in 1950. *Heiress* closed in 1956, bringing to an end the seventy-six-year history of the *Girl's Own Paper*. Both the *Girl's Own Paper* and the *Woman's Magazine*, moreover, published an annual for the Christmas trade.[8]

Who read these magazines? The *Boy's Own Paper* was read by boys aged 12–16; the *Girl's Own Paper* by girls of a similar age as well as their mothers; *Sunday* by all ages—it was described in a 1919 advertisement as 'The Monthly Peal of Joy Bells for the Family Circle'. Ostensibly the papers were also designed with all classes in mind. The weekly price of one penny was within reach of every class; copies were freely passed around, and the Society's papers were among the few 'popular' periodicals stocked by public libraries.[9] *Sunday*, moreover, contained each month a special corner and prizes for 'domestic servants'; and the *Girl's Own Paper* featured articles of interest to single working girls.

[7] *The Girl's Own Paper and Woman's Magazine* for Mar. 1926, for example, contained three short stories and two serial instalments, all of a cheery romantic nature ('Mimosa', by L. G. Moberly; 'The Adventures of a Homely Woman', by Fay Inchfawn); two pages of photographs of 'Wives of the Great' (Mrs Baldwin and the two Mrs Chamberlains); several pages of verse and music; a book page; a travel piece on France; and articles on stitchery, 'Repairing Broken China', and maintaining 'The Bachelor-Girl's Boudoir'.
[8] The Society also published five other fiction annuals for children before the Second World War: *The Empire Annual for Boys/Girls*; *The Schoolboys'/Schoolgirls' Annual* (ages 10–15); *The Light in the Home Annual* (girls, 12–16); and *Little Dots Annual* (8 and under).
[9] Jack Cox, the last editor of the *BOP*, recalled how he and his friends couldn't possibly afford one shilling for the monthly *BOP* in the 1920s, but his Lancashire public library took a copy, in demand by a steady queue of boys (Jack Cox, *Take a Cold Tub, Sir! The Story of the Boy's Own Paper* (Guildford, 1982), 99).

Edward Salmon in 1888 praised the *Boy's Own Paper* as 'the only first-class journal of its kind which has forced its way into the slums as well as into the best homes', and the *Girl's Own Paper* as one of three 'high-class' magazines which fell into the hands of the poor.[10] The magazines also achieved an international circulation through the Society's existing channels for its book trade. Major J. T. Gorman recalled receiving the weekly *Boy's Own Paper* as a schoolboy in Cape Town, and later in the Himalayas, where the arrival of his copy was eagerly awaited and passed around widely.[11]

As circulations declined before the First World War, the core of readers came increasingly from the middle class. The change to monthly publication and corresponding price increase (to 6*d*. and then one shilling) undoubtedly hindered sales among working-class readers. To attract the all-important advertising revenue, publicity highlighted the magazines' 'quality' and appeal to 'better-class' readers and homes; in 1914 the *Girl's Own Paper and Woman's Magazine* was described as being 'For Women and Girls of the Upper and Middle Classes'.[12] The *Boy's Own Paper*, none the less, tried to retain its appeal to all boys. Jack Cox remarked in 1949 that in one village, nineteen boys shared the two copies which arrived in the local newsagent's shop.[13] In 1952 boys at the school in Mather & Platt's engineering works in Manchester were 'very keen' readers of the *Boy's Own Paper*, despite living 'in the poorest quarters of the City'.[14]

The popularity of the *Boy's Own Paper* among girls was recognized by the Society, but no attempt was made to cater for them in the paper. D. C. Thomson adopted the same policy. Salmon, in commenting on an 1884 survey which found the *Boy's Own Paper* to be the second most popular magazine among girls (after the *Girl's Own Paper*), reasoned that girls read the paper to supplement the rather staid contents of their normal reading. 'They can get in boys' books what they seldom get in

[10] Salmon, *Juvenile Literature*, 185–6, 194. The other girls' papers were *Atalanta* and *A–1*. Salmon also quoted details of the 1884 survey of 1,000 boys and 1,000 girls aged 11–19, which revealed the favourite magazines as the *BOP* and *GOP*, respectively.

[11] 'Diamond Jubilee B.O.P.—Major J. T. Gorman', script of television programme 'Picture Page' (19 Jan. 1939), 1 (BBC Written Archives). Gorman, an ex-Indian Army officer, wrote many serials for the *BOP* in the 1930s.

[12] Advertisement, *The Advertisers' A.B.C.* (1914 edn.), 499.

[13] Jack Cox, 'Teen-Age Critics Keep 70-Year-Old "B.O.P." On Its Toes', *TC* (15 Jan. 1949), 5.

[14] Jack Cox, Report, Minutes of Committee, Lutterworth Periodicals Ltd., USCL 143 (4 Mar. 1952), 2.

their own—a stirring plot and lively movement.'[15] The *Boy's Own Paper* correspondence columns often featured replies addressed to 'A Girl Reader'. In 1930 one such reader wrote to say that so many of her girlfriends had now read the *Boy's Own Paper* that it ought to be renamed the *Boy's and Girl's Own Paper*. G. R. Pocklington, then Editor, thought this 'a rotten idea':

The sort of girl who reads the 'B.O.P.' reads it *because* it is a boy's paper, and because she is interested in the sort of things in which boys are interested, and any attempt to provide a sort of milk-and-water 'Boy's and Girl's Own Paper' would almost certainly please neither . . .

As, therefore, we enter upon another year of the work of the 'B.O.P.', I can look forward with growing confidence to the ultimate realization of the aim I have set myself, to make its pages a really powerful agency for drawing together the boys and girls of the world.[16]

As the magazines were treated, at least subconsciously, as propaganda organs of the Society, editors were carefully screened for their religious leanings. For much of the period until 1950, the General Committee, which supervised these appointments in addition to overseeing all workings of the Society (including various subcommittees), was dominated by clergymen. When Charles Peters was appointed the first editor of the new *Girl's Own Paper*, the Committee was satisfied it had 'every assurance that he is truly protestant and evangelical in his doctrinal views'.[17] Flora Klickmann, who succeeded Peters and guided the *Girl's Own Paper and Woman's Magazine* during the height of its popularity, came from the Wesleyan Missionary Society. The Revd Kennedy Williamson, appointed editor of *Sunday* in 1926, pledged to 'loyally uphold the traditions and tenets of the Society, as set forth in the document called Foundation Principles, with which indeed I am in enthusiastic agreement'.[18] Finally, in 1945, 'Mrs Goodall', the new editor of the *Woman's*

---

[15] Salmon, *Juvenile Literature*, 28. In 1903 Arnold Bennett, admitting 'the notorious fact' that girls enjoyed boys' books even more than boys did, wished that girls' papers would learn a lesson. 'The one mistake in policy in that admirably conducted periodical, *The Girl's Own Paper*, has been that it never ran a serial by the late G. A. Henty' (Bennett, *How to Become an Author* (London, 1903), 122).

[16] *BOP* (Sept. 1930), 857.

[17] Minutes of Finance Sub-Committee, USCL 135 (18 Sept. 1879), 1.

[18] Minutes of Committee, USCL 105 (19 May 1926), 101. I have been unable to discover a copy of the oft-referred-to 'Foundation Principles', though the guidelines for readers of tracts and manuscripts submitted for publication probably contained the spirit of these: 'State if the work is written on decidedly evangelical principles, or if the way of salvation by grace, through faith in Christ, by the operation of the Holy Spirit, is clearly pointed out. Or, state whether on other grounds the purpose and character of the work are such as to render it suitable and desirable for publication by the Society.'

Magazine and Girl's Own Paper., impressed the Committee with her religious fervour and commitment:

She felt the sponsoring of the magazines was a most valuable piece of Missionary work and mentioned a letter from a Baptist Minister in Wales congratulating them on the way in which they were reaching girls through the articles in the magazines . . .

She ended by asking members to pray for all associated with the production of the magazines that they might be given wisdom and grace.[19]

Former employees remembered their time with the Society with the same fondness and nostalgia as workers at D. C. Thomson. 'We enjoyed ourselves. We were a happy crew', Michael Foxell, a former general manager, recalled.[20] Some workers remained more for the camaraderie and friendly atmosphere than for the benefits. George Mihill and his wife both started work in 1924, both aged 14, Mihill as an assistant on the new boys' weekly *Rovering*, his wife in the circulation department. Despite difficult working conditions, long hours, and 'terribly poor' pay, they stayed for fifty years. 'I was so happy there,' Mrs Mihill said. 'It was so friendly, a lot of fun. My father tried terribly hard to get me to leave and go to Newnes, who paid much better wages. I went there for an interview and disliked it so much I didn't even wait for the interview.'[21] As at D. C. Thomson, the paternalistic atmosphere at the Society may have been fostered by the ban on unions. According to Foxell, the Society opposed unions, partly out of principle, and partly because, as a charity, it could not afford them. 'There's no way in which the Press and the whole USCL publishing could have survived if it paid union rates', he said.

II

With an apparently solid foundation of readers and the acclaim of the general public, what went wrong? In order to understand the erosion of the Religious Tract Society's leading position as a magazine publisher

[19] Minutes of Committee, USCL 119 (18 Dec. 1945), 125.

[20] Michael Foxell was interviewed in 1988. He joined the USCL in 1949 as an editorial assistant, becoming in turn assistant publicity manager for the periodicals and assistant editor for books, instrumental in reviving the old annuals as *Boy's Own Companions*. He retired as general manager.

[21] Mr and Mrs Mihill were also interviewed in 1988. Mihill eventually became a 'rep', travelling about the country in search of book orders. He maintained that anyone who could sell religious books in the Welsh valleys at the height of the Depression, which he did, could sell, and do, just about anything.

at the turn of the century, we must realize that its titles were flawed from the beginning. Their very success was a handicap. The 'best-seller' by nature has a limited lifespan, as it will inevitably provoke a rash of imitators. These often improve upon the original and ultimately outsell it, whereupon the original is relegated to a kind of sweetly nostalgic, quasi-legendary, but commercially unviable status. This was the fate of the Society's periodicals: their initial success was fleeting, competition intensified, and inexperience, coupled with a resistance to accept change and new ideas, spelled, in the end, financial disaster. The ultimate irony is that the *Boy's Own Paper* and the *Girl's Own Paper*, in attempting to reform the degraded tastes of readers of popular fiction, instead opened the floodgates for less high-minded publishers.

At the outset it should be remembered that the Society was relatively inexperienced in the weekly magazine market. Its forte was books, and books in a highly specialized and 'safe' market. As the Society was a charity, the magazines were regarded as an adjunct to the main book business; any profits were ploughed back into the missionary effort. Losses, moreover, were common among the Society titles; the *Leisure Hour*, for example, continued publishing for decades despite a mounting deficit.[22] Foxell claimed that the *Boy's Own Paper* was unique because it managed to survive 'by the skin of its teeth, because I think it was run by a charity, and they were prepared to, not subsidise it, but to not expect profits from it. They expected it to be self-supporting.' Hence, so long as the magazines paid their own way the Society was satisfied. Panic set in, however, when profits declined and the periodicals began to accumulate large debts.

Despite popular legend, the initial success of the *Boy's Own Paper* and the *Girl's Own Paper* was temporary; within ten years both publications were set in a decline not reversed until after the First World War. In retrospect this seems hardly surprising, as these titles appear old-fashioned and dull beside their competitors, especially those from the Harmsworth stable. Consequently, they were increasingly less attractive to advertisers, and advertising revenue is the life-blood of any magazine, even (in this case) for children's titles. Figure 7.1 shows the net profit and loss accounts for the three Society magazines. Both the *Boy's Own Paper* and the *Girl's Own Paper* peaked within ten years of their débuts, admittedly a long time in the magazine business. The decline of *Sunday* was more severe. Costs of production were one reason why profits were depressed despite healthy sales. The Society

[22] Dunae, '*Boy's Own Paper*', 151.

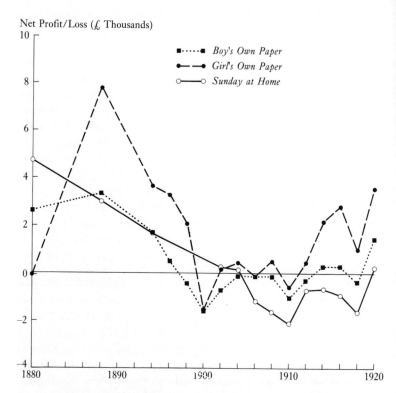

FIGURE 7.1. Net Profit/Loss of Religious Tract Society Magazines, 1880–1920
Source: USCL.

magazines were of higher quality—better paper, gravure printing, photographs—than their competitors, but at the same price. High over-heads and low advertising, therefore, consumed profits.[23] The new century brought some measure of stability, and the First World War set the magazines back in prosperity, although they were saddled with debt. Even in its later, reconstituted formats, the *Girl's Own Paper* was that always the more successful of the titles; one reason was it had much less competition until the real growth of magazines for women in the 1920s and 1930s.[24]

[23] Ibid. 147.
[24] Annual bonuses awarded to the editors of the children's papers, calculated according to circulations, were, in the case of Charles Peters of the *GOP*, consistently double or triple that of his *BOP* counterpart George Hutchison.

The realization in the 1880s and 1890s that the magazines were losing money provoked much discussion, even alarm, in the General Committee and subcommittees. In 1888 the Finance Sub-Committee was informed that circulations had declined by 4.7 per cent for the *Boy's Own Paper* (average weekly circulation: 153,000); 5.4 per cent for the *Girl's Own Paper* (189,000); and 1.4 per cent for *Sunday* (119,000).[25] In 1895 this committee called the attention of the *Boy's Own Paper* and *Girl's Own Paper* editors to 'the *upward* tendency of expenses and the *decrease* in sales'.[26] In 1897 the 'Special Accounts Investigation Sub-Committee' urged the following action:

Will the Committee permit the suggestion that as the November parts commence new volumes, and as the principal advertising expenditure is made to bear upon these issues, that extra efforts should be made to render these the most attractive possible in bulk, matter, illustrations, coloured plates, &c. If the start is a good one, people are likely to continue taking the magazines.

Very much depends upon the first monthly parts. Let us have extra good November parts, and then make special arrangements with the large London & Provincial Wholesale Agents, by personal interviews or otherwise, that they may have the magazine sent, on sale or return to their retail newsagent customers.

There is no better advertisement than showing a good article, but the article must be *good*. No advertising will make people buy what they do not want.[27]

As illustrated in Figure 7.2, sales and advertising revenue were closely linked; a decrease in one prompted a decrease in the other. Here again the *Girl's Own Paper* fared better than the others, largely because its broad-based readership and 'domestic' nature attracted a wider range of advertisers. The sharp increases in revenues from 1915 were as much a result of wartime price rises as of greater demand. It should be noted that the magazines did not disperse advertisements throughout their pages but confined them to their colour covers and between two and three pages at the front and back. Hence, any expansion of revenue from advertisements was limited from the start.

If concern about the state of the periodicals, notably the *Boy's Own Paper*, was expressed around the Committee table, it was never displayed in public. In reply to a correspondent in 1890, the *Boy's Own Paper* was described as having 'a larger circulation than all the other

[25] Minutes of Finance Sub-Committee, USCL 135 (19 Apr. 1888), 239.
[26] Ibid. USCL 136 (13 June 1895), 81.
[27] Minutes of Special Accounts Investigation Sub-Committee, USCL 140 (27 July 1897), unpaginated.

£ (Thousands)

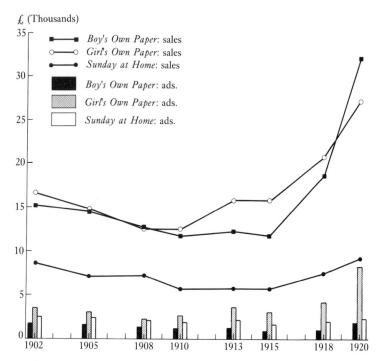

FIGURE 7.2. Sales and Advertising Revenues, Religious Tract Society Magazines, 1902–1920
Source: USCL.

boys' journals put together; and this has been the case for many years—ever since the second volume, in fact'.[28] Given the archival evidence, and the fact that three Harmsworth boys' papers: *Wonder, Marvel,* and *Union Jack,* were selling, respectively, 184,000, 144,000, and 132,000 copies per week in 1894,[29] this was untrue. Similarly, while *The Publishers' Circular* in 1898, on the occasion of the magazine's 1,000th number, stated that 'The *Boy's Own Paper* caught on from the first, soon reaching a circulation of nearly 200,000; and it still holds its own',[30] privately the Finance Sub-Committee admitted that the sales of the

[28] *BOP* (17 Jan. 1890), 256.
[29] Reginald Pound and Geoffrey Harmsworth, *Northcliffe* (London, 1959), 165.
[30] *PC* (12 Mar. 1898), 307.

Boy's Own Paper were 'dropping dangerously'.[31] In 1900 the General Committee was informed that 'The falling off of the sale of *"The Girl's Own Paper"* and *The Boy's Own Paper* is even larger than last year and demands serious attention'.[32] According to Dunae, at the turn of the century the Society was forced to place the *Boy's Own Paper* on its financial subsidy, and it is unlikely that the paper was weaned from this until the Second World War. 'Thus it was largely for altruistic, rather than financial, reasons that the paper continued to be published', he noted.[33] Circulation claims, therefore, must be regarded with suspicion. In 1913, commenting on the death of George Andrew Hutchison, the first editor of the *Boy's Own Paper*, *The Bookseller* said that, under his effective guidance, the *Boy's Own Paper* had become 'an immediate success, and it now has a circulation of over 200,000'.[34] But evidence suggests that sales of this paper had substantially declined by the First World War. Other claims that the *Boy's Own Paper* sold 'approximately' 500,000 copies in the 1880s, 650,000 in the 1890s, and 400,000 from 1900 to 1914, must be qualified.[35]

With its first real crisis in the periodicals at hand, the Society squarely faced the question of market differentiation. 'Is it not time, after twenty years, to start a new series of this magazine also?' a special subcommittee suggested of the *Boy's Own Paper* in 1898. 'Not, perhaps, descending to the *Chums* level but yet catering to a larger extent for the Board School boy.'[36] Similarly, in 1903 the General Committee considered the creation of two new papers, 'A Halfpenny Boy's Own Paper for boys of a humbler grade than the present Boy's Own Paper Readers', and 'A *Monthly Paper for Working Women* at Twopence',[37] and in 1909 a new (but not a replacement) boys' paper that was 'more popular in character' than the *Boy's Own Paper*.[38] None of these recommendations was adopted, perhaps because of the precarious state of

[31] Advertising report, Minutes of Special Accounts Investigation Sub-Committee, USCL 140 (25 Jan. 1898), item 2.
[32] Minutes of Committee, USCL 81 (15 May 1900), 56–7.
[33] Dunae, *'Boy's Own Paper'*, 151. It is unknown whether the other magazines enjoyed such a subsidy; it is probable that *Sunday*, a consistent money loser, did, while the *GOP and Woman's Magazine* managed on its own.
[34] *B* (14 Feb. 1913), 220.
[35] These claims are made in both Dunae, *'Boy's Own Paper'*, 133–4, and Kevin Carpenter, *Penny Dreadfuls and Comics: English Periodicals for Children from Victorian Times to the Present Day* (London, 1983), 46.
[36] Advertising report, Minutes of Special Accounts Investigation Sub-Committee, USCL 140 (25 Jan. 1898), item 2.
[37] Minutes of Committee, USCL 84 (n.d., c.1903), 210–11.
[38] Ibid. USCL 89 (10 Aug. 1909), 356–7.

Society finances. The Committee was therefore resigned to accepting
the increasingly middle-class readership.

The Committee's control of editorial policy at this time also contributed to the waning of the magazines and their diminished competi-
tiveness. Creativity and bold ideas were stifled by clergymen who,
almost inevitably, resisted changes of any kind. The *Girl's Own Paper*,
despite its position as the most successful title, was the worst behaved in
the eyes of the Committee. A series of misjudgments by the editor,
Charles Peters, before the First World War culminated in a Committee
decision in 1908, upon Peters's death, that the *Girl's Own Paper* be
thoroughly proofed before going to press.[39] Peters was frequently requested to 'speak' before the Committee on a number of lapses in the
Girl's Own Paper, many pertaining to 'sexual' references. In November
1900 the Committee decided to eliminate the 'Answers to Correspondents: Medical' column because of 'the character of replies', including
one addressed to 'Ixia Blossom' which contained 'a paragraph apparently referring to a criminal operation'. Peters denied any such intention, adding that the magazine 'would seriously suffer' if the popular
column was removed; the Committee was unyielding.[40] The Revd
W. H. Griffith Thomas, who supported this decision, also raised concern
in 1903 over the first instalment of a *Girl's Own Paper* serial entitled
'Barty's Love Story'. This was the tale of a 24-year-old 'would-be
artist' in London who finds a dishevelled waif on his doorstep on
Christmas Eve. Resurrected from a personal depression, Barty is determined to keep his 'human Christmas Box', taking delight in bathing the
girl (performing a mock baptism in the bath) and laying her down to
sleep in his bed. In a characteristically firm statement after this story
had appeared, it was resolved by the Board members: 'That the Committee view with deep concern the appearance in one of their publications
of the passages to which their attention has been directed and call upon
the Editor for an explanation of the circumstances under which they
have appeared.'[41] The Committee's ire may have been directed at
the following passage, dwelling on Barty's delight in caring for the
child:

[39] Ibid. USCL 88 (14 Jan. 1908), 363.
[40] Ibid. USCL 81 (20 Nov. 1900), 295–6; (27 Nov. 1900), 305; USCL 82 (30 Apr.
1901), 115–16. Peters disregarded the Committee's decision and continued the column
until May 1901, when he was strongly reminded of the Committee's ruling. The reply
to 'Ixia Blossom' was removed from the issue bound into the *Girl's Own Annual* published
in Oct. 1901; the subject matter is unknown.
[41] Minutes of Committee, USCL 85 (27 Oct. 1903), 94.

There are some men who have almost been admitted into the mystery known as mother-love, and among these Barty was to be counted. Heartily masculine as he was, there had been dropped into the ingredients that together resulted in his totality several sparks from female fires. Already he yearned over the Foundling in a manner that was not fully masculine. Jealousy was already showing her teeth; a queer ache for a few minutes troubled his heart.[42]

It is possible that this 'queer ache' could have been mistaken for peculiar leanings. Indeed, sexual references of any kind (as at D. C. Thomson) were strictly taboo. An article in 1900 on 'The Physical Training of Girls' was unanimously condemned by the Committee as 'inconsistent with the tone and character of the Magazine'; Peters was requested 'to avoid anything of the kind in the future'.[43] This article, by 'the Editor of *Physical Culture*', was illustrated with line drawings of women in various poses, including one depicting a woman elevating her legs from a supine position.[44]

The *Boy's Own Paper* also came under the close scrutiny of the Committee, particularly in reference to its treatment of war, patriotism, and current events. By its nature, the Society was susceptible to the concerns of its members, and often had to placate them. In 1903, for example, the Committee strongly denied the claims made in a letter, from Mr T. Pumphery and two other members (all from Newcastle upon Tyne), which protested that 'the inflammatory and warlike character of the Society's *Boy's Own Paper* was an obstacle to their support of the Society'. Given the contents of the *Boy's Own Annual* for 1903, such accusations of militarism were hardly justified. Although these included a serial, 'Val Daintry: His Adventures and Misadventures During the Graeco-Turkish War', colour plates of 'Orders and Medals worn by British Soldiers', and a stirring tune, 'Drilling: Song for Boys—With Chorus', this was, by the standards of the time, tame stuff. The resolution passed by the Committee in response was a reasonable defence of the *Boy's Own Paper*:

the Committee having heard the correspondence are unable to accept Mr Pumphery's characterization of the *Boy's Own Paper*. They feel that the periodical has been conducted with a jealous regard for the danger suggested: they know that during the South African War the Editor's conduct in keeping out of his pages all that could influence the minds of his readers entailed heavy loss

[42] Dr Norman Gale, 'Barty's Love-Story', *GOP* (24 Oct. 1903), 58.
[43] Minutes of Committee, USCL 81 (15 May 1900), 57.
[44] *GOP* (7 Apr. 1900), 422–3.

on the Society and they do not find it their duty to contemplate any change of policy.[45]

The hostility of some of the Nonconformist Churches to the South African War would have prohibited any such mention in the *Boy's Own Paper*, leaving its notoriously xenophobic competitors, Harmsworth's *Boys' Friend* and *Boys' Herald*, to exploit popular opinion and passions. Patrick Dunae has noted that a majority of members of the General Committee were Baptists, one of the principal denominations strongly opposed to the war.[46] Whether the 'heavy loss' incurred by the Society was financial or social in nature is unclear.[47]

But some steps were taken before the First World War to make the *Boy's Own Paper* more competitive. In 1906, on the urgent advice of the Lay Secretary to 'very seriously consider whether anything more can be done to further arrest the falling off in Sales particularly in regard to the B.O.P.',[48] the Committee gave its unanimous approval to George Hutchison's proposals for a series of prizes, including watches, to be awarded to boys who brought new subscribers to the paper. By 1911 a new, reinvigorated *Boy's Own Paper* emerged. Hutchison issued a call to arms in an appeal for new readers:

My dear friends, old and young—

With this week's number of the good ship B.O.P. we start a new voyage, and are arranging to make it the most enjoyable ever attempted.

We are introducing several new features and improvements that we are confident will secure your hearty approval and intensify your interest; and we would now like to make a personal request to all our readers throughout the world.

It is this: that you should each do your best to make this paper still better known than it is in your own immediate circle. A prompt and cheery word of recommendation by one and all just now may do wonders and have far-reaching results.

Yours heartily, George Andrew Hutchison[49]

[45] Minutes of Committee, USCL 84 (28 July 1903), 399–400.
[46] Patrick Dunae, 'Boys' Literature and the Idea of Empire', *Victorian Studies*, 24 (Autumn, 1980), 115.
[47] Robert H. MacDonald has noted that the evangelical tradition of both the Society and the *BOP* was firmly against militarism of any kind: war was presented, in prose and illustrations, as 'cruel, futile and uncivilized', in great contrast to the blazing patriotism of *Chums* and other papers for boys. It was this tradition which made the Society reluctant to support the Boy Scout movement in 1908; when it did, it emphasized the edifying role of Scouting over its military role (Robert H. MacDonald, 'Reproducing the Middle-Class Boy: From Purity to Patriotism in the Boys' Magazines, 1892–1914', *Journal of Contemporary History*, 24 (1989), 519–39).
[48] Minutes of Finance Sub-Committee, USCL 137 (16 Oct. 1906), 65.
[49] *BOP* (7 Oct. 1911), 6.

But it did not take the Committee long to realize that one of the main problems with the *Boy's Own Paper*, as with the *Girl's Own Paper*, was the age of the editors. Hutchison was over 70 when, in 1912, the Committee recommended, in response to 'continued falling off in the circulation', that an assistant be appointed, with a view to his early succession as editor. With A. L. Haydon's appointment, the *Boy's Own Paper* became a monthly magazine.[50] Similarly, Flora Klickmann's election as editor of the *Girl's Own Paper* upon Peters's death in 1908 ultimately ensured the future of the title. Klickmann was one of the first women in Fleet Street to edit a national magazine. The *Girl's Own Paper* also became a monthly, and began its transformation into an elegant magazine for older women. The lack of references to the *Girl's Own Paper and Woman's Magazine* in Committee minutes throughout Klickmann's tenure (until 1931) is an indication of its prosperity. In 1914 *The Bookseller* took the unusual step of announcing that the 'entire edition of the "Girl's Own Paper and Woman's Magazine" for May was exhausted before publication, and a second edition is now ready'.[51]

The transition to monthly publication, combined with increased demand during the First World War, restored a measure of prosperity to the magazines. This is best illustrated by the relative stability of circulation figures for the *Boy's Own Paper* and the *Girl's Own Paper and Woman's Magazine* between the wars (Figure 7.3).[52] Monthly publication meant a higher purchase price (one shilling), and the broadening of the *Girl's Own Paper* attracted new and different advertisers. The First World War, like the Second, was a period of growth for all the magazines, despite higher costs of paper and production. In December 1915, 'a marked increase in the circulation' of the *Boy's Own Paper* was reported, as it was in *Sunday*. The success of the latter was a source of pride for the Society in its *Annual Report*: 'It is felt that the testimony of the magazine was never more necessary than in times like these.'[53] The

---

[50] Minutes of Committee, USCL 91 (27 Feb. 1912), 328. And none too soon. In 1913 Ralph Rollington, a publisher, wrote what is the only history of 'old boys' books' from this period. Admittedly biased towards the author's own publications (including *The Boy's World*) and those of Brett and Fox, Rollington dismissed the *BOP* in a single paragraph: '"The Boy's Own Paper" is also still being issued, though it does not now possess the vitality it did when those grand authors, Talbot Baines Reed, Jules Verne, H. G. Kingston and R. M. Ballantyne were writing for it' (*A Brief History of Boys' Journals* (Leicester, 1913), 107–8).

[51] *B* (1 May 1914), 608.

[52] Although, given the lack of figures for much of the 1930s, the stability illustrated by this graph may not be genuine.

[53] *Annual Report of the Religious Tract Society*, 116th edn. (1915), 159.

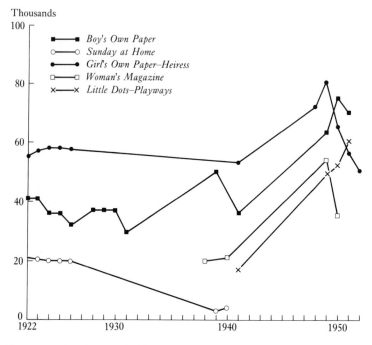

Thousands

Boy's Own Paper
Sunday at Home
Girl's Own Paper–Heiress
Woman's Magazine
Little Dots–Playways

FIGURE 7.3. Circulations of Religious Tract Society/Lutterworth Magazines, 1922–1952
Sources: USCL; *The Publishers' Circular; The Advertisers' A.B.C.*

magazine annuals 'sold better than ever' in 1917, despite the price increase, and in 1919, when the wartime ban on returns was lifted, retailers were urged to order extra copies of the *Girl's Own Paper and Woman's Magazine* and *Sunday* to cope with the anticipated demand.[54] Given their new, middle-class stance, the magazines were able to exploit a dependable (if not mass-market) readership at a time when the market for weekly magazines for working women and for schoolboys was expanding. Apparently, the Society was in a sound enough position financially to launch the *Girl's Own Paper* and *Woman's Magazine* as separate publications in 1930, and to introduce, in 1924, a new title for boys: *Rovering*, 'A Weekly Paper for Young British Manhood'.

[54] *B* (May 1918), 199; advertisement in the *Newsagents', Booksellers' Review and Stationers' Gazette* (20 Sept. 1919), 273.

Rovering was not designed to replace the ageing *Boy's Own Paper* nor even to supplement it. Rather, it was aimed at an older age group, 18–24, with a special appeal to the 'Rovers', the senior members of the Scout Movement. It cast its net widely, aiming to interest 'the many thousands of youths throughout the country and in the Dominions overseas, who stand on the threshold of a new life, and many of whom have no association with any organised body'.[55] *Rovering*, therefore, was to appeal to the boy as he outgrew the *Boy's Own Paper*. The new paper featured 'high-class fiction' ('Held Up in Mexico', by Ashmore Russan), articles on outdoor sport, camping, stamp collecting, the wireless, and books; and competitions for 'thousands' of free gifts (including a 'nickelled match case for tear-off matches'). *Rovering* also reflected its proprietor's missionary zeal with a 'Migration Bureau', containing information on career opportunities overseas, and a weekly column, 'What the Empire *Offers* You'. The Society contended that *Rovering* filled 'a definite gap' in the market,[56] and it did enjoy initial success, achieving a circulation in its first month of 150,000 copies per week,[57] a respectable figure (although pale in comparison with the D. C. Thomson titles). Tag-lines in the paper ran, 'YOU MUST ORDER your copy of ROVERING as the Newsagent is ALWAYS SOLD OUT'.

Despite its limited lifespan (it ended within fifteen months), *Rovering* stands as a good example of the Society's response to the competition through the creation of its first letterpress weekly, price twopence. Its style was strikingly similar to the Thomson papers, with line illustrations, bold headlines, and the use of cheaper quality paper. But its specifically religious tone was obvious, particularly in the '"Up to You" Papers', a series of talks to young men about adolescence and the approach to manhood—'the Gethsemane of life, and every lad worth his salt passes through it'.[58] *Rovering*'s demise can be attributed to poor planning. The Society displayed an amazing ignorance of the magazine market. By the age of 18, boys were already satisfied with newspapers, illustrated magazines (*John Bull*), and 'adult' fiction, and the appeal of religion was waning in an increasingly secular society. Hence, the market for *Rovering* simply did not exist. In June 1925 the Finance Sub-Committee agreed that the considerable sum of '£5,000

[55] *PC* (15 Mar. 1924), 319. The Committee had debated whether 'Manhood' was a better, less restrictive title, but settled on *Rovering*, a rather odd choice given its similarity to *The Rover* of the Big 5 stable.
[56] Ibid. [57] Minutes of Committee, USCL 103 (12 Feb. 1924), 32.
[58] *Rovering* (22 Mar. 1924), 22.

be transferred from Capital Account to the Credit and Profit and Loss Ac. on account of the loss on "Rovering"'.[59]

The 1930s was a difficult decade for magazine publishers in Britain, and the Religious Tract Society was no exception. Public praise for the Society titles 'holding their own' during this time masked yet another crisis behind the scenes. At a special meeting in 1932, the Finance Sub-Committee, 'Having carefully considered the present financial position of the Society, and the best methods of dealing with the circumstances due to the long continued trade depression', recommended a reorganization of the magazine staffs in an effort to cut costs. The *Sunday* editor became responsible for the *Boy's Own Paper* too, and the *Woman's Magazine* took over the *Girl's Own Paper*—which probably resulted in significant staff reduction and savings.[60] In other retrenchment measures, Anne Hepple's annual salary as editor of the *Woman's Magazine* was cut from £600 to £360, and all other Society employees were engaged at not more than £156 per year.[61] Employees, moreover, were no longer paid for magazine contributions, unless directly sanctioned by the general manager.[62] In 1933 the customary free gift of one guinea to new *Sunday* subscribers had to be discontinued, although the Committee was confident that this would not affect circulation.[63] The 1934 *Annual Report* made an unusually direct and frank appeal to members for their support: 'we have to adopt new methods of production and use newer machines which only print on mass production lines; and, to make ends meet, we must have more and more readers. So will our friends remember to recommend Society magazines? All profits go to assist our missionary work.'[64] In 1935 readers were invited to become a 'Companion of the WOMAN'S MAGAZINE' by obtaining as many new subscribers as possible; each one would bring a 'handsome money bonus'. Finally, from October 1935 the *Boy's Own Paper* was reduced in price, from one shilling to sixpence. Presumably, this was a bid to encourage sales, as the *Girl's Own Paper*, already priced at 6*d*., was holding its own.[65] In a suspiciously favourable 'review' of the new 6*d*. *Boy's Own Paper*, a reader in *The Boy*, a club magazine, wrote, 'The price of the

[59] Minutes of Finance Sub-Committee, USCL 138 (9 June 1925), unpaginated.
[60] Ibid. (15, 22 Nov. 1932).   [61] Ibid. (6 Dec. 1932).
[62] Ibid. (24 Jan. 1933).
[63] Minutes of Committee, USCL III (27 June 1933), unpaginated.
[64] *Annual Report of the Religious Tract Society*, 134th edn. (1932–3), 112.
[65] Minutes of Finance Sub-Committee, USCL 138 (4 June 1935), 262.

paper has been reduced, so that there is no reason why any boy should not be able to take the finest boys' paper that is published.'[66]

Coupled with the financial troubles of the Society during the 1930s was a more fundamental problem concerning editorial policy. The growing secularization of British life, evidenced in the expansion of leisure (particularly on Sundays) and the decline in church attendance and in Church schools, 'created grave problems for a society which was founded primarily for Christian evangelism at home', Gordon Hewitt, the Society's historian, wrote.[67] The Committee, beset with money problems, was faced with the dilemma of whether to continue the Society's religious mission through the magazines (not a lucrative prospect) or to make some concessions to the changing tastes of its readers and society in general. The latter path was taken; according to Michael Foxell, by the Second World War the Society had begun to shed its traditional evangelicalism. 'I suppose the Society fell between the stools of piety and secularism, without touching fundamentalism', he said. 'And so this sort of stool probably began to collapse on the pious side. People are no longer pious, are they? Except funda-mentalists.' The insertion of 'Biggles' and "Worrals" serials in the *Boy's Own Paper* and the *Girl's Own Paper* during the war was one example of the extent of this secularization, Foxell claimed. When the Society had previously published 'non-religious' books, such as on gardening or insects, he explained:

All of them had chapters saying, 'God is there, inventing these things', and so on, blessing these things, doing something with them. And so it was very pious. I suppose when you publish in the *Boy's Own Paper* 'Biggles' you begin to say, 'Well, why not publish "Worrals"?'—without any piety in it at all. It begins to sort of release the clamp of being pious.

Consequently, a 'new kind of piety', based on such things as patriotism, was adopted in the magazines, to their commercial gain. This secular-ization, moreover, was promoted through new employees who were recruited according to editorial expertise rather than their piousness. Henry R. Brabrook, general manager from 1921 to 1938, was formerly Glasgow house manager at Blackie & Son, the Society's main rival in the juvenile book trade. Brabrook had been instrumental in preparing Blackie's successful series of rewards and picture books.[68] In 1928 a

---

[66] *The Boy*, 8 (Winter 1935–6), 338. The reviewer was aged 15; this was surely set up.

[67] Gordon Hewitt, *Let the People Read: A Short History of the United Society for Christian Literature* (London, 1949), 73.

[68] *PC* (29 Oct. 1921), 439.

layman, George J. H. Northcroft, was appointed editor of *Sunday*, and the paper's subtitle, 'The Magazine for Christians', was dropped.[69] Similarly, Mrs Len Chaloner was appointed editor of *Woman's Magazine* in 1939 as much on the basis of her previous experience in journalism as her religious beliefs. The general manager believed that 'she was not merely a writer with full knowledge of editorial work, but also an expert on matters of production, and he considered that this was definitely a move in the right direction'.[70] Leonard Halls, the new *Boy's Own Paper* editor in 1942, came from—of all places—the Amalgamated Press, where he was in charge of juvenile papers and annuals.[71] Foxell recalled that the difficulty in obtaining staff during the war also served to change the complexion and outlook of the Society:

In the old Society days, when someone like George Mihill joined, he was expected to know his catechism when he joined the staff. But that began to ease off—it must have been during the war. When I joined, in 1949, we had a Roman Catholic—imagine it, a *Roman Catholic*—assistant book editor. And that, in such a diehard Protestant organization, would *never* have happened in the twenties. No way.

In light of these changes, the demise of *The Sunday at Home* in 1940 is hardly surprising. *Sunday* rarely showed a return on investment; it was principally a propaganda organ for the Society, and maintained for that purpose. Although the First World War brought some prosperity,[72] in 1920, a year which witnessed the introduction of many new magazine titles, *Sunday*'s circulation sagged and caused concern, while its main competitor, the weekly *Sunday Companion*, recorded a healthy circulation of 240,000.[73] A number of proposals to increase circulation were considered by the Committee, including a change of title and the gift of twelve free issues to new subscribers.[74] *Sunday* even assumed a more worldly character: religious verse and evangelical pieces were interspersed with articles on the latest fashions and travel, and semiromantic serials such as 'The Vision and the Deed' by Captain Frank

---

[69] Minutes of Committee, USCL 107 (30 Oct. 1928), unpaginated.

[70] Minutes of Finance Sub-Committee, USCL 138 (24 Oct. 1939), 359.

[71] Minutes of Committee, Lutterworth Periodicals Ltd., USCL 143 (22 Jan. 1942), 17.

[72] In 1919 the editor of *Sunday* was congratulated: 'The Committee expressed its gratification that the loss on the magazine was so small' (Minutes of Finance Sub-Committee, USCL 137 (22 July 1919), unpaginated).

[73] *The Advertisers' A.B.C.*, 36th edn. (1922), 152–4.

[74] Minutes of Committee, USCL 99 (23 Nov. 1920), 226; USCL 100 (31 July 1921), unpaginated.

H. Shaw (September 1928), about a handsome young curate whose comes to see the misguidedness of his ruthless ambition to be vicar. But in the 1936 *Annual Report* the Society admitted that *Sunday* served 'a limited circle of friends ... a striking testimony to their worth when it is remembered how few are at home on Sundays in these days and how few take any time at all, not to speak of thinking great thoughts'.[75] In July 1940 a decision was reached to keep *Sunday* going, 'particularly from the point of view of the use of the magazine as a propaganda medium for the Society's work', but with the general manager commanded to reduce the magazine's loss as much as possible. Just one month later, however, the Committee admitted defeat; *Sunday*'s losses were too great, and an analysis of recent accounts convinced the Committee 'only too clearly that it cannot pay its way'. Although circulation in 1940 had increased slightly, from 3,000 to 4,000,

> From experience it was clear that a circulation of 10,000 was needed, though 6,000 would enable us to scrape through this critical period ... there was a very small public for this type of magazine, and to reach that public we would have to spend a great deal of money with only slender prospects of success: in our present financial situation we could not do this.[76]

Furthermore, as no 'positive connection' could be found between *Sunday* subscribers and the legacies received by the Society's Missionary Department, its closing would not have an adverse effect in this direction. It would also release paper supplies for the other magazines. The Committee 'regretfully moved' to close the magazine in December 1940.

Secularization did not come easily to the other magazines. Before the Second World War, the Society was perpetually falling between stools (to use Foxell's phrase) in terms of editorial policy. This inconsistency, a result of warring camps within the Committee, could only have had a detrimental effect on morale, content, and sales. This is most evident in the Committee's stand on the issues of patriotism and war. The Society, governed by past policy and its evangelical nature, could never have been as aggressively patriotic as, say, D. C. Thomson. They still had to walk a fine line, as during the South African War, between patriotism and the glorification of war. At the height of the First World War, the editor of the *Boy's Own Paper* drew attention not to the fighting itself but to the future, commanding his readers to be prepared for

---

[75] *Annual Report of the United Society for Christian Literature*, 137th edn. (1935–6), 80.
[76] Minutes of Finance Sub-Committee, USCL 138 (20 Aug. 1940), 389.

leadership in a new and changed world, as worthy successors to 'a great imperial heritage' and 'all the great traditions of our country and race, founded on Truth and Justice'.[77] Similarly, in 1933 the Committee extended its congratulations to the editors of the *Boy's Own Paper* and the *Girl's Own Paper* for the 'excellent' articles on the subject of Peace.[78] In the *Girl's Own Paper* this was 'Need there be Another War?' by Hebe Spaull, author of *The World's Weapons*. Spaull encouraged participation in the Junior Branches of the League of Nations Union as well as the Pioneers and called to the attention of young people 'the entirely changed character of modern warfare':

To their parents and grandparents war used to suggest something heroic and full of adventure. This was because war, while morally wrong, did provide opportunities for those taking part in it to display heroic qualities, and the nature of warfare in those days, despite many horrible features, did provide opportunities for adventure and hair-breadth escapes.

To-day the nature of war has so changed owing to the invention of the aeroplane and poison gases that, as a Cabinet Minister said not long ago, in the next war the safest places may be the front-line trenches and the most dangerous the towns where women, children, and old people are living. There can be nothing gallant or heroic about this kind of war.[79]

Significantly, Spaull was careful not to condemn past wars or past soldiers, the fathers of *Girl's Own Paper* readers. The corresponding *Boy's Own Paper* article is harsher, using sporting references to drive the point home to boys. Dr R. Cove-Smith, author of 'Who Wants War?', was described as 'the famous sportsman, the well-known Rugger player, who has forsaken the gallant British winter game for the honourable paths of doctoring. But he knows what war is and he tells us of its stupidity and wickedness.' Striking charts illustrating armament stockpiles and the number of soldiers killed and wounded during the Great War accompanied the article, which condemned the 'glamorous' picture of war which fails to mention the dead, the surviving 'physical wrecks', and the devastation of the countryside. Cove-Smith urged his young sportsmen to foster an international team spirit such as was displayed during the Olympic Games:

The true understanding of the team spirit surely means regarding the whole of mankind as a human brotherhood with the clear vision of their mutual inter-dependence—in matters of money and trade, in matters of social welfare, in

[77] *BOP* (Apr. 1916), 353–4.
[78] Minutes of Committee, USCL III (7 Nov. 1933), 222.
[79] Hebe Spaull, 'Need There Be Another War?', *GOP* (Nov. 1933), 50.

matters of morality and in matters of religion. *The world, after all, is one big family jostled together in one home and it should have the family spirit.* That is why the World Conference will fail to preserve peace if it puts purely national policy before international co-operation—as we read in I Corinth XII, 'The body is one and hath many members', and 'if one member suffer, all the members suffer with it'. [80]

One can imagine how the average reader of *The Wizard* or *The Hotspur* would have groaned when faced with such prose. This endorsement of pacifism did not imply appeasement, however. In 1936 the Committee debated whether the Society 'should or should not permit material appearing in the Society's magazines commending the fighting Services as careers for boys?'. A motion, proposed and seconded by two ministers, to ban all such advertisements was defeated by a vote of 8 to 4. [81] During the Second World War all the magazines vigorously supported the war effort.

III

Having scraped through the 1930s, two events postponed the almost inevitable decline of the Society's periodicals for another decade: the Second World War, which boosted publishing in general, and the creation of Lutterworth Periodicals Ltd. in 1941. The latter, in fact, was arranged following discussions throughout 1940 about the possible winding-up of the periodical business: the uncertainty of obtaining paper (allocations were based on 1939 circulations, an admittedly poor year for the magazines) and the existence of a large debt diminished hopes for a recovery. In December 1940 the general manager reported that despite planned economies, estimated to save £22,500, 'he could not see how we could hope to pay back £30,000 to the bank during 1941. We might be able to do something by the spring of 1942', but 'equilibrium' between expenditure and revenue was not foreseen for at least three years. [82] In order to generate working capital, Lord Luke, president of the Society, announced the creation of the public company in 1941. Of 40,000 £1 shares, the United Society for Christian Literature retained 20,000 (safeguarding its interest in the magazines); the remaining shares were offered to the public to raise capital. [83]

---

[80] Dr R. Cove-Smith, 'Who Wants War?', *BOP* (Nov. 1933), 194.

[81] Minutes of Committee, USCL 114 (20 Oct. 1936), 153; (27 Oct. 1936), 156.

[82] Minutes of Finance Sub-Committee, USCL 138 (18 Dec. 1940), 393.

[83] Report, 'Chairman's Notes on Publishing Business', Minutes of Committee, USCL 118 (25 June 1941), 1.

In retrospect, this bold move was both a bane and a blessing. The periodical and book businesses were separated just in time: the former had already been evacuated to new offices in Surrey when, on 10 May 1941, a bomb completely destroyed the Society's offices and warehouse in London. Over 1.5 million books and tracts were lost, effectively crippling in one stroke the Lutterworth Press. But if the new company saved the periodicals, it also worked against their long-term financial interests. As a charity, the Religious Tract Society/United Society for Christian Literature was exempt from taxation; as a public company Lutterworth Periodicals was not. 'All publishing in the end during the war was very, very profitable', Foxell explained. 'The result was that they made a lot of money and it all went away in tax. If they had not [created the public company], they would have kept all this money.' Indeed, the new company's strong profits during the war, which could otherwise have been ploughed back into magazine development, were virtually eliminated:[84]

Financial year	Profits (£)	Taxation (£)	Surplus left to Company (£)
1941–2	5,401	5,000	401
1942–3	19,994	19,200	794
1943–4	32,240	31,499	741
1944–5	35,508	33,071	2,473
1945–6	28,597	24,912	3,685
1946–7	18,065	11,549	6,516
1947–8	19,760	9,938	9,822
1948–9	8,412	4,257	4,155
1949–50	6,437	3,074	3,363
TOTAL:	£174,414	£142,500	£31,950

None the less, the Second World War did restore some prosperity to the newly formed company. Figure 7.4 illustrates the sales and advertising revenues generated by Lutterworth Periodicals' four remaining titles, including the monthly juvenile magazine *Little Dots– Playways*, which was quite successful in its own right.[85] The steady

---

[84] 'Report on the Trading and Financial Position of Lutterworth Periodicals Ltd.', Minutes of Committee, Lutterworth Periodicals Ltd., USCL 143 (Oct. 1950), 1.

[85] In another example of the bow to secular and commercial concerns, Enid Blyton became a regular contributor to *Little Dots–Playways*, which was eventually renamed

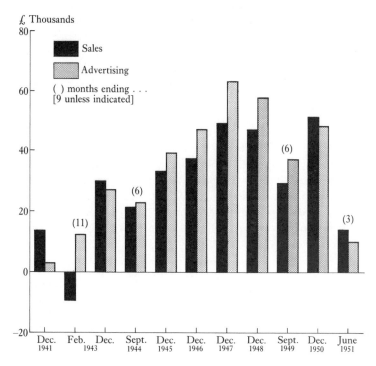

FIGURE 7.4. Sales and Advertising Revenues, Lutterworth Periodicals Ltd., 1941–
1951
Source: USCL.

increase in advertising revenue was crucial in generating profits after
the war. The decline in sales of roughly £9,000 in 1942/3 was caused
by the loss of revenue from the suspension of the magazine annuals. By
1943 the prosperity of the firm was such that Lutterworth Periodicals
could loan its parent, the United Society for Christian Literature,
£15,000; and salary bonuses of 10 per cent were given to staff, 'in view
of the very satisfactory results of the Company's trading operations for

Enid Blyton's Playways. In 1951 the Committee was informed that Blyton was a great fan:
'She was prepared to do anything to help us which did not entail much extra work because
she was so fully occupied. She was very much in sympathy with what the Society
was trying to do' (Minutes of Committee, Lutterworth Periodicals Ltd., USCL 143
(12 Dec. 1951), 180).

COMPANIONS

When I set out to seek a wife,
These homely things I ask of life :
A smile, a joke, a letter gay,
To brighten up a rainy day ;
Warm hearts, two chairs, a book to share,
The look that says, " I'm glad you're there " ;
A silence deep ; a friendly chat,
Keen argument on this and that,
Unstinted praise when life is glad,
Good cheer when sick, kind words when sad ;
A spirit brave, a heart that's true,
With love to last the journey through.
Just simple things of everyday
To help a fellow on his way.

Millicent Westley

Plate 12: 'Companions' by Millicent Westley, a cosy middle-class scene in the *Woman's Magazine,* March 1937.

the last financial year'.[86] Rumours of a takeover of the periodicals were strongly denied, after enquiries were received from W. H. Allen, the Argus Press, and the proprietors of the glossy monthly *Queen*.[87]

In order to account for the astonishing near-collapse of Lutterworth Periodicals in 1950, it should be remembered that the company's wartime prosperity was wholly artificial. This reality was obviously not grasped by the directors of the firm, who, heady from ample (to them) post-war profits after fifteen years of heavy losses, embarked upon what was a reckless programme of expansion. The firm underestimated the costs of the 'circulation war', intense competition which accompanied the lifting of paper rationing in 1949, and consequently was ill-equipped to compete, let alone survive. The titles which were worst affected were the *Woman's Magazine* and the *Girl's Own Paper*.

The monthly *Woman's Magazine* had made a genuine effort during the war to broaden its appeal and model itself on weekly mass-market rivals such as *Woman* and *Woman's Own*. The paper's redesign dated from 1939 when, after a decade of mounting losses, the general manager announced the 'need for a broadening of policy': the latest fall in advertising revenue had been steeper than the fall in sales, an indication that the paper's circulation (then standing at 20,000, about that of the boys' paper *Gem*) was not attractive to advertisers.[88] With unusual frankness, A. H. Sabin, the chairman of the Committee, admitted that in the past the editor of the *Woman's Magazine* 'had been cramped to some extent by a too rigid adherence to what has been understood as "past policy"'. The Committee therefore decided to allow a greater degree of editorial freedom.[89] This was an extraordinary concession for the Committee to make and could only have reflected the precarious state of the magazine. The following proposals, which were approved, would hardly have featured in Flora Klickmann's homely, inspirational magazine:

Articles for dealing with various home problems, such as the young wife's attitude towards the husband preoccupied by his work and the loneliness of the young married woman.

---

[86] Minutes of Finance Sub-Committee, USCL 139 (1 Mar. 1943), 41.
[87] Minutes of Committee, Lutterworth Periodicals Ltd., USCL 143 (2 June 1943), unpaginated.
[88] Minutes of Publications Sub-Committee, USCL 141 (31 Jan. 1939), 1.
[89] Ibid. 2.

Further features such as how to get the best out of life from limited means and articles dealing with the pursuits and recreations of slightly better off women, married and unmarried . . .

It was also agreed to admit 'slightly bolder stories' featuring the more modern type of woman; and the introduction of humour.[90]

Clearly these measures sought to improve circulation among lower-middle- and working-class readers, who might be interested in articles on getting-by, rags-to-riches stories, and the 'bolder' fiction resembling that in the 'blood-and-thunder' papers.

From January 1940, the *Woman's Magazine* shrugged off its dowdy past with a new, sleek look, organized into three sections: Fiction; 'Special Features' (including biographies of 'famous and admirable' people, such as Madame Chiang Kai-shek); and Regular Features (cookery, embroidery, gardening, and an increasingly popular film gossip section). The most striking change was in the character of the fiction. Typical serials in the past included 'So I Retired', the adventures of an elderly widow, and 'A Change for Mrs Carrington', about a 'nervy' woman who gets a rest-cure which changes her life. The magazine's new editorial directives, coupled with the war, opened the door for more exciting tales straight out of Hollywood. 'Breakfast in Bed', by Heather Harrington (May 1941), concerned the spoiled former wife of a factory owner who, newly humbled, applies to her ex-husband for war work. Not only does she save his life *and* foil an enemy sabotage attempt, but they are reconciled. Captain W. E. Johns was a frequent contributor; 'Nocturne Aeronautique' (March 1942) followed the adventures of a British pilot's rescue of a female American ambulance driver in France. At one point he reluctantly agrees to fly her to England, even though the only space in the plane is on his lap:

Thrusting the joystick forward he skimmed the wave-tops in a sweeping rush, and then, as a questing searchlight found him, rocketted like a hard-hit pheasant. Centrifugal force crushed the girl against his breast, her face against his.
    'Sorry,' he murmured as he levelled out.
    'Forget it,' she suggested.
    'I wish I could,' he sighed.

The *Woman's Magazine* had never seen anything like this before. Complementing a vigorous series of articles on civic duty and support of the war effort (their so-called 'Good Neighbour Policy'), the *Woman's*

[90] Ibid.

Magazine also made a direct appeal in its fiction to elevate the status of the working class. 'Dawn for Jessica', by Henrietta Street (February 1943) concerned the attempts of a wealthy woman to persuade her son, the recipient of a DFC, not to marry his 'hopelessly unsuitable' fiancée, a WAAF from 'an ordinary working-class family'. Isobel's prejudices are pitied by her sensible friend Frances, the narrator:

I leaned back and stared at Isobel. She had been shut up in this lovely remote spot since the beginning of the war and she didn't realize what was happening.

The war had taken Graham away, of course, and she'd lost her servants one by one, so that now she was left with the old gardener and his wife and daughter at the cottage to look after her. But she had never experienced the amazing transformation taking place among the people in the towns.

'You know, Isobel,' I said thoughtfully, 'the war has brought great changes and I don't think we can be blind to them. The old barriers of class and, well, money are just disappearing. It's character, courage and sympathy and other qualities that count now.'

Isobel's prejudices disappear when the resourceful working-class girl saves her life during an air raid.

After the war the Committee took steps to maintain the prosperity of the *Woman's Magazine*, which had increased its circulation to a healthy 50,000 copies. The most pressing need was to increase the number of pages (reduced during the war) as the paper ration was slowly increased. In 1945 the Committee appropriated £15,000 for development of all the magazines, with a special sum of £250 per month earmarked in order to obtain 'higher standards of stories'.[91] With the paper allocation increased to 40 per cent (of 1939 levels) in 1946, pages were added to each magazine, resulting in an increase in advertising revenue.[92] In November 1946, with a rise in circulation of the *Woman's Magazine*, the *Girl's Own Paper*, and *Playways* by 10,000 each, an annual increase of £11,000 for 'wider and more varied publicity' was authorized.[93] Along these lines, in 1947 the Committee lifted the old Religious Tract Society's ban on cigarette advertising in the *Woman's Magazine*.[94]

The demise of the *Woman's Magazine* in 1951, however, was a direct result of the end of paper rationing in 1949. Lutterworth Periodicals simply did not have at its disposal the enormous financial resources of

---

[91] Minutes of Committee, Lutterworth Periodicals Ltd., USCL 143 (13 July 1945), 74–5.
[92] Ibid. (28 Mar. 1946), 82.   [93] Ibid. (26 Nov. 1946), 91–2.   [94] Ibid. 93.

its rival publishers (including Odhams and the Amalgamated Press), which would have allowed it to keep pace with their prodigious post-rationing expansions. The Committee anticipated a struggle when the imminent release of paper was first discussed in December 1948: 'The Managing Director considered that it would be necessary, as a first step, to enlarge our magazines to compete with others, especially the new magazines which would be likely to flood the market. In this event cost would, of course, be increased and would need to be offset by economies in other directions.'[95] The *Girl's Own Paper–Heiress* was the first Lutterworth title to be enlarged in size to its pre-war dimensions, despite the fact that the firm could not afford the extra production costs. By August 1949 competition from the larger publishers was beginning to hurt:

The recent national advertising campaign launched by the larger periodical Houses had led to a loss of circulation and during the last few months it had been increasingly difficult to dispose of all copies printed—particularly in relation to Woman's Magazine. Reports of the Publicity Manager and sales staff were read indicating the general trend.[96]

Consequently, the firm worried about the lifting of the ban on returns, upon which it would be faced with the prospect of thousands of unsold copies. To counteract this, it was agreed to increase the dimensions of the other magazines, including the *Woman's Magazine*, from the February 1950 issues. This cost alone was estimated at £10,000 per year, bringing the firm's annual expenditure to £146,104. 'But if sales could be maintained at present level, total income would be £146,000. It was pointed out, however, that if the sizes were not increased the circulations would drop and a net loss sustained',[97] the general manager reported. Hence this was the only way to stem further decline. The measures were successful in terms of sales, but not in terms of attracting advertising revenue, as circulations were still not competitive. In July 1950, given the rate of decrease in advertising revenue (£10,000 per year) and sales (£2,000), it was estimated that the firm would be faced with a deficit of between £14,000 and £15,000 at year's end. Agreement was given to the 'drastic measures' proposed by the managing director (George Martin Lewis), including extra pages and an increase in selling prices (Lewis was an accountant by profession). The *Woman's Magazine* was in the most precarious state, as it suffered

[95] Ibid. (8 Dec. 1948), 128.   [96] Ibid. (25 Aug. 1949), 140–1.   [97] Ibid.

the greatest competition in the market. In a dramatic gesture to boost circulation (which had dipped to 30,000), the paper's advertising rates were reduced, despite the incurred loss of more than £8,000. The editor was also mandated to seek a fine work of fiction: 'a serial by a popular author, such as Frances Parkinson-Keyes, Ernest Raymond or J. B. Priestley should be sought despite the fact that it might well cost between £1,000 and £2,000 to cover six issues of the magazine'.[98]

But, in the end, the firm decided to cut its losses, agreeing to end the *Woman's Magazine* in May 1951. This was accepted during a debate (the first since 1940) on the winding-up of the company during November 1950. Faced with an annual deficit of £35,000, the Committee agreed that the logical step would be the closure of the *Woman's Magazine*, which would result in savings of £11,360 per year. The *Woman's Magazine* was an inevitable choice as it was in the worst state; the following figures were estimated to 31 March 1951.[99]

	Deficit/Surplus (£)	Net Profit/Loss (£)
Boy's Own Paper	Surplus: 7,006	Profit: 180
Heiress	Surplus: 1,134	Loss: 5,672
Playways	Deficit: 1,792	Loss: 4,963
Woman's Magazine	Deficit: 4,768	Loss: 15,075

Reluctantly, the Committee accepted Lewis's proposal for closing the *Woman's Magazine*, although the paper was continued until May 1951 out of deference to readers enjoying the Parkinson-Keyes serial. 'It was with deep regret that the Chairman and Members of the Board agreed that this step was necessary,' the Committee minutes recorded, 'particularly as there was no other magazine published with such a high moral standard.'[100]

While the Committee's handling of the *Woman's Magazine*, from its redesign in 1940 until its demise in 1951, demonstrated some sound judgement and an acute awareness of the market and the competition, its treatment of the *Girl's Own Paper* is astonishing, displaying all the lack of foresight and knowledge which led to the *Rovering* débâcle in

---

[98] Ibid. Frances Parkinson-Keyes was selected, and Foxell worked on the extensive publicity campaign.

[99] G. Martin Lewis, 'Report on Trading and Financial Position of the Company, October 1950', Minutes of Committee, Lutterworth Periodicals Ltd., USCL 143 (16 Nov. 1950), suppl. 5.

[100] Minutes of Committee, Lutterworth Periodicals Ltd., USCL 143 (16 Nov. 1950), 158–9.

the 1920s. Why, in 1947, the Committee should have wanted to fiddle with this prosperous monthly (which was selling 60,000 copies, its largest number in twenty years) is unknown: one can only assume that in this case the Committee truly was misled by the wartime boom in the magazine market.

The new *Girl's Own Paper–Heiress* was doomed from the start. Redesigned as the young woman's equivalent to *Rovering*, it failed—like that old title—to find a market, for the simple reason that one did not exist. In July 1947 the Committee was advised that, as the *Girl's Own Paper* had been 'growing up' over recent years (the same case that was made in 1908), a unique opportunity presented itself to cater for an older, post-school-age girl:

> the change should begin to take place now, *while there is such a demand for a teen-age magazine of high standard.* Furthermore, *the present readers of G.O.P. have no alternative magazine to turn to* while the initial stages of growth are taking place—*and when alternatives can appear* (with freer paper) *the new young Girl's Own Paper will be the first in the field to fill the gap. Thus our present readership should be retained.*[101]

Indeed, before the 'alternatives' appeared, the relaunched *Girl's Own Paper–Heiress* was an initial success. The radical redesign of the *Girl's Own Paper* into a 'teen-age magazine' illustrates the extent of change in editorial policy. An array of new features included articles on character building, psychology, personal careers, fashion, charm, and beauty. The most significant change, however, was in the attitude towards religion. 'Religion will be mostly implicit in the general content, and specific only, probably, in the Revd H. T. Wigley's answers to correspondents', the Committee advised.[102] The *Boy's Own Paper* had already adopted a similar policy; as its editor explained, instead of including a lengthy article written by a clergyman, 'we . . . infer the policy elsewhere, or discreetly arrange for it to be put over in many other ways—an odd line or phrase in a story; the theme of a story; or a line in a reader's letter which may give untold encouragement to other readers'.[103]

At its peak in 1949, *Heiress* was selling 80,000 copies per month. But the same factors which pulled down the *Woman's Magazine*—the

---

[101] Report, 'Girl's Own Paper–Heiress', Minutes of Committee, Lutterworth Periodicals Ltd., USCL 143 (8 July 1947), suppl. 1.

[102] Ibid. 2.

[103] Jack Cox, Report, Minutes of Committee, Lutterworth Periodicals Ltd., USCL 143 (7 Feb. 1952), 4.

de-rationing boom, fall in advertising revenue, and forced economizing measures—also precipitated *Heiress*'s demise. By reorientating the *Girl's Own Paper* to appeal to older 'girls' aged 18–21, the Committee unwittingly encouraged competition from the established women's weekly magazines, which would never have affected the old *Girl's Own Paper* In the end, *Heiress* simply could not attract the readers or the advertising to remain viable. A 1952 report noted the strength of the competition: 'In the case of HEIRESS severe outside competition was felt when WOMAN and WOMAN'S OWN reduced their general age appeal and spent large sums on intensive publicity and sales campaigns. Newnes spent over £50,000 in publicizing one Royal family feature alone in WOMAN'S OWN.'[104] *Heiress* was closed in 1956.

IV

Former employees of the Lutterworth magazines all have views on what went wrong. George Mihill, for example, blamed the contents of the magazines. The fiction was dull and old-fashioned, and it was foolish to attempt to run serial stories in monthly magazines. He believed that the *Boy's Own Paper* should have contained more and better-quality fiction and fewer articles. Given the growth of speciality magazines on all kinds of hobbies, the *Boy's Own Paper* could have dispensed with articles on photography and the like, as serious boy enthusiasts would rather have spent their pocket money on a specialist magazine. 'Well, if the money went on [a] photography [paper], then he didn't have the money for the *Boy's Own Paper*.' Mihill recalled the *Boy's Own Paper*'s heyday and such superior contributors as Henty, Verne, and Westerman. 'In the end I suppose they couldn't afford these good authors. It was a job to keep the circulation going—really hard going.'

Michael Foxell believed that while the Society's finances were just large enough to support the limited circulations of the magazines, they were much too small to contemplate any serious competition with other titles. Overheads were low because staffs were so small: editors and artists were shared, no writers were kept on staff, and there were two sales representatives to cover the entire country. The Hulton Press had thirty-eight full-time salesmen on the *Eagle* comic alone. In terms of the *Boy's Own Paper*, Lutterworth 'didn't spend money. It was running

[104] Ibid. I.

on a shoestring, really. I mean the print order in the end was 10,000 or something, quite inadequate for running a magazine.'

Coupled with the lack of financial resources was the firm's inexperience in dealing with the mass market. In 1952 Jack Cox (who died in 1981) expressed his exasperation over the lack of promotion of the monthlies. 'We have the finest magazines there are for young people—quality, prestige, fine writing, good stuff—they are all there. But they will not succeed unless they are backed up by enterprising sales promotion and publicity.' Cox's own newsagent could not recall whether a Lutterworth salesman had visited in the last five years, while a 'rep' from Newnes checked in weekly. 'We cannot buy our mass circulations as Hultons, Newnes and Odhams do', Cox admitted, but unless Lutterworth was willing to spend money, he maintained, it would not make money.[105] By 1952, it was clearly in a position to do neither.

V

The collapse of the Religious Tract Society and the loss of its once dominant position in the popular magazine market can be attributed to a number of factors: the firm's inexperience in trading within a mass market; inborn resistance to change; inconsistent editorial policies; more ambitious and affluent competitors. This decline, although perhaps inevitable, should not, however, overshadow the Society's achievements in magazine journalism. The initial success of the *Boy's Own Paper* and the *Girl's Own Paper* singlehandedly established the mode for children's papers, laying the foundation upon which the Amalgamated Press and D. C. Thomson built their empires.

But this success was in many respects the Society's Achilles heel. In demonstrating how successful a quality paper could be—and how large the market there was for one—it unknowingly created the conditions for what became a market in free popular taste. And the Society was ill-equipped to survive in this cut-throat market. The contrast between the Society, whose fortunes had started to fade well before the First World War, and D. C. Thomson, with its star firmly in the ascendant throughout this period, could not be more striking. D. C. Thomson kept a much tighter grip on all facets of production; inappropriate passages or references would simply never make it into print. The Society's Committee, on the other hand, usually discussed damage

[105] Ibid. I, 5.

control *after* offending articles had been published. D. C. Thomson, moreover, constantly analysed its readerships in order to keep its titles lively and up-to-date; the Society was much less ambitious, a consequence of smaller financial reserves and inexperience. Indeed, even before the first D. C. Thomson boys' paper had appeared in 1921, the baton of leadership was already being passed on from the Society to the moderns, slowly closing the door on a significant period of British publishing history.

CONCLUSION

I⊤ is clear that Wilkie Collins and George Orwell were largely correct in their conclusions about the reading public and the popular publishing industry. We have seen, for example, that reading among both adults and children in the lower-middle and working classes was a popular leisure activity, as both Collins and Orwell had claimed. In some cases, the amount of 'light' fiction consumed was substantial, particularly in wartime. Collins is also right in that these readers generally sought entertainment, rather than instruction, in their choice of novels and magazines.

Orwell's celebrated claim that attitudes expressed in popular fiction represented a conscious effort on the part of the publishers to try to influence readers towards their view of 'proper' social and moral conduct was also accurate: the moral 'code' in such fiction was always a 'wholesome' one, with the partial exception of some of the grisly thrillers. We can also agree with two of his assertions about the contents of boys' weeklies and romantic novels: the resolution of conflicts in stories was always personal or accidental, or a result of good fortune; there was no social or collective solution, and no alternative image of social improvement or organization was presented. In fact, publishers such as Mills & Boon and D. C. Thomson were careful to make their plots as apolitical and 'uncontroversial' as possible. While Mills & Boon novels contained references to such 'modern' practices as divorce and illegitimacy, these were neither endorsed nor discussed in much detail, nor did they distract from the focus of a story. Both publishers, moreover, insisted on sexual propriety in their publications at all times.

The weaknesses in both Collins's and Orwell's arguments, however, are equally significant and worthy of our attention. This 'Unknown Public', which we have tried to define, did *not* graduate to 'high-brow' novels and non-fiction, as Collins predicted with robust optimism. Although there is some evidence of a trend towards 'serious' reading among these classes, by and large the preference for 'low-brow', 'escapist' books and periodicals predominated. This demand was nurtured after 1914 by personal and national crises (unemployment, war), the wireless and cinema ('the book-of-the-film'), and aggressive marketing techniques adopted by the publishing houses. The relationship between publisher and reader was not as one-sided and indoctrinating as Orwell maintained and feared. With the successful publisher, the relationship was a reciprocal one governed by commercial considerations; the changing tastes of the reader were carefully monitored and accommodated, within certain 'moral' boundaries. Mills & Boon, for example, relied upon its authors and the magazine serial editors to fine-tune its 'formula', while the Religious Tract Society, to its financial ruin, resisted all attempts at modernization until it was much too late.

The major concern of D. C. Thomson editors, moreover, was to keep their publications up-to-date and interesting to children (through such techniques as 'speering'), while at the same time avoiding any controversial insertions which might upset that unseen but omnipotent quantity, the parent. Orwell missed this important point: editors had to tread a fine line between two markets, the positive children's one and the negative parents' one. Without the approval of both, large sales were impossible. The Religious Tract Society was probably aware of these two factors but chose to cater more to the parents. In another sense, the same reasoning probably governed D. C. Thomson's attitude to the women's weeklies, which, being 'family papers', were, they believed, left around a house in view of the children. Clearly, the 'violence' in papers such as *Red Letter* would not have exceeded that which any child would find in the cinema, or indeed in his 'blood', and the moral, 'Crime does not pay', was omnipresent.

The intricate relationship between editorial policy and market forces is hardly surprising. Although publishers of popular fiction, as I have tried to show, were anxious to pass on certain views to their readers, their overriding concern was, in the end, to make a profit. Mills & Boon's transformation to a romantic fiction publishing house during the 1930s was wholly a commercial decision which the Boons have never regretted, as it gave them a large, captive, and loyal readership. A substantial part of D. C. Thomson's success lay in its complete break with the *Boy's Own Paper*—*Magnet* tradition: the 'Big 5' boys' papers offered young readers a whole new kind of weekly magazine: bright, varied, and personal. Although these were still 'penny dreadfuls' at heart, their wrappings were different, exciting and instant attention-grabbers. The Religious Tract Society, on the other hand, resisted change for as long as financially possible. The redesign of its titles in the 1940s, with a diminished emphasis on piety, was an attempt to accommodate to a changing world; but this was too little and too late. It is ironic that the firm which helped to establish the modern mass market in popular fiction in the nineteenth century was ultimately handicapped by its good intentions in the twentieth. The Society lacked the strong centralized control which existed at Mills & Boon and D. C. Thomson and which commanded all facets of policy and production. The commercialization of these two firms is evident in the fact that the author became a non-entity: Thomson serial stories carried no bylines, and the Mills & Boon imprint took precedence over the author's name. Changes in tastes of the readership could, therefore, be swiftly incorporated in the fiction.

The reciprocity between publisher and reader was perhaps responsible for the significant change in the content and style of popular fiction after the First World War. The Big 5 papers, for example, invigorated and democratized a declining genre with exciting (if implausible) plots, international settings and characters, prize competitions, and aggressive attention to its readers ('the personal touch'). These changes paralleled similar developments (commercialization) in adult popular fiction, and the influence of the cinema is obvious. In 1934 James D. Stewart, chief librarian in Bermondsey, claimed that children's reading habits were shaped to an increasing degree by changes in their environment: 'when the actual books could be sampled before being borrowed, boys naturally preferred those authors who knew of the existence of motor cars, aeroplanes, wireless, and other features of the present day . . . It has nothing to do with literary merit, but is governed almost entirely by the contemporary environment.'[1] Editors of popular publications for boys could not ignore these interests.

Similarly, romantic fiction also changed, becoming more 'glamorous' (another nod to the cinema) while at the same time less fantastic in abandoning two strains of storyline: the florid, sensual romances of Marie Corelli and Elinor Glyn; and the gritty, 'mill-girl', rags-to-riches stories popular during the First World War. Plots became more bourgeois in tone and 'realistic'. Taste 'improved', therefore, perhaps as a result of exposure to other mass media. In the 1930s Graves and

[1] James D. Stewart, FLA, 'What Boys Read', *The Boy*, 6 (Mar. 1934), 171.

Hodges observed of adult members of the 'low-brow reading public' that:

the annals of the Land of Tosh no longer carried wide conviction and the mezzo-brow 'Book of the Month' choice of the dailies became (through the Twopenny libraries) the shop-girls' reading too—or such of them as did not sweep all modern fiction aside as 'capitalistic dope'. Even Elinor Glyn's passionate novels then appeared a little grotesque, with their tiger-skin and orchid settings; and, aware of the growing influence of famous book reviewers on the semi-literate public, she ceased to send out review-copies of her new books.[2]

The *Rebecca* plot was now used repeatedly with great success. Mills & Boon heroines, for example, despite their lower-middle/working-class background (of which they are proud), consistently win the respect, even the admiration, of their social superiors through hard work and a natural common sense. The dream embodied in such fiction was not aristocratic, as in the Victorian 'sensation novels', but something more plausible. 'The idea is to give the bored factory-girl or worn-out mother of five a dream-life in which she pictures herself—not actually as a duchess (that convention has gone out) but as, say, the wife of a bank-manager', Orwell correctly noted.[3]

In many respects, the most important influence upon popular publishing between 1914 and 1950 was war. We have seen how little affected service industries, including publishing, were by the economic depression; the First and Second World Wars, on the other hand, had lasting consequences. In general, wartime served to preserve, and perhaps heighten, demand for reading when other leisure activities (wireless, sport, cinema-going hours) were curtailed. It also made the escapist motive less something to be ashamed of, and sales of light fiction boomed—although, it is true, whatever was printed sold. An artificial prosperity for publishers was therefore created: paper rationing, by restricting output, ensured ready sales of all titles in print (which effectively saved the magazine trade after 1939). While these static conditions necessarily inhibited profits, they also served to bolster many shaky publishing houses (the Religious Tract Society is a notable example). Post-war economic conditions, furthermore, served

---

[2] Robert Graves and Alan Hodge, *The Long Week-End: A Social History of Great Britain 1918–1939* (London, 1941), 52.

[3] George Orwell, 'Boy's Weeklies', in Sonia Orwell and Ian Angus (eds.), *The Collected Essays, Journalism and Letters of George Orwell*, i (Penguin edn., Harmondsworth, 1987), 527.

to restructure the publishing industry. Rising production costs promoted commercialization of the book trade during the 1920s and 1930s, at the expense of the magazine trade. The depression in magazine sales favoured the larger publishers with many titles: these firms possessed the financial reserves to corner the market with different, technologically superior, new titles. The Big 5 papers, *Woman*, *Picture Post*, and *Eagle* are some examples, as is the fact that Lutterworth Periodicals Ltd. was crippled after the Second World War by such 'giants' as Newnes and Hulton. The magazine trade was more at risk from the increased expenditure of all classes on leisure between the wars, for, unlike the book trade (bolstered by the 'tuppenny' libraries), no means of cheap distribution existed for magazines, when spending money was directed towards other leisure activities.

Judging from contemporaries and readers, the principal motive of the 'new reading public' during our period appears to have been 'escapism', as it was before 1914. While this was not unique to the poorer classes (Neville Chamberlain said he looked to reading for 'something that takes me out from my daily life and away into a world as remote from reality as possible'[4]), these readers were apparently more dependent upon light fiction. It may be fortunate that the lower-middle and working classes regarded light fiction, with its reliance upon the happy ending and the rule of law, as their 'drug', rather than the real thing. Frederick Cowles expressed this sentiment in 1938:

The highbrow critics who assert that a reader cannot obtain anything of value from a light novel only display their own ignorance. Even the most sensational fiction often contains some out-of-the-way information which can be easily assimilated. The readers of light fiction obtain something more than actual facts and figures—they obtain either a mental opiate or a mental tonic. Both are badly needed in these days when so many of us have to live upon our nerves.[5]

Escapism was not new: in response to a Scottish librarian's claim that 80 per cent of the books she issued were 'disgraceful', Rose Macaulay explained that the reading public through the ages has been obsessed with the 'three S's': sensation, sentiment, and the sordid. 'Most of us like to enjoy with our reading a shudder of excitement, a tear and a smile of sympathy, and a feeling of superiority to the sordid persons

---

[4] 'Prime Minister's Solace', *The Times* (4 May 1939), 9. Chamberlain was fond of Dumas, Conrad—and crime stories. 'I am always swallowing one myself as a sort of literary cocktail, but it is as easy to become an addict to detective stories as to opium and to crossword puzzles. I prefer therefore to treat them as an occasional excess.'

[5] Frederick Cowles, 'Public Libraries and Fiction', *PC* (19 Mar. 1938), 422.

read about.'[6] As a boy in Glasgow during the Second World War, Bob Crampsey purloined his mother's copy of *The People's Friend* to supplement his ravenous appetite for reading. Although the stories 'could scarcely have been further removed from real Scottish life in the 1940s', with women of 'impregnable virtue' and 'dependable and quiet' heroes, it was, none the less, 'a splendid anodyne' for Scottish women.[7] Therefore, escapist reading, and particularly of violent thrillers, may have served as a type of safety-valve, a method to disperse tensions and anxieties which otherwise might have erupted furiously, chiefly among the unemployed. The only harm, it would appear, was that it was so addictive. As such, lower-middle- and working-class readers had no incentive to graduate to high-brow fiction; the continuity between adults and children is evidence of this ingrained dependency.

But, in some respects, the character of escapist reading changed markedly after the First World War. Critics tended to use this phrase loosely, when escapism implied more than just a happy ending. The most striking example is in romantic fiction. Given the shift in emphasis towards more 'realistic' plots, escapism represented, to an increasing degree, aspiration. It is not unreasonable to assume, for example, that readers of Mills & Boon novels thought that the lifestyle presented to them was both socially desirable and 'proper', and was, furthermore, though probably out of reach, not absurdly out of reach. Sara Seale (perhaps Mills & Boon's most successful author) was correct in claiming that the secret of the popularity of romantic novels was that they combined escapism with 'a story which could conceivably apply to many of its readers' lives.'[8] Similarly, Richard Hoggart has noted that working-class readers preferred not a complete escape from ordinary life, but something which 'assumes that ordinary life is intrinsically interesting. The emphasis is initially on the human and detailed, with or without the 'pepping-up' which crime or sex or splendour gives. For them passion is no more interesting than steady home-life.'[9]

This aspiration was ideological. 'What any generation wants to do in its leisure is the expression of its characteristic ideal',[10] C. Delisle Burns wrote in 1932. This was certainly the case with popular fiction:

[6] Rose Macaulay, 'Marginal Comments', *The Spectator* (23 Aug. 1935), 289.
[7] Bob Crampsey, *The Young Civilian: A Glasgow Wartime Boyhood* (Edinburgh, 1987), 70–1.
[8] Sara Seale, 'Who Said Romantic Novel is Dying?', *TC* (29 July 1950), 23.
[9] Richard Hoggart, *The Uses of Literacy* (London, 1958), 94–5.
[10] C. Delisle Burns, *Leisure in the Modern World* (London, 1932), 174.

many of the attitudes contained in novels and magazines reflected the ideological views of the period. According to Kirsten Drotner, the D. C. Thomson boys' papers, for example, satisfied a child's natural need for protest, challenging the infallibility and dominance of adults. This was expressed in the use of two types of character: the 'super-human' hero with extraordinary powers, and the youngster who, through force of circumstances, quite literally saves the (child's) world by foiling Nazis, crazed scientists, and dishonest sportsmen.[11] For perhaps the first time, the child was presented as omnipotent and vital, and readers obviously responded to such flattery. D. C. Thomson may have sensed a popular urge and responded in a relatively harmless, unsubversive way. Similarly, Mills & Boon's emphasis on propriety, companionate marriage, and full-time motherhood reflected the pre-dominant ideological view of sexual relations between the wars. Jane Lewis has suggested that by the Second World War middle-class wives (the role-model of most Mills & Boon readers) 'had greater mobility, more legal freedom and probably increased expectations of sexual pleasure'.[12] The ideal of 'modern marriage', moreover, was togetherness and companionship (paramount in the novels) rather than passivity and separation. Despite a declining birthrate, rising illegitimacy, and divorce, marriage and motherhood were still sacred and sought after, and women were regarded as both the moral guardians of the home and the expression of proper behaviour. Rachel Anderson has noted how the ideal of virginity remained standard in romantic fiction when the reality was quite different:

Despite the new ideas on sexual freedom, free love, and the biological urges which were being advocated in the twenties by writers like H. G. Wells, Aldous Huxley and Bertrand Russell, and the practical advice being offered by Marie Stopes ... free love was by no means what the fictional heroine sought. For her, there was still one man for one woman, and chastity was still a virtue ... marriage was still the ultimate dream.[13]

Significantly, religion was no longer a part of this ideal (although heroines did sometimes 'pray' to an unspecified deity), as we might expect, given the conventional character of such 'wish-pictures'. Thus

---

[11] Kirsten Drotner, *English Children and their Magazines, 1751–1945* (New Haven, Conn., 1988), 222–3.

[12] Jane Lewis, *Women in England 1870–1950: Sexual Divisions and Social Change* (Sussex, 1984), 135.

[13] Rachel Anderson, *The Purple Heart Throbs: The Sub-Literature of Love* (London, 1974), 200–1.

the Religious Tract Society, as we have seen, was forced to accommodate the increasingly secular nature of society between the wars.

Finally, popular fiction reflected changing attitudes towards class divisions and differences encouraged by both wars. 'Discretion and reticence about class became the hallmarks of the two most public of all the media, films and radio', Arthur Marwick observed; popular fiction was no exception.[14] In a decided departure from the Victorian and Edwardian literary tradition, class divisions were blurred. The Big 5 papers, for example, were more 'classless' than the *Gem*, and tales of boys set around the world reflected the spirit of Anglo-Saxon internationalism and social mobility, as they did in the *Boy's Own Paper*. Similarly, but with less success, the Religious Tract Society during the 1930s and 1940s made a conscious effort to broaden the appeal of its magazines to all classes. Mills & Boon also managed to transcend class by championing the lower-middle/working-class heroine, accentuating the value of her class—such qualities as its common sense, propriety, and fortitude.

Hence, it is arguable that publishers of popular fiction reinforced the predominant stereotypes and ideals of the period rather than imposed them. Attitudes expressed in novels and magazines often reflected what people thought they should be, even if reality was different. Consequently, it is doubtful whether such publishers could have had as direct and immediate an influence upon the reading public as, say, a tabloid newspaper proprietor might have had.[15] But Mills & Boon, D. C. Thomson, and the Religious Tract Society all believed that they were reaching and helping their publics, at least in an instructive way. D. C. Thomson, for example, prided itself on introducing proper spelling and grammar to children. 'The vital thing was, in a prose story there's only one way of spelling a word, and that's the right way', Jack Mackersie said. 'And they were being taught good English, and good spelling, and loving it, and not knowing they were being directed in this fashion, which is what I suppose good education is all about.' The boys' papers also served to nurture the reading habit in young people by

---

[14] Arthur Marwick, 'Images of the Working Class since 1930', in Jay Winter (ed.), *The Working Class in Modern British History: Essays in Honour of Henry Pelling* (Cambridge, 1983), 234.
[15] Lord Beaverbrook, publisher of the *Daily Express*, unashamedly told the Royal Commission on the Press (1947–9) that his main purpose in publishing was power and influence: 'I run the paper purely for the purpose of making propaganda, and with no other object' (published in Royal Commission on the Press, *Minutes of Evidence*, 26th day (18 Mar. 1948), p. 4, question 8656).

providing 'a good read'. The Religious Tract Society regarded its magazines as propaganda arms of the organization's missionary efforts overseas. Similarly, Mills & Boon believed that its novels had the potential to influence a readership which it considered both gullible and vulnerable. Mary Burchell expressed well the sense of responsibility which Mills & Boon authors felt in approaching their readers:

The thing I can truly say is, I have never got out of my mind that romantic fiction has more influence than anything to do with its literary worth. That is because it is read by unsophisticated people.

I truly don't think I have ever let a girl of mine do anything that I wouldn't like to see a girl of that age do, or if she does, she's punished.

Publishers of children's books also assumed a role *in loco parentis*, as did such prolific and popular authors as Captain W. E. Johns. This management of popular fiction was, we have seen, the legacy of the 'improving' and 'optimistic' movement initiated in the 1870s by such pioneering publications as the *Boy's Own Paper*.

In the end, however, the extent to which readers were actually influenced by such fiction, and by the publishers' views on morality, class, and patriotism, is difficult to gauge. We can determine how successful a magazine or a novel was by the number of copies sold, but whether financial success implied an endorsement of editorial policy by readers is another matter. Drotner's assertion, for example, that children's magazines were excellent 'seismographs' of taste is flawed because of the degree of parental supervision in the choice of reading matter. The answer may lie in what Cynthia White called 'the cornerstone of modern publishing for women': the 'all-important concept of "reader-identification"'.[16] Each publisher went to great lengths to accommodate his publications to the personal taste of each reader. The *Boy's Own Paper* appealed to all young men; *The Wizard* to all 'chums'; *My Weekly* to all 'friends'; and Mills & Boon addressed a personal notice ('the bait') to each reader. The trust undoubtedly established between publisher and reader, reflected in the fierce loyalty of women and children to their publications, must have inculcated attitudes and values through countless repetitions. Given the extent of market research, moreover, there must have been much common ground. 'I think we published what we thought represented the state of play in general', Alan Boon claimed. Similarly, George Moonie believes that the Thomson boys' papers represent fifty years of social history, as the need

---

[16] Cynthia L. White, *Women's Magazines 1693–1968* (London, 1970), 87.

for the child to identify was constantly encouraged among editors: 'All the time we are subconsciously aware of the social conditions of the time when we are creating these characters in a story. We are drawing upon things that are happening, and we've seen happening, when the papers are published, using these as props in a story.'

Popular fiction in Britain during our period embodied a number of common attitudes and concerns. In general, it was fiercely patriotic and pro-Empire, but decreasingly xenophobic. The importance of good manners, respect, and public service was emphasized. Good always triumphed over evil, and the consequences of crime and 'sinful' behaviour were depicted, often graphically. Marriage, motherhood, and 'middle-classery' were all endorsed, in a kind of pan-class crusade. In many respects, therefore, the status quo owed much to D. C. Thomson, Mills & Boon, the Religious Tract Society, and other publishers. Editors acted as educators, both openly and subliminally, for as long as it was financially possible. Fortunately for the predominantly Conservative Government, as Orwell observed, popular publishing was wholly a preserve of the Right, and thus non-confrontational. These publishers were consequently never troubled by censorship laws, as the cinema was. But if they represented the ruling moral system of the period, as well as the kind of party Conservatism which was politically dominant, the one was not dependent upon the other. Popular fiction was immune to political change: the Mills & Boon 'formula', for example, succeeded as well in the 1940s as in the 1930s. It was as profitable under Attlee as under Chamberlain.

It is unlikely, however, that popular publishers cast themselves—or could cast themselves—as agents in a master plan for social control and domination, as Bridget Fowler has suggested they did. Of popular literature she writes: 'Archaic elements litter its pages, both in style and the images of society it employs. . . . At its most conscious, such social control is exerted by editorial selection on the basis of practical rules of thumb about the genre and "what the audience wants" which filter out any ideologically or stylistically alien product.'[17] This is certainly true, but, as we have seen, financial misfortune could lay waste to even the holiest of intentions, as Lutterworth Periodicals discovered after the Second World War. Lutterworth, moreover, could not make such an 'archaic element' as religion sell papers.

---

[17] Bridget Fowler, 'True to Me Always: An Analysis of Women's Magazine Fiction', in Christopher Pawling (ed.), *Popular Fiction and Social Change* (London, 1984), 105.

Popular fiction, moreover, is an organic genre subject to change. Even the most successful publishers have had to adapt in order to maintain their momentum. The launching of the *Eagle* comic in 1950 hit the Big 5 papers hard, presaging their transformation in the late 1950s to picture-story papers. This was the first serious challenge to the Thomson supremacy, and the firm, not surprisingly, reacted, following the lead of its two best-selling comics, *The Dandy* and *The Beano*.[18] Similarly, romantic fiction, although littered with stereotypes, was not regressive for its period, and in the 1970s and 1980s Mills & Boon has faced some of the same problems that the Lutterworth Press did. The 'formula' which it projected in the interwar years was well suited to the predominant 'romantic' ideals of companionate marriage and motherhood. But post-war changes in gender role allocation and in women's aspirations have, to some extent, cut the ground from beneath its feet. Despite its confidence that it was purveying timeless ideals, Mills & Boon has always struggled to fit the 'formula' to the times. During this period the firm acknowledged 'modern' problems such as unemployment and single parenthood, and began to admit more passion between spouses. The inclusion of premarital sex in the novels today is embarrassing to some; the Boon brothers feel resigned. Mary Burchell was scornful of the fact that commercial concerns have had such an influence, standardizing the 'product', which is marketed like soap-flakes. 'The paperbacks, of course, changed the whole scene. We weren't all very pleased', she said. 'I think that the influence today is very much for what sells. We're in the business to sell.' As were all publishers of 'popular' fiction.

[18] According to Audit Bureau of Circulations records, the *Eagle* averaged a weekly sale of 735,000 copies between Jan. and June 1950. *The Wizard*, the best-selling Big 5 title, only sold 460,500 (according to D. C. Thomson). After the Second World War most of the Big 5 papers experimented with picture stories: *Adventure* featured a continuing picture serial on its cover from 1947.

BIBLIOGRAPHY

I. *Archives consulted*

AUDIT BUREAU OF CIRCULATIONS LTD., LONDON
THE BBC WRITTEN ARCHIVES CENTRE, READING
  1939 script of 'Picture Page' programme.
THE BOOTS COMPANY PLC, NOTTINGHAM
  Information pertaining to the Boots Booklovers Library: catalogues, usage
  statistics, library policy.
D. C. THOMSON & CO., LTD., DUNDEE
  Circulation figures, bound files of magazines, library of newspaper cuttings,
  and editorial information.
THE JOHN JOHNSON COLLECTION, BODLEIAN LIBRARY, OXFORD
  First numbers of magazines for women and children, circulating library
  catalogues and ephemera.
JOHN MENZIES PLC, EDINBURGH
  Statistical data on advertising at bookstalls, library of newspaper cuttings,
  Menzies publications.
NATIONAL FEDERATION OF RETAIL NEWSAGENTS, LONDON
  Bound files of newsagent publications, list of retired newsagents.
THE TOM HARRISSON MASS-OBSERVATION ARCHIVE, UNIVERSITY OF SUSSEX
  Topic Collections 'Reading', 'Newspaper Reading', 'Town and District',
  'Air Raids', 'Posters', 'Women in Wartime', 'Youth', 'Children and Educa-
  tion'; File Reports nos. 1–3194 (selected).
THE UNITED SOCIETY FOR CHRISTIAN LITERATURE ARCHIVE, SCHOOL OF
  ORIENTAL AND AFRICAN STUDIES, UNIVERSITY OF LONDON
  Minutes of General Committee, Finance, Publications and Copyright sub-
  committees, annual reports, financial statistics.
W. H. SMITH & SON LTD., MILTON HILL, ABINGDON
  Trade publications, library catalogues, and statistics.

II. *Oral evidence*

Anderson, Alfred	10 April 1986, Dundee
	11 August 1987, Dundee
Boon, Alan	30 May 1986, London
	5 August 1986, London
	4 December 1986, London
	10 August 1988, Richmond

Boon, John   30 May 1986, London
                                4 December 1986, London
                                10 August 1988, Richmond
Burchell, Mary   18 June 1986, London
Cartland, Barbara   26 May 1988, Hatfield
Cooper, R. D.   17 May 1988, Oxford
Doig, David   17 July 1986, Dundee
Fowler, Norman   9–10 April 1986, Dundee
Foxell, Michael   22 June 1988, Farnham
Mackersie, Jack   10 April 1986, Dundee
                                11 August 1987, Dundee
Macleod, Jean S.   10 July 1986, York
Marsh, Jean   3 August 1988, Bewdley
Mihill, George (Mr and Mrs)   3 August 1988, Clevedon
Moonie, George   17 July 1986, Dundee
                                14 August 1987, Dundee
Paterson, Maurice   10 April 1986, Dundee
                                16 July 1986, Dundee
                                12 August 1987, Dundee
Russell, Shirley   5 July 1988, London
Thompson, Philothea   26 February 1987, Woodstock
Wyatt, H. R.   18 March 1988, Oxford

III. Publications by firms studied (and quoted in text)

MILLS & BOON, LTD.

BRADSHAW, NINA, *The Net Love Spread* (1935).
BRAYBROOKE, FRANCIS, *Anne Finds Reality* (1940).
BURCHELL, MARY, *Call-And I'll Come.* (1937).
—— *Wife to Christopher* (1936).
CARFRAE, ELIZABETH, *Lady by Marriage* (1935).
CHANDOS, FAYE, *Away From Each Other* (1944).
COLE, SOPHIE, *Arrows from the Dark* (1909)
DORIEN, RAY, *Anchor at Hazard* (1935).
EVANS, CONSTANCE M., *Enter—A Land Girl* (1944).
GERARD, LOUISE, *Secret Love* (1932).
—— *A Sultan's Slave* (1921).
—— *The Witch-Child: A Romance of the Swamp* (1916).
MACLEOD, JEAN S., *Life for Two* (1936).
—— *This Much to Give* (1945).
MARTIN, STELLA, *The Transformation of Philip Jettan* (1923).
SARK, SYLVIA, *Once to Every Woman* (1940).

SEALE, SARA, *The Gentle Prisoner* (1949).
TRENT, GUY, *Be Patient with Love* (1937).

D. C. THOMSON & CO., LTD. (JOHN LENG & CO., LTD.)

Adventure	*Red Star Weekly*
Annie Swan Annual	*The Rover*
Dixon Hawke Library	*Secrets*
Family Star	*The Skipper*
Flame	*Topical Times*
The Hotspur	*Weekly Welcome*
My Weekly	*The Wizard*
The People's Friend	*Woman's Way*
Red Letter	

THE RELIGIOUS TRACT SOCIETY
(USCL; LUTTERWORTH PERIODICALS, LTD.)

Annual Report of the Religious Tract Society
Annual Report of the United Society for Christian Literature
Boy's Own Annual
The Boy's Own Paper
Girl's Own Annual
The Girl's Own Paper (*The Girl's Own Paper and Woman's Magazine, The
   Woman's Magazine and Girl's Own Paper, Girl's Own Paper–Heiress, Heiress*)
The Religious Tract Society Record
Rovering
The Sunday at Home
The Woman's Magazine

IV. Annuals, newspapers and periodicals used as sources

The Advertisers' A.B.C.
Annual Abstract of Statistics
The Bee (Boots)
The Board of Trade Journal
The Bookseller
The Book Window (W. H. Smith)
Library Association Record
May's (Willing's) British and Irish Press Guide
The National Newsagent, Bookseller, Stationer and Fancy Trades' Journal
   (continued as *The National Newsagent, Bookseller and Stationer*)
The Newsagent and Booksellers' Review (continued as *The News and Book Trade*

Review and Stationer's Gazette; The Newsagents' Booksellers' Review and Stationers' Gazette)

The Newsbasket (W. H. Smith)

The Newspaper (Benn's) Press Directory

The N.F. Year Book: The Official Organ of the National Federation of Retail Newsagents, Booksellers and Stationers

The Publishers' Circular

The Scottish Newsagent, Booksellers' and Stationers' Guide

The Times

The Times Higher Education Supplement

The Times Literary Supplement

The Trade Circular (W. H. Smith)

The Writers' and Artists' Year Book

Young Opinion: A Literary Review (The Junior Book Club)

V. Secondary Material

ACKLAND, JOSEPH, 'Elementary Education and the Decay of Literature', *The Nineteenth Century*, 35 (Mar. 1894), 412–23.

Advertising World, 'Press, Advertising and Trade under War Conditions' (London, Oct. 1940).

ALDERSON, BRIAN, 'Tracts, Rewards and Fairies: The Victorian Contribution to Children's Literature', in Asa Briggs (ed.), *Essays in the History of Publishing in Celebration of the 250th Anniversary of the House of Longman 1724–1974* (London, 1974), 247–82.

ALDGATE, ANTHONY, and RICHARDS, JEFFREY, *Britain Can Take It: The British Cinema in the Second World War* (Oxford, 1986).

ALEXANDER, WILLIAM, 'Literature of the People—Past and Present', *Good Words*, 17 (1876) 92–6.

ALLEN, R. G. D. and BOWLEY, A. L., *Family Expenditure: A Study of its Variation*, (London, 1935).

ALTICK, RICHARD, *The English Common Reader: A Social History of the Mass Reading Public 1800–1900* (Chicago, 1957).

—— 'English Publishing and the Mass Audience in 1852', *Studies in Bibliography* vi (1954), 3–24.

'An Analysis of Child Reading', *The Publishers' Circular* (20 Nov. 1926), 759.

ANDERSON, RACHEL, *The Purple Heart Throbs: The Sub-Literature of Love* (London, 1974).

ANDERSON, SIDNEY W., 'Catering for the Adolescent', *Library Assistant*, 420 (Sept. 1934), 192–5; 421 (Oct. 1934), 215–19; 423 (Dec. 1934) 254–9.

'The Appetite for Books', *John O'London's Weekly* (4 June 1943), 91.

'A Bad Time for Good Books', *Manchester Guardian*, 14 Sept. 1921; quoted in *The Publishers' Circular* (15 Oct. 1921), 397.

BAILEY, PETER, *Leisure and Class in Victorian England: Rational Recreation and the Contest for Control, 1830–1885* (London, 1987).

BARCLAY, FLORENCE L., *The Rosary* (London, 1909).

—— *Through the Postern Gate* (London, 1912).

'The Basic Paper Ration: The Situation of the Small General Publisher', *The Bookseller* (4 May 1944) 410, 412; (18 May 1944), 442.

BATTY, RONALD F., *How to Run a Twopenny Library* (London, 1938).

BEABLE, WILLIAM HENRY, *Romance of Great Businesses* (London, 1926).

BEAUMAN, NICOLA, *A Very Great Profession: The Woman's Novel 1914–1939* (London, 1984).

BELL, FLORENCE EVELEEN E., LADY, *At the Works: A Study of a Manufacturing Town* (Virago edn., London, 1985).

BELTON, F. L., 'Library Episode', *The Bee* (20 Oct. 1949), 28.

BENNETT, ALAN, 'Alan Bennett Remembers the Treachery of Books', *The Independent on Sunday Review* (28 Jan. 1990), 8–9.

BENNETT, ARNOLD, *How to Become an Author* (London, 1903).

BENNETT, SCOTT, 'Revolutions in Thought: Serial Publication and the Mass Market for Reading', in Joanne Shattock and Michael Wolff (ed.), *The Victorian Periodical Press: Samplings and Soundings* (Leicester, 1982), 225–57.

BERRY, WILLIAM EWERT, 1st VISCOUNT CAMROSE, *British Newspapers and Their Controllers* (London, 1947).

'A Best-Seller in Search of a Publisher', *The Bookseller* (5 Apr. 1945), 406–7.

'"Biggles" is the Boys' Hero', *News Chronicle* (17 Nov. 1938), 3.

BIGLAND, EILEEN, *Ouida: The Passionate Victorian* (London, 1950).

BLAKE, GEORGE, 'The Press and the Public', *Criterion Miscellany*, 21 (1930) 5–36.

BLAKE, NICHOLAS, 'Detective Stories and Happy Families', *The Bookseller* (13 Mar. 1935), 268.

BLOOM, URSULA, *Life Is No Fairy Tale* (London, 1976).

Board of Trade, *Census of Distribution and Other Services 1950* (London, 1953).

BODEN, F. C., 'Fiction in the Mining Districts', *The Bookseller* (6 Feb. 1935), 106, 108.

'Book Publishing in Britain To-day', *The Bookseller* (8 June 1944), 495.

'Books a Cure for War-Weariness: The Need for Good Fiction', *The Times* (11 Oct. 1939), 3.

'Books and the Public', *The Newsbasket* (May 1930), 104.

'"Books *are* a Commodity"', *The Publishers' Circular* (11 Oct. 1930), 513–14.

'Books for Days of Crisis', leading article, *Times Literary Supplement* (1 Oct. 1938), 627.

'"Books Library": Select Reading for a Troopship', *The Times* (29 June 1916), 11.

'The Bookstaller', 'Round the Bookshops: Boys' "Bloods"', *The Times* (1 July 1922), 14.

BOON, JOHN, 'The Early Years of Mills & Boon', *The Bookseller* (2 May 1959), 1650–2.

—— 'A Plague O' Both Your Houses!', *The Bookseller* (18 Oct. 1945), 498–9.

Boots Booklovers Library, *Modern English Literature: A Selection of the Best Known Works circulated by Boots Booklovers Library with which is embodied a Guide to Popular Works of Fiction* (Nottingham, 1903).

Boots the Chemists, *Behind the Scenes: Glimpses of the Immense Organization behind Boots the Chemists* (Nottingham, 1930).

BOSANQUET, HELEN, 'Cheap Literature', *Contemporary Review*, 79 (May 1901), 671–81.

BOWLEY, A. L., *Studies in the National Income 1924–1938* (Cambridge, 1944).

—— *Wages and Income in the United Kingdom Since 1860* (Cambridge, 1937).

——, and BURNETT-HURST, A. R., *Likelihood and Poverty: A Study in the Economic Conditions of Working-Class Households in Northampton, Warrington, Stanley and Reading* (London, 1915).

BOX, KATHLEEN, 'Cinema and the Public', Social Survey, NS 106 (London, Mar. 1948).

—— 'Wartime Reading', File Report 47, M-O (London Mar. 1940).

—— 'Selection and Taste in Book Reading', File Report 48, M-O (London, Mar. 1940).

'The BOY'S OWN PAPER: Memories 1879–1929. A Souvenir of the B.O.P. Jubilee' (London, 1929).

BRADDON, M. E., *Lady Audley's Secret* (first edn. London, 1862; Virago edn. London, 1985).

BRADLEY, IAN, *The Optimists: Themes and Personalities in Victorian Liberalism* (London, 1980).

BRATTON, J. S., *The Impact of Victorian Children's Fiction* (London, 1981).

BREW, J. MACALISTER, *Informal Education: Adventures and Reflections* (London, 1947).

—— *In the Service of Youth: A Practical Manual of Work among Adolescents* (London, 1943).

BRIGGS, ASA, *The B.B.C.: The First Fifty Years* (London, 1985).

BROWN, LUCY, *Victorian News and Newspapers* (Oxford, 1985).

BUCKLAND, FRANK, 'What We Read in the Army', *John O'London's Weekly* (31 Dec. 1943). 121–2.

BURNS, C. DELISLE, *Leisure in the Modern World* (London, 1932).

Business Statistics Office, *Historical Record of the Census of Production 1907 to 1970*, HMSO (1979).

'By Favour of the Public', *The Bookseller* (10 Dec. 1949), 1488.

CADOGAN, MARY, *Frank Richards: The Chap Behind the Chums* (London, 1988).

—— *Richmal Crompton: The Woman Behind William* (London, 1986).

——, and CRAIG, PATRICIA, *You're a Brick, Angela!: The Girls' Story 1839–1985* (London, 1976).

CALDER, ANGUS, *The People's War: Britain 1939–45* (London, 1969).

CALLENDER, T. E., 'The Twopenny Library', *Library Association Record*, 3rd Ser. 3 (Mar. 1933), 88–90.

CAMERON, JAMES, *Point of Departure* (London, 1967).

CARADOG JONES, D. (ed.), *The Social Survey of Merseyside* (London, 1934).

CARPENTER, HUMPHREY, and PRICHARD, MARI, *The Oxford Companion to Children's Literature* (Oxford, 1984).

CARPENTER, KEVIN, *Penny Dreadfuls and Comics: English Periodicals for Children from Victorian Times to the Present Day* (London, 1983).

CARR-SAUNDERS, A. M., and CARADOG JONES, D., *A Survey of the Social Structure of England and Wales* (Oxford, 1937).

——, and MOSER, C. A., *A Survey of Social Conditions in England and Wales* (Oxford, 1958).

——, MANNHEIM, HERMANN, and RHODES, E. C., *Young Offenders: An Enquiry into Juvenile Delinquency* (Cambridge, 1943).

CARTER, JOHN, 'Detective Fiction'. in John Carter (ed.), *New Paths in Book Collecting* (London, 1934), 33–63.

CARTLAND, BARBARA, *Jig-saw* (London, 1923).

—— *Sawdust* (London, 1925).

Centenary of the Religious Tract Society (London, 1898).

Central Statistical Office, *Annual Abstract of Statistics*, no. 86 (London, 1938–48).

—— *National Income and Expenditure 1946–1951* (London, 1952).

—— *National Income Statistics: Sources and Methods* (London, 1956).

—— *Statistical Digest of the War* (London, 1951).

CHASE, JAMES HADLEY, *No Orchids for Miss Blandish* (London, 1939).

'The Cheap Movement in Literature', *Book-Lore*, 4 (19 June 1886), 10–12.

CHESTERTON, G. K., 'A Defence of Penny Dreadfuls', *The Defendant* (London, 1914).

CHEVERTON, A. G., 'The Vogue of Zane Grey', *The Publishers' Circular* (27 Mar. 1920), 345.

'Children and the "Library Habit"', *The Publishers' Circular* (17 Aug. 1929), 219.

CLARK, ALAN, *The Children's Annual* (London, 1988).

CLOUD, HENRY, *Barbara Cartland: Crusader in Pink* (London, 1979).

COLBY, ROBERT A., '"The Librarian Rules the Roost": The Career of Charles Edward Mudie (1818–1890)', *Wilson Library Bulletin*, 26 (Apr. 1952), 623–7.

—— '"That He Who Rides May Read": W. H. Smith & Son's Railway Library', *Wilson Library Bulletin*, 27 (Dec. 1952), 300–6.

COLE, G. D. H., and POSTGATE, RAYMOND, *The Common People 1746–1946* (London, 1938).

COLLET, COLLET DOBSON, *History of the Taxes on Knowledge: Their Origin and Repeal* (London, 1933).

[COLLINS, WILKIE], 'The Unknown Public', *Household Words*, 18 (21 Aug. 1858), 217–22.

COLWELL, EILEEN H., 'Some Trends in Children's Books', *The Bookseller* (1 Sept. 1937), 195–6.

—— 'What the Children Want From the Publishers', *The Bookseller* (4 Sept. 1935), 839, 841.

—— 'Which Books Delight Children?' *The Trade Circular* (28 Aug. 1948), 9.

CONNOLLY, RAY, 'A Childhood: Kingsley Amis', *The Times* (24 Mar. 1990), 35.

CORELLI, MARIE, *The Mighty Atom* (London, 1896).

—— *Ziska: The Problem of a Wicked Soul* (London, 1897).

CORP, W. G., *Fifty Years: A Brief Account of the Associated Booksellers of Great Britain and Ireland 1895–1945* (Oxford, 1948).

'The Cost of Printing: Mr Pett Ridge on Love in Fiction', *The Times* (17 Mar. 1920), 14.

COTTERELL, LAWRENCE, 'Before the "Juvenile" Reaches the Shop Window', *The Trade Circular* (25 Sept. 1948), 5.

COWLES, FREDERICK, 'Children's Reading in Wartime', *The Publishers' Circular* (23 Aug. 1941), 92.

—— 'Libraries in Wartime', *The Publishers' Circular* (24 May 1941), 221–2.

—— 'Public Libraries and Fiction', *The Publishers' Circular* (19 Mar. 1938), 422.

COX, JACK, *Take A Cold Tub, Sir! The Story of the Boy's Own Paper* (Guildford, 1982).

—— 'Teen-age Critics Keep 70-Year-Old "B.O.P." On Its Toes', *The Trade Circular* (15 Jan. 1949), 5.

CRAIG, PATRICIA, and CADOGAN, MARY, *The Lady Investigates: Women Detectives and Spies in Fiction* (Oxford, 1981).

CRAMPSEY, BOB, *The Young Civilian: A Glasgow Wartime Boyhood* (Edinburgh, 1987).

CRANFIELD, G. A., *The Press and Society: From Caxton to Northcliffe* (London, 1978).

CRUSE, AMY, *After the Victorians* (London, 1938).

—— *The Victorians and their Books* (London, 1935).

CURWEN, HENRY, *A History of Booksellers, The Old and the New* (London, 1874).

CUTT, MARGARET MARY, *Ministering Angels: A Study of Nineteenth-Century Evangelical Writing for Children* (Wormley, Herts., 1979).

DARK, SIDNEY, *After Working Hours: The Enjoyment of Leisure* (London, 1929).

—— *The Life of Sir Arthur Pearson* (London, 1922).

—— *The New Reading Public* (London, 1922).

DARTON, F. J. HARVEY, *Children's Books in England: Five Centuries of Social Life* (Cambridge, 1932; 1958).

DAVIDSON, JULIE, 'Speak Softly and Say Yes Please', in *The D. C. Thomson Bumper Fun Book* (Edinburgh, 1977), 105–16.

DAWSON, JOHN, *Practical Journalism: How to Enter Thereon and Succeed. A Manual for Beginners and Amateurs* (London, 1885; 1904).

'Death of Mr Charles Garvice', *The Publishers' Circular* (6 Mar. 1920), 255.

'The Decline in Magazine Sales', *The Newsbasket* (July–Oct. 1927), 157–61, 181–5, 209–11, 229–30.

'Decline in Novel Reading: Librarians' Findings', *The Times* (22 Aug. 1950), 6.

'Decline of Book Reading: Rivalry of the Newspaper', *The Times* (4 June 1928), 19.

DELL, ETHEL M., *The Knave of Diamonds* (London, 1912).

DELL, PENELOPE, *Nettie and Sissie: The Biography of Ethel M. Dell and her Sister Ella* (London, 1977).

'Diamond Jubilee B.O.P.—Major J. T. Gorman', script, 'Picture Page' programme, 209th edn. (broadcast 19 Jan. 1939); BBC Written Archives Centre, Reading. Interviewer: Dorothy A. Cannell.

DIBBLEE, G. BINNEY, *The Newspaper* (London, 1913).

Disinherited Youth: A Report on the 18+ Age Group Enquiry Prepared for the Trustees of the Carnegie U.K. Trust (Edinburgh, 1943).

DIXON, R. H., and TATTERSALL, G. K., 'Literature and Morals: A Boy's View and a Man's Reply', *The Boy* viii. 3 (Winter 1935/6), 332–6.

'Does Filming Stories Help their Sale?', *The Publishers' Circular* (8 May 1920), 515, 517.

DROTNER, KIRSTEN, *English Children and their Magazines 1751–1945* (New Haven, Conn., 1988).

—— 'Schoolgirls, Madcaps, and Air Aces: English Girls and their Magazine Reading Between the Wars', *Feminist Studies*, 9 (Spring 1983), 33–52.

DUNAE, PATRICK, 'Boys' Literature and the Idea of Empire', *Victorian Studies*, 24 (Autumn 1980).

—— '*Boy's Own Paper*: Origins and Editorial Policies', *The Private Library*, 2nd Ser. 9.4 (Winter 1976), 123–58.

—— 'British Juvenile Literature in an Age of Empire: 1880–1914', D. Phil. thesis, Victoria University of Manchester, Dec. 1975.

EASTON, FRED, 'Capture the Book Trade! Don't Blame Others—Act Yourself', *National Newsagent, Bookseller, Stationer and Fancy Trades' Journal* (23 Mar. 1935), 1.

'Effect of Films on Girls', *The Times* (30 Dec. 1950), 2.

ELLIOTT, GEORGE H., 'Our Readers and What They Read', *The Library*, 7 (Sept. 1895), 276–81.

ELLIS, PETER BERRESFORD, and WILLIAMS, PIERS, *By Jove, Biggles! The Life of Captain W. E. Johns* (London, 1981).

'The Encouragement of Reading: Practice in the West Riding and in Norfolk', *Times Educational Supplement* (7 Oct. 1913), 155.

'Encouraging Young Readers: Book-Borrowers Aged Five', *The Times* (16 Jan. 1937), 9.

ENGLEDOW, J. H., and FARR, W. C., 'The Reading and Other Interests of School Children in St Pancras', *Passmore Edwards Research Series*, no. 2 (London, 1933).

ESCOTT, T. H. S., *England: Its People, Polity and Pursuits* (London, 1885).

—— *Masters of English Journalism: A Study of Personal Forces* (London, 1911).

—— *Social Transformations of the Victorian Age: A Survey of Court and Country* (London, 1897).

ESDAILE, ARUNDELL, 'Books and the War: The Functions of Libraries', letter, *The Times* (11 Sept. 1939), 4.

'Favourite Books of Children: "Treasure Island" A First Choice', *The Times* (8 Sept. 1932), 12.

FAYNE, ERIC, and JENKINS, ROGER, *A History of the Gem and Magnet* (Maidstone, 1978).

FENN, G. MANVILLE, 'Henty and His Books', in Lance Salway (ed.), *A Peculiar Gift* (London, 1976), 424–36.

FORRESTER, WENDY, *Great Grandmama's Weekly: A Celebration of The Girl's Own Paper 1880–1901* (Guildford, 1980).

FOWLER, BRIDGET, 'True to Me Always: An Analysis of Women's Magazine Fiction', in Christopher Pawling, (ed.), *Popular Fiction and Social Change* (London, 1984), 99–126.

FRASER, W. HAMISH, *The Coming of the Mass Market 1850–1914* (London, 1981).

FRIEDERICHS, HULDA, *The Life of Sir George Newnes* (London, 1911).

From the Beginning: An Amalgamated Press Record in Outline (1888–1944) (London, 1944).

'From Comics to Conrad: The Librarian as Readers' Guide', *The Times* (21 Sept. 1950), 2.

FROST, THOMAS, *Forty Years' Recollections: Literary and Political* (London, 1880).

'The Future of the Newsagent-Bookseller', *The Bookseller* (1 Feb. 1947), 114–16.

GALLUP, GEORGE (ed.), *The Gallup International Public Opinion Polls: Great Britain 1937–1975* (New York, 1976).

—— *A Guide to Public Opinion Polls* (Princeton, NJ, 1948).

GANNET, J. B., 'Selling Down', *The Bookseller* (3 July 1935), 634–5.

'George Mackay Brown', *Contemporary Authors Autobiography Series*, 6 (1988), 61–76.

GISSING, GEORGE, *New Grub Street* (Penguin edn., Harmondsworth, 1987).

GLYN, ANTHONY, *Elinor Glyn* (London, 1956).

GLYN, ELINOR, *Three Weeks* (Duckworth edn., London, 1974).

GORDON, R. J., 'Child Reading', letter, *The Times* (25 Jan. 1949), 5.

GOWER, A. E., 'Children and the Reading Habit', *The Publishers' Circular* (5 Oct. 1929), 435.

GRAVES, ROBERT, and HODGE, ALAN, *The Long Week-end: A Social History of Great Britain 1918–1939* (London, 1941).

'A Great Librarian: Mr William Faux On His Half-Century's Experiences', *The Book Monthly* (Oct. 1903), 19–28.

GREEN, BENNY, 'George Orwell, Great Wilson and the Tuppenny Bloods', *The Spectator* (26 Dec. 1970), 840–1.

GREENWOOD, JAMES, *The Wilds of London* (London, 1874).

GREENWOOD, THOMAS, *Free Public Libraries: Their Organisation, Uses and Management* 1st edn. (London, 1886); 4th edn. (London, 1894).

—— *Greenwood's Library Year Book 1897* (London, 1897).

GREENWOOD, WALTER, *Love on the Dole* (Penguin edn., Harmondsworth, 1987).

GRIBBLE, LEONARD, *Who Killed Oliver Cromwell?* (London, 1937).

GRIEST, GUINEVERE L., *Mudie's Circulating Library and the Victorian Novel* (Newton Abbot, 1970).

GRIGSON, GEOFFREY, 'Novels, Twopenny Libraries and the Reviewer', *The Bookseller* (20 Mar. 1935), 286–7.

HAINING, PETER (ed.), *The Penny Dreadful: Or, Strange, Horrid and Sensational Tales!* (London, 1975).

HALSEY, A. H., *Trends in British Society since 1900* (London, 1972).

HAMPDEN, JOHN (ed.), *The Book World* (London, 1935).

HANNAY, A. C., 'Are Lending Libraries Really a "Menace"?', *The Bookseller* (11 Apr. 1934), 200.

HARRISON, MAJOR G., and MITCHELL, F. C., *The Home Market* (London, 1936; 1939; 1950).

HASLAM, JAMES, *The Press and the People: An Estimate of Reading in Working-Class Districts* (Manchester, 1906).

HAWEIS, REVD H. R., 'Marie Corelli as I Know Her,' *The Temple Magazine*, 1 (Oct. 1896), 54–6.

HENREY, MRS ROBERT, 'Why Deride Teen-Ager and Her Magazines?', *The Trade Circular* (27 May 1950), 19.

HEWISON, ROBERT, *Under Siege: Literary Life in London 1939–45* (London, 1988).

HEWITT, GORDON, *Let the People Read: A Short History of the United Society for Christian Literature* (London, 1949).

HILTON, JOHN, *Rich Man, Poor Man* (London, 1944).

HIMMELWEIT, HILDE T., OPPENHEIM, A. N., and VINCE, PAMELA, *Television and the Child: An Empirical Study of the Effect of Television on the Young* (London, 1958).

HITCHMAN, FRANCIS, 'The Penny Press', *Macmillan's Magazine*, 43 (1881), 385–98.

HOBSON, J. W., and HENRY, H. (comp.), *The Hulton Readership Survey* (London, 1947–53).

HODGE, JANE AIKEN, *The Private World of Georgette Heyer* (London, 1984).

HOGGART, RICHARD, *The Uses of Literacy* (London, 1958).

HOPE[-HAWKINS], ANTHONY, *Memories and Notes* (London, 1927).

The House of Menzies (Edinburgh, 1958).

HOWATT, J. REID, 'Characteristic Library Readers', *The Readers' Monthly*, 1 (Nov. 1898), 8–9.

HOWE, GARFIELD, 'What the Public Likes', *The Bookseller* (19 June 1935), 580, 583.

'How I Drew for a Boys' Paper', *The Anglo-Saxon* (27 May 1899), 17–19.

'How to Write Detective Novels', *The Times* (19 July 1935), 12.

HUMPHERY, GEORGE R., 'The Reading of the Working Classes', *The Nine-teenth Century*, 33 (Jan.–June 1893), 690–701.

HUMPHRIES, STEPHEN, *Hooligans or Rebels? An Oral History of Working-Class Childhood and Youth 1889–1939* (Oxford, 1981).

HUNTER, PENROSE, 'Selling through the Schoolboy: How National Adver-tisers can Make Use of the Magazines of Youth', *Advertising World*, 60 (Sept. 1931), 192–6.

INGE, REVD W. R., 'School Stories May Become History', *Evening Standard* (4 Aug. 1937), 7.

Investigated Press Circulations (London, 1932).

IREMONGER, LUCILLE, 'Our Girls Deserve Better', *The Trade Circular* (10 June 1950), 26, 29.

IRWIN, RAYMOND, 'The English Domestic Library in the Nineteenth Century', *Library Association Record*, 56 (Oct. 1954), 382–9.

'Is a Library an Advantage?', *The Scottish Newsagent, Booksellers' and Stationers' Guide*, 12 (Jan. 1930), 11; (Feb. 1930), 1–5.

C. M. J., 'Young People and the Reading Habit During Wartime', *The Publish-ers' Circular* (18 Dec. 1943), 678–9.

JAMES, H. E. O., and MOORE, F. T., 'Adolescent Leisure in a Working-Class District', *Occupational Psychology*, 14 (July 1940), 132–45.

JAMES, LOUIS, *Fiction for the Working Man 1830–50* (Harmondsworth, 1974).

—— 'The Trouble with Betsy: Periodicals and the Common Reader in Mid-Nineteenth-Century England', in Joanne Shattock and Michael Woolf (eds.), *The Victorian Periodical Press: Samplings and Soundings* (Leicester, 1982), 349–66.

JAST, L. STANLEY, *The Child as Reader* (London, 1927).

—— 'Libraries in War Time', letter, *The Times* (1 Sept. 1939), 6.

JENKINSON, A. J., 'Children and their books: New Methods of Education Are Needed', *The Bookseller* (19 Sept. 1940), 310–14.

—— *What Do Boys and Girls Read?* (London, 1940).

JEPHCOTT, PEARL, A., *Girls Growing Up* (London, 1942).

—— *Rising Twenty: Notes on Some Ordinary Girls* (London, 1948).

JOHNS, CAPTAIN W. E., 'What the Modern Boy Expects of his Hero, Biggles', *The Trade Circular* (20 Aug. 1949), 15.

Jones, Stephen G., *Workers at Play: A Social and Economic History of Leisure 1918–1939* (London, 1986).

Joy, Thomas, *Bookselling* (London, 1952).

—— *The Right Way to Run a Library Business* (Kingswood, Surrey, 1949).

'Jubilee Presentation to Mr D. C. Thomson', *Dundee Courier and Advertiser* (18 Dec. 1934).

'Juvenile Best-Sellers', *The Bookseller* (3 Nov. 1933), 10.

Kaldor, Nicholas, and Silverman, Rodney, *A Statistical Analysis of Advertising Expenditure and of the Revenue of the Press* (Cambridge, 1948).

Keating, Peter, *The Haunted Study* (London, 1989).

Kelly, Thomas, *Books for the People: An Illustrated History of the British Public Library* (London, 1977).

Keverne, Richard, 'Need It Always Be Murder?', *Constable's Quarterly* (Spring 1931), 23–6.

Knight, Charles, *Passages of a Working Life During Half a Century* (London, 1873).

Koss, Stephen, *The Rise and Fall of the Political Press in Britain*, vols i, ii (London, 1981–3).

Lane, Allen, 'All About Penguin Books', *The Bookseller* (22 May 1935), 497.

Lane, Margaret, *Edgar Wallace: The Biography of a Phenomenon* (London, 1939).

Lang, Andrew, and 'X', A Working Man, 'The Reading Public', *Cornhill Magazine*, ns xi (Dec. 1901), 783–95.

Lazell, David, *Flora Klickmann and her Flower Patch* (Bristol, 1976).

Leavis, Q. D., *Fiction and the Reading Public* (London, 1932).

Lee, Alan J., *The Origins of the Popular Press in England 1855–1914* (London, 1976).

LeMahieu, D. L., *A Culture for Democracy: Mass Communication and the Cultivated Mind in Britain Between the Wars* (Oxford, 1988).

John Leng & Company, *How a Newspaper is Printed* (Dundee, 1898).

Lennon, Bernard, 'Books in an Industrial Town', *The Bookseller* (9 Jan. 1941), 26–8.

Lewis, Jane, *Women in England 1870–1950: Sexual Divisions and Social Change* (Sussex, 1984).

Leyland, Eric, *The Public Library and the Adolescent* (London, 1937).

'Libraries in War-time: Plea for Maintenance as "A Vital Function"', *The Times* (27 June 1939), 16.

The Library Association, *A Century of Public Library Service: Where Do We Stand Today?* (London, 1949).

The Life of Florence Barclay: A Study in Personality, by One of Her Daughters (London, 1921).

Lines, Kathleen (compiler), *Four to Fourteen: A Library of Books for Children* (Cambridge, 1950).

'The Literature of the Rail', *The Times* (9 Aug. 1851), 7.

'The Literature of Snippets', *Saturday Review*, 87 (15 Apr. 1899), 455–6.

'The Literature of the Streets', *Edinburgh Review*, 165 (Jan. 1887), 40–65.

'The Literature of Vice', *The Bookseller* (28 Feb. 1867), 121–3.

LITTLE, JAS. STANLEY, 'Some Aspects and Tendencies of Current Fiction', *Library Review*, 1 (Mar. 1892), 1–16.

LLEWELLYN SMITH, SIR HUBERT (director), *Life and Leisure*, vol. ix, *The New Survey of London Life and Labour* (London, 1935).

LOANE, MARGARET, *An Englishman's Castle* (London, 1909).

LOFTS, W. O. G., letter, *The Spectator* (30 Jan. 1971), 169.

——, and ADLEY, DEREK, *The British Bibliography of Edgar Wallace* (London, 1969).

——, —— *The Men Behind Boys' Fiction* (London, 1970).

London Research and Information Bureau, *Press Circulations Analysed 1928* (London, 1928).

LOWELL, RUSSELL, 'Our Trade Organisations Then and Now', *The N.F. Year Book* (1921–2 edn.), 160–7.

LUBBOCK, PERCY, *The Craft of Fiction* (London, 1921).

MACAULAY, ROSE, 'Marginal Comments', *The Spectator* (23 Aug. 1935), 289.

MACDONALD, ROBERT H., 'Reproducing the Middle-Class Boy: From Purity to Patriotism in the Boys' Magazines, 1892–1914', *Journal of Contemporary History*, 24 (1989), 519–39.

MACLEOD, ROBERT, 'Scottish Publishers Past and Present', *The Bookseller* (2 Mar. 1934), 144–5.

MACNAB, BRYCE, 'Searching for a Film Story: The Type of Novel Which Film Producers Want', *The Bookseller* (3 July 1935), 646, 648.

MAGENIS, WALTER J., 'Changes Have Taken Place', *The Publishers' Circular* (5 Oct. 1929), 427, 431.

—— 'Twopence a Week: No Deposit, No Subscription', *The Publishers' Circular* (3 June 1933), 605, 607; (10 June 1933), 624–5.

MAGNUS, GEORGE G., *How to Write Saleable Fiction*, 14th edn. (London, 1924).

MANN, PETER H., *A New Survey: The Facts about Romantic Fiction* (London, 1974).

MARCH, JERMYN, 'The World of Fancy', *The Trade Circular* (19 Feb. 1927), 3–4.

MARGOLIES, DAVID, 'Mills & Boon: Guilt Without Sex', *Red Letters* (Winter 1982–3), 5–13.

MARSH, JEAN, *Death Stalks the Bride* (London, 1943).

MARWICK, ARTHUR, *The Deluge: British Society and the First World War* (London, 1965).

—— 'Images of the Working Class since 1930', in Jay Winter, (ed.), *The Working Class in Modern British History: Essays in Honour of Henry Pelling* (Cambridge, 1983), 215–31.

Mass-Observation, *Books and the Public: A Report for the National Book Council*, London (File Report 2018, M-O), 11 Feb. 1944).

—— *The Press and its Readers* (London, 1949).

—— *Reading in Tottenham: An Interim Report on a Survey carried out by Mass-Observation on behalf of the Tottenham Borough Council*, London (File Report 2537, M-O), Nov. 1947.

—— *Report on Books and the Public: A Study of Buying, Borrowing, Keeping, Selecting, Remembering, Giving, and Reading* BOOKS, London (File Report 1332, M-O), 2 July 1942.

—— *A Report on Penguin World*, London (File Report 2545, M-O), Dec. 1947.

—— 'War Themes in Entertainment', London (File Report 1380, M-O), Aug. 1942.

MASTERMAN, CHARLES F. G., *England After War: A Study* (London, 1923).

MASTERS, BRIAN, *Now Barabbas Was a Rotter: The Extraordinary Life of Marie Corelli* (London, 1978).

MELLER, H. E., *Leisure and the Changing City 1870–1914* (London, 1976).

MIDGELEY, WILSON, 'Reading in Wartime', *John O'London's Weekly* (4 June 1943), 81–2.

MILES, PETER, and SMITH, MALCOLM, *Cinema, Literature and Society: Elite and Mass Culture in Interwar Britain* (London, 1987).

Mills & Boon, Ltd., 'And Then He Kissed Her . . .,' promotional cassette (London, 1986).

MINNEY, R. J., *Viscount Southwood* (London, 1954).

'Mischievous Literature', *The Bookseller* (1 July 1868), 445–9.

'Miss Ayres Shares her Ideas', *The Trade Circular* (22 Apr. 1933), 10.

'Miss Braddon's Work', *The Publishers' Circular* (13 Mar. 1915), 231–2.

MOGRIDGE, STEPHEN, 'Percy F. Westerman', *The Publishers' Circular* (29 July 1950), 911–12.

—— *Talking Shop* (London, 1949).

MOSS, LOUIS, and BOX, KATHLEEN, 'The Cinema Audience', Social Survey, NS 37b (London, June–July 1943).

MOULDER, PRISCILLA E., 'The "Story Interest" Only: What Working Boys and Girls Read and What They Miss', *The Book Monthly* (May 1913), 543–5.

MOWAT, CHARLES LOCH, *Britain Between the Wars 1918–1940* (London, 1955).

'Mr Manchester', 'To-night's Diary: Book Psychology', *Manchester Evening News* (22 Feb. 1926), 3.

'Mrs Florence Barclay', *The Publishers' Circular* (19 Mar. 1921), 309.

Mudie's Library Ltd., *Mudie's Catalogue of the Principal Works of Fiction in Circulation at the Library* (London, May 1934; Oct. 1935).

MULLAN, BOB, *The Enid Blyton Story* (London, 1987).

NAUGHTON, BILL, *On the Pig's Back* (Oxford, 1988).

NEUBURG, VICTOR E., *Popular Literature: A History and Guide* (London, 1977).

'The New Editor of "The Woman's Magazine"', *The Publishers' Circular* (4 Apr. 1931), 426.

270 *Bibliography*

The News Chronicle, Behind the Gallup Poll (London, 1951).

NORRIE, IAN, *Mumby's Publishing and Bookselling in the Twentieth Century*, 6th edn. (London, 1982).

NOWELL, CHARLES, 'The Public Library', in John Hampden (ed.), *The Book World* (London, 1935), 181–94.

'Of Boys' Books', *Times Literary Supplement* (11 Apr. 1918), 165–6.

OLLÉ, JAMES G., *Library History: An Examination Guidebook* (London, 1967).

'130 Years in the Publishing World', *The Publishers' Circular* (14 Dec. 1929), 823.

'One 2s. 6d. Novel: Library Profit—£9', *The Trade Circular* (6 May 1950), 22.

ORWELL, GEORGE, 'Boys' Weeklies', in Sonia Orwell and Ian Angus, (eds.), *The Collected Essays, Journalism and Letters of George Orwell*, vol. i (Penguin edn., Harmondsworth, 1987), 505–31.

ORWELL, SONIA, and ANGUS, IAN (eds.), *The Collected Essays, Journalism and Letters of George Orwell*, vol. i. (Penguin edn., Harmondsworth, 1987).

OSBORNE, JOHN, *A Better Class of Person* (London, 1981).

'Our Favourite Authors and Books', *The Trade Circular* (20 Aug. 1949), 11, 13.

PALMER, CECIL, 'The Thriller Is Everyman's Fiction', *The Publishers' Circular* (30 Sept. 1939), 330–1.

—— 'The Working Classes and Books', *The Publishers' Circular* (15 Feb. 1941), 93–4.

PARKER, PETER, *The Old Lie: The Great War and the Public-School Ethos* (London, 1987).

PARRINDER, PATRICK, and PHILMUS, ROBERT (ed.), *H. G. Wells' Literary Criticism* (Sussex, 1980).

PAYN, JAMES, 'Penny Fiction', *The Nineteenth Century*, 9 (Jan. 1881), 145–54.

PEER, EDMUND H., 'Best-Selling Books', *The Newsbasket* (Mar.–Sept. 1912), 67, 92–3, 111, 141, 166, 186, 196.

'Penny Fiction', *Blackwood's Edinburgh Magazine*, 164 (Dec. 1898) 801–11.

'Penny Fiction', *Quarterly Review*, 151 (July 1890), 150–71.

PERKIN, H. J., 'The Origins of the Popular Press', *History Today*, 7 (July 1957), 425–35.

PHILLIPS, MARGARET, *The Young Industrial Worker: A Study of his Educational Needs* (Oxford, 1922).

The Pilgrim Trust, *Men Without Work* (Cambridge, 1938).

PLAYFAIR, PETER, 'Literary Tastes of Working Lads', letter, *Times Literary Supplement* (30 Nov. 1916), 574.

'Post-Sherlockism', *The Times* (8 Feb. 1922), 8.

'Post-War Developments in Publishing and Bookselling: J. M. Dent Memorial Lecture', *The Publishers' Circular* (29 Oct. 1938), 633–5; (5 Nov. 1938), 682, 684; (12 Nov. 1938), 744–6.

POUND, REGINALD, and HARMSWORTH, GEOFFREY, *Northcliffe* (London, 1959).

PRESTON, WILLIAM C., 'Messrs. W. H. Smith & Son's Bookstalls and Library', *Good Words*, 36 (July 1895), 474–8.

—— 'Mudie's Library', *Good Words*, 35 (Oct. 1894), 668–76.

PRIESTLEY, J. B., *Blackout in Gretley* (Dent edn., London, 1987).

—— 'No More "Best-Seller"!', *The Bookseller* (2 Mar. 1934), 146.

'Prime Minister's Solace: Dumas and Conrad', *The Times* (4 May 1939), 9.

'Profile—D. C. Thomson', *Sunday Observer* (18 May 1952).

'Public Taste in Books: Value of Libraries in Speeding Education', *The Times* (20 Sept. 1950), 5.

The Publishers' Association, 'Book Publishing in Britain To-day', *The Bookseller* (8 June 1944), 495.

'Publishers' Profits and their Losses', *The Publishers' Circular* (27 Dec. 1919), 591.

QUIGLEY, ISABEL, *The Heirs of Tom Brown: The English School Story* (Oxford, 1984).

C.R., 'What the People Read', *The Academy*, 52 (Oct.–Dec. 1897), 283, 303, 327, 378–9, 429, 498–9, 577; 53 (Jan.–June 1898), 59, 156–7, 209, 293–4, 377–8, 689–90; 54 (July– Sept. 1898), 91–2, 156, 180.

RADWAY, JANICE A., *Reading the Romance: Women, Patriarchy and Popular Literature* (North Carolina, 1984).

'The Railway Bookstall', *Chambers's Journal*, 6th ser. 8 (13 May 1905), 375–8.

'Readers in the City', *Times Literary Supplement* (25 Apr. 1942), 205.

'Reading Habits of the Public: Librarians and Effect of Broadcasting', *The Times* (30 Sept. 1927), 8.

'Reading in Industrial Centres: Interesting Analyses', *The Times* (8 Aug. 1924), 8.

'Reading in Youth Clubs', *The Bookseller* (18 Feb. 1950), 224.

'Reading Rationally: The Adolescent's Choice', *The Librarian and Book World*, 19 (Mar. 1930), 242–4.

'Reading in the Time of War', *The Times* (13 Apr. 1915), 6.

'Reading and War Worry', *The Times* (12 Apr. 1917), 8.

'Real Reading', leading article, *The Times* (14 June 1939), 15.

REED, BRYAN H., *Eighty Thousand Adolescents* (London, 1950).

RICE, MARGERY SPRING, *Working-Class Wives* (London 1939).

RICH, ARTHUR T., 'Boys Who Never Grow Up', *Evening News* (London, 17 Jan. 1939), 8.

RICHARDS, FRANK, *The Autobiography of Frank Richards* (London, 1952).

'Frank Richards Replies to George Orwell', in Sonia Orwell and Ian Angus (eds.), *The Collected Essays, Journalism and Letters of George Orwell*, vol i (Penguin edn., Harmondsworth, 1987), 531–40.

RICHARDS, JEFFREY, 'The Cinema and Cinema-Going in Birmingham in the

1930s', in John K. Walton and James Walvin (eds.), *Leisure in Britain* (Manchester, 1983), 32–52.

—— *Happiest Days: The Public Schools in English Fiction* (Manchester, 1988).

RICHARDSON, F. R., 'The Circulating Library', in John Hampden (ed.), *The Book World* (London, 1935), 195–202.

ROBERTS, ELIZABETH, *A Woman's Place: An Oral History of Working-Class Women 1890–1940* (Oxford, 1984).

ROBERTS, K. A. L., 'The Evolution of a Non-Borrower', *The Library Assistant*, 32 (Nov. 1939), 243–51.

ROBERTS, ROBERT, *The Classic Slum* (Penguin edn., Harmondsworth, 1987).

—— *A Ragged Schooling* (Manchester, 1987).

ROLLINGTON, RALPH, *A Brief History of Boys' Journals* (Leicester, 1913).

The Romance of the Amalgamated Press (London, 1925).

ROOFF, MADELINE, *Youth and Leisure: A Survey of Girls' Organisations in England and Wales* (Edinburgh, 1935).

ROSIE, GEORGE, 'The Private Life of Lord Snooty', *Sunday Times Magazine* (29 July 1973), 8–16.

ROWNTREE, B. SEEBOHM, *Poverty and Progress: A Second Social Survey of York* (London, 1941).

——, and LAVERS, G. R., *English Life and Leisure: A Social Study* (London, 1951).

Royal Commission on the Press, *Minutes of Evidence* (London, 1947–8).

—— *Report* (London, 1949).

SADLEIR, MICHAEL, 'Yellow-Backs', in John Carter (ed.), *New Paths in Book Collecting* (London, 1934), 127–61.

'The Sale of Penny Periodicals in Victoria's Early Days', *The Publishers' Circular* (21 Apr. 1923), 421.

SALMON, EDWARD, *Juvenile Literature As It Is* (London, 1888).

—— 'What Girls Read', *The Nineteenth Century*, 20 (July–Dec. 1886), 515–29.

—— 'What the Working Classes Read', *The Nineteenth Century*, 20 (July–Dec. 1886), 108–17.

SANDERS, F. D. (ed.), *British Book Trade Organisation: A Report on the Work of the Joint Committee* (London, 1939).

SAVAGE, ERNEST A., 'Rakes' Progress', *Library Association Record*, 2 (Dec. 1935), 548–9.

SAVILLE, MALCOLM, 'What Children Tell Me', *The Trade Circular* (9 Apr. 1949), 13.

SAYERS, R. S., *A History of Economic Change in England, 1880–1939* (London, 1967).

SAYERS, W. C. BERWICK, *A Manual of Children's Libraries* (London, 1932).

SCHMOLLER, HANS, 'The Paperback Revolution', in Asa Briggs (ed.), *Essays in the History of Publishing in Celebration of the 250th Anniversary of the House of Longman 1724–1974* (London, 1974), 285–318.

'School Reading', *Times Educational Supplement* (27 May 1920), 275.

'School Speech Days', *The Times* (15 July 1935), 7.

'School Staffing', *The Times* (9 Jan. 1925), 7.

SEALE, SARA, 'Who Said Romantic Novel is Dying?', *The Trade Circular* (29 July 1950), 13, 23.

'Sensation Novels', *Quarterly Review*, 113 (Apr. 1863), 481–514.

SHAYLOR, JOSEPH, *Sixty Years a Bookman: With Other Recollections and Reflections* (London, 1923).

SIMONIS, H., *The Street of Ink: An Intimate History of Journalism* (London, 1917).

Sixpenny Wonderfuls: 6d. Gems from the Past (London, 1985).

Six to Sixteen: A Classified Catalogue of The Children's Book Club, 2nd edn. (London, Christmas 1934).

'Sixty New Books a Day', *The Publishers' Circular* (5 Oct. 1929), 425.

SLADEN, DOUGLAS, *My Long Life: Anecdotes and Adventures* (London, 1939).

—— *Twenty Years of My Life* (London, 1915).

'The Small Bookseller After the War'. *The Publishers' Circular* (25 Sept. 1943), 472–6; (2 Oct. 1943), 494–5; (9 Oct. 1943), 530–2.

SMITH, THOMAS, and OSBORNE, J. H. (eds.), *Successful Advertising: Its Secrets Explained*, 7th–9th, 21st edns. (London, 1887–89, 1902).

W. H. Smith & Son, Ltd., 'Books in Great Demand', London, Library Department, 12 Jan.–15 June 1935 (W. H. Smith archives (Milton Hill), PA.167).

Souvenir of Banquet, Held at The Fleetway House (London, 7 Nov. 1912).

SPENDER, J. A., *Life, Journalism and Politics* (London, 1927).

SPICER, ALBERT, 'The Paper Trade', in Harold Cox (ed.), *British Industries under Free Trade: Essays by Experts* (London, 1903), 201–13.

Spring-Heeled Jack, the Terror of London, by the Author of Turnpike Dick (London [c.1870s]).

STEAD, W. A. H., 'Best-Sellers as the Small Man Sees Them', *The Bookseller* (5 Feb. 1936), 115–16.

STERN, C. M., 'Bloods', *Library Assistant*, 34 (Sept. 1941), 160–5.

STEVENS, GEORGE, and UNWIN, STANLEY, *Best-Sellers: Are They Born or Made?* (London, 1939).

STEVENSON, JOHN, *British Society 1914–45* (London, 1984).

——, and COOK, CHRIS, *The Slump: Society and Politics During the Depression* (London, 1977).

STEWART, J. A., 'Sir Hall Caine: Our Most Popular Novelist', *The Publishers' Circular* (4 June 1921), 571–2.

STEWART, JAMES A., 'What Boys Read', *The Boy*, 6 (Mar. 1934), 169–72.

STONE, LAWRENCE, 'Literacy and Education in England 1640–1900', *Past and Present*, 42 (Feb. 1969), 69–139.

STRAHAN, ALEXANDER, 'Our Very Cheap Literature', *Contemporary Review*, 14 (July 1870), 439–60.

'Study of Reading Habits: Surveys Suggested', *The Times* (22 Sept. 1950), 2.

'Subjects of General Reading: Popularity of Fiction', *The Times* (26 Oct. 1933), 11.

'A Survey of Reading', *The Bookseller* (1 May 1948), 888–90.

SUTHERLAND, JOHN, *Victorian Novelists and Publishers* (London, 1976).

SWAN, ANNIE S., *My Life: An Autobiography* (London, 1934).

SYMONS, JULIAN, *Bloody Murder: From the Detective Story to the Crime Novel: A History* (Harmondsworth, 1985).

TATTERSALL, G. K., 'Books—Boys' Books—and "Bloods"', *The Boy*, 6 (Sept. 1933), 80–4.

TAYLOR, A. J. P., *English History 1914–1945* (Oxford, 1965).

TAYLOR, W. G., ''Publishing', in John Hampden (ed.), *The Book World* (London, 1935), 49–88.

'Teen-Agers' Reading Preferences', *The Bookseller* (6 Aug. 1949), 512–14.

'Television and Children's Reading', *Times Literary Supplement* (13 June 1952), p. ii.

THOMPSON, FLORA, *Lark Rise to Candleford* (Penguin edn., Harmondsworth, 1987).

THOMPSON, PAUL, *The Voice of the Past* (Oxford, 1978).

THOMPSON, THEA, *Edwardian Childhoods* (London, 1981).

THOMSON, D. C., 'Memorandum by Mr D. C. Thomson, Chairman and Senior Managing Director, D. C. Thomson & Co., Ltd. and John Leng & Co., Ltd', published in Royal Commission on the Press, *Minutes of Evidence*, 27th Day (31 Mar. 1948), 8–11.

The D. C. Thomson Bumper Fun Book (Edinburgh, 1977).

D. C. Thomson Firsts: 1921–1939 (London, 1978).

THORNICROFT, JANE, 'What Children Tell Me', *The Publishers' Circular* (6 May 1933), 473.

'*The Times* Cinema Number', supplement, *The Times* (21 Feb. 1922).

TRACEY, HERBERT (ed.), *The British Press: A Survey, A Newspaper Directory, and a Who's Who in Journalism* (London, 1929).

'"The Transiency of Trash": Lord Shaw on Public Taste in Literature', *The Times* (16 Dec. 1921), 9.

TREVOR, MCMAHON, 'Who Buys Novels?', *The Publishers' Circular* (28 May 1921), 555.

TURNER, E. S., *Boys Will Be Boys* (London, 1975).

'Twopenny Libraries and the Shops Act', *The Publishers' Circular* (10 Aug. 1935), 219.

'Types of Popular Fiction: The Fast, the Sensational and the Simple', *Times Literary Supplement* (1 May 1937) 343–4.

UNWIN, STANLEY, *The Book in the Making* (London, 1931).

—— *The Status of Books* (London, 1946).

—— *The Truth about Publishing*, 3rd edn. (London, 1929).

'Value of English in Education: Children Reading Less', *The Times* (7 Jan. 1949), 2.

'Value of Libraries in War-Time: Mental Refreshment from Books', *The Times* (25 Jan. 1940), 4.

VULLIAMY, C. E. (ed.), *The Letters of the Tsar to the Tsaritsa, 1914–1917* (London, 1929).

WAGNER, LEOPOLD, *How to Publish a Book or Article, and How to Produce a Play* (London, 1898).

WAITES, BERNARD, *A Class Society at War: England 1914–18* (Leamington Spa, 1987).

WALLER, JANE, and VAUGHAN-REES, MICHAEL, *Women in Wartime: The Role of Women's Magazines 1939–1945* (London, 1987).

WALLER, P. J., *Town, City and Nation: England 1850–1914* (Oxford, 1983).

WALVIN, JAMES, 'Children's Pleasures', in John K. Walton and James Walvin (ed.), *Leisure in Britain* (Manchester, 1983), 228–41.

'Wanton Blemish Cut from Shakespeare', *The Times* (15 May 1939), 19.

WARD, J. C., 'Children and the Cinema', Social Survey, NS 131 (London, Apr. 1949).

—— 'Children Out of School', Social Survey, NS 110 (London, June 1948).

WARNER, PHILIP (ed.), *The Best of British Pluck: The Boy's Own Paper* (London, 1976).

WATSON, COLIN, *Snobbery with Violence: Crime Stories and their Audience* (London, 1971).

WEBB, R. K., *The British Working Class Reader 1790–1848: Literacy and Social Tension* (London, 1955).

—— 'Working Class Readers in Early Victorian England', *English Historical Review*, 65 (1950), 333–51.

WEBB, W. S. K., *The Truth about Wilson* (London, 1962).

WEST, REBECCA, 'The Tosh Horse', in Rebecca West, *The Strange Necessity: Essays and Reviews* (Virago edn., London, 1987), 319–25.

'What Children Read', *The Publishers' Circular* (12 Nov. 1932), 561.

'What Children Read', *The Times* (24 Sept. 1927), 13.

'What Children Read', *The Times* (26 Nov. 1921), 11.

'What East End Children Read', *The Times* (23 Sept. 1926), 14.

'What Girls Read', *Daily Mail* (2 Aug. 1921), 8; *The Publishers' Circular* (13 Aug. 1921), 161.

'What IS the Function of the Public Library?', *The Publishers' Circular* (18 Apr. 1931), 465.

'What to Read: A Librarian's Lure', *The Times* (29 Dec. 1925). 13.

WHITE, CYNTHIA L., *Women's Magazines 1693–1968* (London, 1970).

'Who Are the Most Popular Authors of Boys' Books?', *The Publishers' Circular* (16 Apr. 1927), 452; (1 Oct. 1927), 477, 479.

'Why Boys Read: Decline of Robinson Crusoe', *The Times* (15 Feb. 1950), 8.

'Why We Read', leading article, *The Times* (7 Feb. 1930), 15.

WILLIAMSON, KENNEDY, *Can You Write Magazine Stories?* (London, 1939).

WILLMER, JOHN C., 'The Commercial Library: Its Organization, Administration, and Service', *Library Association Record* 28 (15 Mar. 1916), 98–108.

WILSON, CHARLES, *First with the News: The History of W. H. Smith 1792–1972* (London, 1985).

WINTER, J. M., *The Great War and the British People* (London, 1986).

WODEHOUSE, P. G., *Eggs, Beans and Crumpets* (London, 1940).

WOOD, MRS HENRY, *East Lynne* (Everyman edn., London, 1984).

WOOLF, LEONARD, 'Mining Town—1942', London (File Report 1498, M-O), 8 Apr. 1944.

WOOLF, ROBERT LEE, *Sensational Victorian: The Life and Fiction of Mary Elizabeth Braddon* (London, 1979).

'Working Girls' Reading: The Queen's Gift of Books', *The Times* (7 Aug. 1917), 9.

WRIGHT, THOMAS, 'On a Possible Popular Culture', *Contemporary Review*, 49 (July 1881), 25–44.

YOUNG, TERENCE, *Becontree and Dagenham: The Story of the Growth of a Housing Estate* (London, 1934).

INDEX